Max Weber

Max Weber

AN INTELLECTUAL BIOGRAPHY

Fritz Ringer

The University of Chicago Press CHICAGO & LONDON

FRITZ RINGER is the Mellon Professor of History Emeritus at the University of Pittsburgh. He is the author of *The Decline of the German Mandarins, Education and Society in Modern Europe, The Rise of the Modern Educational System, Fields of Knowledge, Toward a Social History of Knowledge,* and *Max Weber's Methodology.*

The University of Chicago Press, Chicago 60637
The University of Chicago Press, Ltd., London
© 2004 by The University of Chicago
All rights reserved. Published 2004
Printed in the United States of America

13 12 11 10 09 08 07 06 05   2 3 4 5

ISBN: 0-226-72004-7 (cloth)
ISBN: 0-226-72005-5 (paper)

Portions of chapter two previously appeared in Lindenfeld and Marchand, eds., *Germany at the Fin de Siecle,* Louisiana State University Press.

Library of Congress Cataloging-in-Publication Data

Ringer, Fritz K., 1934–
    Max Weber—an intellectual biography / Fritz Ringer.
        p.   cm.
    Includes bibliographical references and index.
    ISBN 0-226-72004-7 (cloth : alk. paper) — ISBN 0-226-72005-5 (pbk. : alk. paper)
    1. Weber, Max, 1864–1920. 2. Sociology. I. Title.

HM479.W42R56 2004
301—dc22

                                                    2004004092

        ♾ The paper used in this publication meets the
        minimum requirements of the American National
        Standard for Information Sciences—Permanence of Paper
        for Printed Library Materials, ANSI Z39.48-1992.

To my children & grandchildren,

MONICA & MAX,
SORAYA & LOGAN

CONTENTS

ACKNOWLEDGMENTS

Much of this book was written during an exciting year, 2001–2002, at the *Wissenschaftskolleg* / Institute of Advanced Study in Berlin. I want to thank Wolf Lepenies for inviting me there—and for holding my place open while I struggled with a health problem. My wife and I fondly remember the wonderful staff of the Institute for their unfailing kindness in matters large and small. The book was finished and revised in Center Lovell, Maine, and Washington, DC, after fine critical readings by Tony LaVopa, John McCole, Bill Scheuerman, Paul Vogt, and Dennis Wrong. Thank you all!

Washington, DC
December 20, 2003

Max Weber was born in 1864. His father, Max Weber Sr., was a legally trained politician and a prominent member of the National Liberal Party, which had accepted Bismarck's autocratic leadership and the bureaucratic monarchy of the German Empire. Weber's mother, Helene Fallenstein Weber, was a deeply pious and morally rigorous woman, who became estranged from her conventional husband. Max Weber himself was profoundly interested in religion, but he was never a believer. A brilliant youth, Max learned more from his own reading than from his traditionally humanistic secondary schooling. Following in his father's footsteps, he enrolled as a student of law at the University of Heidelberg in 1882, while also taking courses in history, economics, and philosophy. At the same time, he joined a dueling fraternity, drank beer, and generally enjoyed the forms of sociability characteristic of German student life in those days.[1]

After a year of military service in 1883–1884, Weber interned in the courts and continued his legal studies, mainly in Berlin. Working on the borderline between legal and economic history, he eventually published his doctoral dissertation on the history of medieval trading companies in 1889. A second thesis on Roman agrarian history earned him the right to teach commercial, German, and Roman law in 1891. After a brief stint at the University of Berlin, Weber accepted a full professorship in economics at the University of Freiburg in 1894, at the age of thirty. Two years later, he moved to the University of Heidelberg, apparently launched on a successful academic career. During the early and mid-1890s, he organized a survey of agrarian working conditions, personally analyzing the returns for the East Elbian regions. In the process, he became an opponent of the Prussian landowners and a champion of German industrialization.

In 1893, while still teaching at Berlin, Weber married Marianne Schnitger, a distant cousin. Max and Marianne Weber were devoted to each other, but their marriage was almost certainly never consummated. This has been reported on good authority in Arthur Mitzman's psychobiography of Weber, which also mentions an extramarital affair he had sometime after reaching age forty in 1904. Mitzman's main interest was in the profound depression that virtually paralyzed Weber for over three years between about 1898 and 1902 and pursued him intermittently for the rest of his life. In all likelihood, Weber inherited a predisposition to manic-depressive illness, which also occurred in some of his relatives. Mitzman convincingly argues, however, that the first manifestation and most extended episode of Weber's depression grew out of the guilt he took away from a conflict with his father in 1897. The overt issue in that conflict was whether Helene could visit Max and Marianne without her husband. When the senior Weber intruded upon such a visit, the son ordered his father out of the house, and the father died unreconciled soon thereafter.[2]

In any case, Weber's extended illness between 1898 and 1902 had at least two substantive consequences for his work. First, the direction of his thought changed substantially after 1902. His questions became broader and deeper. He moved from economic and legal history to methodological issues, on the one hand, and to the study of Protestant asceticism on the other. In 1904, he joined Werner Sombart and Edgar Jaffe as an editor of the *Archiv für Sozialwissenschaft und Sozialpolitik,* the opening issue of which contained his famous essay on objectivity in the social sciences. Later that year, the first part of *The Protestant Ethic* appeared. The other significant consequence of his illness of 1898–1902 was his resignation from his teaching duties at the University of Heidelberg; he did not teach again until 1918, when he accepted a position at the University of Munich. While his brother Alfred achieved public recognition as a distinguished academic, Max was confined to the role of a private scholar for much of his life. Recurrent episodes of sleeplessness and nervous exhaustion plagued him until his premature death from pneumonia in 1920.

During the intervals between these episodes of depression, however, Weber was able to work in extraordinary bursts of manic energy. He usually had two or three projects under way at the same time. Before his illness, while working on the agrarian question, he also studied the stock exchange. In 1904, after launching *The Protestant Ethic,* he spent over three months in the United States. In 1906, he published a commentary on the Russian Revolution of 1905, having taught himself Russian for the purpose. In 1908 and 1909, he launched a survey of the psychophysical conditions of productivity among factory workers, while carrying out an exemplary local study himself. In the years before the First World War, he organized the German Association for Sociology, helping to define and launch its conference topics and empirical studies. At the same time, he began two major projects, the results of which were not published in their final versions until after his death. One of these was a handbook of economics, politics, and society that was posthumously published as *Economy and Society;* the other was a monumental comparative study on the economic ethics of the world religions. During the war, he administered a military hospital in Heidelberg. He also wrote passionate polemics in behalf of parliamentary reform and against the annexationist hysteria that seized many of his colleagues. He remained politically active—and influential—during the opening years of the Weimar Republic. Thus, despite his illness, Weber turned out a staggering amount of scholarship and reflection between 1904 and his death at the age of 56 in 1920.

In the chapters that follow, I propose to analyze some of Weber's most intriguing texts. I want to concentrate on those of Weber's works that seem to me essential to his intellectual enterprise as a whole. I hope in this way to provide an advanced introduction to Weber for students and scholars in the cultural and social studies, and for the broader educated public as well. I want to lead people to Weber's texts, not to serve as a substitute for them. For Anglo-American readers, a number of excellent translations are available. In a serious readings course on Weber, his texts—or translations of them—could be combined with sections of this book to arrive at a manageable reading assignment. My purpose, in short, is to provide a solid foundation both for the reading of Weber's own works and for more intensive studies of his thought.

The chapters that follow are *interpretations* of Weber's most interesting texts. They sometimes encompass brief critical commentaries; but they mainly try to articulate what Weber actually wrote, or to restate it in terms that are as lucid and accessible as possible. I mean to apply the rules of interpretation that Weber himself proposed. I begin by assuming that his works are coherent, both in themselves and in relation to each other. But even when I encounter ambiguities or contradictions, I will ask how they might have arisen, and what they tell us about Weber's thought. I will *not* seek to *transcend* Weber, to arrive at a social theory more comprehensive than his own. For Weber was exemplary even when struggling with paradoxes. He was the first to address the crucial problems of modern social life. His analysis of capitalism is particularly salient now that the vision of total planning has faded. More intensely than any other thinker, Weber pondered the apparently inescapable expansion of private and public bureaucracy, with its links to the pervasiveness of educational qualifications and credentials. He struggled with the implications of mass politics for the liberal tradition. He asked himself about the prospects for the autonomous individual in the rationalized environment of modernity. He pondered the relationship between scientific knowledge and human values in a post-religious world. And he sought to redefine the role of the intellectual in a pluralistic and democratic society. Altogether, Weber was surely the most important social thinker of our time.

The ongoing critical edition of Max Weber's collected works (*Max Weber Gesamtausgabe*) has been of great help to me. It is richly annotated, but it is not yet complete. The final analysis of Weber's thought certainly could not be attempted now, if ever. Moreover, I know less about the vast secondary literature on Weber—or about the Weber debates among political and legal theorists, for example—than I know about Weber's works themselves. I have been decisively influenced by eminent authorities on Weber, but it would be too cumbersome to specify exactly where I do or do not agree with my numerous predecessors. Colleagues who want to know more about my intellectual obligations may want to consult the bibliography, which surveys the whole corpus of Weber's works, spells out the full titles of volumes cited in abbreviated forms, and lists the most important English translations. (Unless otherwise indicated, passages quoted in English from Weber are my own translations, and any italics are Weber's.) Let me add that I am not a philosopher or a social theorist, but a practicing social and intellectual historian. On the other hand, I have taught Weber's works for more than forty years. Weber has been my methodological mentor and was the hero of my first book. He has figured in everything I have written, and not only as a part of my subject matter. Rather, his ideas have guided me in my understanding of modern German social and intellectual history, of the comparative history of modern secondary and higher education, and of the decisive methodological questions in the cultural and social sciences. My students and friends know that I have been a passionate Weberian throughout my academic career. For me, therefore, this study is not a last-minute extension of my scholarly work, but its completion. To the experts among the sociologists, what I write may seem old or outrageous. Nevertheless, if I succeed in increasing Weber's influence, especially in the United States, I will have achieved my goal.

As I will try to show, the unity of Weber's thought does not lie in his methodology, and most certainly not in his intellectual obligation to Heinrich Rickert. Nor can I accept the thesis that Weber was primarily a German nationalist. Like virtually every European intellectual of his day, he ranked his nation's interests above those of others; but he was more moderate and more realistic in his conception of German national interests than the vast majority of his colleagues. Finally, I reject the view that Weber's account of plebiscitarian leadership democracy made him an unwitting prophet of National Socialism. On the contrary, I take it to be a tragedy for contemporary German liberals that too many of them have lost touch with one of their memorable forebears. For Weber was primarily a liberal. I do not want to say only that he was a rare academic supporter of the Weimar Republic, prepared to work with the moderate Social Democrats, and a fierce opponent of the reactionary myths and cliques that ultimately brought it down and gave Hitler his chance. I also mean to insist that the underlying unity of Weber's thought lay in his liberal pluralism. So profound was this commitment that I see it as the core of the *intellectual personality* whose portrait I propose to draw.

CHAPTER ONE

A Man in His Time

To read Weber's texts as an intellectual historian is to locate them in their context. Following Pierre Bourdieu, I want to describe Weber's cultural world as an *intellectual field.* In Bourdieu's account, the intellectual field at a given time and place is made up of agents taking up various intellectual positions. Yet the field is not an aggregate of isolated elements; it is a configuration or network of relationships. The elements in the field are not only related to each other in determinate ways; each also has a specific authority, so that the field is a distribution of symbolic power as well. The agents in the field compete for the right to define what shall count as intellectually established and culturally legitimate. But the main point of Bourdieu's definition lies in the positional or relational attributes of ideas. The views expressed in a given setting are so thoroughly interdefined that they can be adequately characterized only in their complementary or oppositional relationships to each other. The intellectual field is influenced by the concerns of the larger society; but its logic is its own.[1]

All sectors of an intellectual field or subfield are profoundly affected by the orthodoxies that are dominant within it. Even the most heterodox positions are partly shaped by their more or less deliberate orientations toward the orthodoxies they contest. At the same time, orthodoxies and heterodoxies alike are grounded in a cultural preconscious of tacit assumptions or "doxa" that are perpetuated by inherited practices and social relations. During periods of change and conflict, at least some of these doxic beliefs may become explicit— and thus subject to analysis and clarification. Under the impact of unusual experiences—or from sheer intellectual penetration, a creative minority of intellectuals may critically reexamine their tradition. They will clarify important tenets, abandon others, and thus begin to transcend the limits of their world. I am convinced that original and coherent thought is always a kind of clarification, a gaining of analytical distance from the unexamined assumptions of a culture. I find this model of clarification less mystifying than the unreconstructed idealist's notion of a new idea as an uncaused cause. Max Weber is one of the greatest clarifying thinkers of our age. Even while sharing some of the doxa of his time and place, he reexamined, restated—and partly transcended—the dominant assumptions of his intellectual field. That is why his work is of interest to us even today—and why we must begin by trying to chart his intellectual field.

WEBER'S INTELLECTUAL FIELD

The German academic tradition that Max Weber both continued and transformed originated in the late eighteenth and early nineteenth centuries. Sometime around 1800, an educational revolution took place in the German states; it occurred much earlier there than it did in England or France, and it did so long before the Industrial Revolution reached Germany. One element in this transformation was the emergence of the research imperative, the expectation that university faculty would do original research and prepare their students to do the same. The other component in the revolution was the establishment of formal examinations and credentials for future secondary teachers, and the ultimate introduction of similar qualifications for other learned professions as well. In all modern European societies, advanced education eventually became almost as important a source of middle-class self-images as wealth and economic power, and this was especially true in Germany, where the educational revolution took place earliest, and the industrial revolution followed relatively late.

The radical renovation of the universities in Prussia and in other German states during the decades around 1800 assigned an especially important place to the faculties of "philosophy," as against the professional faculties. The reform movement was inspired by the new German Idealist philosophy, but also by a neo-humanist enthusiasm for classical Greece, and by the ideal of *Bildung*, meaning education in the sense of self-cultivation. According to this ideal, the learner's interpretive or "hermeneutic" interaction with venerated texts, chiefly those of classical antiquity, enhanced his whole personality. This view informed the ideology of the *Bildungsbürgertum*, the German educated upper middle class. I have elsewhere used the term *mandarins* to characterize an elite that owed its social standing primarily to its educational qualifications, rather than to aristocratic birth or to wealth and economic power. This mandarin elite consisted of high officials and teachers, clergymen, and members of the liberal and learned professions; the university professors were its natural spokesmen. In a precapitalist or early capitalist environment, only *Bildung* could compete with noble birth as a source of self-esteem and social honor. Similar visions of advanced education emerged in other cultures. But in Germany, the ethos of *Bildung* took on an almost metaphysical pathos. In the language of the German Idealists, the world exists so that, in coming to know it, the human mind may realize its potential.

If most German academics were more or less consciously committed to the concept of *Bildung* from the late eighteenth century on, then much is explained that would otherwise seem disconnected. Thus the German research university of the nineteenth century drew much of its vitality from a neo-humanist enthusiasm that was initially focused more upon Greece than upon Rome. The birth of the research seminar and the subsequent expansion of the philosophical faculties were linked to the emergence of the interpretive, philological, and historical disciplines. It was these disciplines, not the natural sciences, which initially defined the norms of rigorous scholarship. The word *Wissenschaft* broadly encompassed all systematic disciplines, including the interpretive ones, of course. There was a common belief that productive involvement in research usually would, and certainly should, have the effect of *Bildung*. The original scholar was meant to emerge from his activity enriched in mind *and person*. From the late nineteenth century on, this expectation was also expressed in the proposition that scholarship or science (*Wissenschaft*) should engender a "worldview" (*Weltanschauung*), a comprehensive and partly evaluative view of the world. The pursuit of truth was to lead to something like integral insight and moral certainty, or personal knowledge, or wisdom. In any case, the yen to derive *Bildung* and a "worldview" from learning or science was almost universal at German universities during Weber's time. Weber himself, however, stood against this pervasive assumption. He challenged the belief that the German universities could offer their students anything more than specialized training, and he insisted upon a rigorous separation of learning from value judgment.

As problematic as the expectation that *Wissenschaft* would produce "cultivation" was a traditional insulation of *Wissenschaft* from practical concerns. Although mathematics had a place in German classical secondary schooling, hermeneutic studies clearly ranked as the primary source of *Bildung*. To the extent that *Wissenschaft* was linked to the objective of *Bildung*, therefore, "practical" and experimental knowledge was undervalued—and difficult to conceptualize. Laboratory science depends upon controlled intervention in the environment. Yet German treatises on *Bildung* and *Wissenschaft* rarely included positive references to practical activity. On the contrary, they usually inveighed against instrumental or "utilitarian" conceptions of knowledge, and they tended almost automatically to identify "pure" *Wissenschaft* as impractical. A symbolic hierarchy extended downward from abstract theory to experimental and causal analysis, and on to merely "technical" or "applied" studies. Thus the German research universities of the nineteenth century were generally firmer in their repudiation of "utilitarian" infringements upon the "purity" of *Wissenschaft* than in their defense of heterodoxy and intellectual diversity. Weber was painfully aware of this bias.

The modern German universities were funded by the territorial states. Princely governments needed trained officials and sought to supervise the education and certification of clergy, secondary and university teachers, and liberal professionals as well. In theory, the statutory rights of university faculties guaranteed their academic freedom, along with their independent role in the appointment and promotion of their colleagues. In practice, the state ministries of education managed to assert considerable influence in these matters, and the de facto control of the bureaucratic monarchy found increasing acceptance among most German academics. More ominously, the abstract purity of *Wissenschaft* was eventually taken to prohibit openly "partisan" social and political views. On the other hand, university faculty typically thought it their duty to champion the "national cause" and the "good of the whole" against the "egotism" of openly "interested" parties. The mandarin doctrine of the "cultural state" (*Kulturstaat*) could be read to imply that government derives its legitimacy not from pursuing the interests of the governed, but from supporting the intellectual life of the nation. The result of these converging attitudes was a tendentious but supposedly apolitical politics of national "idealism." Weber himself was a fervent nationalist. But he exposed the misuse of "national" phrases to protect the Prussian landowners and the bureaucratic monarchy. He also castigated the view that there was true academic freedom in Germany, as long as heterodox and radically critical views were not tolerated as a matter of principle.

I shall say little here about the emergence of *Bildung* as a new concept by around 1800. There was a certain unity in the several currents of thought that converged in Germany during the late eighteenth and early nineteenth centuries, and the organizing principle behind this unity was a set of partly conscious beliefs about education, interpretation, and learning. Wilhelm von

Humboldt is considered the intellectual founder of the modern German university. But his theory of *Bildung* and of *Wissenschaft* was affected not only by the doctrines of German neo-humanism and Idealism, but also by the pedagogical debates of his day, and by the philological and interpretive *practices* that converted the neo-humanist impulse into a paradigm of systematic scholarship. Even in France and England, education was an important intellectual issue in the eighteenth century, along with economic individualism and political rationality. But in Germany, education became the primary concern of the new intellectual stratum, while economic individualism remained a comparatively minor theme.

My other historical point is that there was a change in the meaning of *Bildung* sometime between 1800 and 1900, a change best described as a shift from a forward-looking or "utopian" emphasis to a defensive or "ideological" one. Around 1800, the idea of self-enhancement through *Bildung* was a socially progressive and universalist challenge to permanent social distinctions based upon birth. Advanced education was not in fact available to everyone, but it seemed universally accessible in principle. The emerging educated middle class could in good conscience regard itself as an open, or merit, elite, a new aristocracy of intelligence and personal worth. To speak for education was in some sense to speak for all men against unjust and humanly irrelevant social barriers. By around 1900 or 1920, in sharp contrast, advanced education itself had taken on the character of a socially distinguishing privilege. With the institutionalization of secondary and higher education and of the credentials system, educational qualifications had become routine sources of social status. The educated upper middle class now sought to check the influx of new social groups into the universities and thus to reduce the competition for places in the academic professions.

As the concept of *Bildung* took on a socially confirmative character, some of its other implications changed as well. In some of Humboldt's early writings, he had insisted that human improvement could come only from the development of free individualities in interaction with each other. This was the cultural individualism that so impressed John Stuart Mill. Even in Humboldt's projects for the reorganization of Prussian higher education in 1909–1910, he saw the state as providing no more than a material environment for the autonomous life of learning. Yet he ultimately conceded opportunities for state intervention in university affairs. More important, to many university professors of later eras, this seemed less and less troublesome. Especially as they began to see themselves as a threatened minority, they tended to see the existing regime as an adequate embodiment of the *Kulturstaat*, the disinterested supporter and representative of the national culture. Most of them displayed an ever-firmer commitment to the bureaucratic monarchy, which protected their social position and accepted their claim to speak for the nation as a whole.[2]

Bildung around 1800, it must be added, had been invested with a collective and even transcendent significance that was gradually dissipated in the century that followed. The early German neo-humanists had seriously looked to antiquity for universally and eternally valid cultural norms. The Protestant antecedents of German Idealism, too, had conferred a religious meaning upon the pursuit of *Bildung*. Although that meaning was affected by the individualist element in Protestantism, it still linked *Bildung* to a universal vision of human salvation. In the metaphysical language of German Idealism, the self-realization of Mind was the transcendent aim of human existence. As that spiritual connotation gradually faded, however, it became ever more damaging that neither Humboldt nor the great Idealists had taken a clear position on the social preconditions of individual *Bildung,* or on its this-worldly consequences for all members of the community. Left in a kind of spiritual and social vacuum, the cultivation of the isolated self ultimately became a gratuitous and strictly private enterprise, a higher form of selfishness. Weber understandably felt the need radically to redefine the role of higher education, of systematic knowledge, and of the intellectual in the modern world.[3]

From around 1890 on, German university professors in the humanities and social sciences expressed a sense of crisis that reached its greatest intensity during the interwar period. Among the causes of their concern, some were broad trends in the political and cultural life of their time; others were changes in the situation of the universities and of *Wissenschaft* itself. Included in the latter category were structural transformations in the educational system that were widely perceived as forms of modernization and democratization. Thus from the late 1870s to the turn of the century, public controversies took place over the accreditation of the so-called technical institutes (*technische Hochschulen*), and of the nonclassical or incompletely classical secondary schools that were collectively termed *Realschulen.* Rightly or not, contemporaries considered the growth of these practically oriented institutions a functional adjustment of the educational system to the requirements of a modern technological society. Even opponents of the nontraditional programs thought them necessary; what they denied, at least until 1900, is that they should be accredited equally with the classical *Gymnasium* or with the universities themselves. The prevailing sentiment in the university faculties of philosophy was against them. In this context, it proved remarkably easy to use the language of *Bildung* in defense of the status quo. The inherited animus against "utilitarian" conceptions of learning virtually dictated a hierarchic ranking of educational institutions according to their more or less exclusively impractical character. The traditional defense of "pure" learning thus served to justify a social divide between the gratuitously cultivated and those schooled for useful employments.

During the late nineteenth century, and especially during the Weimar period, German academics also faced the questions raised by a substantial growth in secondary and university enrollments. While these increases probably did not substantially increase social mobility through education, contemporaries perceived them as forms of educational democratization or "massification." In these circumstances, the theory of *Bildung* was repeatedly brought forward to challenge the notion that school and university places should be distributed on the basis of tested academic aptitude. Since *Bildung* was thought to fulfill an individual's unique potential, statistical approaches to academic selection almost had to seem inappropriate. Thus in 1917, the pedagogue and philosopher Eduard Spranger saw "a connection between democracy and rationalism in the growth of technical methods by which the intellectual characteristics are to be measured." He objected that "individuality can only be grasped through vital intuition." In 1923, the psychiatrist and philosopher Karl Jaspers, Weber's friend and not usually a reactionary, conceded that certain specific aptitudes might be tested, but not "intelligence as such," "intellectuality" (*Geistigkeit*), and "creativity, genius." Jaspers reminded his readers that "the masses" had always been known to have a low intelligence. A student's receptivity to learning would be deficient, he thought, unless he came from a "cultured family."[4] These exclusionary views had little left in common with the universalist optimism of Wilhelm von Humboldt.

At a broader social and political level too, the mandarin intellectuals felt deeply threatened. Industrialization was under way well before 1870, but the pace of change increased dramatically during the late nineteenth and early twentieth centuries. Gigantic combines and producers' associations concentrated huge masses of capital, while exerting a growing influence in politics and in the press. The Free Trade Unions and the Social Democratic Party expanded sharply, to counterbalance the power of capital. In the pseudo-constitutional regime of the bureaucratic monarchy, the elected parties of the Reichstag were too weak to develop coherent policies of their own, but they were strong enough to bargain for petty concessions as Chancellors tried to construct governing majorities. Politics became less and less a matter of reasoned debate and more and more a conflict among competing quantities of organized monetary and electoral weight. Even moderate academics viewed this transformation with a kind of moral horror. The Frankfurt Parliament of 1848 had been dominated by the educated elite, and by university professors in particular. But by the turn of the century, party secretaries, journalists, and representatives of producers' associations held an increasing share of seats in the Reichstag. The narrow interests of the political parties seemed to predominate over larger national and cultural objectives. Economically and socially, the high industrial class society seemed to overwhelm the traditional status system, in which the highly educated had held a place of honor.

The typical mandarin was by no means uncritical of capitalism, not to mention laissez-faire economic individualism. To be sure, the educated and the entrepreneurial upper middle classes merged to some degree from the late nineteenth century on. Still, the ordinary German academic ranked the German cultural heritage and the cause of the German nation above the uncontrolled rule of capital. The dominant tradition in German economics focused upon the institutional and cultural setting of economic activity. The idea of the economic agent as a rational profit-seeker was widely rejected on both empirical and moral grounds. Few academics believed in timeless and culture-free "laws" of economic behavior; even fewer were outright socialists. This left many of them committed to a paternalist "social policy" and to the protection of agriculture against the inroads of commercial capitalism. It was easy for them to see the monarchical state and bureaucracy as "standing above" the political parties, ensuring social harmony and defending the welfare of the nation as a whole.

In Germany as in other countries, the outbreak of war in 1914 was greeted with an outburst of enthusiasm that seems shocking in retrospect, given the massive slaughter that ensued. Almost unanimously, German university professors supported their nation's war effort, and that requires no more explanation than the similar reactions of intellectuals in other countries. What does call for comment is the German mandarins' interpretation of the war as a triumph over the social conflicts of the prewar years, and as the subordination of private and group interests to the cause of the nation. In their wartime speeches and proclamations, the German mandarins were able once again to assume their traditional role of cultural leadership. They wrote of a profound struggle between German "culture" and Western "civilization." They castigated Western commercialism, rationalism, and utilitarian individualism, as against the uniqueness of Germany's cultural traditions, political institutions, and sense of "community." Invoking the "ideas of 1914," they envisaged a German alternative to the opposition between unfettered capitalism and radical socialism, a system in which both capital and labor were organized to serve the larger objectives of the nation. At the same time, the large majority of German professors called for extensive territorial annexations, even while resisting the political reforms that might have brought the Prusso-German polity closer to the English model of parliamentary government. It became painfully obvious during the war that the rhetoric of the national cause represented an exclusionary tactic, a right-wing attack upon liberal reformers and Social Democrats.

Of course there were differences of opinion among German university professors of this period. I have distinguished two major groups, the "orthodox" and the "modernists." The orthodox majority perpetuated the antidemocratic implications of their ideology without much reflection. They saw their time as one of shallow utilitarianism, social "dissolution," and moral corruption. They castigated the "interest politics" of the political parties and the "materialism" of the Social Democratic electorate. During the First World War, they celebrated the resurrection of the nation while opposing political reform and supporting the demands of the ultra-annexationists. They despised the Revolutions of 1918–19 and the Weimar Republic. The foreign and domestic enemies of Germany, they believed, had combined to impose an intolerable regime, an outgrowth of lower-class envy and partisan egotism. They responded with a rhetoric of cultural despair, an ostensibly "apolitical" repudiation of modernity in all its aspects. They called for an "intellectual revolution" and a renewal of "idealism." Some of them openly linked modernity with the Jews, as if anti-Semitism were an acceptable alternative to the despised politics of material interests. Among their students, they encouraged messianic expectations of a vague and violent character. Their ideological attacks materially weakened the Weimar Republic, along with the norms of reason and civility.

In both the Imperial and Weimar periods, to be sure, a substantial minority of German university faculty took less one-sided positions on the political issues of their time. They were more critical than their colleagues of the existing political and social system, and they resisted the annexationist hysteria that infected the German academic world during the First World War. After 1918, they supported the genuinely republican parties. They were guided less by enthusiasm for democracy, not to mention socialism, than by a sense of realism, and by the hope that the Republic might be encouraged to pursue moderate policies. Among the members of this relatively progressive minority, some were determined cultural individualists and therefore "liberals" in some sense of that term; others more closely resembled the type of the enlightened conservative; only a handful directed truly radical criticisms at the political assumptions prevailing among their colleagues. Yet I have applied the term *modernists* to all the members of this group, because they held one definitive belief in common. This was that the German intellectual heritage had to be systematically reexamined in the light of modern conditions; socially indefensible accretions had to be stripped away, so that the vital core of the tradition could be transmitted to a wider audience in an inescapably more democratic age.

In pursuit of the modernist program, such scholars as Ernst Troeltsch, Georg Simmel, and Max Weber in fact became critical "translators" of German neo-humanism, Idealism, and Romanticism, as well as analysts of the interpretive or hermeneutic method. In almost every discipline, and especially in the social sciences, some of the more prominent innovators were modernists. This is not surprising, for the modernists were open to the creative experience of intellectual incongruity. While the orthodox almost unconsciously perpetuated the ideology of *Bildung* in its socially confirmative form, the modernists had to raise this ideology to critical consciousness. Thus my distinction between orthodoxy and modernism is meant to capture something more than a divide between the right and the left center in the political spectrum. It is also intended to point up the crucial difference between the unreflected transmission and the conscious clarification of an intellectual tradition. As a matter of fact, it is possible to locate the German academic modernists of the Weimar period on a scale of increasing critical distance from mandarin orthodoxy. Varying degrees of heterodoxy were not only individual responses to distancing experiences of all kinds; they were also immediate consequences of intellectual crisis. Once dislodged from the position of naive adherence, the critics of orthodoxy were precipitated into a chain of reversals that nonetheless reflected the tradition they challenged. Thus German Idealism ultimately provoked self-conscious anti-idealisms that are hard to imagine in any other intellectual field.

A final symptom of the German cultural crisis of the decades around 1900 was a widespread dissatisfaction with specialized research. German academics were troubled by the problem of disciplinary specialization or by a whole cluster of issues they associated with specialization. They faced a dilemma, since most of them were deeply involved in specialized work. They enjoyed the prosperity and renown of German science and scholarship. Yet they could not shake the sense that something vital to them was being lost, and that their practice was becoming incongruent with their ideals. The branching out of existing disciplines into autonomous subfields, and the decreasing breadth of scientific and scholarly works: these seemed to portend an intellectual atomization, in which researchers lost sight of the interrelationships among their findings. Even beyond this cognitive disjunction, specialization was widely held to threaten the unity of knowledge, or the relationship between empirical *Wissenschaft* and fundamental philosophy. Interpreted in the light of the German tradition, incoherence in specialized science and scholarship stemmed from the loss of the integrative framework that had once been provided by German Idealist philosophy.

This helps to account for the almost automatic association of specialization with "positivism." The latter in turn was rarely described in detail. Disciples of Auguste Comte or self-confessed positivists were rare among German university faculty between 1890 and 1930. The label "positivist" was almost always used in a derogatory sense, and those accused of positivism were typically thought guilty of unacknowledged fallacies. Chief among the errors ascribed to positivists was the belief that the concepts of the natural sciences could be extended to the humanities and social studies, or that the search for law-like regularities was the main task of the interpretive and historical disciplines as well. Indeed, even unreflected research practices could be viewed as positivist, if they were guided by a naive objectivism (envisaging a theory-free adding up of facts) or by a strong causalist program. Obviously, all forms of determinism, "materialism," or doctrinaire Marxism were considered positivist in inspiration or tendency, as were mechanical, "atomistic," or otherwise reductive analyses of organic processes, cultural meanings, or social wholes.

By the 1920s, German academics wrote and spoke not only of a "crisis of culture," but of a "crisis of *Wissenschaft*" as well. In describing this crisis, they typically repeated the established view that excessive specialization had eroded the vital ties between research and morally significant insight. To deal with the resulting loss of meaning, they called for scholarly "synthesis." Moreover, the divide between the orthodox and the modernists, which had widened a great deal during the First World War, now affected methodological positions to an unprecedented degree. The demand for "synthesis," though initially expressed by modernists as well, became ever more clearly an orthodox device. Indeed, "synthesis" itself was more and more broadly conceived. While it initially meant no more than cognitive integration, it ultimately acquired extraordinarily broad connotations. In German academic addresses of the period, one senses a desperate groping for morally elevating "lessons." The revival of the humanistic disciplines (*Geisteswissenschaften*) since the 1880s, which we have yet to discuss, was thought to promise a more integral and spiritually profitable engagement with the values embodied in great texts. References to "vital experience" (*Erlebnis*) suggested an intuitive identification with objects of interpretation, while "phenomenological" methods were taken to authorize a direct "viewing" (*schauen*) of "essential" meanings (*Wesensschau*). It was in this context that Weber insisted upon the inescapability of disciplinary specialization, denigrated academic "prophecy," and warned students against placing their hopes in intuition and vital experience. People who want to "view," he grumbled, should go to the cinema.[5]

THE GERMAN HISTORICAL TRADITION

Max Weber developed much of his methodological position in a critique of the German historical tradition, which was decisively shaped by the ideology of *Bildung*. Thus a persistent model of *Bildung* implied that the self-cultivating reader could reproduce or "relive" (*Erleben*) the experiences or "values" embodied in his texts, or that he could intuitively identify with the authors.[6] What may be called the *principle of empathy* long remained a temptation within the German interpretive and historical disciplines. It dictated, for example, that historians must "put themselves in the place of" the historical agents they seek to understand. Indeed, there is nothing wrong with this injunction, as long as it is understood in a loose and metaphorical sense. Taken literally, however, it implies a process of empathetic reproduction that cannot be communicated, validated, or falsified. Successful historians become geniuses with mysterious powers. The more they succeed in identifying with agents in cultures other than their own, moreover, the more they raise what came to be called the "problem of *Historismus*": Knowing only historically specific worldviews, we have no reason to exempt our own values and beliefs from the contingent flow of historicity.

The other element in the concept of *Bildung* that helped to shape the German historical tradition may be called the *principle of individuality*. The self-cultivating individual was consistently portrayed as absolutely unique, imbued with a distinctive potential for personal fulfillment. German theories of advanced education thus diverged sharply from a recurrent French emphasis upon the "socialization" of the younger generation in the light of inherited norms. Nor was *Bildung* conceived as the enhancement of a universal capacity for rationality; it was the development of an incomparable individual. This radical cultural individualism could acquire a utopian significance. It encouraged a positive view of both individual and cultural diversity; this is the implication that attracted John Stuart Mill to the thought of Wilhelm von Humboldt, and it certainly appealed to Max Weber as well. Yet the principle of individuality could also make a mystery of the relationship between the incomparable individual and his group or culture. The principle of individuality excluded additive views of aggregates, including political groupings. Moreover, the commitment to individuality in the study of history raised serious difficulties about the issue of change. Since "mechanical" causal processes were excluded, change could only be a teleological unfolding of preexistent potentialities, or an "emanation" of intellectual or spiritual forces.

Leopold von Ranke was commonly regarded as the dean of nineteenth-century German historians. He attained that status because he rigorously applied the source-critical methods transmitted by the philologists to an unprecedented range of historical sources. He was a great practitioner of the historian's craft. What he mainly recommended in his theoretical and methodological writings was a past-mindedness that recalled the *principle of empathy*. He wrote of "placing oneself back into [a given] time, into the mind of a contemporary." In line with the concept of the "cultural state," moreover, he saw states as the outward embodiment of "intellectual forces," "moral energies" that could be understood only by means of "empathy."[7]

At the same time, Ranke persistently championed the *principle of individuality*. He not only believed that great statesmen and thinkers truly stood for their nations, and thus legitimately led them; he also saw states themselves as "individualities," with their own distinctive "tendencies." Indeed, he repeatedly insisted upon the discontinuity between "the general" and "the particular." "From the particular," he wrote, "you may ascend to the general; but from general theory there is no way back to the intuitive understanding of the particular." What the historian must start from, therefore, is "the unique intellectual and spiritual character of the individual state, its principle."[8] As a profoundly religious thinker, Ranke was able to accept each culture and epoch as utterly distinctive and yet find meaning in world history as a divinely instituted plenitude of cultural individualities.

Among nineteenth-century German theorists of history, only Johann Gustav Droysen equaled Ranke in authority. His reflections on history rested upon a sharp contrast between explanation and interpretive understanding (*Verstehen*). Droysen associated the latter with intuitive insight, but also with the recovery of past human actions and beliefs from the "traces" they have left in the present. Like Wilhelm Dilthey after him, Droysen distinguished processes "internal" to the human agent from their outward "expressions." He also insisted that "the state is not the sum of the individuals it encompasses; nor does it arise from their wills or exist for the sake of their wills." Following

the theory of *Bildung*, he described the course of history as "humanity's coming to consciousness." Droysen developed some of his views in opposition to
H. T. Buckle's two-volume *History of Civilization in England* (1858–1861),
which sought to transform history in the image of the natural sciences. In response, Droysen reemphasized the divide between the scientist's search for
regularities and the historian's predominant concern with the interpretive understanding of the unique and particular.[9]

Max Weber did not comment directly upon the writings of Ranke or Droysen, but he did review a book closer to his own early research specialization in
economic history. This was a famous 1853 opus by Karl Knies, a cofounder of
what came to be called the "older" German historical school of economics.
Along with a handful of precursors, including Wilhelm Roscher, Knies
launched a tradition in political economy that was distinctly German in its
emphasis upon the historicity of economic institutions and ideas. Knies's
point of departure was the rejection of English classical economics. He utterly
repudiated the notion that economic analysis can be based upon axioms that
are independent of time and place. For Knies, there could be no exclusively
economic field of study, for economic activity cannot be separated from its political and cultural settings, which are products of history. The idea that permanent "laws" of economic behavior can be based upon the universality of
"private egotism" struck Knies as a "fiction" to be rejected on ethical as well as
methodological grounds.[10]

Insisting upon the relevance of spiritual forces in history and upon the integration of the economy into the surrounding culture, Knies had recourse to
such entities as the "spirit" of a nation. The individual economic agent was influenced not only by changing political and social arrangements, but also by his
national culture. Knies sometimes wrote of the "causal" interconnections between economic life and the other elements of a national culture. Yet he was
clearly uncomfortable with ordinary causal formulations. His problem was that
he equated causal connection with "natural necessity." To him and to other
German historians, causal explanation was inherently nomological (*naturgesetzlich*): It was explanation in terms of laws like those of the natural sciences.
While excluding such regularities from the domain of historical economics,
Knies hit upon two fairly plausible substitutes. First, he argued that in his field
the action of causes was not universal but modified by specific cultural conditions. This accounted for the centrality of "the individual and the concrete" in
history. Second, he claimed that "analogies" might be discovered where strict
laws could not be found. Incomplete regularities might be detected, not only
within the several subsections of a culture and in the way these subsections

affected each other, but also in the stages that followed each other in the historical development of nations. Finally, Knies was deeply concerned with the "freedom" of both individuals and nations to depart from pre-established patterns. Although he saw the individual as a product of his culture, he insisted upon the "personal element" in history. It was his commitment to "freedom" that mainly motivated his objection to nomological "causality."[11]

Knies' works in economic history were still used in Weber's time, including by Weber himself. The leadership of the "younger" historical school of economics, however, had by then passed to Gustav Schmoller, who also dominated the famous Social Policy Association (Verein für Sozialpolitik). This was an academic and semipublic forum for the study and advocacy of moderate social reform. The social policies championed by the association under Schmoller's influence came to strike Weber and a few of his colleagues as problematic. They seemed excessively paternalistic and bureaucratic in tendency, and they reflected ad hoc policy compromises, rather than fully reflected—and debated—objectives. This eventually provoked a controversy about value judgments in scholarship, in which Weber played a leading part. But even before that debate was launched, Schmoller's brand of historical economics was challenged by the Austrian neo-classical economist Carl Menger, one of the initiators of the marginal utility theory that has become a fundament of modern economic analysis. In 1883, Menger published a programmatic tract that set off a protracted "methods controversy" and that clearly impressed Weber. Menger's central thesis was that economic theory should not be confused with historical accounts of economic practices, or with the practical policy studies that Menger termed "political economy."[12]

In specifying his conception of *theoretical* economics, Menger raised crucial issues, not only for the historical school of economics, but also for the German historical tradition as a whole. He began by distinguishing two divergent perspectives upon empirical phenomena: "Our cognitive interest is directed either at the concrete phenomena in their position in space and time . . . or . . . at the recurrent patterns in which they appear. The former research direction aims at knowledge of the concrete or . . . individual, the latter at knowledge of the general." While insisting upon the divide between theoretical and historical economics, Menger further stipulated that "typical relations" or "laws" observable in the empirical world are not equally strict or invariant in their application to individual cases. He concluded that the theorist cannot hope to know the typical relations of particular phenomena in their "totality and their whole complexity." Rather, theoretical economics must be further subdivided into a "realistic-empirical" and an "exact" branch. The realistic-empirical direction may seek to discern "real types" and "empirical laws"; but these will inevitably be imprecise and subject to exceptions. The exact direction, on the other hand, must analyze complex phenomena into more elementary constituents and relationships that *can* be represented in strictly invariant laws; but these will rarely be applicable to the empirical world. Thus exact economics may theorize about the behavior of fully informed and rational economic agents, knowing full well that few such agents are to be found in real life. In the natural sciences too, as Menger pointed out, empirically observed regularities are usually not exact, while rigorous and universal laws are products of analysis and abstraction.[13]

For German historians, the issue of "positivism" became particularly acute during the controversy over the publication of the first volume of Karl Lamprecht's *German History* in 1891. Rejecting the predominant emphasis upon the state and upon great individuals in the German tradition, Lamprecht proposed a "cultural history" that gave attention to everything from economic conditions to popular culture and also drew heavily upon the history of the arts. In a 1905 collection of lectures, Lamprecht urged the replacement of narratives organized around "heroes" with comparative analyses of changing "conditions." His early interest in economic history may have earned him the reproach of "materialism," but his mature program for "modern" scientific history was based upon a theory of "psychic differentiation." He saw the individual progressing from total integration into the clan, via looser ties to the family and social group, toward increasing differentiation and autonomy. In a sequence of distinctive "cultural epochs," humanity thus moved from the "symbolic" age, through the "typical" and "conventional" periods, to the modern era of "individualism" and "subjectivism."[14]

Lamprecht explicitly drew upon the psychology of Wilhelm Wundt. He characterized history as "applied psychology," especially social psychology. While "psychic differentiation" was presumably a singular trend, Lamprecht observed regularities in the "psychic mechanisms" of cultural epochs. As one epoch gave way to its successor—or an earlier to a later phase of "subjectivism," older modes of thought and feeling underwent "dissociation," while new stimuli intruding from the environment gradually converged in a new psychic "dominant" or "synthesis." Thus the subjectivist era at first entailed an "increase in the activity of the nervous system" and a new "susceptibility to stimuli" (*Reizbarkeit*). Once fully developed, however, the standpoint of the self-conscious subject permitted the organization of chaotic sensations into formed experience.

In tracing the second phase of the subjectivist epoch to the stimuli provided by urbanization and technological change, Lamprecht evoked the psychological pressures of modernity. This allowed him to move on with remarkable ease to the "search for a new dominant," the "yearning of the age" for a new *Weltanschauung* or religion, the displacement of artistic naturalism by a new "idealism," and the new primacy of the humanistic disciplines. Reading Lamprecht's lectures today, one is struck by the looseness of his descriptions, in which virtually anything could be integrated into a broader "psychological" dynamic—and thus "explained" at will. In any case, Lamprecht's program struck most of his colleagues as subversive, not only in its methodology, but in its social and political implications as well. He was deservedly criticized for his slovenly scholarship, and he was suspected of "economic materialism." Indeed, it proved so easy to repudiate Lamprecht as a dilettante and a "positivist" that he probably retarded the opening to the social sciences that was beginning to transform historical studies in France by the turn of the century.[15]

In 1902, Eduard Meyer, a respected historian of antiquity, wrote a methodological essay that was affected by the Lamprecht controversy and that later drew a critical response from Max Weber. Meyer scoffed at the "modern" direction in historiography, which insisted on imitating the natural sciences. He was particularly offended at the equation of history with "applied psychology," the emphasis upon mass phenomena rather than the individual. What the new historians ignored, according to Meyer, was the "free will" of the human agent, the role of ideas and of chance in history. Like Knies before him, Meyer believed that causal relationships between events could only be based upon deterministic laws. Yet he found it hard to escape the conviction that "accidents" and deliberate actions can shape historical outcomes. Like Knies, he sought to escape this dilemma by means of ad hoc adjustments. Perhaps laws are replaced in history by "analogies" that may be altered by human agency or chance. Meyer also believed that the whole antithesis between necessity and contingency could be restated as the difference between a completed and an ongoing sequence of occurrences. Once events have taken place, we must accept them as necessary effects of their antecedents. While matters are still in flux, however, we may consider particular developmental paths as more or less probable, while also acknowledging that outcomes may be altered by intervening accidents or human actions.[16]

In 1883, just as Menger launched his critique of German historical economics, Wilhelm Dilthey published his *Introduction to the Humanistic Disciplines* [*Geisteswissenschaften*], which launched a whole chain of reflections upon the German interpretive and historical disciplines. Dilthey's purpose was to codify the concepts and methods of these disciplines, particularly as they contrast with those of the natural sciences. While human beings as bio-logical entities are part of nature, Dilthey held, practitioners of the interpretive disciplines deal essentially with the human mind (*Geist*) as it has expressed it-self in the historical world. They do not seek regularities but direct their at-tention to the unique and to freely chosen action. Human agency can only be understood "from the inside," in terms of intentions and beliefs. Thus the *Geisteswissenschaften* must be grounded in a "descriptive and analytical psy-chology" that does not rely on psychophysical laws or on other reductive tac-tics.[17]

The project Dilthey thus initiated in 1883 did not mature until 1907, with his *Construction of the Historical World in the Humanistic Disciplines* [*Geis-teswissenschaften*], which was further elaborated in later years. In a classic statement of the interpretive position, Dilthey here worked with a threefold scheme of "immediate experience" (*Erlebnis*), "expression" (*Ausdruck*), and "interpretive understanding" (*Verstehen*). He was particularly emphatic about the primacy of immediate awareness. Our lived experience, he argued, is an initially unanalyzed complex of sensations, memories, desires, and value ori-entations. The fullness of this totality provides the raw material for any obser-vations we may transform into organized experience (*Erfahrung*), or integrate into the cognitive frameworks of the disciplines. This part of Dilthey's thought inspired what came to be called "philosophy of life" (*Lebensphiloso-phie*). It also affected Dilthey's own further reflections in important ways. Above all, Dilthey always believed that *Nacherleben*, the empathetic repro-duction of immediate experience, played a role in the genesis of interpretive understanding. Primitive forms of *Verstehen*, he suggested, might be virtually unconscious—though culturally conditioned—insights into the meaning of gestures, facial expressions, and simple actions.[18]

Yet even while retaining this subjectivist view of empathetic understand-ing, the mature Dilthey also developed a more complex account of *Verstehen*. To capture the sense of reconstructing human meanings from their manifesta-tions, he loosely adapted the Hegelian terminology of "objectification." Texts, artifacts, and institutions can be considered externalized, or "objectified," traces of "mind"; the interpreter's task is to reconstruct the historical world from such objectively available traces. Among the objects of interpretation, Dilthey distinguished the expression of an immediate experience, a purposive human action, and a purely intellectual judgment. Even with respect to imme-diate experience, he suggested, we seek the distanced articulation of objective knowledge (*Erfahrung*). The most interesting aspect of Dilthey's late work, however, was his attempt to explicate the interpretation (*Verstehen, Ausle-*

gung) of intellectual "structures" or "patterns of thought." His point was that we can understand such products of mind as legal codes and mathematical theorems by retracing the reasoning on which they are based. The way in which the parts of a text are related to form a coherent whole, too, may be rationally reconstructed with some degree of reliability. As an objectification of mind, Dilthey noted, a text becomes independent of the author's psyche; it is integrated into a set of texts that jointly form an intellectual tradition. The relationship among texts is one of mutual adaptation and influence (*Wirkungszusammenhang*), which extends over time, right to our own day, for we live in a historical world of inherited meanings.

While fascinating in their scope, Dilthey's formulations never became fully clear. Perhaps his difficulty stemmed from his overriding commitment to the separation of the humanistic studies from the natural sciences. He contrasted the "freedom" of the human mind with the lawfulness of nature. Indeed, he identified causal relationships with "nomological" (*naturwissenschaftlich*) laws and with necessity, which made him all the more anxious to dissociate intellectual influence from causal connection. History is "immanently teleological," he wrote; human purposes and values are realized in the meanings that make up the historical world. *Verstehen* provides access to the "inner" connections within that world, which further distinguishes the humanities from the natural sciences. The historian is not interested in regularities, but in individualities, including distinctive cultures and epochs. Finally, Dilthey never lost his conviction that empathy is an element in interpretation. *Verstehen,* he wrote, always contains "something irrational."

Some of the positions Dilthey thus fully articulated after the turn of the century were actually anticipated by the sociologist and philosopher Georg Simmel as early as 1892. This is important because Simmel ultimately influenced Weber more than Dilthey did. Simmel's short treatise on *Problems in the Philosophy of History* was completed in 1892, then revised and extended in 1905. Like Dilthey, Simmel focused upon the relationship between inner "movements" of the "soul" and their outward expressions. In all human interactions, he noted, we presuppose mental states in others; we infer their thoughts and feelings from their actions and gestures, reasoning from visible "effects" to inner "causes." Asking how historians achieve their understanding of past human behaviors and beliefs, Simmel assigned a special place to the "theoretical contents of thought," which can be reconstructed independently of the intentions of their originators. Obviously, much greater difficulties arise in the understanding of subjective states. Interpreters may never fully grasp emotions too far beyond their own prior experience, Simmel believed;

but some degree of insight is possible even with respect to partly unfamiliar feelings. While insisting that we can know human history in a way that we cannot know nature, Simmel firmly rejected the notion of understanding as a kind of telepathic reproduction. The historian's ability to identify with others, he argued, is not a fact but a heuristic assumption, one that allows us to begin the process of interpretation at all.[19]

In a particularly interesting chapter, Simmel addressed the issue of "laws in history." Following Hume, he defined a law as the assertion that the occurrence of a set of facts is invariably followed by the occurrence of certain other facts. But in the world we know, he wrote, the states of the world that succeed each other are infinitely complex. We cannot judge whether they are lawfully linked, unless we first analyze them into their elements—but that is impossible. Thus a fully lawful connection between two historical events as totalities can never be established. Simmel's clear purpose was to undermine the vision of history as a sum of regularities. He saw scientific laws as "ideal" and thus different in logic from descriptions of particular events. History, he wrote, is not a *Gesetzeswissenschaft,* a nomological science, but a *Wirklichkeitswissenschaft,* a discipline concerned with concrete realities. The borderline between these two forms of inquiry did not seem to him unbridgeable; but he insisted that historical knowledge is of great human interest independently of the search for universal regularities.[20]

Having effectively excluded invariant laws in history, Simmel was prepared to recommend more loosely conceived "laws." By way of example, he cited such statistical regularities as suicide rates in given societies. He observed that we can arrive at rough generalities about such phenomena without knowing much about the particulars they aggregate. He also mentioned the "law of differentiation," which asserts a generally increasing specialization of functions and traits among human beings through the ages. Imperfect laws, he argued, should be expected to conflict on occasion, but they are nonetheless useful in the organization of data, in the identification of "typical" developments, and as preliminary steps toward more exact knowledge. One is reminded of Menger's distinction between abstract-but-exact and empirical-but-inexact regularities. Yet Simmel drew an even sharper line between all empirical approaches to history and inquiries into its "meaning." Whether historical change adds up to "progress," for example, can only be decided on the basis of extrahistorical value judgments. Nevertheless, historical studies must be guided by concerns about the human significance of the issues taken up, for the complex realities of the past cannot simply be enumerated. Historians must have questions to put to their data.[21]

Weber owed a great deal to Simmel; but he also benefited from a line of analysis that began with Wilhelm Windelband's 1894 address entitled "History and the Natural Sciences." Windelband criticized the division of the empirical studies into the natural sciences and the humanistic disciplines. He observed that this divide was based upon the "substantive" difference between "nature" and "mind," but he cited psychology to show that this distinction was hard to maintain. In its place, he proposed a "formal," or methodological, divide. The empirical disciplines usually identified as humanistic, he argued, seek "exhaustively" to describe particular events. Their "cognitive purpose" is to "reproduce and understand" a "form of human life" in its "unique actuality." Methodologically, the empirical disciplines fall into two groups: The *Gesetzeswissenschaften* pursue "nomothetic" knowledge of the general in the form of invariant "laws"; the *Ereigniswissenschaften* strive for "idiographic" knowledge of singular events or patterns. Windelband held that the same set of phenomena can be studied in both the nomothetic and the idiographic modes, and that the borderline between the two approaches is not absolute.[22]

As a theoretician of the German historical tradition, Windelband shifted the focus from the *principle of empathy* to the *principle of individuality*. He virtually ignored not only "nomothetic" psychology but Dilthey's reflections upon the humanistic disciplines as well. In this and other respects, Heinrich Rickert continued Windelband's perspective in his 1902 *Limits of Scientific Conceptualization*. According to Rickert, the world is an infinitely extensive set of objects, each of which is infinitely subdivisible, so that we confront an "extensively" and "intensively" infinite "manifold" of particulars. Obviously, our knowledge cannot be a reproduction of reality; indeed, we cannot know an object or event in all of its aspects. To comprehend reality is conceptually to simplify and to transform it in the light of a cognitive strategy. The strategy of the natural sciences is to analyze objects into their simpler components, trying to arrive at elementary constituents, while also subsuming selected aspects of reality under universal generalizations or laws that hold independently of time and place. The "limitation" of scientific conceptualization, in Rickert's view, is that it leaves behind the intuitive immediacy (*Anschaulichkeit*) of ordinary experience, so as to achieve the coherence embodied in its hierarchy of laws. For Rickert, it followed that the infinite manifold of reality may also be approached with a cognitive strategy other than that of the natural sciences.[23]

Like Windelband before him, Rickert found fault with the traditional division of the academic specialties into the natural sciences and the humanistic disciplines. Traditionally, these disciplines were held to deal interpretively with the world of "mind." Rickert did not object to this usage, which he expected to endure in practice. What he opposed, however, was a substantive or ontological divide between the realm of physical nature and that of the mental or psychic (*Geist, Psyche*). Instead, expanding Windelband's antithesis between "nomothetic" and "idiographic" knowledge, he recommended a logical distinction between the disciplines searching for nomological laws and those interested in the "individual," or singular. As the main alternative to the nomological disciplines, "history" is concerned with what occurred at specific times and places, with the distinctive, with personal and collective "individuals." "All empirical reality . . . becomes nature when we consider it with regard to the general; it becomes history when we consider it with regard to the particular. Every discipline has its point of departure in immediately experienced reality." The last sentence is important, for it reaffirms that reality itself cannot be reproduced. To illustrate the point, Rickert commented upon the widely held view that the great individuals resist generalization. According to Rickert, this is true simply because they are real. For all of reality is "irrational" in the sense that it cannot be encompassed by our concepts. Nevertheless, Rickert clearly believed that history comes closer than the natural sciences to conveying the fullness of ordinary experience. In that sense, history is what Simmel said it was: a discipline dealing with reality (*Wirklichkeitswissenschaft*) (250, 255, 258–60).

Of course, as Rickert conceded, the methodological divide between the natural sciences and the historical disciplines is not absolute. Elements of history—and singular developments—can be found in biology, in evolutionary theory, in geology, and in astronomy. Conversely, historians often use limited generalizations, or what Rickert called "relatively historical" concepts (309–10). Moreover, the historical "individual" too is a construct, not a concrete person or collectivity, although its description is meant to point up its distinctive qualities, not those of its traits that lend themselves to generalization. "Historical individuals" are conceptually isolated and defined in the light of their *cultural significance.* Historians of modern Germany are interested in the fact that Frederick William IV refused the crown offered by the Frankfurt Parliament; they do not care who made his coats (325–26). Most of the objects of historical study encompass mental events, which partly justify the term *Geisteswissenschaften.* Yet the central role played by cultural values and culturally significant "historical individuals" suggests that the real alternative to the natural sciences is the "historical study of culture" (*historische Kulturwissenschaft*) (339).

While mainly concerned with the particular, the historian must also search for causes, since the world is an infinitely complex network of singular causal connections. Having said that, however, Rickert sharply distinguished the interrelationships among historical individuals from the necessary connections implied by deterministic laws. On occasion, he actually equated "causal explanation" with nomological (*naturwissenschaftlich*) explanation. But his main point was that the mutual influences among historical individualities are not deducible from invariant laws (128–29, 307–8). Like earlier theoreticians of the German historical tradition, he fled the specter of determinism, leaving himself the problem of articulating an alternate model of singular causal analysis. He did offer a cogent distinction between "primary" and "secondary" historical individuals. "Primary historical individuals" derive their significance from their relationship to cultural values, whereas "secondary historical individuals" are *causally* relevant to "primary historical individuals" or "intellectual centers" (409–14, 475–80).

Rickert's overriding interest was in the problem of values. To begin with, he distinguished value judgments from judgments of "value relatedness." Without making value judgments in their own behalf, he argued, historians may judge certain "individuals" to be culturally relevant or value related. Thus two scholars may differ in their values and yet agree that some singular object or issue is culturally relevant (389–90). At any rate, as Rickert argued, the values involved in the historian's judgments must be *general* in some sense. But values are evolved by human beings living in communities; they are *cultural* values. Thus values may be empirically general in two ways: They may be commonly accepted as valid in the historians' own cultures or in the cultures they choose to investigate. Finally, Rickert suggested that values may be considered normatively general if they *ought* to be recognized as such by all educated persons within a culture (560–88).

Some of Rickert's formulations do not stand up to close examination. Thus his judgments of "value relatedness" do not remove the need for underlying value judgments. Moreover, the distinction between values held in the historians' own cultures and those held in the cultures they study is problematic, because it fails to specify how the commitments of past "intellectual centers" are known to historians. Rickert here either tacitly accepted the view that the past can be directly understood "in its own terms," or he forgot that his "intellectual centers" must first be selected—or constructed—as significant in the light of the historians' own values (641–42). Even more damaging, finally, is Rickert's tendency to confound values that are shared in reality with values that *ought* to be respected by educated members of a cultural group. The grounds for such obligatory commitments could lie only in the *absolute* validity of the values involved. This raises problems, because Rickert equated the *objectivity* of historical accounts with the *general validity of the values* that guide them. Historians attain the highest possible degree of "objectivity," he argued, if their judgments of significance are informed by values that are empirically valid in their culture. What remains in doubt is only their *universal* validity, the counterpart in the historical disciplines of *universal* truths in the sciences. While acknowledging that the absolute validity of cultural norms cannot currently be demonstrated, Rickert suggested that on a "supra-empirical plane," they can be posited as orienting ideals in the individualizing disciplines. Thus historical accounts will change, along with the empirical values of the historians' cultures; but they may nevertheless converge, along with the universal history of human culture, toward a single set of absolute values. The standpoint from which Rickert advanced these speculative claims was that of a transcendental subjectivism, in which the supra-individual subject was a valuing as well as a knowing one. He repeatedly emphasized that truth itself has to be posited as an unconditional value in the realm of science and learning (660–94).

Like Windelband, finally, Rickert virtually ignored the problem of interpretation. He apparently failed to consider Simmel's early suggestions on this subject, while the mature work of Dilthey was not yet available to him. When he wrote about interpretation at all, he restated the most crudely subjectivist account of "understanding" as an empathetic identification. As a theorist of "individuality," he used the term *Individuum* to designate not only persons, but also particular objects and events (10–14, 18–22). At the same time, he considered every such "individuality" unique and indivisible. Extending the metaphor of individuality, Rickert urged that historical development be conceived as a movement through unique stages that is value related not only in its elements, but also as a whole. Historical ages and groups too are unique and "teleologically" significant constellations of particulars. Rickert contrasted this holistic approach with the "atomizing individualism" of the Enlightenment, in which society seems a mere aggregate—and thus ultimately a "mass phenomenon." The historical whole, he argued, is more than the sum of its parts; it is their "essence" (*Inbegriff*) (360–61). Max Weber was influenced by aspects of Rickert's work, but he never accepted Rickert's holism or his "philosophy of values."

THE RISE OF GERMAN CLASSICAL SOCIOLOGY

With respect to the German historical tradition, Max Weber's posture was that of a heterodox critic; politically as well, he dissented from the orthodox mandarin views current among the large majority of historians. One has to know something about the historians to understand what Weber *opposed*, both methodologically and politically. The opposite is true, however, of the tiny handful of individuals who launched the fledgling discipline of sociology in late nineteenth-century Germany. Ferdinand Tönnies and Georg Simmel, the two most prominent early sociologists, stood fairly close to Weber, not only personally and politically, but also intellectually. Weber respected their works and was influenced by them. To know something about them is to understand a line of thought and analysis that Weber judged in positive terms and that he actively extended.

Indeed, German classical sociology was a true child of mandarin modernism. It dealt with the impact of commerce, bureaucracy, and capitalism upon traditional social relations. It echoed concerns that had first been expressed by the Romantic conservatives of the early nineteenth century, and it drew on Marx's analysis as well. Tönnies, Simmel, and Weber did not share the revolutionary hope of the Marxists; but they knew that there was no returning to the past, no escape from modernity. So they proposed to accept some facets of modern life, while seeking to understand and perhaps to moderate its most problematic aspects. Unlike their orthodox colleagues, they controlled their emotional response to their new environment, rejecting reactionary illusions and upholding a heroic ideal of rational clarification. This spirit, along with the German tradition of interpretive individualism, shaped the new discipline in Germany. Interpersonal relations, the network of social *interactions* or "bonds" among members of a group had to be conceptually isolated so that modern social problems could be studied in abstraction from both Marxism and Romantic holism.

Ferdinand Tönnies's *Community and Society* appeared in 1887, and went through six more editions between 1912 and 1926. For Tönnies, two contrary conceptions of law, two types of association, and two divergent styles of thought arose from a fundamental dichotomy between two forms of the will: *Wesenwille* and *Kürwille*. The German word *Wesen* refers to the "essence" or "nature" of something, so that the compound *Wesenwille* may be translated as the "essential" or "natural will." One must imagine a situation in which an individual's will with respect to some issue is determined by her "nature" or by her primary concerns. Thus a mother's devotion to her child or a nun's religious beliefs might be part of her "essence." There was always some suggestion of the primitive, unreflected drive in Tönnies "natural will," and yet he included habits and intellectual commitments among its sources. By contrast, the verb *küren* means "to choose," and the compound *Willkür*, which Tönnies used at times in place of *Kürwille,* suggests an arbitrary willfulness. More specifically, Tönnies associated *Kürwille* with what Max Weber later called "purposively rational" behavior, meaning action that is rational with respect to a given end. An act of *Kürwille,* in Tönnies' scheme, is very much a calculated act. It presupposes a distinction between means and ends, and a series of mental operations in which possible choices are located in a chain of means-ends relations. In describing a specific act of rational will, one refers to a particular place in such a chain; one does not have to characterize the individual chooser. Rational will proceeds upon emotionally and morally neutral modes of analysis, whereas natural will links thought to the whole personality and to its primary goals.[24]

All human relationships and groups, according to Tönnies, may be classified with respect to the quality of the will that creates them and holds them together. The members of a "community" are united in and through their "natural will"; the partners of a "society" come together to pursue objects of "rational will." The adjectives "communal" and "societal," when applied to a given "social entity," describe the character of the associative bond that is involved. Among social entities of a communal type, Tönnies included family and clan relationships, along with friendships, villages, guilds, and religious groups. On the other hand, the temporary agreement between the partners in an exchange, along with most modern business associations and interest groups, fell into the category of societal entities. Tönnies often used organic analogies to describe communities, while he tended to picture societal relationships in mechanical or contractual terms. In his view, the Romantic and the rationalist modes of social analysis each legitimately expressed one side of the permanent antithesis between the two forms of the will and of association, and he extended this argument to the field of political and legal theory as well. The fictions of the social contract and of natural law, it seemed to him, were excellent typical descriptions of societal legality, whereas communal law was a product of organic evolution, of custom and tradition.

In Tönnies' descriptions of communal relationships, customs and inherited practices fostered common expectations and obligations. A tacit consensus engendered communal actions, which might be rational but not explicitly rationalized. In the father of a family, the guildsman, and the small-town mayor, the person and the role were not clearly separated; gradations of power were experienced as degrees of "dignity," and there was unanimity or harmony of views (*Eintracht*) on major issues confronting the group. This pattern was threatened when interregional commerce led to a specification of exchange values, when state officials codified and articulated rights and obligations, and when capitalism created "free" labor and the wage contract. The destruction of community was a kind of rational articulation, in which explicit contracts and calculated equivalences replaced traditional expectations. Tönnies envisaged an inescapable long-term shift from communal to societal relationships. Drawing upon a distinction initially suggested by Immanuel Kant, he further associated this shift with the decline of inner "culture" and the rise of external "civilization." He did not hide his revulsion against developments that nonetheless seemed to him inevitable. Agriculture, the small-town guild, communal customs, and even the family itself had to be sacrificed, so that there could be worldwide markets, rational patterns of social organization, mass production, and an army of uprooted workers to be exploited in the factories. Of this he had no doubt, and he could not abide "idealistic" phrases designed to disguise these realities.[25]

Not surprisingly, Tönnies' *Community and Society* was ultimately simplified and appropriated by the orthodox critics of modernity. Especially during the First World War and during the interwar period, his work was used to lament the decline of "culture," to attack technological and liberal "civilization," and to preach the revival of a Germanic "community." But Tönnies himself explicitly repudiated the reactionary conclusions that others derived from his theories. He simply did not believe that the language of mandarin orthodoxy could restore the realities of community. He repeatedly warned against the illusion that "a dead ethic or religion can be brought back to life through any sort of compulsion or instruction." In a short autobiographical sketch and elsewhere, he made every effort to explain his position and to separate himself from his reactionary interpreters. He did not believe in social revolution, but he was actively interested in producers' and consumers' cooperatives, and especially in labor unions. He regarded these associations as the most promising exemplars of community in modern social life. His long-term pessimism did not prevent him from advocating radical measures in the field of social policy. He acquired the reputation of being a "socialist," which plainly hurt his academic career. In letters to his friend Friedrich Paulsen, Tönnies expressed his contempt for the class politics of the National Liberals, the self-serving "patriotism" of the Conservatives, and the servility of the German academic community. Very much an outsider, he finally became an associate professor at the age of fifty-four, and he did not receive an official teaching assignment in sociology itself until he was sixty-five, in 1920.[26]

Tönnies most abiding commitment was to the ideal of rational clarification. He included modern *Wissenschaft* among the products of the "rational will," but this did not prevent him from identifying with "the rigorously scientific manner of thinking, which rejects all belief in spirits and spooks." During the 1920s, in the face of widespread attacks on liberalism, he announced his "full personal sympathy" with "the freeing of thought from the bonds of superstition and delusion," and with "all movements of liberation against feudalism and serfdom." He admitted that many of the Romantic and conservative ideals that he now opposed had originally been rooted in community. The difficulty was that they had long since become "empty," "fundamentally untrue and hypocritical," so that "a vital individualism and the [forms of] society" were the only real alternatives to "force and tyranny." While remaining pessimistic about the course of modern life, he sought to block the escape into obscurantist illusion. In 1909, when Max Weber and others founded the German Society for Sociology, they chose Ferdinand Tönnies as its first president.

Georg Simmel ranks as the second founder of sociology in Germany. Among his many works, three proved particularly important for the emerging discipline. The essay "On Social Differentiation" (1890) and the more systematic *Sociology* (1900), explicate Simmel's vision of sociology as a discipline; his *Philosophy of Money* (1908) is the most suggestive application of his method. Some of the essays he wrote develop particular themes in his foundational works, so that they have become classics in their own right. Simmel's loose use of analogies and his infrequent reference to specifically relevant empirical data can be frustrating. Yet he is extraordinarily rich in insights and suggestions. Thus if his sociological works are added to his extended essays in the philosophy of history, he must be considered among Max Weber's most important precursors.

In the German tradition of interpretive individualism, Simmel defined "sociation" (*Vergesellschaftung*) as the sum of "interactions" (*Wechselwirkungen*) among individuals. Such interactions, he believed, can create patterns that attain a degree of autonomy in relation to the particular individuals and behaviors involved. Thus, on the one hand, the "social" must not be conceived holistically as existing apart from the interactions that constitute it. On the other hand, there is a borderline between the exclusively individual and the social, "where the interaction among persons does not consist only in their subjective states and actions, but engenders an objective formation (*Gebilde*), which has a certain independence from the participating personalities." Thus sociology deals with the patterns of interactions in so far as these are not purely subjective or ephemeral.[27]

In his systematic *Sociology* of 1908, Simmel distinguished between the "forms" and the "contents" of social interactions. Under the heading of "forms," he cited such recurrent relationships as superordination and subordination, and such groupings as voluntary associations. The "content" of these social forms might vary over the range of human concerns, from the economic and political to the cultural and personal. Thus hierarchies of superiors and subordinates may occur in a shoe factory as well as in a political party, and voluntary associations may be founded to pursue or oppose all kinds of objectives. As Simmel stressed, the forms and the contents of sociation are always conjoined. By separating the forms alone for analysis, therefore, sociology, like other disciplines, abstracts from reality. It conceptually isolates particular aspects of sociation for special attention. The generalizations of the sociologist, like the "laws" of the historian, according to Simmel, are not invariant. They do not deal with microscopic and law-like regularities, but with macroscopic generalizations that may be altered by unexpected circumstances. Moreover, they often one-sidedly "exaggerate" typical traits of the "forms" they analyze, thus positing hypothetical relationships that may not have full counterparts in reality. Simmel's vision of "formal" sociology anticipated some of what Max Weber was to say more clearly about the "ideal type."[28]

Unlike Tönnies, Simmel took a positive view of conflict and competition. He believed that the limits and norms of conflict were gradually defined in the process of conflictual interactions—and were thus important elements in sociation. Like the French sociologist Emile Durkheim, moreover, Simmel valued dissensus, within limits, as a source of social change and vitality. Also like Durkheim, he saw modern societies evolving toward a degree of internal differentiation in proportion to their quantitative expansion. He considered this one of the imperfectly invariant laws that formal sociology could detect. Members of small groups, Simmel thought, would engage in relatively similar means of sustaining themselves and their families. With growth in the size of the group, increased competition was likely to lead to a degree of occupational specialization. While the reasons for this drift were at least partly economic, Simmel also suggested a propensity of human beings to distinguish themselves from their fellows: "As the circle expands in which we act and to which our interests are directed, so there is more scope for the development of our individuality." Thus the individual emerged with the quantitative growth of modern populations.[29]

Simmel detected a long-term evolution from small, uniform, and highly integrated social groups to larger and internally more differentiated social systems. Complex modern societies, Simmel argued, are composed of many loosely integrated "social circles," from occupational and status groups to voluntary associations of all kinds. They also provide a setting for the development of distinctive personalities. At first constrained by the norms and practices of a small group, the individual is later more loosely affiliated with a larger number of less binding "social circles." Indeed, modern individuals can be described as the "intersections" of many social circles, and therein lies their opportunity for individuation. This conclusion of "formal sociology" may be considered a more complex—and less pessimistic—restatement of Tönnies's vision of the progression from "community" to "society."[30]

In his fascinating *Philosophy of Money,* Simmel used the term *philosophy* to designate lines of analysis that lie either below or above the level of abstraction of an ordinary discipline like economics. Thus, looking into the foundations of economics, Simmel proposed to "construct a floor beneath historical materialism." He accepted the neo-classical economics of marginal utility and marginal cost, and proceeded to ground it in a set of "philosophical" considerations. He posited a dialectical tension, in which a desiring self confronts a desired object that is not automatically available, but stands at a "distance" from the self. This distance must be overcome through effort, or through the sacrifice of other potential objects of enjoyment. Even solitary individuals can compare the "distances"—or levels of sacrifice—that lie between them and various goods. More typically, it is the sum of social interactions of exchange that jointly define the relative value of goods. Rejecting the labor theory of value, in sum, Simmel saw prices as intersubjective effects of exchange relationships. In its origins, Simmel suggested, money was a particularly valued good, something scarce, perhaps decorative, and ideally subdivisible. Then, over time, its substantive qualities lost significance, and it ultimately came to play the purely symbolic role of measuring the value relationships involved in economic interactions.[31]

The presence of money in modern social systems, Simmel argued, facilitates the long-term process of social differentiation and individuation. Money encourages the emergence of an extensive network of social interactions that are less intense than the few binding interpersonal relationships characteristic of small groups. When I make a cash contribution to a voluntary association, I do not commit much of myself to the group I thus join. When I buy a commodity produced in a distant country, I do not have to see the producers and merchants with whom I interact. The immense system of exchanges in a modern money economy makes possible the complexity and variety of the social circles in which the individual participates, most often at a relatively modest level of engagement. Without money, the modern territorial state could not exist; for it needs salaried administrators to function at all. Eventually, it becomes the guarantor of a purely symbolic currency. Technological innovation can reach unprecedented rates in the presence of money; for money can concentrate resources, much as scientific concepts concentrate our knowledge. The abstractions involved in the establishment of quantitative relationships among qualitatively dissimilar objects requires complex calculations that foster the "intellectuality" of modern culture.[32]

Like Tönnies, Simmel saw the beginnings of interregional trade as a crucial step in the emergence of the modern money economy. The traders who entered economically self-sufficient regions to buy goods highly valued in distant markets were typically strangers to the local community. Very often, they were excluded from other local activities, which helped to channel their energies toward trade and monetary exchange. Simmel particularly emphasized the role of the Jews in that connection. Unhampered by Christian restrictions upon usury, they performed economic functions that others neglected. They were easily exploited by territorial princes, who collected taxes from them in exchange for "protection." Given their "pariah status," Simmel argued (before Weber), the Jews were suited to the role of the "stranger"; their exclusion from alternate occupations and their geographic dispersion made them ideal agents of interregional trade, currency exchange, and the lending of money.[33]

Toward the end of his *Philosophy of Money*, Simmel turned to the impact of money upon the modern "style of life." Anticipating Weber, he grounded this part of his exposition in a theory of action. He insisted that mere "intentions," images of actions in terms of their outcomes, could not be considered the causes of actions. Instead, there had to be a kind of energy that was directed at the imagined outcome, but that existed separately from it and served as its "cause." He also sharply distinguished actions aimed at an immediate end from actions in pursuit of *means* to an end. In modern life, many of our actions aim at intermediate links in ever-lengthening chains of means-ends relationships. Money, of course, may serve as a means to a large variety of ends; it becomes a kind of universal tool—and it may easily be misperceived as an end in itself. Simmel occasionally sounded a pessimistic note, not only about the predominance of means over ends, but also about human estrangement in a world of increasingly impersonal relationships. Yet he also recognized the benefits to be derived from the replacement of intensely personal obligations by a network of economically or rationally mediated relationships. Money and social complexity can engender "freedom" as well as isolation. Young American women prefer factory work under contractually regulated conditions to the personal dependence associated with domestic service in traditional European households. Superiority and subordination cannot be eliminated from organized social action. But in a complex environment, a superior with respect to some field of activity may find himself a subordinate in another realm. Above all, there is a marked difference between delimited, objective social relations and outright personal dependence.[34]

Simmel's most striking occasional essays were generally extensions of his foundational works, and several of them deal with modern individuation. He distinguished between an Enlightenment and a post-Romantic idea of individual freedom. The Enlightenment was guided by the vision of a universal human essence that only had to be freed from the distorting forces of prejudice for the autonomous individual to emerge. "Freedom" in that context meant freedom from the bonds of tradition. But this universalist project of enlightened Reason was transformed during the Romantic era by a new emphasis upon the distinctive character of the ideal individual. "Freedom" now came to mean room for the development of each individual's unique potentialities. The diversity of human individuals—and of distinctive cultures—thus moved to the center of the stage. The change of emphasis was attuned to the individuation possible in large and complex modern societies. In a lecture on Schopenhauer and Nietzsche, Simmel argued that the lengthening of means-ends chains stimulated a countervailing quest among modern individuals for ultimate ends or values. Inherited from Christianity, the need to locate an ultimate purpose of life led, in Friedrich Nietzsche, to a paradoxical reversal—an apotheosis of life itself. Simmel saw Nietzsche as the champion of such life-affirming qualities of extraordinary human individuals as strength, beauty, and, above all, *dignity (Vornehmheit)*. Suspicious of the typical roots of beneficence and of humility, Nietzsche spoke for the perfection of rare individuals, rather than the comfort of the mediocre majority. For Simmel, at any rate, Nietzsche was the radical prophet of individuation.[35]

In a cluster of essays on "cultivation" and on "culture," finally, Simmel offered another striking analysis of his world. He began with a definition of "cultivation" (*Kultiviertheit*) that fully articulates the idea of *Bildung* current in his intellectual field.

> Every kind of learning, virtuosity, refinement in a man cannot cause us
> to attribute true cultivation to him if these things function . . . only as
> super-additions that come to his personality from a normative realm external to it . . . In such a case, a man may have cultivated attributes, but
> he is not cultivated; cultivation comes about only if the contents absorbed out of the supra-personal realm (of objectified cultural values)
> seem, as through a secret harmony, to unfold only that in the soul which

exists within it as its own instinctual tendency and as the inner pre-figuration of its subjective perfection.

The terminology of the neo-Idealist revival of the *Geisteswissenschaften* is here used to specify (1) that cultivation entails the absorption of values from "the supra-personal realm," (2) that it can only "unfold" the "pre-figuration" of the individual's "perfection," and (3) that the cultivated individual is a unique totality, not a mere aggregate of "cultivated attributes." The formulation explicates the principles of empathy and of individuality. It also reveals both the utopian and the socially confirmative uses of "cultivation." The utopian thrust emerges if one focuses upon the *obstacles* to perfection encountered by most contemporaries. The confirmative or ideological implication comes to the fore if one assumes that a minority has actually achieved full cultivation. The formulation then suggests that these few, unlike the many, have *become* what they always *were,* in their *essence.*[36]

Enlarging upon his model of learning as "cultivation," Simmel characterized the development of human culture as a dialectical interaction between "objective mind" (*Geist*) and "subjective mind" or "soul." In Simmel's adaptation of a common idiom, "personal culture" was identical with "cultivation"; "subjective mind" or "soul" stood for the thought of the individual knower and, by extension, of humanity in general. "Objective mind" or "culture" encompassed the external expressions of subjective mind, the social and material forms in which it is fixed and transmitted. Simmel emphasized that subjective and objective mind can only develop in dialectical interaction; an exclusively subjective life can never attain any degree of complexity or coherence. On the other hand, the inescapable need for objectification leads to consequences that have a tragic aspect. The fullness and pliability of subjective culture gives rise to the diversity and fixity of objective mind. As the latter grows more extensive, there is an increasing "incommensurability between the subjective and the objective poles in the dialectic of cultural development and of individual *Bildung.*" Alienation occurs as well; for the reified elements of the objective culture acquire a life of their own. Man is constrained by the artifacts, institutions, and theories he has invented; they do not seem to him malleable; he does not recognize them as his creatures. The division of labor and scholarly specialization are the two great exemplars of the disjunction between subjective and objective mind. The subjective mind of the producer is drained into machines and commodities that enslave him. Subjective mind cannot intellectually encompass its former creations, and harmonious individual cultivation becomes ever more difficult.

Influenced by Marx, Simmel sometimes described the division of labor as the cause of the growing incongruity between objective and subjective culture. But his formulations also allow the interpretation that the division of labor is only one facet of the broader alienation of subjective mind from its creations. The other is the loss of philosophical coherence and personal mastery associated with scientific specialization. Moreover, Simmel failed to explain why the timeless "tragedy of culture" became particularly acute during his own time. One can only speculate that it was the rapid acceleration in the growth of objective culture that left a relative deficit of subjective culture, or a loss of soul. Reading Simmel, it is hard to imagine that progressive French humanists and social scientists, including the sociologist Emile Durkheim, greeted the decades around 1900 as a promising new age of scientific specialization, cultural vitality, and political reform. But that only confirms that Simmel was a penetrating analyst of German academic culture.

Until the early 1920s, I should add, German sociology was essentially a modernist enterprise. It was therefore furiously attacked by such orthodox historians as Georg von Below. Indeed, Max Weber himself long remained indifferent to or skeptical of the emerging discipline. Even in his posthumous conceptual introduction to *Economy and Society,* the term *sociology* is characterized as "highly ambiguous." Nevertheless, there was a shift in Weber's emphasis sometime around 1909, when he helped to found the German Society for Sociology. From the methodology of the cultural and social sciences, the introduction of the "ideal type," and a predominantly historical approach, Weber moved toward the categorical analysis of "social relationships," even as his work on the sociology of the world religions and the preconditions of modern capitalism took on a nearly universal scope. I believe that this change of emphasis in Weber's work did not alter the foundations of his methodological individualism. But what I mainly want to suggest for the moment is that Weber became the greatest of the German classical sociologists, and that the questions he pursued in his own rigorous fashion were first raised by Ferdinand Tönnies and Georg Simmel.

CHAPTER TWO

Weber's Politics

Throughout his life, Weber was deeply engaged in the political issues of his time. Immediately after the First World War, he came close to taking up the calling of politics; but regional party officials, his health—or his innermost instincts—ultimately prevented that step across the line between political commentator and politician. The early portions of this chapter deal with his political writings from 1892 to the First World War. This was, for him, a particularly distressing phase in German politics. The "new era" announced when William II chose to govern without Bismarck in 1890 was soon followed by a period of political reaction. Two attempts to replace the antisocialist laws by new exceptional legislation against the Social Democratic Party failed to pass the Reichstag, but police and judicial harassment of the workers' organizations continued. At the same time, the last two decades before the war were dominated by a regime of high import duties in support of the East Elbian landowners and of heavy industry. Along with commercial exporters, it was the workers and other consumers who bore the cost of this policy. Indeed, the Agrarian League (1893) and the Conservatives imposed a distortion upon the German economy, retarding commercial and industrial development while artificially maintaining the socially and politically significant tradition of agrarian predominance. One of the consequences was a huge migration of former peasants from the eastern provinces, not only to the western industrial centers, but also to the United States and elsewhere abroad.

Max Weber began to comment upon the pertinent economic and social questions shortly after beginning his academic career at the University of Berlin in 1892. He was asked to participate in a survey of German agrarian conditions by the Social Policy Association (Verein für Sozialpolitik). As the forum of the German Historical School of Economics, the Association had been chaired, since 1890, by Gustav Schmoller. Its aim was to bring academic expertise to bear upon current social problems, typically by considering draft laws and by directly influencing the leading government officials. The young Max Weber's participation in the agrarian survey was to facilitate his movement from legal to economic and social history, to launch him into a series of protracted political controversies, and ultimately to bring him into conflict with the leadership of the Social Policy Association itself.[1]

THE AGRARIAN QUESTION
AND WEBER'S NATIONALISM

In Weber's *Situation of the Agricultural Workers in East Elbian Germany* (1892), he focused upon the most sensitive portion of the nationwide survey, the part that dealt with the great landed estates of the eastern provinces. The survey was based upon two questionnaires sent to all German agricultural *employers,* including the East Elbian estate owners, or *Junkers.* Weber was aware of the one-sided character of the information gathered in this way; but the critical acumen with which he approached the portion of the responses allocated to him effectively disarmed potential critics. Even the *Junkers* found something to praise in Weber's report, since he included an appreciation of their former services to Prussia and Germany. At the 1893 meeting of the Social Policy Association, Weber's report became the main subject of discussion.

Weber's analytical tactic in his report on East Elbian conditions was to distinguish a single dominant trend for the eastern provinces from subordinate local variations that were consistent with his overall thesis, and thus actually reinforced it. He drew upon the most reliable data reported by agrarian employers: land costs, population changes, prices, consumption patterns, and similarly objective statistics. He then constructed a set of subjective attitudes that were both internally coherent and consistent with the quantitative results. In areas where relatively poor soil encouraged cereal production, he found large estates, on which a traditional form of day labor still prevailed. The so-called *Instmann,* a dependent sharecropper who subsisted there, lived in a separate household that was nevertheless still partly integrated into the lord's manor. The lord allocated a garden plot and a small share of agricultural land to his dependent, which he cultivated in the latter's behalf. In return, the *Instmann* and his family worked with the landowner's unmarried domestic servants, occasionally supplemented by auxiliary hands, especially during the summer. In addition, the day laborer threshed out the lord's harvest during the winter months, taking a small fraction of the yield for himself.[2]

Instmann and *Gutsherr* (lord) stood in a dependency relationship that entailed some degree of mutuality. The sharecropper raised his own potatoes, a couple of pigs, and a cow or two. He thus partly sustained himself and his family, but he also enjoyed a fraction of the cereals produced by the estate. He thus shared his lord's interest in adequate harvests and grain prices. He relied upon the competence as well as the good will of the *Gutsherr;* and, as Weber insisted, the patriarchal context was not devoid of "personal feelings of honor and duty." Indeed, the intense relationship involved laid the basis for the Prussian military system, which served Prussia and Germany well, at least until 1871.[3]

But there was a second set of relationships among agricultural employees and workers in the east Elbian provinces, one that predominated in the fertile valleys south of the sandy northern lands, and it was rapidly growing in quantitative significance. Typically associated with the cultivation of sugar beets, it was linked more broadly to the advance of agrarian capitalism. In regions of rich soil, the trend was toward wage labor, which proved more profitable for the proprietor than remuneration in kind. Instead of resembling small homesteads, worker settlements were concentrated, essentially barracks, and poor in garden land. The emerging "free" agricultural laborer was better protected against poor harvests than the traditional *Instmann;* but he was a proletarian, with interests directly opposed to those of his employer, and of course he was highly mobile. Weber traced his situation to excesses committed by the landowners in the distribution of land after the liberation of the serfs in the nineteenth century. Technical improvements in capitalist agriculture seemed less significant to Weber than the erosion of traditional agrarian relationships in the most advanced regions.

The chief symptom of the conditions created by capitalist agriculture was an ever more pressing demand for seasonal labor. The raising of sugar beets was much more labor intensive than the cultivation of cereals on sandy soil. But the relatively self-sufficient *Instmann* system was incompatible with agrarian capitalism. What interested Weber about the results was not the agrarian owners' well-advertised labor shortage, but two related dimensions of population movement. On the one hand, Polish and Russian migrant workers made up an increasing share of the population in such regions as Silesia; on the other hand, the eastern provinces were rapidly losing German workers, not only to the industrial centers of Western Germany, but also to the United States and to other foreign countries. In the 1880s, the eastern borders had been largely closed against immigrants; but the barriers were lowered again in 1890 to help the landowners. Worse, migrants who came to work in Germany during the summer—for low wages—could be forced back across the border for the winter. Permanent German smallholders found it hard to survive the resulting competition.

When Weber summarized his findings in the conclusion of his report and in his comments before the Social Policy Association, he highlighted three themes. To begin with, he warned against blaming the *Junkers* for the ominous trends in the eastern provinces. The *Junkers* had been a main support of the monarchy, sustaining a crucial service elite of military officers and civil servants. The changes that undermined their economic position were driven by technological and market forces beyond their control, and especially by shifts in the *psychology* of their employees. The most reliable of their workers now sought to escape the relationship of personal dependence they had formerly tolerated. When agrarian spokesmen cited Weber's recognition of the *Junkers*' former role to justify further subsidies, he refused to concede that a former governing elite should be rewarded for services it was no longer able to perform.[4]

The loss of population in the east might have been explained in purely economic terms, but Weber also insisted on "psychological" changes. The *Instmann* was no longer willing to accept his former dependence. "It is the powerful and purely psychological magic of 'freedom'" that causes precisely the best-situated German workers to leave areas in which the *Instmann* relationship still survives. The aspirations of the migrants may be illusionary, as may be their hope for their heirs. Still, "the changes in the psychological needs of human beings are almost greater than the transformations in the material conditions of life." Weber's formulation recalls Simmel on the impact of money on social relationships, for money and social complexity can engender "freedom," along with impersonality and isolation. Above all, there is a great difference between a precisely delimited and "objective" relationship and personal dependence.[5]

What Weber recommended as a result of his survey was the creation of various types of smallholdings in the eastern provinces. Economically threatened Polish or German estates could be bought and divided up, and the Prussian domain administration should take the lead in settling new generations of German farmers in the threatened regions. At the same time, the further immigration of Polish agricultural workers should be prohibited. Weber recommended "inner colonization," arguing for a tough brand of cultural nationalism: "Our cultural standards, the nutritional status of our agrarian populations and their needs are being pushed down to the level of a lower, more easterly cultural stage . . . We hope to raise (our) domestic Polish proletariat to the level of German culture—but that will become impossible if the continuing influx of . . . eastern nomads . . . destroys this cultural work."[6] Weber here unhesitatingly wrote as an enemy of a "lower eastern" culture.

While working on his survey for the Social Policy Association, Weber also helped to launch a supplementary inquiry in collaboration with the Protestant Social Congress. That congress brought together Protestant pastors with lay social reformers. Its program was to ameliorate agrarian as well as industrial working conditions. Its course soon drew criticism from William II and from the orthodox leadership of the Protestant church. As a result, the organization split along ideological lines and relapsed into passivity during the mid-1890s. Between 1892 and 1894, however, the congress sponsored its own survey of agrarian working conditions. With Weber's advice, questionnaires were sent to Protestant pastors all over Germany, with the hope that those in rural posts would consult agricultural workers, rather than employers. Only a modest share of the questionnaires were returned, and the conclusions Weber had drawn from the Social Policy Association's survey were not substantially modified. At the 1894 meeting of the Protestant Social Congress, Weber largely reaffirmed his established position, but he also conveyed a degree of resignation. As a "class-conscious bourgeois," he again argued that the East Elbian landowners had once been an economically secure ruling class, but that the conditions of their ascendancy could not be resurrected. The former relationship between lords and peasants, brutal or not, had been replaced by the impersonality and the "objective hatred" of class antagonism. Once again, Weber underlined the "idealistic" aspirations of the peasants who left their homes, including their partly conscious "thirst for intellectual culture."[7]

Toward the end of his presentation, Weber apparently felt the need to signal the difference between his viewpoint and that of Naumann. A leading champion of Protestant social reform, Naumann had given the welcoming address at the meeting, and Weber registered his dissent.

> In the welcoming address of pastor Naumann yesterday, we heard an infinite yearning for human happiness, which surely moved us all. But precisely from our pessimistic standpoint . . . I believe we must renounce the idea of fostering . . . happiness by means of . . . social legislation. We want something else. . . . That which seems to us of value in human beings, autonomy, the profound drive upward, toward the intellectual and moral goods of mankind, that is what we want to . . . support even . . . in its most primitive form.[8]

The formulation is highly characteristic of Weber in its aversion to charity as a motive of social policy, and in its emphasis upon character formation rather than "happiness."

During the years between 1894 and 1912, Weber continued to pursue the issues raised by his work on eastern agrarian conditions, but he broadened his position. His critique of the status quo became less hopeful and decidedly more bitter. Shortly after presenting his findings to the Social Policy Association, he published an overview of the East Elbian situation in a neutral journal and in terms that echoed Marx. The eastern provinces had once produced a surplus based upon the labor-intensive exploitation of land. This surplus depended more upon personal domination than upon entrepreneurial skill, and it maintained a ruling elite that could afford to supply the state with military officers and high civil servants. But as this system of production faced increasing economic competition from abroad, the political capital accumulated by the agrarian landowners was increasingly used to bargain for domestic economic concessions. The result was a system of high tariffs and export subsidies that barely maintained the lifestyle of the landowners—at the cost of two fundamental transformations. First, the *Junkers* came to play the role and to speak the language of "dissatisfied alms receivers." They claimed to be entitled to surplus incomes that ultimately came out of the pockets of working-class consumers. Second, the continuing threat of economic decline forced the landowners to become agricultural capitalists, to think entrepreneurially about maximizing profits and minimizing costs. The old personal ties to their dependents were dissolved, and farm workers came to prefer money wages to remuneration in kind. Like their urban cousins, they became participants in the capitalist class war. The landowners' chief weapon against them was the employment of cheap migrant laborers, especially Poles.[9]

Weber's animus against Polish immigrants may strike us as unacceptable, but it was not inconsistent with his position on social policy questions. He insisted that Germany did not face a "natural law" of economic development from which there was no escape. He saw no reason to tolerate a situation in which freedom had become synonymous with homelessness for a large segment of the population, and he again insisted on a vigorous program of colonization. But he clearly doubted that his recommendations would be followed under prevailing political conditions.[10]

Apparently, his pessimism was justified, for in 1904 we find him bitterly opposing a proposal that reversed the thrust of his recommendations. A draft law was introduced to establish entailed estates (*Fideikommisse*) to be inherited by male primogeniture, inalienable, and associated with a family council.

The potential owners' "noble conduct of life" was to be guaranteed by a mere ten years of titular aristocratic rank, and the emperor himself was to consider the worthiness of the families thus privileged. The family of entailed estate owners could expect preferred access to the officer corps and the high civil service. Weber anticipated even higher grain tariffs, which under existing arrangements would yield substantial export subsidies as well. The drafters of the proposed law wrote in sentimental terms about future estate owners finding "a home for themselves and their families for all time," but they ignored the impact of the proposal on the makeup of the agrarian population in general and on the fate of agricultural workers in particular.[11]

In his scathing commentary, Weber characterized the draft law as an outright capitulation of the state to agrarian capitalism. Land prices were bound to rise; small farmers would be forced to move to more marginal lands or to leave the region; the "artificial protection of large-scale ownership and production" would deprive thousands of their homes. The proletarianization of the agricultural work force would accelerate, and so would the recourse to migrant labor. But the most devastating effect of the proposed measure would be its seductive effect upon the German bourgeoisie. Entrepreneurial capitalists were in effect offered the chance to become privileged rentiers, while ensuring their families' claims to public employment. Responding to the "contemptible yen for aristocratic titles," they would be "compensated for their minimal political influence" with a "second-class courtier's status." They could be expected to react to their *parvenu* status by pliability toward their superiors and "mandarin haughtiness" toward their "subjects." An arrogant bureaucracy committed to the preservation of the status quo was bound to turn Germany into a "vassal state."[12]

Weber's Freiburg Inaugural Address of 1895 must be understood in the light of his position on the agrarian question and on "social policy" more generally. The empirical focus of his address was on the province of West Prussia. Here too, Weber observed, German day laborers left regions of fertile estates, while Poles actually increased in relatively infertile counties. Once again, Weber wrote of the "primitive idealism" and the "magic of freedom" that drew German laborers away from a world in which traditional working relationships were being replaced by agrarian capitalism. Again he called for the closing of the border and a program of German resettlement.[13]

But Weber's emphasis in the inaugural address was not upon agrarian conditions themselves, but upon two other issues. First, he observed that Germans and Poles had for some time been in economic competition; yet victory in this contest had not gone to the "economically more highly developed or talented nationality." Instead, the Poles had shown greater "adaptability" to the prevailing "conditions of existence." The "Slavic race" was able to adjust to a lower standard of living and thus to emerge victorious from the "process of selection" that caused Germans to leave the eastern provinces. Weber tried to avoid the issues posed by the variability of a "population's physical and psychological qualities" under changing "conditions of life." Nevertheless, he had certainly introduced the issue of "racial qualities," of "selection" and "adaptability" into the discussion of the agrarian question, and he had identified the Poles as a backward group.[14]

The other main point Weber wanted to make had to do with the role of value judgments in "social policy." He thought there was no escape from economic competition, and he once again repudiated the aim of maximizing human happiness or comfort.

> The question that moves us when we think beyond the grave of our own generation is not whether the human beings of the future will *feel* well, but what sort of human beings they will *be*. . . . Not well-being but the qualities . . . that make up human greatness and the nobility of our nature are what we want to breed into human beings.

Whether explicitly or not, Weber claimed, some have believed that the discipline of economics can find its standards in its own subject matter. They have stressed the pursuit of productivity; or they have sought justice in the distribution of goods. But economics is a "human science," and as such it must ask primarily about the "quality of human beings that are developed by economic and social conditions." Indeed, we "disciples of the German historical school" too easily succumb to the illusion that "we can avoid conscious value judgments altogether." But the consequence is that we are moved by "uncontrolled instincts, sympathies and antipathies." Instead we must be consciously guided by the "power-political interests of the nation." In economics too, our ultimate standard of judgment must be *"reason of state."*[15]

Turning to the issue of political maturity, Weber warned against the assumption that economic success guarantees a vocation for politics. As an economist and a member of the middle class, Weber insisted that the Prussian landowners could no longer act in behalf of the whole nation, and that neither the bourgeoisie nor the working class was politically mature enough to exercise power. That is why Germans relied on Bismarck's Caesarian rule. The clear and present danger to Germany stemmed not from economic causes or from the much-lamented "interest politics" but from lack of political experience among large segments of the burgher stratum, from their "apolitical past." Neither the illusion of a value-free social policy nor the substitution of "ethical" for political objectives could reverse the drift toward passivity and impotence. A great effort of political education was needed. The suffering of the masses may "weigh upon the political conscience of the new generation; but what weighs upon it even more heavily today is the consciousness of our responsibility before history."[16]

Weber's inaugural address should not be read *only* as an expression of his commitment to power politics or to nationalism. For he also identified the ultimate aims of social policy with "human greatness," the aspiration to "freedom," and the desire to share in the "intellectual and cultural goods of mankind." His purpose was not only to exclude charitable grounds to pursue human well-being, but even more urgently to deny that social policy could be based upon such intra-economic norms as "productivity," or upon such implicit aims as the preservation of rural values or the disarming of radical Social Democrats. There may even have been a tactical element in Weber's choice of nationalism as the ultimate norm of social policy, for the typical use of nationalist rhetoric among agrarian conservatives and members of the educated middle class was directed against the Social Democratic Party, who were explicitly *excluded* from the "national" consensus that took itself to be "apolitical." To say merely that Weber was a nationalist would be to say very little, for almost all European intellectuals before the First World War were nationalists. What requires explanation is that Weber's nationalism was deliberately *inclusive,* and that this was extremely rare, at least in the German political context. It was backed, moreover, by the specific *rationale* he offered for his nationalism. What he really intended, as he insisted, was to foster valued *human qualities.*

Of course, that still leaves us with the need to account for Weber's hostility to the Poles, and for his introduction of racist language into the debate over agrarian conditions. Here he was guilty of prejudices that we certainly cannot share. As it happens, Weber recognized this flaw in his position, and he made the necessary corrections well before the First World War. Intervening in a debate on "the concepts of race and society" at the 1910 meeting of the Social Policy Association, for example, he challenged a colleague's racial speculations as "mystical." He saw no evidence that racial theory contributed in any way to the analysis of sociohistorical processes. On the contrary, as he pointed out, if "race" played a role at all, "we do not know it and will never know it." But where we have "known and sufficient grounds" for a particular phenomenon, "it conflicts with scientific method to put them aside in favor of an uncontrollable hypothesis." Two years later, he similarly registered his objection to any essentialist definition of "the nation": "A concept of the nation could presumably be constructed only . . . as follows: It is a community of feeling, the adequate expression of which would be a national state, and which thus normally tends to generate such a state. But the causal components that will lead to the emergence of national feeling in this sense may differ radically." Weber cited shared religious beliefs and a common language as possible grounds of experienced national identities, but he also stressed shared political memories or aspirations as sources of national feelings.[17]

In two sections of *Economy and Society,* sections that were written in 1910 or shortly thereafter, Weber came back to the issues of "race," "ethnicity," and "nationalism." His approach was conditioned by his definition of "communal" relationships in terms of the participants' feeling of belonging together. Thus he did not ask what racial or national attributes *were,* but how particular social groups came to *feel* and to *act as if* they shared "racial" or "national" characteristics, for "racial membership" will create a sense of community only "when it is subjectively experienced as a common quality." The "communal actions" that then arise express themselves as contempt or superstitious reserve toward those who are different. But the antipathy involved is "by no means tied only to inherited, but also to other conspicuous differences in the outward *habitus.*" Religious beliefs as well as status differences may limit intermarriage and thus ultimately produce "genuine anthropological differences," as among the Indian castes or among "pariah peoples," who are "despised and yet sought as neighbors, because they have monopolized indispensable techniques." Divergences of language and of custom may encourage the belief in distinctive ethnic identities, which may be associated with certain forms of social honor as well.[18]

Weber simply no longer believed in the reality of "racial qualities."

All in all, "ethnically" determined communal action subsumes phenomena that would have to be carefully distinguished by a really exact sociological analysis. . . . The actual subjective effect of customs conditioned by heredity on the one hand, and by tradition on the other; the impact of all the various contents of "custom"; the effect of common language, religion and political action, past and present . . . the degree to which such factors engender attraction and repulsion, and especially the belief in affinity or disaffinity of blood; the consequences of this belief for . . . sexual relations (and) for the chances that various forms of communal action will develop . . . all this would have to be separately investigated. In the process, the collective concept "ethnic" would surely be thrown overboard. For it is totally useless for any rigorous analysis.

Weber has here adopted a sociological terminology that highlights the "chance" that the *belief* in common ethnicity will result in "communal action." He took a similar stance with respect to "the nation." The *belief* in a common national identity may but need not be encouraged by a common language, by similar customs, and especially by shared political memories or aspirations. Thus the allegiance of German-speaking Alsatians is reflected in the Colmar museum's collection of tricolored flags and other "relics" of the French Revolutionary regime, which are valued as symbols of the *grande nation*'s destruction of feudalism. It is these political memories that condition the German Alsatians' sense of civic and national identity; neither language nor ethnicity play a comparable role.[19]

In another early section of *Economy and Society*, Weber argued against the Marxist theory of imperialism. He noted that political expansion does not always follow the routes of export trade. The ancient Roman roads served military purposes, and this is true also of modern railroads. The governing objective of "imperialist capitalism," beginning with that of Rome, was the capture of rent-yielding land. The interests that have driven expansionist wars have been those of state creditors and, increasingly, of arms manufacturers. Military conflicts have yielded profits for these groups that have exceeded the earnings derived from rational entrepreneurship and peaceful commerce, and this regardless of the outcome of these conflicts. Moreover, successful aggression has normally enhanced the prestige and domestic power of the status groups that have led the nation in wartime. Weber's theory of imperialism, like his commitment to social reform, in other words, was prototypically *liberal*.[20]

More specifically, Weber pointed out that a "realm of honor" comparable with the "status order" affected the rivalries among the great powers in his own day. Feudal ruling strata, along with officers and officials, were the principal sponsors and beneficiaries of this striving for prestige. They were joined in their sentiments not only by those materially interested in capitalist imperialism, but also by intellectually privileged strata who saw themselves as the "bearers" of a specific national culture. Under their influence, the naked prestige of power became a "cultural mission" in behalf of a distinctive nationality. National identity is not always based upon language, and a shared ethnic background is neither necessary nor sufficient for the emergence of national feeling. Again according to Weber, it is the subjective *belief* in nationhood that really matters.[21]

Weber certainly remained a German nationalist, but he rejected essentialist conceptions of the nation as well as of "race"; he championed an exceptionally inclusive form of nationalism, and he was as committed to the aspirations he associated with "human greatness" as he was to Germany. Fully to understand his political stance, moreover, one must consider it in relation to the broader field of German academic opinion. When the First World War finally came in August 1914, most German academics greeted it with passionate enthusiasm. For the vast majority among them, the obligation "apolitically" to preach the national cause also implied the duty to ensure Germany's future by means of extensive territorial annexations, especially in Western Europe. They characterized the military conflict as a "cultural war" in behalf of German alternatives to such "Western" values as French democratic rationalism and English commercial individualism. In the "ideas of 1914," they tried to articulate distinctively *German* traditions and ways of dealing with the problems of modernity.

Weber shared his colleagues' enthusiasm for the war. Indeed, he believed that the cause of the nation could give meaning to the sacrifice of the individual. In a short popular essay published in 1916, he contrasted the radical pacifism of the Christian ethic with the wartime values of German patriots. While the smaller West European countries could play the role of neutrals, the German Empire had the responsibilities of a great power. Much that was of value in German culture originated at the margins of the German power state. Nevertheless, precisely because we are a great power, Weber argued, it is our duty "before history" to ensure a future *alternative* to "the regulations of Russian officials on the one hand, and the conventions of Anglo-Saxon 'society' on the other." A German defeat in the World War, he suggested, would reduce the diversity of cultural alternatives available to future generations.[22]

It is difficult for us today to reproduce the intensity of Weber's national feelings, but he shared those feeling with most of his colleagues. As an intellectual biographer, I am primarily interested in Weber's *deviation* from the widespread use of nationalist rhetoric to justify extensive annexations and to define a specifically German response to modernity in the "ideas of 1914." Despite the official proclamation of "peace within the fortress" (*Burgfrieden*), a virulent war-aims debate was launched by a right-wing coalition shortly after the war began. The ultra-annexationists subsequently organized the Independent Commission for a German Peace; after the Reichstag peace resolution of 1917, they formed the so-called Fatherland Party. In opposition to them, a minority of "modernists" called for moderation. Thus the German academic community quickly moved from the ostensibly harmonious enthusiasm of August 1914 to a confrontation between two hostile camps of unequal size. Weber not only opposed outright territorial acquisitions, trying to construe the war as a defensive one, but he also became one of the most penetrating critics of the ultra-annexationist coalition.[23]

Weber first publicly expressed his position on war aims toward the end of 1915, framing his case as a reconsideration of Bismarck's foreign policy so as not to offend against the *Burgfrieden*. His main point was that Bismarck's diplomacy had been essentially defensive, that he never dreamt of a "greater Germany," and that he resisted colonial expansion. Bismarck understood that Germany could not afford to alienate both England and Russia, given the determination of the French to recover Alsace-Lorraine. While the English long avoided entangling commitments, it was post-Bismarckian Germany's program of naval construction, not German economic competition, that ultimately brought England to the side of France. The "madness" of annexing Belgium, of course, did not occur to a single German politician before 1914. Above all, Bismarck knew that German foreign policy should not be dictated by military leaders. In two important respects, however, events had superseded Bismarck's policy toward the east. The close alliance with Austria-Hungary and Russian support of Pan-Slavism had nullified Bismarck's Reinsurance treaty with Russia, and that set the stage for a redirection of Austro-German policy in Central Europe. It was now possible to envision a Polish-German federation based upon a favored-nation relationship in economics and upon military "guarantees" in favor of Germany. But if such an arrangement could be achieved—with the agreement of Austria-Hungary—it required the acceptance of full Polish cultural autonomy.[24]

In early 1916, Weber was embittered by a ruthless public campaign in behalf of unrestricted submarine warfare, which was directed against the government of Bethmann Hollweg by the military leaders and the political right. Weber responded with a memorandum sent to the Foreign Office and to nearly twenty parliamentary leaders in early March of 1916. He pointed out that the proposed policy was likely to bring the United States into the war. The English could then draw upon the vast resources of their new ally; they could expect "many hundreds of thousands (of) well-armed and athletically trained American volunteers" to arrive on the Western front. Any realistic estimate of Germany's capacity to produce additional submarines made the total blockade of England "utopian" in any case. Weber was appalled by the moral cowardice of those unable to stand against the hysteria of the warmongers. He could not tolerate the fact that fateful decisions were reached without consideration of the probable consequences. He accordingly insisted that all pertinent "calculations" be made with great care, and that all those involved in these calculations be formally "documented as responsible." In the face of an irrational outburst that signaled desperation, Weber called for political responsibility.[25]

Weber's most comprehensive critique of the ultra-annexationist program appeared in a late 1916 article entitled "Germany among the European World Powers." Because of its geopolitical situation, he argued, Germany had to avoid policies that alienated all of its neighbors or that drastically reduced its freedom of negotiation with potential allies. Yet precisely such policies were being urged by Pan-Germans and other "national" agitators. German annexations in northern France were bound to be unacceptable to the rest of Europe. The "absurdity" of German suzerainty in Belgium ignored the "dignity and sense of honor of a civilized people." Though currently without friends in Western Europe, Germany did have a close ally in Central Europe. This circumstance, together with the defeat of Pan-Slavism, offered a chance to extend German influence in Eastern Europe. Strengthened ties between Austria-Hungary and Germany might provide the basis for a larger "federation of nationalities," within which an autonomous Poland might enjoy "full self-government." Weber hoped that the Poles would accept German military "guarantees" against Russia. But what he emphasized against the ultra-annexationists was that Germany's eastern policy could not be "German national." The Polish language and Polish cultural autonomy had to be accepted without reservation. The vision of a "greater Germany" had to be abandoned. The German state would become multinational—and could thus act as the champion of the small nations. We may find it hard to imagine the Poles consenting to German suzerainty or a victorious German army making the required concessions. Still, it is worth noting that Weber here envisioned a political entity that encompassed a plurality of autonomous nationalities.[26]

Weber left no doubt that Germany was, and would continue to be, a great power. Therein lay the ultimate cause of the war: "Our honor," not territorial change or economic gain, he wrote, is at stake in it. Our survival is vital, Weber argued, and not only to ourselves. For "the small nations around us live in the shadow of our power." A defeat would force Germany into a "pariah position" that would disastrously affect all segments of society. Weber thus reintroduced the theme of defense to counter the prevalent rhetoric of conquest. He also questioned the motives of the ultra-annexationists. During a visit to Berlin, he reported, he was repeatedly told that a reconciliation with England would "lead to parliamentarianism," or he was challenged to name the domestic political consequences of a German withdrawal from Belgium. Do-

mestic political issues and interests were thus helping to shape the foreign political demands of supposedly "national" politicians.[27] A policy of vanity and
hate was stirring up emotions, where cool reflection and a "matter-of-fact" approach in foreign affairs were urgently needed.[28]

Reading Weber, one begins to ascribe to him a distinctive intellectual personality. He had a pronounced penchant for heterodoxy and a deep-seated commitment to liberal pluralism. His character was reflected, to begin with, in his
choice of friends. He was close to a few senior colleagues, including the political scientist Georg Jellinek. He respected the economist Lujo Brentano, although they certainly had their disagreements. Among valued political allies
were Friedrich Naumann and the jurists Gustav Radbruch and Gerhard Anschütz. All of these were "modernists" in my terminology; they voted with the
liberal left or, more rarely, with the Social Democrats. But Weber also developed close relationships with many junior faculty and students. These he encouraged and supported with great constancy, almost regardless of their
views. As a matter of fact, he typically disagreed with them in important respects, but liked them precisely because they took heterodox positions based
on principle or because they were in need of support against orthodox senior
colleagues. A good many of them were Jews, but he also appreciated the Russian and Polish students who valued him as a teacher.

   His voluminous correspondence testifies to his enduring support, despite
occasionally heated debates, for the young sociologist Robert Michels.[29]
Michels was a Social Democrat who did not have his children baptized. In
Prussia, a law had been passed to ensure that members of the Social Democratic Party could not become university instructors (*Privatdozenten*), even
though that rank did not entail the status of a civil servant. When Michels tried
to find a place at a non-Prussian university, moreover, he was turned away
even in the absence of such a law. He therefore emigrated to Italy, where he
joined the faculty at the University of Turin. In 1908, an annual conference of
German university teachers (*Hochschullehrertag*) discussed the freedom of
learning and teaching, primarily in order to exclude specified religious affiliations for certain positions. In response, Weber reported on Michels' experience to a liberal newspaper and confessed himself unable "to behave as if we
possessed anything like 'freedom of teaching'" that someone could threaten
to take away. "In the interest of good taste and of *truth* [there should be no further talk] of the "freedom of learning and teaching" in Germany. For the fact is

that . . . the *freedom of learning exists only within the limits of political and confessional acceptability*—not outside it." In a more extended commentary, he further insisted that faculty should not use the classroom to convey their "world views" or to stipulate the ultimate norms of social policy. They should confine themselves to empirical and logical analysis, while announcing their personal commitments only in the public arena, where they were subject to criticism.[30] Many German academics linked academic freedom to the abstract "purity" of learning and to the "apolitical" posture. Weber was not satisfied with that; he demanded the principled *toleration of diversity,* along with a distinction between classroom teaching and public debate.

In 1908, the Faculty of Philosophy at the University of Heidelberg had to recommend a candidate for the second senior position in philosophy to the state Ministry. Max Weber wanted to bring Georg Simmel to Heidelberg, but the posture of Wilhelm Windelband, the remaining senior philosopher, was deliberately ambiguous. Moreover, a negative reaction to Simmel reached Karlsruhe from Berlin, where Simmel taught in a junior position. We now know that Professor Dietrich Schäfer of Berlin wrote to Karlsruhe to signal that Simmel was an "Israelite through and through." Schäfer further contrasted "our German-Christian *Bildung*" with Simmel's "world view," which was characterized by "acid and negating" criticism. Windelband too had written of Simmel's "destructive" (*einreissend*) criticism, and these terms were part of a hateful code intended to contrast "Jewish" with "German" modes of thought. Weber did not know about Schäfer's letter; but he was certain that some sort of intervention from Berlin had ruined Simmel's chances, and he found out enough about Windelband's position to feel deeply disappointed and, indeed, disgusted.[31]

The young economist Franz Eulenburg published a solid and courageous report on the difficulties faced by poorly paid instructors (*Privatdozenten*), who made up a rapidly increasing portion of the teaching faculty at German universities. This attracted Weber's attention and caused him repeatedly to recommend Eulenburg for an associate professorship. Since Eulenburg was Jewish, Weber once again ran into the prejudices then faced by Jewish academics at German universities. In a letter to Brentano, he complained of always "having to see the least intelligent 'Arian' preferred to the ablest Jew." This reaction lends credibility to the story told by Paul Honigsheim that Weber once fantasized about teaching a seminar made up entirely of Russians, Poles, and Jews. Honigsheim also recalls Weber's sympathy for the young economist Emil Lederer. Mommsen and Schwentker have collected essays that analyze Weber's relationships not only with Michels, with the Protestant Social Congress, and with Naumann, but also with such pronounced outsiders as Ernst Toller, Ernst Bloch and Georg Lukacs.[32]

I dwell on these particulars, not only to challenge speculations about Weber as an anti-Semite, but also—and mainly—to portray Weber as an instinctive liberal. I mean to point up his *cultural individualism,* which echoes Wilhelm von Humboldt and is recaptured in John Stuart Mill's ideal of an open intellectual community. In such a community, radical differences among a plurality of conflicting beliefs and ways of life are preconditions of intellectual progress. The model suits not only Weber's insistence upon the toleration of heterodoxy, but also his vision of economics as a "human science" that tries to affect the *qualities* of future populations, rather than securing their welfare. Weber admired autonomous individuals who act upon carefully considered principles. He insisted that intellectuals must be capable of swimming against the tide of established opinion, and he despised those whose pliable natures could adjust to almost anything in their environment that would help them succeed.

Another ingredient in Weber's liberal orientation was his commitment to "the rights of man" or "human rights" (*Menschenrechte*). Since he can easily be misunderstood on the subject, we have to trace his views back to the reasoned convictions of Jellinek, which he largely shared. Though a political scientist, Jellinek traced the historical origins of the idea of human rights not to the French Revolution but to declarations attached to the constitutions of several American states at the time of the Continental Congress, beginning with that of Virginia. These in turn were rooted in the principle of the freedom of religion that motivated the English Puritan Levelers, along with such American religious sectarians as Roger Williams. In the American setting, the insistence upon freedom of religion was transformed into the broader doctrine of "subjective" rights, rights that limited the power of the state over the individual. Jellinek distinguished this religiously motivated restriction of state power from the idea of natural law. In any case, he saw the "rights of man" as a product of history—or as a foundational commitment laid down in a constitution, not as an axiom discovered in nature. Moreover, he recognized the contribution of what Weber was to call the "Protestant ethic" to this fundament of modern freedom.[33]

Weber expressed his own view of "human rights" in his 1906 assessment of the prospects for liberalism in Russia. His comments on the Russian Revolution of 1905 were originally intended as notes to a translated draft constitution produced by an alliance of Russian émigré liberals and social revolutionaries (*Befreiungsbund*). These notes became a lengthy essay because of Weber's passionate interest in the cause of Russian "Semstwo" liberalism. Though the Semstwos themselves were indirectly representative bodies of the estate type, the draft constitution that attracted Weber's attention envisaged a bicameral legislature (duma) with a directly elected lower and an indirectly elected upper house. The intention was to transform the Tsarist regime into a constitutional monarchy. The Russian liberals expressed none of the disdain for parliamentary institutions that had become fashionable in Germany, but the central planks of their agenda were the "four-part" (general, equal, direct, and secret) suffrage, and constitutionally anchored "human rights." The Semstwo liberals took it to be their duty to introduce fully equal suffrage, even though they knew that this was risky, given the cultural backwardness of the Russian peasants. As a social group, the Russian liberals were middle-class intellectuals, not capitalist bourgeois, and they were seconded by the more radical "third element" of officials attached to the Semstwos. Weber thought them comparable in their principled individualism to the members of the Frankfurt Parliament of 1848.

The main point of Weber's commentary was that the fight for individual freedom in Russia faced very heavy odds, since the extended historical developments that allowed individual rights to emerge in Western Europe had not had time to do their work in Russia. The problem of differences among nationality groups had not been resolved, and the separation of church and state had not been achieved. More important, the Russian peasants were interested primarily in land redistribution, which in itself posed formidable problems. The belated advent of capitalism, moreover, awakened class conflicts that might well foster revolutionary violence and bureaucratic centralization, rather than middle-class liberalism and gradualist social reform. The Leninists explicitly rejected the thesis that the development of capitalism—and of its contradictions—had to be complete before the proletarian revolution could take place. Weber even detected an affinity between the bureaucratic centralism of the anarcho-syndicalists and that of the Tsarist regime. "The political 'individualism' of the West European 'rights of man'. . . was created partly by former religious convictions . . . and (partly by) the optimistic faith in a natural harmony of interests among free individuals that has now been destroyed forever by capitalism." The old middle-class individualism, having been abandoned by the propertied and educated strata, was unlikely to convert the lower middle class, not to mention the revolutionary masses.[34]

In the last six pages of his essay on the revolution of 1905, Weber brought his themes together in an extraordinary sequence of tension-ridden paragraphs. Once again, he insisted upon the unique historical conditions that gave rise to modern freedom: the expansion of Europe, the distinctive economic and social structure of the early capitalist epoch in Western Europe, the rise of modern science, and especially religious ideas that interacted with specific political constellations and material preconditions to form the cultural values of modern man. Current developments, unfortunately, were pointing away from "democracy" and individualism, not only in Russia, but elsewhere as well. Weber was thinking mainly of bureaucratization: *"Everywhere, the steel housing (Gehaüse) for the new bondage stands ready."* The slowing down of technical and economic "progress," the victory of "rent" over "profit," and the exhaustion of the remaining "free soil and free markets" might well make the masses pliable enough to enter that housing. Certainly if everything depended only upon the "interest constellations" created by material conditions, then all the signs pointed toward "unfreedom": "It is ridiculous to ascribe to high capitalism . . . an elective affinity with 'democracy' or 'freedom.' The question can only be: under its domination, how are these things 'possible' at all in the long run?"[35] This, for Weber, was the burning question of his time.

The pessimistic tone of Weber's analysis, however, must not be interpreted as resignation. While acknowledging that Semstwo liberalism faced great obstacles in the short run, he thought, it might ultimately play the role of an inspiring memory, much as the Frankfurt Parliament did in Germany. Indeed, Weber expected liberalism to retain its power as an ideal, and this for quite specific reasons: The current estrangement between the upper-middle-class intellectuals and their "proletarian" cousins could be overcome. The influence of "populist romanticism" was bound to be undermined by the further development of capitalism. It might be replaced by Marxism, but the "immense and fundamental agrarian problem" could not be mastered by the "intellectual means" embodied in Marxism. On the contrary, it could be solved only by the organs of self-government. This, indeed, could eventually bring the two wings of the intelligentsia back together again. "Thus it seems a life-and-death question that liberalism continue to find its vocation in fighting against bureaucratic as well Jacobin centralism, and to try to infuse the masses with the old individualistic principle of the inalienable rights of man, which has become as 'trivial' to us West Europeans as rye bread is to those who have enough to eat." Liberals must act while there is time. The "much-maligned 'anarchy' of production and the equally maligned 'subjectivism'" may offer a last chance to "construct 'free' cultures from the ground up," in America as in Russia. And that is why we must regard the "Russian war of liberation" with profound sympathy, regardless of national differences and even of national interests.[36]

National interests were important to Weber, but so was the "freedom" of the autonomous "personality." This is clear also from Weber's interventions in debates at meetings of the Social Policy Association during the decade before the First World War. In a 1905 session on working relationships in large-scale industry, for example, he explicitly identified his "value perspective" as a "characterological" one; he wanted to know what "becomes of the human beings" who are placed in specific conditions of existence. He called attention to the language used in the disciplinary rules set down for workers in German factories. These spelled out punishments for various kinds of transgressions in what Weber termed "police jargon." The less "German citizens have to say in political matters," Weber concluded, the more they will insist upon their right to rule in their own enterprises. But this "philistine yen to dominate" has not only been costly for Germany; it has also "distorted the character of our working population." Seconding Brentano, Weber then protested the one-sidedness of German labor law, which elaborately protected strikebreakers, while allowing employers to threaten workers with dismissal if they joined unions. For labor, however, unions were valuable in themselves, whether or not they achieved much in their conflict with management. For they alone fostered and sustained the "comradely honor" and "idealism" of the working class. One is reminded of Tönnies's sense that the trade unions represented a rare new source of "community" in the modern world. The Social Democratic Party, though less desirable than the trade unions, was nonetheless indispensable as a shield in the "petty war against the Prussian state and its police."[37]

In another session of the 1905 meeting, Weber confronted Gustav Schmoller on the question whether government representatives should be added to the boards of large combines and cartels. Schmoller had apparently spoken deprecatingly of "parliamentary chatter." In an admittedly exaggerated simplification, Weber answered that Germany's "pseudo-constitutional" regime had none of the advantages but all the disadvantages of the parliamentary system, including party patronage. He therefore suspected that state positions on corporate boards would not attract "altruists," as Schmoller had suggested. Instead, they would serve as "benefices" for the clients of the dominant parties. Weber further believed that an alliance between heavy industry and the Prussian civil service would simply reinforce the stultifying effects of bureaucratization. Indeed, he asked whether the industrialists were not actually *interested* in the survival of the Social Democratic Party (as a threat to the middle class), just as the Social Democrats were *interested* in the repression that strengthened their following among the workers.[38]

In a 1907 debate on German municipal government, Weber challenged Adolf Wagner, another senior member of the association. Wagner had urged modifications of universal suffrage in municipal elections that would prevent the Social Democrats from taking control. Weber countered that the time was long past when tinkering with universal suffrage was politically acceptable. Besides, who had more to fear from Social Democratic access to local government: "bourgeois society or Social Democracy," particularly "those elements within it that are the bearers of revolutionary ideologies"? Like other mass organizations, the Social Democratic Party was undergoing bureaucratization. Visible tensions between the interests of party functionaries and the aspirations of revolutionary ideologues within the party were bound to be aggravated if allowed to develop. Certainly if Social Democrats were admitted to veterans' organizations and the like, their revolutionary sentiments would be seriously threatened.

> I would have liked to take our German princes to the Mannheim (Congress of the Social Democratic Party) and show them [how the delegates behaved]. . . . The Russian Socialists . . . threw their hands up at . . . this party, which they . . . worshiped as the bearer of a grand revolutionary future . . . and in which the . . . lower-middle-class physiognomy emerged so plainly: a lame . . . carping . . . in place of the revolutionary energy of belief to which they were accustomed from their own assemblies.

In control of a municipal government, the Social Democrats might at first do some posturing. But in the interests of their constituents, they would ultimately pursue neo-mercantilist policies, offering inducements to attract employers to their towns. The commune of Catania in Sicily, currently in the hands of the Social Democrats, was one of the most flourishing towns on the island. Policies inspired by middle-class fear of Social Democracy, Weber suggested, were more damaging to German politics than Social Democracy itself. Certainly nothing impaired German prestige abroad as much as the withholding of domestic freedoms that other nations had achieved.[39]

In 1909, the Social Policy Association discussed the public enterprises of municipalities. In his comment, Weber again opposed Wagner in particular, but he also charged many of the senior members with an excess of enthusiasm for bureaucracy. Indeed, he referred to the younger generation as "we who think differently." He could not agree that private entrepreneurs should be replaced, where possible, with public officials. He repeated that to add state representatives to the boards of large corporations would tend to adjust social policy to the needs of employers. He fully acknowledged the "technical superiority of the bureaucratic mechanism" and the high moral standards of the German civil service. He also pointed out, however, that France, the United States, and even Britain did very well without reliable officials, especially in foreign affairs. But many of us, as Weber insisted, take the power of the nation to be our ultimate value.[40]

Weber thus at least partly reinvoked the standpoint of his Freiburg Inaugural Address. Yet his formulations seem to highlight another, equally salient concern. He called up a dark vision of the ancient Egyptian bureaucracy, which might be reincarnated in a technically perfected form.

> The question that concerns us is not: How can one change anything in this development?—For one cannot do that. Rather: what follows from it? . . . We recognize . . . that, in spite of all exceptions, [honorable and able] people do have a chance to rise in the hierarchy of officialdom, just as the universities . . . claim that they [offer] a chance . . . for the gifted. But awful as the thought may seem that the world will some day be made up of nothing but professors . . . even more dreadful is the thought that it will be inhabited only by those little cogwheels, those human beings . . . glued to a little post and striving for a little bigger one—a condition you will find, just as in the papyri, so increasingly in the spirit of today's civil service, and above all among its *heirs, our students.*
>
> [It is as if we were] human beings who need "order" and nothing but order, who become nervous and cowardly when that order is weakened for a moment. . . . That the world should know nothing but such men of order—that is the development in which we are involved . . . and the central question is not how we are to support . . . it, but what we have to set against [it] . . . to preserve a remainder of humanity . . . from this total domination of bureaucratic ideals.[41]

This vision of the human cost of bureaucratization is surely more passionate than anything Weber wrote about the primacy of the national cause.

Weber's 1909 response to Wagner was a symptom of increasing tensions among divergent policy preferences within the Social Policy Association. By 1909, after all, Weber had challenged all of the prominent senior members of the association except Brentano, who shared his commitment to trade union rights. Weber was worried about the impact of internal dissensus upon the public influence of the association—and upon the cause of social policy itself. It did not help that influential industrialists and employers' associations became increasingly vocal in their complaints about the "Socialists of the Lectern"—and in demanding that their viewpoint be represented among academic economists. In the so-called "Bernhard Case" of 1908, Weber publicly objected to the Prussian Ministry of Culture's "imposition" of a pro-entrepreneurial economist upon the University of Berlin. Shortly thereafter, he chose not to attend the celebration of Gustav Schmoller's seventieth birthday, but wrote a letter instead. Early in 1912, he tried to organize a meeting in which younger members of the organization were to express their continued support for the overall objectives of their elders—and thus to stem the tide of public sentiment against reform. But Brentano refused to go to Berlin, and Schmoller cited reasons of health to excuse himself. Weber then attempted to launch a less formal demonstration by middle-class supporters of socially progressive policies, but substantive and personal differences caused this initiative to fail as well. In fact, Weber broke off relations with Brentano during the negotiations, which must have increased his sense of isolation.[42] It was as if the whole tradition of academic social policy was now at risk, even as Germany moved toward the First World War.[43]

TOWARD A DEMOCRATIC COALITION

In 1917, Weber's political commentary entered a new phase as he began to outline reforms that were to be completed before the end of the World War. He published two brief articles on the democratization of the Prussian electoral system as well as a series of essays for the liberal *Frankfurter Zeitung* that he subsequently revised and expanded into a treatise on "Parliament and Government in Germany under a New Political Order." Published before the collapse of the old regime, this treatise will be our main source in the following pages. In the preface to "Parliament and Government," Weber announced that his arguments would not be confined to the realm of science but would encompass value judgments, as would his attacks upon the reactionary speculations of the "academically educated." "We . . . who have stayed at home," he wrote, "have no business distinguishing 'German' political forms from 'Western' alternatives, as if we had no liberal traditions of our own. We certainly should not tell our men at the front that they will have bled in vain unless extensive new territories are annexed. Instead, we must transform our political institutions, so that the returning soldiers will be able to participate in shaping the nation's future. To that end, we must be willing to deal with 'sober civic' issues of political technique that may not satisfy the cultural pretensions of our 'literati.'"[44]

Weber began a systematic critique of the Wilhelmian sociopolitical system with an attack on the "Bismarck legend" that had been created by politically immature publicists. According to the current "literati's fashion," Bismarck's liberal collaborators and rivals in the construction of the German Empire were people without talent, political instinct, or vision; they were unrepresentative of the "German spirit." In the face of this orthodoxy, Weber conceded the limitations inherent in the laissez-faire economics of the old liberal leaders, but he identified with their determination to create a politically liberal framework that could endure beyond the era of Bismarck's personal dominance. The fact that they failed was due not to their lack of leadership but to Bismarck's profound contempt for mankind and to his inability to tolerate men of independent views among his competitors. To defeat his liberal rivals, Bismarck engaged in the worst sort of demagogic tactics, using the seven-year military budget and the anti-Socialist law not only to obtain the concessions he needed, but also to impose illiberal solutions that destroyed his principled opposition. In an analogous way, he refused to accept the trade unions' right to represent the interests of the workers, while unsuccessfully wooing the working class with social insurance payments from a state in which they played no role. The police and judicial harassment institutionalized by the anti-Socialist law virtually forced the Social Democratic Party into the fruitless posture of unconditional opposition, while the dramatized threat of revolution kept the middle class pliant from sheer cowardice. A state that based its military system on honor and comradeship deprived the proletariat of comradely honor, the only possible source of working-class idealism. Thus Bismarck's heritage left (1) a huge deficit in the political education of the nation, (2) a powerless Parliament unable to attract political talents, and (3) the unchecked rule of the government bureaucracy (437–50).[45]

According to Weber, the modern world is characterized in any case by the steady advance of bureaucracy. Just as economic modernization is equivalent with progress toward capitalism, so the modernization of the state entails the emergence of a bureaucracy based upon specialized training, secure salaries, pensions and promotions, designated spheres of competence, systematic record keeping, and a clearly defined hierarchy of ranks. Municipal government, the modern army, and private capitalist enterprise too are characterized by bureaucratic organization and thus by the separation of the official, the officer, and the employee from the means of administration, warfare, and production. The parallel development of capitalism and bureaucracy is no accident, for modern Western capitalism rests upon rational calculation; it therefore needs a system of public administration and justice whose workings are predictable, like the operations of a machine (450–54).

Modern political parties too are increasingly bureaucratic in structure. They have always been voluntary organizations, dependent upon solicitation to increase their membership and influence. In recent times, however, they have evolved from associations of notables to mass organizations administered by salaried officials. The parties must still compete for votes, but the ordinary voter and party member has played a decreasing role in determining party programs. Notables have continued to be important, whether as financial patrons or as figureheads, but much of their former influence has passed to party secretaries, publicists, and other professionals (454–55). Modern parties have been of two main types: Some have primarily pursued the patronage of offices captured by a victory at the polls. Particularly in the United States, such patronage parties have adjusted their platforms to attract as many votes as possible; party "bosses" have traded in patronage to deliver elections. But even in the United States, as resources become scarcer, the efficiency of specialized training is pointing the way toward bureaucratization. The second type of party has been more characteristic of Germany; it has been committed to a "worldview," and has accordingly pursued fixed *substantive* ends. The Catholic Center is an example, and so is the Social Democratic Party; yet particularly the latter, the largest and most democratic party in the German political system, also illustrates the increasing convergence between the patronage and the "worldview" types of modern political parties (457–58).

Against this background sketch of bureaucratization, Weber developed a penetrating critique of the existing German political system. The fatal flaw of that system, he thought, lay in the absence of responsible political leadership. Ever since Bismarck's time, the German state had been governed by honorable civil servants, who tried to stand "above" the political parties in the Reichstag rather than taking responsibility for a deliberate political course. Emperor William II's misguided determination to govern in person led to offensive and pointless gestures rather than to reflected policies, for the monarch was surrounded only by an interested courtly clique and by men who ignored their elementary duty to *resign* when egregious mistakes were made. In short, there were no responsible political leaders, no one to restrain the administrative rule of the bureaucracy, and no genuine intermediary between the government and the Reichstag. In England, by contrast, a monarch retained a measure of political influence precisely by withdrawing from day-to-day political decisions; a working Parliament represented the citizens in the face of officialdom, and genuine political leaders guided a state that was able to attract the largely voluntary submission of much of the globe. Yet this polity was denigrated as a "night watchman's state" by the German "literati" (467–72).

Article 9 of the German Constitution of 1871 forbade leading statesmen, who had to be members of the Federal Council, from holding or retaining their seats in the Reichstag. Thoughtlessly adapted from the English separation of Lords and Commons, this disastrous provision prevented party leaders from taking ministerial positions without severing their parliamentary roots—and thus condemning themselves to impotence. As a result, young aspirants for political leadership were shunted away from the Reichstag, which really became a recruiting ground for civil servants. This seemed a "German" solution of the parliamentary problem to the academic "literati," who "examine officials, and feel themselves to be officials and the fathers of officials," and who sneer at "West European" and "democratic" place hunting (476–77). Weber countered that the conventions of the civil service hierarchy do not favor personal independence and the talent for politics, which requires conflict and the ability to recruit allies and followers. Of course there are flaws in the selection of leaders by the parties, as there are in any human arrangement. The rule of the parties may force us to accept imperfect individuals, but the authoritarian regime leaves us no choice; it simply gives us functionaries to obey (481–82, 484). "Philistine moralists" harp upon the obvious fact that the "will to power" motivates aspirants to political leadership, while the "egotistic striving for office" moves their followers. Candidates for civil service posts, by contrast, are presumably never conformist "climbers" *(Streber)*—or hungry for salaries. The truth is that we must create a framework in which such all-too-human traits will help to select political talents. That is why party leaders must have a real chance at power and responsibility. That too, Weber wrote, is why we need a *working* Parliament, in which service on commissions and acquired expertise will be as important as good speeches. We need true political leaders, not mere demagogues. Politically neutral officials can never take their place (485–87).

Weber contrasted the parliamentary system that made England a "democracy" (*Volksstaat*), with the "negative politics" of Germany's "authoritarian state." Since the Reichstag could only grant or refuse budgetary provisions, and accept or reject policies proposed to it, it was bound to confront the government as a hostile force. It could express the dissatisfaction of its constituents, but it was never asked to participate in the formulation of political programs. The highest places in the monarchical regime were occupied by successful civil servants or courtiers. Neither the struggles for power nor patronage ceased under these circumstances. But they took covert and subaltern forms, and they consistently favored policies acceptable at court. The political parties consequently developed a "will to powerlessness," while extra-parliamentary forces were encouraged to intervene in the decision-making process (473–76). In this "pseudo-constitutional" context, it was taken for granted that Prussian officials and district administrators (*Landräte*) must be politically conservative, for that was what the claim to "stand above the parties" really meant (500–501). The Social Democratic Party actually collaborated in "negative politics." Its members cultivated their class solidarity and the antipolitical vision of "brotherliness." Its leaders were given no incentive to break out of the "ghetto existence" that was thus perpetuated. "Negative politics" was perfectly consistent, moreover, with blatant concessions to the material interests of government supporters. That is why the representatives of big capital stood united behind a regime that obviously benefited them (503–5).

Weber's account of English parliamentary government was highly specific. The leading statesmen needed the confidence of the strongest political party or of a parliamentary majority. The members of the government had to answer critical questions put to them by the opposition and to control the administrative apparatus in the sense desired by the people's representatives. To help them in that task, they had the right of parliamentary inquiry (*Enqueterecht*); they could compel civil servants to testify before them under oath. They could thus partly match the specialized knowledge and penetrate the administrative records of the bureaucracy, overriding the official secrecy invoked by administrators to protect their prerogatives. The proceedings of the Parliament and of its commissions were public, so that they contributed to the political education of the citizens. To Weber, it was ludicrous that German literati looked down upon the proceedings of the British parliament from the height of their impotence (488–91).

The key question for the German polity, according to Weber, was how to make the Reichstag fit to exercise power. Article 9 and various procedural rules must be altered to meet this objective. But above all, Germany needed parliamentarians who could make politics their full-time occupation. This is the context in which Weber introduced the distinction between living *from* and living *for* politics. The employees of political parties and pressure groups earn their living *from* their positions. Among people in nonpolitical occupations, some are more "available" (*abkömmlich*) than others, in that they can free themselves from their ordinary duties to take on political work; lawyers are the outstanding example. Party officials can no longer be dispensed with, but they can make it difficult for independent leaders to reach high office, and that difficulty must be overcome. The notion that the winners of political contests are typically unscrupulous "demagogues" is almost certainly exaggerated, but some sort of demagogic solicitation of voters really is indispensable. Nevertheless, the exposure of candidates during elections is no worse a means of selection than the collegial assessment of candidates for academic appointments, for example (533–37). In modern mass democracies, the selection of leaders is likely to take on a plebiscitary character. Yet unlike pure Caesarism, plebiscitary leadership is relatively stable and controllable, limited by legally guaranteed civil rights, and by the leader's apprenticeship in the usages of parliamentary work. Besides, the plebiscitary leader whose *program* fails can be peacefully replaced (539–40).

My reading of Weber here conflicts with that of Wolfgang Mommsen. Stressing Weber's commitment to plebiscitary leadership democracy, Mommsen claims that he did not believe in the sovereignty of the people: "Political leaders create for themselves a majority in parliament as well as amongst the people at large . . . not so much on the basis of a positive program, but by displaying their charismatic power of persuasion and positive demagogy. . . . Hence decisions arrived at by debate and rational deliberation [are] gradually superseded by plebiscitarian decisions." Mommsen's case, I believe, is based upon an incomplete understanding of the relationship between the charismatic leader and his followers, in which the claim to obedience seems unconditional, and the role of the political program is ignored. But one has to remember Weber's insistence upon an *active* Parliament, one that can play a controlling role, and a politically educative one. I am sympathetic to the view that liberalism implies rational deliberation and debate, rather than the de facto buying of votes, for example. But I cannot agree that the chief threat to such deliberation in the contemporary world stems from the plebiscitarian element in such institutions as the American presidency. And the American presidency was Weber's main example of plebiscitarian democracy. More important, I would point to Weber's clear distinction between Caesarism and plebiscitary leadership, which lies in the role of the Parliament, its committees, its norms and usages. Finally, I want to stress Weber's commitment to *constitutional* democracy and, in that context, to "human rights" as well.[46]

In part 1 of *Economy and Society,* which was written *after* part 2, Weber referred to the "division of power" as a means of limiting, reducing, or "minimizing" domination. He was particularly interested in the *constitutional* division of power, in which there is a functional subdivision and distribution of powers among governing individuals and bodies that force them to reach a "compromise" before issuing legitimate directives. In such small-scale polities as Swiss cantonal governments and American "town meetings," he saw an opportunity for "direct democracy," and he called attention to the more or less consensual rule of "notables" as well. He reserved his most intensive analysis, however, for uninstructed or "free" parliamentary representation in large polities, which cannot really function without the active intervention of voluntary political parties, whose "candidates" and "programs" are presented to "politically passive" citizens. In mass polities, this is the only viable means of establishing and articulating the political preferences of the electorate. In "constitutional" government, according to Weber, a traditional ruler participates in a regime based upon the division of power. The other alternatives are "plebiscitary-representative government," in which a plebiscitary president shares power with a parliament, and "purely representative government," in which the political leader is chosen by a parliament, as in England. The several organs of representative government can be further "limited" and "legitimized" by means of referenda. Free representation combined with parliamentary institutions as a political form, Weber added, is unique to the "West."[47]

When Weber asked himself why there were *democratic* opponents of parliamentary government, he pointed to the *voluntary* character of party politics. The popular leader does not emerge directly from a mass constituency. Rather, he seeks power and responsibility to "realize specific political ideas," and he begins by seeking party support *for his program.* Thus the leader *proposes* both policy ends and political means, and the voters dispose of his recommendation by accepting or rejecting it (547). The safeguard against merely demagogic leaders lies in their prior political work and in their commitment to the norms of their political system. The "masses," regardless of their social status, are too easily led by transitory emotions. But the setting of a political course demands cool heads, which is why it should be left to leaders clearly designated as responsible for the programs they recommend. Weber expected the First World War to be followed by years of economic and political crisis, and he was prepared for syndicalist uprisings. But he hoped that the response would not be dictated by the social fear of the propertied. While violence would have to be met with violence, the "proud traditions" and sound "nerves" of a mature people demanded that the underlying issues be addressed and the civil guarantees of a free political order quickly restored (549–51).

Weber also called for a variety of particular measures that reflected the conditions of 1917 and interest us less than the principles he laid down. The Germany of the future, he believed, should be a federally structured constitutional monarchy. Parliamentary governments should continue to be headed by a Prussian chancellor; but the elected representatives of the other German states should participate more actively in the parliamentary leadership (583–87). Still, the foremost task of 1917 was to replace the three-class suffrage in Prussia with the universal suffrage introduced by Bismarck for the Reichstag. This would put an end to the anomalies arising from the disproportionate weight of the Prussian landowners and industrialists in German politics. It would make room for a genuine parliamentary democracy, in which soldiers returning from the front could not be outvoted by people who prospered while staying at home. This seemed to Weber a moral imperative. "Politics may not be an ethical business," he wrote. But there is a "minimal feeling of shame" and a "duty of common decency" that cannot be disregarded, even in politics.[48]

Max Weber's 1917 political essays can only be understood as challenges to orthodoxies he meant to contest. We have to remember that the harmonious mood of August 1914 had been quickly dissipated by what Weber considered a class war from the right. The campaigns in behalf of expansionist policies and unlimited submarine warfare deeply embittered Weber and some of his colleagues. The division between an orthodox majority and a "modernist" minority among German academics deepened to the point of undisguised hostility. Weber could not help but feel that the "apolitical" rhetoric of his conservative and "national" opponents was designed to preserve the status quo at home through conquest abroad. He was not surprised that the beneficiaries of the distorted domestic balance of power should press for the total victory of a distinctively "German" polity. What really angered him was the complicity of many German university professors in this disastrous course. Tensions ran so high within the German academic world that false rumors described the liberal *Frankfurter Zeitung* and Weber himself as recipients of English funds. Weber in turn increasingly portrayed his orthodox colleagues as either empty-headed or mendacious (532).

One of the public political speculations that provoked Weber's anger was the plan to privilege advanced education in the assignment of individuals to the Prussian voting classes. Weber saw higher education as a major source of *status* advantages, as against the economic roots of *class* positions. "Differences of *Bildung,* much as one may regret it, are today one of the very strongest inner barriers in society. Especially in Germany, where almost all privileged positions within and without the civil service are tied not only to specialized knowledge, but also to 'general *Bildung*.' . . . All our examination diplomas also and primarily certify this important *status* quality." But Weber insisted that German "doctoral factories" had no more to offer their students than "specialized knowledge" (*Fachwissen*). Their graduates might be suitable as counselors to political leaders or as members of an advisory upper house of the legislature. Beyond that, however, Weber could not imagine a politically less qualified stratum. The lack of measure demonstrated by university professors during the war left no doubt about that. The steadily increasing demand for certified professional qualifications was nothing but a quest for prebends, for secure salaries and pensions appropriate to the status of the diploma holders. Weber was not kind in his comments upon the social pretensions of the highly educated, who habitually looked down upon modern entrepreneurs, labor leaders, politicians, and journalists. He could not think of a group less eligible for electoral privileges.[49]

In some of the darkest passages of his 1917 essay on "Parliament and Government," Weber traced the links between (1) the interests and ideological propensities of German university faculty, (2) the stubborn resistance to parliamentary democracy, and (3) the advance of bureaucracy. In what was clearly an attack on his colleagues, he wrote again of the "academic literati," their resentment of anyone not examined and certified by them, and their "fear for the prestige of their own stratum." Such attitudes, he thought, were behind their repeated diatribes against democracy and "parliamentary dilettantism." Their "instincts" blinded "the mass" of them to political realities. Their "typical snobbism" caused them to dismiss the "subaltern" problems of political reform in favor of more elevated speculations about "the ideas of 1914," "true socialism," and the like. But a people that is ruled by an uncontrolled bureaucracy, that is not master of its own fate at home, should certainly not try to play the master abroad. The "will to powerlessness" in domestic matters is incompatible with the "will to power" in foreign affairs (591–95).

More than other people, Weber thought, the Germans have displayed a talent for rational administration in every kind of organization. They have applauded bureaucratization as a "form of life," and again the prebends and status claims of the highly educated have been their real objectives. "The fact of *universal bureaucratization* is really hidden behind the so-called ideas of 1914, behind what the literati euphemistically term the 'socialism of the future,' behind the slogan about 'organization,' the 'communal economy,' and . . . behind all similar contemporary turns of phrase." In a double-edged analogy, Weber claimed that "the old Chinese mandarin was not a specialized official, but . . . a humanistically educated gentleman." The modern official, by contrast, is increasingly dependent upon specialized training, and thus not really a man of *Bildung*. There are literati who believe that private capitalism could be domesticated through state control. But instead of weakening the "steel housing" of modern industrial work, this would leave the bureaucracy in sole command. A bureaucracy is a human machine, Weber wrote. Together, the animate and inanimate machines are constructing "the housing for the new bondage," to which "future human beings . . . may have to submit, *if a technically good, and that means: rational bureaucratic administration is the ultimate value that will guide the regulation of their affairs*" (461–64).

But if that is the fate that awaits mankind, Weber added, one has to "smile at the fear of our literati" that we might have too much "individualism" or democracy, and at their belief that "true freedom" will arise only when the "anarchy" of contemporary production and the parliamentary jostling of our parties will have been replaced by social order and "organic stratification." Given the advance of bureaucratization, the questions about our political future could only be put as follows:

1. How is it . . . *still possible* . . . *to salvage* . . . individualistic freedom of movement? For it is . . . crude self-deception to believe that we could nowadays bear to live . . . without the achievements of the age of the "rights of man."
2. How, in view of the increasing . . . dominance of . . . state officialdom . . . will there be powers to keep . . . this growing stratum . . . under effective control?
3. A third issue, the most important of all, emerges from a consideration of what bureaucracy as such does *not* achieve . . . The guiding spirit: the entrepreneur here, the politician there, after all, is something other than an official. (465–66)

These formulations have much in common with Weber's outwardly pessimistic reflections on the problems of liberalism in Russia. Again, the image of the "housing for the new bondage" functions as a prophecy of doom that cries out, against the tide of history, for whatever sources of human vitality may yet be mobilized. Weber's emphasis upon the technical training of the official was meant to contribute to his image of the bureaucracy as a machine, which underscored the need to mobilize residual sources of individualism and of liberty.

In the summer of 1918, while briefly at the University of Vienna, Weber agreed to give a "political education" lecture to Austro-Hungarian army officers. His analysis of "socialism" drew upon the critique of orthodox Marxism by Eduard Bernstein and other Social Democratic "revisionists." The Communist Manifesto of 1848, Weber argued, had proved both theoretically stimulating and emotionally powerful as the prophecy that capitalism would in time be replaced by a temporary dictatorship of the proletariat and ultimately by the end of "man's domination over man." But Marx was wrong in his predictions: The bourgeoisie failed to shrink, and economic crises failed to deepen. Instead, finance and monopoly created new forms of capitalist organization; small producers survived, including in agriculture; joint stock companies created substantial numbers of new rentiers; and the expanding white-collar hierarchy separated itself from the working class. At the same time, a system of collaboration between private enterprise and public authority, far from controlling big industry, greatly increased the political power of capital. Finally, the advance of bureaucratization in government, in the economy, and even in party politics, transformed the landscape of early entrepreneurial capitalism.[50]

The lessons Weber distilled from his presentation were essentially reformist. He explicitly sympathized with the labor unions, which sought to improve the workers' lot *within* the capitalist framework, although he believed that employers could demonstrate that there were limits to the concessions they could make. What Weber really approved about the unions was their sense of "comradely honor." As a political party, he thought, the Social Democrats should sponsor social reform and democracy through parliamentary means. His sharpest criticism was directed against radical *syndicalism*, its exclusivist (*ouvrierist*) animus against politics, and its idea of the general strike as the ultimate weapon. Paradoxically, in Weber's view, the syndicalist movement attracted the support of radical intellectuals, who were inspired by the romantic vision of revolutionary transformation, and perhaps by the temptations of power as well. What worried Weber, clearly, was the possibility of pacifist and syndicalist sympathies among exhausted soldiers, who yearned primarily for peace.[51] He was deeply concerned about the Bolshevik Revolution in Russia.

The months that followed upon the November Revolution in Germany, from late 1918 through March 1919, saw Weber more actively engaged in current politics than ever before. It looked for a time as if he might be elected a representative of the new German Democratic Party. But after party officials had undercut that possibility—and Weber had failed to fight for a mandate—he continued to campaign energetically for the new party, to sit on constitutional commissions, and to travel to the peace conference at Versailles. In substance, he favored a constitutional monarchy until the behavior of William II made that impossible. He was dismayed by the revolutionary disorders of November 1918 and appalled at German pacifists who seconded the Allied claim that Germany was solely responsible for the war. He preached "dignity" in defeat. As the terms of the Versailles settlement began to emerge, his outrage and his pessimism deepened. Yet he soon recovered his characteristic sense of reality. He recommended a program of cooperation between the revisionist Social Democrats and the progressive elements within the German middle class. For a while, he even gave lip service to limited forms of "socialization."[52]

If we leave Weber's famous lecture "Politics as a Vocation" aside for the moment, we can find his postwar political views in a sequence of short articles he wrote for the liberal *Frankfurter Zeitung* in late 1918 that was republished as a pamphlet in January 1919 and supplemented by a note entitled "*Der Reichspräsident*" two months later. His main purpose in these writings was to prepare the ground for a democratically elected National Assembly that would reestablish the authority of the German central government and lay the constitutional foundations for a Republic. The legitimacy of the new regime, according to Weber, could only be based upon the "natural law" conception of popular sovereignty. More specifically, Weber's political plan extended the institutions of the old empire, including its federal structure, though with significant modifications. The hegemony of Prussia within Germany, which perpetuated the disproportionate influence of the agrarian magnates and heavy industrialists, was to be reduced. The chancellor of the German Republic would no longer be identical with the Prussian prime minister, and Prussian control of the military and of the Federal Council would be tempered as well. The state of Prussia would not be subdivided, but due weight would be given to the rights of the other large states, including Bavaria and possibly German Austria. Yet Weber eventually modified his initially federalist emphasis in a unitary direction. He excluded anything like the autonomy of the American states, partly in view of the need for an active social policy. With respect to primary and secondary education, moreover, Weber intended the national legislature to stipulate "norms" for the policies of the several states.[53]

The president of the German Republic, Weber believed, should be directly elected by the voters, rather than by the Reichstag. Like the president of the United States, he would have an independent political mandate, based upon the plebiscitary principle of popular sovereignty. He was also to be equipped with a suspensive veto, and with the right to dissolve the Reichstag and call for new elections, particularly if no prime minister or chancellor succeeded in forming a governing majority. Weber's long-standing interest in the selection of political leaders culminated in this call for a plebiscitary presidency. Yet Weber was not alone in recommending either a strong president or a partly federal structure. Moreover, his views were not decisive for the constitution of the Weimar Republic as drafted by Hugo Preuss and others. More interesting for us are Weber's insistence upon the control of the bureaucracy by means of a parliamentary right of inquiry and his call for a set of fundamental "human rights" (*Grundrechte*) to be anchored in the Constitution.

Tactically, Weber insisted upon the need for political cooperation between the moderate working class and middle-class progressives. Since a Social Democratic majority could not be expected in elections to a National Assembly, he argued, the new regime required the support of the German bourgeoisie or of genuinely democratic elements within it. A purely socialist government was impossible in any case, since Germany needed economic credits that would not be granted unless expropriation was formally excluded. This was no time to listen to radical intellectuals, who lived "from" and not "for" the revolution, or to flirt with the fantasies of "academic literati" about a "communal economy" and the like. Above all, the German middle class had to do without the "security" it had enjoyed under the authoritarian regime, and it had to abandon its fear of innovation and its "will to powerlessness." For broad segments of the German population, sound administration and material welfare had provided a "framework" (*Gehäuse*) that had suppressed the "pride of citizenship, without which even the freest institutions are mere shadows." The Republic would put an end to this security. The middle class would have to learn to fend for itself, as the working class has always done. New political parties would need to be formed, without the politicians who had campaigned against Western democracy, for extensive annexations, and for unlimited submarine warfare. Indeed, Germany would have to abandon its imperialist dreams, so as peacefully to cultivate its national traditions within a League of Nations.[54] Here again, Weber's position was plainly liberal.[55]

CHAPTER THREE

Weber's Methodology

Beginning in 1903, Weber wrote a series of methodological essays that drew upon the relevant controversies of his time.[1] In the process, he clarified and extended the German vision of the *Geisteswissenschaften.* He brought together two divergent perspectives that have divided theorists of the historical, social, and cultural sciences since the nineteenth century: the *explanatory* and the *interpretive* traditions. In the explanatory model, investigators try to identify the causes of events, processes, and outcomes, often with the aid of laws. In the interpretive mode, which was dominant in Weber's intellectual field, the chief task of scholars is the interpretation of human meanings: Historical actions are to be understood, not causally explained, in relation to the agent's motives and beliefs. Texts and cultures are to be conceived as systems of interrelated meanings that can be elucidated only internally, "in their own terms."

Dissatisfied with the limitations and misuses of interpretation in German philological and historical scholarship, Weber bridged the divide between the interpretive and the explanatory traditions by means of two crucial reformulations. First, he adopted a scheme of *singular causal analysis,* in which particular events, changes, or outcomes are traced to their causally relevant antecedents. The word *singular* is not meant to suggest a mono-causal approach; rather, it indicates that what is explained is singular in the logical sense that it is not universal (like the ideal gas law, or Gresham's law) and that it can be located in space and time. Weber's account of singular causal analysis was based upon probabilistic and counterfactual reasoning, not upon deductions from general laws. He thought in terms of processes and outcomes that are more or less probable or favored by relevant causes. Second, Weber developed a model of interpretation based upon the hypothetical attribution of rationality that dispensed with naturalist assumptions while also redefining interpretation as a form of singular causal analysis. In the interpretation of past actions, according to Weber, we begin by supposing that the relevant agents rationally pursued appropriate ends. The agents' *reasons* for acting were the *causes* of their acting as they did.

Weber wrote his methodological essays as a critical practitioner of the cultural and social sciences—and as a rebel against his own scholarly tradition, not as a philosopher. Technically philosophical problems he left to "the logicians," chiefly Simmel and Rickert. The starting point of his methodological reflections was Rickert's characterization of reality as an extensively and intensively infinite manifold of objects and events within and outside us. Since our knowledge cannot *reproduce* that manifold, we need deliberate strategies of selection and *description*. In Simmel's terminology, Weber distinguished the nomological sciences (*Gesetzeswissenschaften*) from the sciences of reality (*Wirklichkeitswissenschaften*). The former abstract from the world of phenomena in search of regularities; what is *significant* or worth knowing in these disciplines is what can be subsumed under universal laws. The sciences of reality, including history and the cultural sciences (*Kulturwissenschaften*), by contrast, seek knowledge of concrete particulars. They deal with those aspects of the world that interest us in their distinctiveness. They work with isolating descriptions that pick out what is significant, directly or indirectly, in the light of our values. To know history is thus to know neither timeless laws nor any portion of the past in its totality; it is to know what is worth knowing about the past in the light of our concerns.[2]

Moreover, we want to understand the significant actions and events of the past as parts of a network of singular causal connections. Links in this network too are singular, and some of them involve interpretable human actions as causes or effects. In such cases, our desire for causal knowledge is not satisfied by evidence of behavioral regularities; we want to grasp the "meaning" or "sense" (*Sinn*) of an action. So we must *interpret* in order to *explain*. In any case, the causal connections that interest us are not usually instances of causal laws; what we aim at is *singular* causal analysis, in which *particular* outcomes are explained in terms of *specific* causal antecedents. Indeed, following Rickert, Weber distinguished "primary" historical facts, which are significant in their own right, from "secondary" historical facts, which figure among the *causes* of primary facts. On the other hand, he rejected a definition of the historical as the causally effective; for the causal connections of the past too are infinitely numerous, while many historical outcomes are plainly trivial.

Therefore, no matter what heuristic means historians may draw upon, they still need judgments of significance to identify the individual outcomes they seek to explain.[3]

Weber accepted Rickert's view that judgments of significance or of "value relevance" guide historians in the choice of their objects of study. To investigate the cultural world is to select from the infinite manifold of reality in the light of human interests: "Culture is a finite segment of the infinitude of the world process that has been invested with meaning and significance from a human point of view." The imputation of cultural significance is a presupposition, not a result, of research in this domain. Weber never wavered from that position, but he did not share in Rickert's broader quest for a "philosophy of value" (*Wertphilosophie*). Rickert argued that the values guiding historians could be "empirically general" either in their own cultures or in those they investigated, without specifying how the beliefs of other cultures could be established in advance of relevant research. Weber gave much thought to the problem of understanding other cultures, but he left no doubt that the normative commitments that move social scientists are those of their own culture, or even simply their own. Indeed, he expected the viewpoints inspiring historical and social inquiry to vary—and to be renewed again and again, unless an "ossification" of intellectual life put an end to inquiry itself.[4]

According to Weber, "objectivity" in the cultural and social sciences is thus attainable only in the form of well-founded claims about some defined aspect of cultural reality, not in the value considerations that initially suggest certain lines of inquiry. The values that inspire scholars may be "subjective," but "it does not follow . . . that research in the cultural disciplines can only have results that are 'subjective' in the sense that they are valid for some and not for others. What changes, rather, is the degree to which they *interest* some and not others." The point is central for Weber:

> (The causal) attribution is undertaken, in principle, with the aim of being an "objectively" valid truth of experience, . . . and only the adequacy of the evidence determines . . . whether that aim is actually reached. . . . What is "subjective" . . . is not the determination of the historical "causes" for a given "object" of explanation, but the delimitation of the historical "object" . . . itself.[5]

In short, Weber thought it possible to reach objectively valid claims in the cultural and social sciences, despite the subjectivity involved in the selection and delimitation of their objects of study.

In his view of singular causal analysis, Weber borrowed from the physiologist and statistician Johannes von Kries, who in turn built upon an established tradition in German legal philosophy as well as upon the broader idea that certain social characteristics are objective statistically measurable properties of particular societies. The specific problem von Kries addressed was that of assigning responsibility in civil law cases, in which there is no question of criminal intent. To do this, one has to attribute effects to causes in particular circumstances, and thus engage in singular causal analysis. Like Weber, von Kries knew that reality cannot be fully described. Our statements of prior conditions are thus typically incomplete and conceptually generalized, as are our descriptions of consequences. We can only hope to estimate the likelihood of certain results in the light of stated antecedents. Before throwing a die, to be sure, we can specify the chance of a given result with mathematical precision, but the probability involved is low, and the outcome is thus "accidental." In other cases, however, we may be able to judge that a certain broadly described event is "objectively probable," given a generally stated antecedent.

According to von Kries, we have nomological knowledge not only of invariant causal laws, but also of probable causal connections, and it is this probabilistic knowledge we draw upon when we ask, in retrospect, to what extent various causal factors, or "moments," contributed to a particular result. To inquire into the importance of a specific antecedent, we imagine it (counterfactually) absent or altered. In assessing the role of negligence in an accident, for example, we "compare" the sequence of events that actually occurred with what could have been expected if "normal" caution had prevailed. We consider a factor causally relevant to an effect if the effect would not have occurred without it. Our probabilistic knowledge allows us to estimate the course of events in the absence of that factor, but we also seek to generalize upon the closeness of the relationship between "the cause" and the actual outcome. Consider a carriage driver who gets drunk and loses his way. At some distance from his normal route, his passenger is struck by lightning. We do not hold the driver responsible for two related reasons: (1) his wandering from the regular route did not (unless it prolonged exposure to the weather) increase the objective probability of the passenger being struck by lightning, and (2) we have no basis for a probabilistic generalization linking drunkenness in coachmen to their passengers being struck by lightning. But suppose that the drunk driver's carriage turns over in a ditch: He is responsible because his drinking certainly increased the chance of the accident, and we are prepared to generalize upon the incident.[6]

Von Kries explicitly rejected a model of causation involving the invariable succession of two events or types of events, a model that can be traced to David Hume. It is typically linked to the idea of "the cause" as a *sufficient* condition for the effect. Von Kries' objection to this conception was the practitioner's observation that events can rarely if ever be traced to single antecedents or causal factors. Nevertheless, we are often quite certain that a particular "moment" within a set of anterior conditions increased the probability of a given result, and that it would have done so even if some of the conditions had been altered. Von Kries further insisted that we ordinarily and rightly think of a causal factor as "acting" (*Wirken*) to bring about an outcome. These considerations led von Kries to term an antecedent factor the "adequate cause" of a given result, and that result the "adequate effect" of the antecedent, if the cause "favored" the occurrence of the effect.[7]

Von Kries clearly thought of a causally relevant antecedent as a *necessary* condition or cause, rather than a sufficient one. His causes had to be present for the result to occur, although they brought it about only in conjunction with various additional conditions. In the light of this conception, one can understand most of von Kries' remaining suggestions: He called attention to two particularly clear cases of adequate causation. First, we securely ascribe a *deviation* from a regularly recurring course of events (a train not passing safely through a junction) to an *alteration* in the normal antecedents (a switch not being properly set). Second, if a state of affairs has remained stable over a period of time, we confidently trace a change in it to the intrusion of a new causal factor. In both of these cases, moreover, the idea of causation as an active effecting is reinforced, for a cause is seen to change a set of initial conditions, to alter a course of events, and thus to bring about a deviation in the outcome that could have been expected in its absence. The whole conception is *dynamic;* it deals in sequences and processes, rather than in successive but unconnected events. It also forced von Kries into the complexities of counterfactual reasoning. Even without following von Kries' reflections on these difficult issues, however, we may safely conclude that he recommended probabilistic generalizations primarily because he had to ground legal judgments about what would have happened if "the cause" had been absent or altered.[8]

After first mentioning von Kries' main concepts in his 1904 essay entitled "Objectivity," Weber explicitly followed von Kries in the concluding section of his 1906 critique of Eduard Meyer, which is subtitled "Objective Probability and Adequate Causation in Historical Analysis." The context was provided by passages in Meyer's works that seemed to call for clarification. Meyer traced the outbreaks of the Second Punic War, the Seven Years' War, and the War of 1866 to the relevant decisions of Hannibal, Frederick the Great, and Bismarck. Other personalities might have chosen differently and thus changed the course of history, he claimed, but the question of whether these wars would have occurred in any case was unanswerable and therefore "idle." On the other hand, Meyer elsewhere described the untraced shots that provoked street battles in Berlin during March of 1848 as "historically irrelevant," since social and political conditions made some sort of upheaval inevitable in any case. In his history of antiquity, finally, Meyer portrayed the Battle of Marathon as a turning point in Western history, in that it ensured the survival of Hellenic culture in the face of a theocratic alternative that was a distinct possibility—until the threat of Persian domination was turned aside.[9]

In response, Weber systematically examined the methodological foundations of singular causal claims. "To begin with, we ask . . . how the attribution of a concrete "result" to a single "cause" is . . . feasible . . . in principle, given that in reality it is always an infinity of causal factors that brought about the single "event," and that strictly all of these . . . causal factors were indispensable for the achievement of the result." Excluding the idea of reproducing the totality of concrete conditions jointly sufficient for an outcome, Weber outlined the analytical tactics proposed by von Kries. Somehow, a set of antecedent conditions has to be conceptually isolated that more or less strongly "favored" the result to be explained. The judgments of probability required for this purpose typically cannot be quantified; but one can focus upon selected potential "causes" and compare the ranges of additional conditions under which they would, and would not, have brought about the effect in question. Meyer's thesis about the historical significance of the Battle of Marathon, for example, ultimately depends upon the judgment that a changed outcome of the Persian Wars would have made theocracy "objectively probable." Judgments of objective probability could seem problematic, because they require the historian to imagine alternate causal sequences and outcomes. But as Weber pointed out, one does not have to know exactly what would have followed upon a Persian victory at Marathon to conclude that the Hellenic tradition might well have been altered by theocratic influences.[10]

When Weber first mentioned "objective probability" and "adequate causation," he cited two characteristic examples, one of which he repeated in his 1906 response to Meyer. The first was of a boulder dislodged from a cliff, which falls, fragments upon impact below, and disperses rock splinters over a certain area. Weber's point was that we could neither predict nor fully explain the resulting distribution of splinters. We would be satisfied if, after the event, the outcome did not contradict our nomological knowledge about the processes involved. We could safely identify the dislodging of the boulder as the cause of what followed, and we would seek further explanation only if the final location of a particular rock fragment seemed radically inconsistent with our expectations. Weber further observed that in our explanation of the actual out-come, as in many similar cases of causal attribution, no empirically grounded judgments of necessity would be involved. The postulate of universal "determinism" would accordingly remain extra-empirical, a "pure a priori." In a second example, Weber referred to the throw of a die, which presumably causes a given result, but again in ways we cannot specify. We therefore regard the particular outcome as "accidental," although we can state the probability of its occurrence with mathematical precision. If, after many throws, we find that certain outcomes are markedly more frequent than others, as a matter of fact, we confidently trace this (quantifiable) *deviation* from the "accidental" distribution to some physical abnormality in the die. Weber provided a quantitative example, but his real intention was to argue for a looser, typically qualitative application of probabilistic reasoning to human affairs.[11]

Weber relied extensively upon the interlinked concepts of "objective probability" and "adequate causation," but he insisted even more strenuously upon the role of counterfactual reasoning in causal analysis. If history is to rise above the level of the chronicle, he wrote, the historian must be explicit about possible developments that *did not occur*. Meyer had claimed that a defeat of the Greeks at Marathon would have had far-reaching cultural consequences; yet he had elsewhere rejected "idle" speculations about what would have happened if leading statesmen had not decided in favor of war on certain occasions. In response, Weber stressed the need for just the sort of conjectures that Meyer accepted in practice but rejected in theory; for we cannot assess the causal significance of a political decision—or other possible cause—without trying to imagine what would have ensued in its absence. After all, a potentially infinite number of causal "moments" or antecedent conditions have to be present to produce any concrete outcome. To identify significant singular causal relationships at all, therefore, we must inquire into the degree to which a particular cause "favored" a given effect. But this in turn requires us hypothetically to "compare" the result that actually followed with alternate possibilities. Thus historians cannot avoid reasoning counterfactually about historical events that *did not occur,* in order to identify the significant causes of what *did occur.*[12]

Here is Weber's simplest statement about the role of counterfactuals in singular causal analysis: "The judgment that if a single historical fact in a complex of historical conditions (had been) missing or altered this would have brought about a . . . divergent course of historical events (is crucial in) the determination of the "historical significance" of that fact." Here "historical significance" means something like "causal influence" as further defined by the notions of "favoring" and of "adequate causation." There is no reference to the issue of "cultural relevance" or to the grounds of the historian's interest in what is to be explained. The weighing of possible causes is somewhat more completely described as follows. "The first . . . [abstraction involved in causal analysis] is just this: that among the actual causal components of a course [of events], we think of one or several as altered in a certain direction, and we ask ourselves whether, under the changed conditions . . . the same—or what other—outcome was 'to be expected.'" The point of counterfactual reasoning, for Weber, is a conjectural ranking of possible causes. That ranking takes place in the context of counterfactual reflections upon possible courses of events, paths of historical development that were more or less probable in the light of the possible causes under consideration. Weber's formulations about these matters were notably dynamic.[13]

A final point Weber made again and again in his discussion of adequate causation has to do with the inescapably "abstract" character of causal analysis. In Weber's view, causal "moments" are not simply "given"; they are constructs. On the one hand, we analyze the given into components, isolating possible causes from the vast complex of surrounding conditions. On the other hand, we have to describe such potential causes at a certain level of generality. Like Simmel before him, Weber dismissed the project of following causal relationships to the microscopic level of necessary connections among elementary constituents of reality. Freed from the tacit identification of explanation with reproduction, he emphasized the role of *description* in the formulation of singular causal claims. Thus he saw no logical difference between causal questions about such specific events as the Defenestration of Prague, and causal questions about such broad but singular phenomena as the rise of Western capitalism. Indeed, Weber demystified the rhetoric of "uniqueness" that typically accompanied the defense of "idiographic" knowledge. To sustain individual causal claims at all, he pointed out, both "causes" and "effects" must be described at a level of abstraction that will permit them to be related to "rules of experience" (*Erfahrungsregeln*). In Weber's account of these rules, they resemble imperfect empirical generalizations; they are incompletely universal and less rigorously formulated than scientific laws. Often expressed in the language of common sense, they are subject to modification by various "outside" influences. Even so, Weber explicitly considered them forms of nomological knowledge.[14] His model of singular causal analysis thus really excluded the illusion of a radically "idiographic" historiography.

To place Weber's account of causal analysis into the broader framework of his methodology, and to explore some of its practical implications, we must consider a passage in Weber's "Objectivity" that conveniently brings together the several elements of his program. Drawing upon the contrast between "nomological sciences" and "sciences of reality," Weber called for a social science that deals with social realities in their "distinctiveness," that seeks to comprehend the "interconnection and the cultural significance" of particular phenomena "in their present-day form," along with "the grounds of their having historically become thus and not otherwise." The formulation is not elegant, but it does identify the elements of his program. He begins by focusing upon the singular phenomenon to be explained. This explanandum is selected for analysis because it is culturally significant—or seems significant to the investigator—in its distinctive contemporary form. The passage reflects Weber's enduring concern with the *description* of singular objects, descriptions that must point up both what is significant about them and how they fall under the terms of empirical "rules." Finally, Weber calls for the kind of causal analysis that will explain why the course of historical development ultimately produced the explanandum rather than some other outcome.[15] The projected investigation is clearly expected to deal in "objective probability" and "adequate causation," but the formulation also implies counterfactual reasoning and a dynamic vision of alternate paths of historical change.

In his critique of Meyer, Weber urged practicing historians not to confound the genesis with the justification of particular interpretations or explanations. He conceded that historians might depend upon their "intuition" in their reconstructions of the past. They might "understand" historical agents by drawing directly upon their own experiences. In writing their narratives, moreover, they might try to evoke the total character of persons and situations, so as to give their readers a sense of "reexperiencing" a historical world. Weber did not repudiate these aspects of historical practice, but he pointed out that mathematicians and natural scientists too may be inspired by initially unsubstantiated intuitions. In any case, he insisted upon separating the psychological origins of historical insights, along with their literary representations, from the "logical structure of cognition" and the validity of causal claims about the past. He saw the reconstruction of what he called the "causal regression," not literary evocation, as the historian's main task.[16]

Elsewhere in "Objectivity," Weber enlarged upon the role of nomological knowledge in singular causal explanation. The attribution of particular outcomes to definite causal antecedents, he wrote, is impossible without such knowledge. The ways in which historians make use of their experience and schooled imagination may vary from case to case, but the *validity* of their causal claims is bound to depend upon the reliability and comprehensiveness of what they know about recurrent connections. To be sure, their recourse is not likely to be to the strict laws typical of the natural sciences, but to "adequate causal connections expressed in rules." These rules function more as means than as ends in the cognitive strategies of the cultural sciences. Often, there is no point in articulating the everyday knowledge of human behavior that more or less dependably warrants a singular explanation. While the laws of the natural sciences are both general and abstract, the historian's rules of adequate causation tend to be richer in qualitative content but also correspondingly less general. Nevertheless, the cultural and historical disciplines are by no means uninterested in the use—and even in the attempt to establish—relatively reliable "rules of adequate causation."[17]

These rules do have a degree of predictive power; their fallibility is due to the fact that their terms—and the parameters of their applicability—are imprecisely specified, so that they are subject to alteration by unexpected intervening processes. Weber pointed out that even such "lawful" processes as the development of a fetus may be modified in unanticipated ways. The main problem of historical explanation lies in the sheer number of possibly relevant considerations. This also helps to explain why the cultural and social sciences are so much more successful in their retrospective explanations than in their predictions; they simply need the additional information that becomes available about a course of events only after it has been completed. After the fact, too, the historian knows much more about a situation in the past than the agents who confronted it at the time.[18]

Referring back to the examples of the falling boulder and the thrown die, Weber pointed out that we are often satisfied if what actually happens does not contradict our nomological knowledge. Even so, Weber regarded the study of singular cultural and social phenomena as valuable not only because they interest us in their own right, but also because the admittedly tentative discriminations involved in singular causal analysis may pave the way for more reliable "rules of adequate causation." In his 1907 critique of Stammler, Weber distinguished between causal laws and empirical generalizations that offer no insight into causal relationships. He then argued that the term *science (Naturwissenschaft)* could be broadly defined to encompass all disciplines committed to the "empirical-causal explanation" of reality.[19]

Any remaining doubts about Weber's causalism can be removed, at the cost of some repetition.

> The weighing of the causal significance of a historical fact begins with the question: whether with its elimination from the complex of factors under consideration . . . or with its alteration in a certain manner, the course of events could, according to general rules of experience, have taken a direction that somehow diverged in character [from the actual one] in aspects decisive for our interest.

The sentence again posits a dynamic model of alternate historical sequences or paths. The influence of the presumptive cause is such that its removal or change would have led to a *deviation* from the course of events that has actually been observed. Weber further insisted upon the recourse to "general rules of experience." Yet the role of such rules in the above passage is not to link the cause to the actual effect, but to support the claim that the absence of the cause would have been followed by a divergent course of events. We need not infer that Weber was uninterested in rules that connect causes to effects; however, at least in the formulation just cited, he drew upon nomological knowledge exclusively to sustain a projection about events that did not occur. In his 1905 article on Knies, Weber further argued that the notion of causation actually encompasses two separate components. One of these is the idea of the cause "acting" (*Wirken*) to *bring about* an effect. The other element in causation is the idea of conformity to observable "rules" or laws. Where the sciences reach the level of quantitative equations, according to Weber, the idea of the cause as agency can in practice be bracketed. Conversely, the idea of lawfulness becomes less important as the focus shifts to the links among particulars. But in history and in the cultural sciences, Weber suggested, both components of causality come into play. The predominant cognitive aim is to identify causal connections among singular elements of reality, but there is a simultaneous interest in the use—and the extension—of nomological knowledge.[20]

What ultimately emerges from Weber's formulations is a *triadic* scheme of the causal relationships—and of causal analysis—that deals in *courses* of events, and in *divergences* between alternate paths and outcomes. By way of illustrating Weber's scheme, we must begin by positing a *hypothetical* sequence of events from an initial state (A) to an eventual result (B). We next focus upon a distinctive element within the initial state (A') or a *change* in initial conditions (A-A') that can be isolated as causally significant with respect to an *ob-*

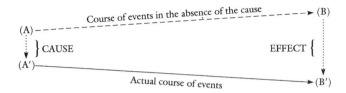

FIGURE 1 Diagram of Cause and Effect. Reprinted by permission of the publisher from *Max Weber's Methodology: The Unification of the Cultural and Social Sciences* by Fritz Ringer, p. 78, Cambridge, Mass.: Harvard University Press, copyright © 1997 by the President and Fellows of Harvard College.

served path of development (A′-B′) that *diverges* from the hypothetical sequence. If this element (A′) or change (A-A′) were absent, then the hypothetical sequence would ensue. In Weber's thinking, the *effect* of this element or change in initial conditions is a *deviation* in the subsequent course of events (A′-B′) and in its outcome (B′), such that the hypothetical sequence (A-B) is replaced by the observed path (A′-B′), and the ultimate effect is the substitution of the actual outcome (B′) for what would have occurred if the cause had not intervened (B). Figure 1 is a schematic representation of Weber's model of causal analysis.

The object of causal analysis is to explain the actual course of events from the region of the starting point to the observed endpoint, rather than the hypothetical alternative, by specifying the causally significant elements or changes within the initial conditions, which "act" to change the direction of historical development. The causal relationship is not a "constant conjunction" of two events. Instead, an alteration in a set of initial conditions "makes a difference" by *bringing about* an outcome that could not have been expected in the absence of the cause. The claim that this alteration "adequately caused" the replacement of the hypothetical outcome by the observed one rests upon the claim that without the intervention of the cause, the objectively probable outcome would have been the hypothetical one. Explicitly or implicitly, historians who explain what actually happened must draw upon more or less formal "rules of experience" or upon other forms of nomological knowledge. Weber recognized that particularly convincing causal claims often trace divergences from expected courses of events to deviations in the normal initial conditions. Particularly in retrospect, it is much easier to chart what actually followed upon the Battle of Marathon—or upon the untraced shots of 1848— than to defend counterfactual claims about the course of events in the absence of these possible causes. Nomological knowledge may thus be more often required to sustain counterfactual claims about hypothetical sequences than to link alleged causes to particular effects. Weber's model is complex, but I believe it represents the historian's reasoning more fully than simpler schemes.

Notice that a counterfactual supposition about a course of events can become the explanandum in a further stage of causal analysis. In a statistical study of access to higher education, for instance, one might find oneself explaining a short-term upswing in the rate of university entry against the background of long-term increases at a more moderate pace. Obviously, these long-term trends in turn demand explanation, which might depart from the counterfactual supposition of essentially unchanging rates of enrollment per age group. Stable rates of access, finally, would be treated as a normal causal process, not as a deviation from an alternate course of events. Practicing historians have probably always known that long-term changes must be traced to long-term causes, while short-term phenomena must be linked to chronologically more specific antecedents. In any case, Weber's model of singular causal analysis can easily be extended to encompass several stages of short-term as well as long-term relationships, in each of which a deviation from a "normal," or expected, path of development is traced to an alteration in the initial conditions. Notice, finally, that Weber's account of causal analysis is particularly hospitable to the interpretation and explanation of human actions. Thus if social scientists trace changes in rates of marriage to shifts in economic conditions, Weber argued, they seek "causal interpretations in terms of motives," trying to link alterations in the contexts of choice to changes in the behaviors of typical agents.[21] Weber left no doubt that the interpretive inquiry into motivations is a *form of causal analysis* in the same sense as any other search for "adequate causes," even though the causal connection between a motive and an action is not an instance of natural necessity.[22]

INTERPRETIVE INDIVIDUALISM AND THE IDEAL TYPE

Many of Weber's methodological writings were critical essays, so it seems reasonable to ask what positions he *opposed*. In fact, his critical targets fall under the three main headings of "holism," "naturalism," and "psychologism." His repudiation of "holism" was explicitly directed against dominant assumptions of the German historical tradition, which grew out of the *principle of individuality*. His position on this subject emerges most clearly in his commentaries upon Wilhelm Roscher and Karl Knies, two founding fathers of the older historical school of economics. Both Roscher and Knies treated peoples or nations as organic totalities, rather than organized groups of individuals. In trying to avoid the isolation of economic practices from the rest of a nation's culture, they ended by assigning a peculiar guiding force to the "spirit" of the people. That spirit could come to serve as the source of its expressions, or "realizations." Weber detected a form of teleological reasoning in this line of argument, which he called "emanationism," though I believe "essentialism" would have done as well. In the case of Roscher, the syndrome became oddly linked with the search for "laws" of historical development. But as Weber noted, the pertinent generalizations had to be about the class of nations; indeed, they had to deal with parallels in the "life cycles" of these "individualities." Fortunately, Roscher's commitment to this form of "historical economics" did not prevent him from drawing upon classical theory in his accounts of particular phenomena.[23]

Under the heading of "naturalism," Weber opposed doctrines that many of his contemporaries called "positivist." He traced naturalistic fallacies to the belief that the search for universal laws is the only legitimate aim of knowledge. Despite the resistance of German Idealism and of the German historical tradition, Weber wrote, the dramatic success of the natural sciences in Darwin's century fostered a commitment to the strategy of abstracting from reality what can be subsumed under predictive generalizations. This commitment further suggests both that the singular as such is not worth knowing, and that reality may be fully deduced from universal laws. Weber also challenged the type of reductionism he loosely associated with Comte's "hierarchy of sciences." He opposed the view that the more "general" disciplines near the bottom of the cognitive "hierarchy" provide the foundations for the "higher," more complex disciplines, a thesis that again implies the deducibility of singular realities from general laws. Weber's most explicit repudiation of this view was a critique of the chemist Wilhelm Ostwald, a member of the scientistic Leipzig Circle that also included the psychologist Wilhelm Wundt and the historian Karl Lamprecht. Ostwald provided Weber with an ancillary account of "naturalism" as a dilettante's attempt to raise the insights of his discipline, most often a natural science, to the status of a *Weltanschauung*. What Weber particularly disliked about such speculations was the false aura of scientific exactitude that enhanced their popularity. The various forms of Social Darwinism were perfect examples of this syndrome. In some of his letters, as well as in notes and asides, he specifically expressed his contempt for Lamprecht's vision of history as "applied psychology."[24]

Prominent among the naturalistic reductions that Weber sought to discredit, indeed, was the doctrine that interpretations of human actions and beliefs can be *deduced* from the *laws of psychology*. Psychologists might some day clarify the relationship between the mental and the physiological, he conceded, but in the meantime, the two are separate realms. Historians develop their terms and methods in the light of their own cognitive strategies. The understanding of some irrational states may be facilitated by an informally interpretive psychology or "folk" psychology *(Vulgärpsychologie)*. But psychophysical regularities and the findings of psychopathologists are mere "givens" for the historian. They may be causally relevant to singular actions and events, but they function as background conditions, not as elements in interpretations. "In so far as psychological concepts and rules or statistical data are not accessible to 'interpretation,' they are . . . accepted as 'given,' but . . . do not satisfy . . . [our] specifically 'historical interest.'" Thus Weber drew a sharp line between the interpretation of human actions and beliefs, and the "laws" of psychology.[25] What is called his *methodological individualism* rests upon the claim that the smallest unit to which the interpretive method can be applied is the human individual.

A more specific target of Weber's attack upon "psychologism" was the view held by prominent historical economists, including Lujo Brentano, that the Austrian theory of marginal utility was an application of a psychophysical law. Brentano claimed that the declining utility of added increments of a good could be deduced from the Weber-Fechner law. According to that law, added increments of a physical stimulus call forth decreasing sensory responses. (The difference between weights of 51 and 52 pounds is harder to "feel" than that between weights of 1 and 2 pounds.) Weber could find no more than a vague analogy between this psychophysical finding and the marginalist model in neo-classical economics. He pointed out that the personal "needs" weighed by economic agents are not simply physiological and that the weighing takes place in the context of scarce means and market competition. The economic agent is engaged in purposive rational action, not in reflex reactions to physical stimuli. Like Menger, Weber saw economic theory as a hypothetical construct rather than an empirical generalization; it predicts how the "ideal" economic man would act under certain circumstances, not how real individuals actually behave in complex situations. The analytical tactics pursued by the theoretical economist thus differ radically from those of the German psychophysical tradition. Too many methodologists simply assume that what is not "physical" must be "psychological"; yet the "meaning of a mathematical problem is surely not 'psychological.'" As he wrote in a 1909 letter to Brentano, "our theory is 'rational,' not 'psychological' in its foundations."[26]

In any case, Weber persistently emphasized the role of interpretation in the cultural and social sciences. He used the terms "interpreting" *(Deuten)* and "interpretive understanding" *(Verstehen)* to characterize this part of his program; more rarely, he referred to "empathetic understanding" *(nachfühlendes Verstehen)*. At the same time, he always regarded interpretation as an element, or even a subset, of causal explanation, writing of "interpretive explanation" and recommending an "interpretive sociology" *(verstehende Soziologie)*. In his 1904 essay entitled "Objectivity," he touched upon the social scientist's effort to "understand" intellectual processes and human actions, the latter on the basis of informal observation and "rules of rational action." He challenged the view that the historical, cultural, and social sciences depend upon "teleological" reasoning about human intentions and purposes. To undermine this position, he redefined the *aim* of an action as its *cause*. For the cultural scientist, he wrote, a purpose is "the *image of an outcome* that becomes the cause of an action." Agents envisage the outcomes they desire to bring about, along with the means of doing so, and that is what moves them to act. The specific characteristic of "this kind of cause" is that we can "understand" it.[27] From Weber's causalist perspective, in other words, the peculiarity of the cultural sciences has nothing to do with "teleology," but it does depend upon accounts of actions that entail the "interpretive understanding" of their "causes."

Weber's strenuous causalism and his insistence upon the rationality model of interpretation cannot be understood apart from his comments upon what he called the "problem of irrationality." He himself occasionally characterized reality as "irrational," in that it cannot be encompassed by our descriptions. When he wrote about the "problem of irrationality" in the work of Knies and others, however, he was referring to an altogether different issue. He noted that many German historians divided reality into two distinct realms. One of these was the world of "necessity" and causal determination; the other was the realm of "accident" and of "free" human action. The use of this binary scheme was a reaction to the view that causality implies lawfulness and determinism, a view held by such targets of Weber's criticism as Roscher, Knies, Schmoller, Meyer, and Stammler. Apparently, it was the specter of determinism that drove many historians into a problematic defense of "free will." They took it to be the dignity of human beings that their actions were "free" in the sense of being incalculable. But this made history inexplicable in principle, and of course it encouraged an emphasis upon the deeds of "great men," as against the causal role of structural "conditions."[28]

Weber dealt with the "problem of irrationality" in several ways. If "freedom" means incalculability, he wrote, we will find no more of it in the interactions of human beings than in the evolution of local weather conditions. More important, as Weber insisted, both "determinism" and "free will" are metascientific speculations that have no relationship to the analytical practices of historians. For the work of the cultural and social sciences, Weber held, "necessity" in the sense of full explicability is an infinitely distant goal, but also a guiding maxim in Kant's sense of that term. Conversely, the incalculability of individual actions cannot serve as a framework for the historians' practice, for historians do *seek* to explain such actions. The choice among a plurality of possible actions, considered as an object of empirical investigation, is quite as "determined" in principle as any particular event in nature.[29]

Both Meyer and Stammler tried to rescue the "freedom" of actions by distinguishing between a prospective and a retrospective view of them. In retrospect, they argued, what has been done seems "necessary," or at least explicable, but courses of action still in progress are open to alternate choices. Stammler added that without the awareness of multiple options, the agent's sense of *choosing* would be an illusion, which is hard to believe. In response to these arguments, Weber pointed out that in "dead" nature too, particular series of events are more fully describable in retrospect than in prospect. We simply know more about processes after than before they have occurred. As for the agent's sense of choice, it is certainly not an illusion, and there is no need to deny its causal significance. What *would* be illusory is an insistence upon the *causelessness* of actions on the basis of an "indeterminist metaphysics." The claim that "free action" is causally relevant can only mean that the agent's "resolve" to act in a certain way is both understandable and productive of consequences. Even a rigorous determinist, Weber thought, would not object to that.[30] The whole debate about "free will" and "determinism" in history is thus radically misconceived—and certainly irrelevant to empirical inquiry.

Finally, Weber argued that individual actions are less "irrational" than events in nature, for human actions may be interpretable as *rational* ones. The relevance to the issue of "freedom" and "determinism" is clear; for, as Weber pointed out, it is precisely "free" actions that are least "irrational" in the sense required by the champions of indeterminism. "Free" agents are unconstrained by physical and psychological forces beyond their control. They can pursue deliberate ends by means rationally selected to achieve them. And the "freer" they are in this respect, the more "calculable" are their actions. While human behaviors may be predictable as the effects of psychological or other natural *causes,* no one is more predictable than the principled and rational agent, whose actions are the effects of deliberate principles and sound *reasons.* The romantic counterimage of gratuitous deeds actually violates our sense of what it means to act freely, for our sense of freedom requires that we be aware of our ultimate commitments and that we exclude all but rational considerations in making our choices. Of course most human actions are not fully rational in this sense. Yet the specific incalculability suggested by the romantic view of "freedom," Weber wrote, is the "privilege of—the madman."[31] "Freedom" and "explicability" just aren't opposed to each other in the way some historians think they are.

It was the "motivational understanding" of actions that Weber chiefly had in mind when he stressed the explanatory significance of interpretation. "Any . . . science about human behavior . . . [including about] any intellectual act and any psychic *habitus* . . . seeks to understand this behavior, and thereby interpretively to explain its progression [*Ablauf*]." The difficulty of the passage stems from the fact that it refers to an outward *course of action,* but that this *progression* can be understood only in terms of inner dispositions. Weber agreed with Simmel's observation that human behaviors are difficult to predict, since individuals may react to similar situations in dissimilar ways, but he pointed out that "rules of adequate causation" often fall short of full predictive power as well. He thus felt free to insist that the "interpretive investigation of 'motives' is a form of 'causal attribution,'" and thus an integral part of the larger project of causal analysis in the cultural and social sciences. Consistent with this position, Weber held that the interpreter must try to determine what actually moved persons to act in particular cases. He warned against the view that the agents themselves are reliable informants about the grounds of their actions. Nor was he content to know what considerations *might reasonably* have motivated certain behaviors. It is the agent's actual motive that the investigator must seek to identify, since it was the true cause of the action to be explained.[32]

For Weber, an agent's "motive" might be any meaningful "reason" for behaving in a certain way. Of course some actions are the expressions of a normative standpoint or of an emotion. Nevertheless, Weber argued, interpreters are well advised to begin by supposing that the actions they observe are rationally selected to *achieve specific ends.* It is such purposively rational action that can create the false impression of "teleology." In reality, the *image* of the result is the *cause* of the action, and it can play that role only if it is joined to beliefs about how to attain it. Of course Weber knew perfectly well that many actions are not purposively rational and that some are not rational at all. Yet even for such cases, Weber recommended the model of purposively rational action as a useful *starting point,* if only to "measure" the *deviation* between the course of action that would have been rational and the behaviors actually observed.[33]

Weber distinguished the "inner" processes that define the "meaning" or "sense" (*Sinn*) of an action from the "outer" behaviors that are shaped by that meaning. The cultural and social sciences, he held, deal primarily with the causal relationships between "inner" meanings and their "outward" expressions; indeed, a motivational interpretation can be empirically validated only in terms of the outward behaviors it actually accounts for. At no point did Weber suggest that the identification of an agent's "subjective" motive depends upon the "subjectivity" of the interpreter. On the contrary, following Simmel, he repeatedly stressed that one does not have to be Caesar to understand him. Much of Weber's commentary on Knies, in fact, was written to challenge the subjectivist fallacy that interpretation is an intuitive *identification* with the persons who are "understood," or an empathetic *reproduction* of their inner states. Of course we may at times "experience" (*erleben*) an apparently unmediated sense of another person's feelings. Still, we must leave the realm of intuitive insight to reach justifiable interpretations, which are deliberate constructions, not intuitive flashes. Weber suspected that irrationalist views of interpretation reflect a confusion between the genesis of interpretive understandings and their justification. For in the cultural and social sciences as in other disciplines, new knowledge often originates in intuitions, which then must be validated in more formal arguments and procedures.[34]

Nothing is more central to Weber's methodology, in any case, than the maxim that interpreters must *begin* by supposing that the actions and beliefs they seek to understand are "rational" in some sense of that term. Clearly influenced by Menger's understanding of marginal utility theory as an abstraction from a more complex reality, Weber repeatedly used economic examples to explicate his views. What the "economic principle" stipulates, he argued, is how agents would behave if they fully knew their present and future needs, and effectively related them to the resources available to them. Such omniscient and rational economic agents may not exist in the real world; but the model is *heuristically* useful, especially in an age of increasing economic rationality. In the same way, we may imagine a perfectly informed and rational military commander, if only to judge to what extent the decisions of a real general matched those of his ideal colleague. Not only economics, but all the social sciences need such "rational constructions." Economics, especially in its historical form, "interpretively understands human actions in their motives and consequences," and is thus "intimately linked to interpretive sociology."[35]

Weber left no doubt that the rationality he proposed to attribute to the agents and beliefs to be investigated was "our" rationality, the rationality of the investigator. "We obviously 'understand' without difficulty that a thinker solves a certain 'problem' in a way that we ourselves consider normatively correct." Weber used the term "right rationality" (*Richtigkeitsrationalität*) to refer to what *we* consider "correct" reasoning. Of course the norm of "right rationality" is "the a priori of all scientific investigation," but it may also serve more specifically as an aid to interpretive understanding. On the other hand, "wrong" thinking is accessible to interpretation as well. The hypothetical attribution of "right rationality" to an agent or a text is therefore just an especially useful point of departure for the interpretive enterprise. "Even to 'understand' an incorrect . . . logical statement, and to . . . assess . . . its influence, one not only has to . . . recheck it by means of correct . . . thinking, but also explicitly to identify . . . the precise point . . . at which [it] deviates from what the [investigator] himself considers 'correct.'" The point of deviation may be causally relevant or culturally interesting, especially if the "truth value" of a line of reasoning is a source of its "value relatedness," as in the history of a discipline. Consistent with his emphasis upon "right rationality" as a point of departure, Weber insisted that art historians, for example, must be capable of *substantive* artistic judgments.[36]

In his 1907 essay on Stammler, Weber defended his vision of causal analysis against what he considered fashionable obscurantism. Stammler had characterized group life as essentially "rule-governed" (*geregelt*), regarding legal and conventional norms as *constitutive* of social systems. In response, Weber distinguished several senses of the word *rule:* A rule may be an observed *regularity,* one less strict than a scientific law, yet sound enough to sustain a judgment of "adequate causation"; it may be a legal or customary *norm* of conduct; or it may be a behavioral *maxim,* the "rule" actually guiding an action. Legal or conventional norms considered valid within a social group may nonetheless be circumvented in practice. Furthermore, agents may be partly or wholly unaware of the maxims guiding their behavior, so that only "outside" investigators can fully articulate them. Thus social scientists cannot be content to understand the "rules" of a society; they must interpret and explain the actions and beliefs of social agents. Of course juridical laws may function as *causes,* affecting *expectations* about the consequences of actions, especially if they are reinforced by sanctions. For the sociologist, Weber remarked, the "validity" of a law is just the empirical "chance" that its breach will be sanctioned. Moreover, laws and maxims alike may serve as hypothetical models of social practice, if only to "measure" the distances that separate them from the observed realities. Investigators themselves may construct such maxims as that of economic rationality for analytical purposes. Still, no matter by what cognitive means, social scientists must seek to know the causes and consequences of social actions; their task cannot be limited to understanding "rules" in Stammler's sense of that term.[37]

Among Weber's methodological writings, one stands out as particularly significant, because it summarizes Weber's own position without commenting upon the work of others. "Basic Concepts of Sociology" was written as an introduction to *Economy and Society,* Weber's famous socioeconomic handbook, which was published after his death. Here are the well-known definitions that form the opening of the essay.

> Sociology . . . seeks interpretively to understand social action and thereby causally to explain it in its progression and in its effects. "Action". . . [is defined as] human behavior (whether outer or inner and including failure to act) in so far as the agent or agents associate it with a subjective meaning. "Social" action . . . is . . . related in its intended meaning, and oriented in its progression, to the behavior of others.

While the principal subject matter of sociology is thus defined as social action, Weber acknowledged that much of the action of interest to the sociologist is oriented toward the nonmeaningful objects in the world. In fact, he devoted less attention to the obvious distinction between *action* and *social action* than to the more difficult topic of meaningful action in general. When he wrote about the "progression" of an action, he pointed not only to behavioral *sequences,* rather than isolated events, but also to the outer manifestations of inner processes. The interpretive sociologist, he specified, is interested in *action,* especially in action that is "co-determined by . . . its meaningful relatedness to the behavior of others and . . . interpretively explainable in terms of . . . [its] intended meaning."[38]

As in other contexts, Weber insisted that an action must be understood in terms of the agent's actually intended meaning, rather than a logically "valid" one. The investigator must know what the agent or agents really had in mind—what actually made them act as they did. As for the intended meanings of actions, they may be those of a single individual, those prevailing on the average within a particular group, or those attributed to a hypothetically constructed "typical" agent.

> "Understanding" . . . signifies the interpretation of the meaning or complex of meanings (a) actually intended in a particular case, . . . or (b) intended on the average and approximately, . . . or (c) to be constructed . . . for the pure type (ideal type) of a frequent phenomenon. The con-

cepts and "laws" posited by pure economic theory, for example, are such ideal-typical constructions. . . . Real action proceeds only rarely . . . and . . . approximately as projected in the ideal type.

While thus charting the methods of "interpretive sociology," Weber also called attention to the limits of interpretive understanding. Along with pathological states, he cited such "meaningless" (*sinnfremd*) phenomena as the onset of epidemics and the facts of the human life cycle, such psychophysical processes as changes in reaction times, rates of rote learning, and fatigue. Discoverable regularities in these areas, Weber held, are no more closely related to the cognitive objectives of the cultural and social sciences than the more typical laws of the natural sciences. Of course, "meaningless" realities may be of great significance as conditions and consequences of human actions. At the same time, human actions are thoroughly integrated into a wider network of causal relationships, which also encompasses "meaningless" phenomena.[39]

In a systematic approach to the varieties of "understanding," Weber used the German term *Evidenz* to signify something like "verisimilitude." Like all cognition, he argued, interpretation strives for *Evidenz,* which in the case of "understanding" may be either rational or empathetic. The "rationally evident" is "intellectually understood," fully penetrated in its "meaning relationships." The "empathetically evident" is "reexperienced." Thus, on the one hand, we completely understand the Pythagorean theorem, along with "right" reasoning, or the choice of empirically proven means to attain given ends. Somewhat less fully, we understand errors that we ourselves might have made. On the other hand, we can empathetically reexperience irrational states only to the extent that we have passed through them ourselves. Weber clearly considered this kind of projection from the interpreter's own experience less reliable than rational understanding. The ability to reexperience another's feelings on the basis of one's own may enhance the verisimilitude of an interpretation; but the fact that it "possesses this quality of *Evidenz* to a particularly high degree," Weber wrote, "does not . . . in itself prove anything about its empirical validity." Wherever possible, the "understanding" of a meaning relationship must therefore be "checked with the ordinary methods of causal analysis."[40]

Weber actually distinguished four types of action: "Purposively rational" (*zweckrational*) action is "adequate" to bring about desired ends; "value-rational" (*wertrational*) action is grounded in coherent normative commitments; "traditional" action follows accustomed practices; and "affective" action is driven by emotional states. In his substantive writings, Weber stressed the differences between these four kinds of behavior, especially that between purposively rational and value-rational action, but in his methodological essays, he emphasized the divide between rationality and irrationality. He also pointed out that the line between meaningful action and merely reactive behavior is far from clear in reality; traditional orientations in effect straddle the border between the two realms.[41]

Weber firmly anchored the tactics of interpretation in the hypothetical models of purposive and of "right" rationality. Interpretation based upon the assumption of the agent's purposive rationality, according to Weber, achieves a high degree of verisimilitude. To suppose that an action was indeed purposively rational is to say that certain means had to be chosen to reach the ends in view. The model of purposively rational action may thus be linked to the ideal type of "right rationality" (*Richtigkeitstypus*), which applies to the interpretation of value-rational actions and of beliefs as well: Maximally "evident" to us is reasoning that meets our own standards of rationality, along with actions and outcomes demonstrably brought about by appropriate means. Of course we must not automatically attribute rationality to a text or agent. A tactical construct of action based upon errors of judgment (*Irrtumstypus*) may be just as relevant in a particular instance as the type of right rationality. It follows that interpretation on the rationality model is a strategic device, not an ultimate goal of sociology, and that sociology is not inherently "rationalistic." On the contrary, as Weber insisted, practitioners of the cultural and social sciences rarely encounter purely rational actions and beliefs in reality. Their "rationalism" is purely heuristic.[42]

All the more important is the tactical role Weber assigned to observed *deviations* from purposive and/or right rationality. Having projected the course of action that would follow from purposive rationality, sociologists must chart the *divergence* between it and the actual "progression" of behavior, since that alone will permit "the causal attribution of the deviation to the irrationalities" that account for it.

> The more clearly an action . . . [conforms to] right rationality, the less . . . [need is there for] psychological considerations. Conversely, any explanation of "irrational" processes . . . requires the sociologist to determine how the action would have proceeded in the limiting case of purposive and right rationality. For only . . . [then can the sociologist] undertake the causal attribution of the [behavior] to . . . objectively and subjectively "irrational" components . . . [or judge] what aspects of the action . . . are "only psychologically" explicable . . . based upon . . . er-

roneous orientations, or upon . . . motives that are either wholly incomprehensible and knowable only through rules of experience, or else understandable but not purposively rational.[43]

The passage suggests a rich hierarchy of interpretive strategies, from the model of right rationality to other forms of "understandably" meaningful or "psychologically" comprehensible action and belief, and finally to behaviors that can only be explained by reference to "rules of experience."

More specifically, Weber noted that investigators may encounter purposively rational actions based upon assumptions they cannot share; magical practices based upon animist beliefs may serve as examples. In a catalogue of possibilities confronting the interpretive sociologist, Weber distinguished the following six alternatives: (1) the more or less fully realized type of right rationality, (2) the type of subjectively purposive rationality, (3) action more or less unconsciously or incompletely oriented in a purposively rational sense, (4) action that is not purposively rational but understandably meaningful, (5) behavior that is less than fully understandable as meaningful and codetermined by nonmeaningful relationships, and (6) wholly incomprehensible psychic or physical states. These six possibilities, according to Weber, are not clearly separated in reality; rather, they are linked by gradual transitions on a single continuous scale. Nevertheless, Weber was particularly interested in the divergence between the ideal type of right rationality and empirically observed beliefs and behavioral "progressions." He added that both right rationality and deviations from it may be culturally as well as causally significant, depending upon the investigator's value-related concerns. "Not only for a history of logic or of other disciplines, but in all other areas as well . . . [the] seams at which tensions between the empirical and the type of right rationality can break open are of the highest significance." One clear instance of the tension Weber refers to is that between rational reconstruction and attention to empirical contingency in the history of knowledge.[44]

At the same time, Weber was extremely cautious about the reliability of interpretation itself. In his deliberately broad definition, a *motive* is a *meaning relation* that is taken to be a "reason" (*Grund*) for an action. But as he pointed out, motives may be feigned, mixed, or unconscious. More generally, a highly "evident" interpretation, one that is unquestionably "adequate at the level of meaning," may nevertheless be causally "inadequate." Thus a plausible motivational interpretation can never be more than a promising hypothesis about the real cause of an action—until it is checked against the relevant "progression" of external behaviors. In the case of group actions, statistical data may help to confirm the causal adequacy of a meaningful interpretation, even though statistical regularities cannot, by themselves, satisfy our need for a causal understanding of actions. Comparative analysis, too, may aid us in identifying reasons that are causally as well as meaningfully adequate. Otherwise, our only recourse is to counterfactual analysis. Though aware of the great difficulties involved, Weber nonetheless saw "understandable" meaning relationships as crucial elements in the cultural and social sciences. Indeed, he described reasons or motives as potential "links in a causal chain" that "begins in external circumstances and ultimately terminates again in outward behaviors." Sociology, he concluded, "would have to protest against the assumption that 'understanding' and causal 'explanation' have no relationship to each other."[45]

Weber's methodology, and especially his theory of interpretation, can scarcely be imagined apart from his concept of the "ideal type," which Weber first extensively discussed in his 1904 essay entitled "Objectivity." His point of departure was "abstract economic theory," which can provide an "ideal portrait" of the processes resulting from rational action in a "free market" economy. This "construction" has a "utopian" character, in that it is obtained by conceptually "heightening" certain aspects of reality. Where we suspect the presence of relationships resembling those emphasized in the "ideal type," the type can help us to understand these connections. "Ideal types" are not normatively exemplary, of course; they are "pure constructs of relationships" that we conceive as "sufficiently motivated," "objectively probable," and thus causally "adequate" in the light of our nomological knowledge. They are valuable as cognitive means to the extent that they lead to knowledge of "concrete cultural phenomena in their interconnections, their causes, and their significance."[46]

On the other hand, the line between the ideal type and reality must not be blurred. Cultural and social scientists must avoid a fallacy that Weber traced to essentialist assumptions. Thus a historian may be tempted to "hypostatize" his interpretive ideas, making them generative forces that are somehow "realized" in the historical process. In the face of this danger, it is imperative for investigators to distinguish between *their* constructs and the beliefs and attitudes of the historical agents they hope to understand. In order to emphasize the difference, Weber pointed to agents who are incompletely conscious of their motives, though the "outside observer" can detect and account for the maxims implied in their practices.[47]

What really strikes me about Weber's ideal type is its tactical role in his model of singular causal analysis. The ideal type is deliberately constructed to project a hypothetical "progression" of external behaviors that *could be* fully explained in terms of understandable motives and beliefs about means of action. In the analysis of virtually all real actions, such ideal-typical projections become secure—though counterfactual—bases for the causal ascription of *deviations* from the rationally understandable "progression" to *divergences* between the motivations stipulated in the type and those actually moving the agents involved. Here are two particularly revealing formulations on this subject.

> The rational construction [of an ideal general's decisions] . . . functions as a means of causal "attribution." Exactly the same purpose is served by those utopian constructions of error-free and rigorously rational action that are created by "pure" economic theory. . . . Whatever content the ideal type is given, . . . its only value . . . for empirical investigations lies in its purpose: to "compare" empirical reality with it, so as to ascertain . . . the distance or degree of approximation between [reality and the type], and thus to be able to describe and causally to explain [reality] in terms of clearly understandable concepts.[48]

Once again, neo-classical economic theory serves as an example of ideal-typical construction, and the overall aim is to reach optimally clarified concepts.

Though the rational agent provides a starting point for the investigator who constructs interpretive types, Weber clearly considered other possibilities, as in the following sentence: "Right rationality serves [interpretive sociology] as an ideal type with respect to empirical action; purposive rationality [plays an analogous role] with respect to . . . meaningfully understandable [action, and] meaningfully understandable [action] with respect to not meaningfully understandable action, by comparison with which the causally relevant irrationalities . . . can be ascertained for the purpose of causal attribution."[49] The analytical strategies suggested by these formulations are complex; they call for stepwise approaches to reality by means of increasingly fruitful interpretive constructs. In its underlying structure, however, the typological approach closely parallels Weber's triadic scheme of singular causal explanation.

The positing of the ideal type allows the investigator to "compare" an actual sequence of behaviors with the sequence "predicted" by the ideal type and thus to "measure" the *deviation* that must be causally attributed to the *difference* between the motives hypothetically ascribed to the ideal-typical agent and the motivation of the real agent involved. Note that the scheme represents only one step in what may become a more extended analytical sequence, for the investigator may begin by positing an ideal-typical agent whose action was entirely motivated by "right rationality." Having found that this supposition falls short of accounting for the observed progression of behaviors, the investigator may next stipulate a purposively rational agent who drew upon identifiably false or vacuous assumptions, or upon other "meaningfully understandable" considerations. In principle, the investigator must supplement the motives ascribed to the ideal-typical agent until the behaviors projected on that basis "match" those actually observed. This aim must be maintained even if it ultimately requires partial or total recourse to irrational causes of action.

To interpret a text or an action, in short, we begin by assuming that it is (or was) rational in the light of relevant criteria ("rightly rational"). We then check whether the actual sequence of sentences in the text—or of observed behaviors—is (or was) consistent with this initial assumption. To the extent that we observe inconsistencies, we introduce supplementary hypotheses: Perhaps an understandable error was made, or assumptions were involved that are interpretably "meaningful" but not rational in *our* sense. Alternately, we may be dealing with unreflected beliefs or traditional actions, which must be traced to inherited institutions or practices. Or irrational attitudes may be involved that are best deduced from empirical "rules" of commonsense "psychology." This is just a partial list of the possibilities. Weber named others; he did not try to exhaust the alternatives, and he insisted that the borderlines between the options were imprecise in any case. What he mainly conveyed was the vision of a hierarchy of interpretive constructions that begins with the hypothesis of "right rationality," extends through a spectrum of more or less "meaningful" actions and beliefs, and ends in the realm of the purely irrational. Consistent with his view that interpretation is a form of causal analysis, Weber saw the explanation of irrational behaviors as the endpoint of a continuum that also encompasses meaningful action. To imagine his overall scheme, one has to conceive of observed *incongruities* with initially posited lines of interpretation as *deviations* from expected paths.

Understood in this context, Weber's "ideal type" has three main functions. First, it spells out the stages in the process of interpretation, along with the broader strategy of causal analysis. In a theoretically heightened form, it demonstrates how the elements in a sequence of behaviors may be ascribed to various factors within the complex of causally relevant motives, beliefs, and other conditions. Second and more specifically, it allows interpreters to articulate the relationships of meaning they take to be involved in particular actions or texts. One has to remember that Weber deliberately distinguished the "adequacy" of an interpretation from the "adequacy" of a singular causal claim. A plausible account of a meaning relation, he held, was a necessary but not sufficient condition for a valid explanation in the realm of action. This suggests that the meaning relation alleged by an interpreter should be fully articulated in an ideal type, and thus separated from the empirical procedures necessary to assess its applicability to observed behaviors. Third and finally, the "ideal-typical" approach emphasizes the active role of the investigator in the interpretation of actions and beliefs. Against the illusion of empathetic reproduction, it highlights the engagement of the interpreter's own norms of "right rationality." It also portrays the interpretive process as a complex *interaction* between the conceptual world of the investigators and that of the agents and texts they seek to understand. Such intellectual interactions are likely to clarify the interpreters' relationships to their own cultures, even while confronting them with other possibilities. Interpretation may thus have some of the broadly educative effects envisioned in the German ideal of *Bildung*.[50]

OBJECTIVITY, VALUE NEUTRALITY,
AND VALUE PLURALISM

To clarify what Weber wrote about "objectivity" and "value neutrality" in the cultural and social sciences, I propose to distinguish his partial adaptation of Rickert's philosophy from his contribution to a significant debate within the Social Policy Association, and to separate his relevant writings between 1904 and 1910 from his more systematic statements of 1913 and afterwards. Weber came closest to Rickert's doctrines in his distinction between "nomological sciences" and "sciences of reality." Interested in singular phenomena and unable to reproduce them in their totality, cultural and social scientists need criteria to select and delimit their objects of study.

> There is no purely "objective" scientific analysis of cultural or . . . "social phenomena," independent of particular and "one-sided" perspectives, according to which they are . . . selected . . . [and described]. The reason lies in the . . . cognitive aim of social scientific projects. . . . We want to understand reality . . . in its distinctiveness—the interconnectedness and the cultural significance of its particular phenomena in their contemporary form . . . and the grounds of their having historically become thus-and-not-otherwise.

The "objective" analysis Weber here repudiates is the misconception of knowledge as a reproduction of the world; the term "objective" appears in quotation marks. The argument is that the singular objects of the cultural and social sciences are selected and described in the light of their cultural significance, and explained in causal terms. Some phenomena are significant primarily as causes of other, "value-related" particulars. But this still leaves the need for "perspectives" to guide the choice and description of objects that are significant in their relationship to contemporary cultural commitments.[51]

In short, the constructs of the cultural and social sciences reflect the values of the investigators; they do not emerge from a passively observed reality. But if that is true, then the "objectivity" of these disciplines can only lie in the fact that their inquiries, though "oriented toward . . . value ideas," do not and cannot "prove the validity" of the values involved. Our cultural concerns *launch* our investigations; once we are at work on a set of phenomena, however, we must analyze our evidence for its own sake, without further regard for our value interests. Ordinarily, our concerns tend to be stable. "Nevertheless, at some point there is a change in the atmosphere: the significance of unreflectively applied perspectives becomes uncertain; the path is lost in the dusk. The light of the great cultural problems has moved on. Then science too prepares to change its viewpoint and its conceptual apparatus."[52] The last three sentences are often cited and sometimes overinterpreted. What they show is that Weber accepted—and even valued—the energizing impact of contemporary concerns upon the cultural and social sciences, but they do not make him a "subjectivist" in the broader sense of that term.

Weber did not, like Rickert, envision the prospect of universal norms of the culturally valuable or value-related. He simply conceded the "subjectivity" of the personal or collective interests that shape the investigators' perspectives. This was consistent with his *cultural pluralism,* but of course it made portions of Rickert's philosophy irrelevant to his work. At the same time, Weber found it fruitful to investigate potential objects of the cultural and social sciences for their possible relationships to contemporary cultural values. That is what he meant by "value analysis" (*Wertanalyse*). Such analysis may serve to articulate the relevance of singular phenomena for our values, but it may also be merely "dialectical," exposing the *conceivable* value relations of cultural objects. Thus our understanding of a particular text or institution might initially be vague and unconsciously affected by personal commitments. "Value analysis" then transforms our inchoate appreciations into explicit judgments of value-relatedness. It clarifies the grounds of our interest in certain objects, if only to separate those grounds from the causal analysis of these phenomena.[53]

In his 1906 critique of Eduard Meyer, Weber related his conception of value analysis to the German tradition of *Bildung* on the one hand and to ordinary historical explanation on the other. Approaching such sources as the Sermon on the Mount or *Capital,* we might ask ourselves about the relationship of their "intellectual contents" to our values. Even if we do not share the commitments they articulate, our engagement with them will tend to broaden our "intellectual horizons" and enhance our "inner life." Weber's account of this prospect was consistent not only with his sense of the interaction between interpretation and self-understanding, but also with a sophisticated version of the theory of self-development through textual interpretation. At the same time, Weber saw "value analysis" as a step toward a more complete, historical, and causal explanation. In partial agreement with Meyer, he postulated an initially unhistorical reading of a text, one that naively locates it in the interpreter's intellectual field rather than its original context. Yet he also insisted that such a reading is a mere preliminary to a more properly historical analysis: "Obviously, the kind of 'interpretation' we have here termed 'value analysis' is the introductory guide to that other, 'historical,' i.e., causal 'interpretation.' The former analysis pointed up the 'valued' elements of the object, the causal 'explanation' of which is the problem of the latter."[54] Weber left no doubt that a text can be fully understood only in the cultural field that actually shaped it. His distinction between "value analysis" and historical interpretation is thus purely theoretical; nevertheless, it served to underline the logical divide between the grounds of an interpreter's interest in certain objects and the methods involved in its contextual interpretation and causal explanation.

In any case, it would be an error to see Weber as a relativist. While conceding the "subjectivity" of the value preferences that affect the selection and delimitation of subject matters, he repeatedly and explicitly stressed the "objectivity" of research *results* in the cultural and social sciences.

> Unquestionably, the value ideas [that make us decide what is worth investigating] are "subjective." . . . And of course they are historically changeable. . . . But . . . it does *not* follow that research in the cultural sciences can only have results that are "subjective" in the sense that they are valid for some people and not for others. What changes, rather, is the degree to which they *interest* some people and not others. . . . What becomes an object of research, and how far the investigation extends into the infinity of causal connections, that is determined by the value ideas

that dominate the researcher and . . . shape his constructs. In the use of these constructs, however, the researcher is bound . . . by the norms of thought. For only that is scientific truth which *wants* to be valid for all. . . . A methodically correct . . . demonstration in the social sciences . . . must be acknowledged as correct by a Chinese as well . . . [and so must] the logical analysis of an ideal . . . even though [the Chinese] may reject the ideal itself.[55]

These passages leave no doubt that Weber intended to draw a sharp line between the "subjective" grounding of the questions raised in the cultural and social sciences and the "objectivity" of what adequate answers are actually found.

The only path left open to the persistent relativist, therefore, is to argue that Weber's distinction between subjectively motivated problem definitions and objective research results cannot be as consistently maintained as he believed. He admitted, after all, that the value orientations of investigators enter into the very *constitution* of their objects, setting the boundaries of their topics and defining their concepts. How could he expect the "Chinese" to acknowledge the validity of answers to questions he considered uninteresting or badly put? But those who read Weber in this way overlook his belief in the possibility of interpretation across cultures. In any case, there can be no doubt about what Weber *took away* from his reflections on the role of cultural interests in the selection and delimitation of research problems. While subjective judgments do enter into our decisions about what is worth knowing, he argued at scholarly conferences in 1909 and 1910, they should not affect our research itself.

> When we consider an "interesting" fact as empirical scientists, then the question of why it is interesting lies behind us. . . . And even the parties that are in conflict over [value-related policy questions] have an interest in there being someone who says: I do not say that you are right or wrong; I cannot say that with the means of empirical science; instead, I can tell you: [T]hese are the facts; . . . these are the consequences of things being what they are. Thus if what you want is to happen, you have to put up with these . . . means and . . . side effects.[56]

The emphasis upon policy disagreements is symptomatic, since debates within the Social Policy Association did as much to shape Weber's views on objectivity as the problems raised by Rickert.

In 1904, Werner Sombart, Max Weber, and Edgar Jaffe took over as editors of the *Archiv für Sozialwissenschaft und Sozialpolitik,* the former *Archiv für soziale Gesetzgebung und Statistik.* Supporting Sombart, Weber helped to shape the joint introductory statement by the new editors, and his "Objectivity" was written to enlarge upon that statement. Indeed, the joint declaration itself called for a clearer distinction between social science and value judgment. The editors recalled that the Social Policy Association was founded to study and recommend reforms within a capitalist framework. Its members repudiated the claim that economic "laws" could be deduced from the self-interested behavior of economic agents, and many of them believed in socially ameliorative legislation. As a result, many of them came to disregard the divide between the empirically real and the ethically desirable, between what is (*das Seiende*) and what ought to be (*das Seinsollende*); they tried to derive "scientific" prescriptions from the empirically given. But that cannot be done. An age that has eaten from the tree of knowledge, Weber wrote, must acknowledge that ideals are human creations; values cannot be "read off" from the realities around us. To be sure, certain formal (Kantian) *categories* of ethical argument are universally valid, but they do not suffice to dictate full-bodied *cultural ideals* or action orientations in specific situations. We are thus inevitably confronted with competing cultural values—and with ideals that are as holy to others as ours are to us.[57]

Weber particularly disliked the idea that socioeconomic policies can be "scientifically" grounded in an ethical common ground or a "happy medium" that excludes only extreme positions. He explicitly attributed this position to Schmoller; but as we know, he deeply disliked the bureaucratic paternalism favored by Schmoller as well. As a methodologist and a coeditor of the *Archiv,* Weber urged a rigorous divide between scientific findings and value judgments, along with the fullest possible discussion of both. He certainly did not recommend indifference to policy questions; indeed, he welcomed the energy of passionate commitments. He believed that explicit value preferences could and should be examined for their logical coherence, their relationship to other possible ideals, and their grounding in ultimate value orientations. He suspected that the superficial consensus on policy questions pursued by Schmoller would not survive full examination and debate. And finally, as he insisted again and again, the social sciences can provide reliable answers to causal questions. The objective social scientist is able to identify the probable consequences of particular policies, along with potentially undesirable side effects or ancillary means to the ends in view.

In 1909, Weber reviewed a book by the economist Adolf Weber, which seemed to second the call for a separation between science and value judgment. Adolf Weber suggested a reconciliation between the entrepreneurs and the academic champions of social reform, in which the ethically motivated prescriptions of academics were adjusted in the light of the economic "realities" (*das Seiende*). Adolf Weber claimed that a more realistic science of economics could educate the nation "beyond the limits of partisan politics," reducing the antagonism between capital and labor, and showing that wage levels depend upon productivity. In response, Max Weber observed that the antagonism between capital and labor was not only a matter of wages. At the same time, he expressly identified himself with the "Socialists of the Lectern," who were united in opposition to the Manchesterite dogma that economic policy must follow from purely economic "realities," as Adolf Weber implied. Moreover, Max Weber deeply distrusted the supposed exclusion of "party political" positions. "The . . . rejection of partisan political positions . . . [only] . . . aggravates the situation, by fostering the illusion that such a contradiction . . . as an 'impartial' judgment could ever be meaningful, or that such ambiguous terms as 'the interests of the whole' . . . could ever be less 'subjective' than any party slogan, no matter how extreme!"[58] Sensing the danger of a new scientistic economism, Weber called for intellectually radical debate.

In discussions at the 1909 meeting of the Social Policy Association, Weber joined Sombart in urging a clearer distinction between social science and value judgment. His repeated interventions were deliberately provocative. The concept of "national welfare" (*Volkswohlstand*), he said, is loaded with value implications. It can be more precisely defined as per capita income, but that may be attained by an economic unit made up of a few great landowners and many dependent shepherds, or by one composed of independent farmers. And what if large agrarian producers destroy some of their crops to maximize their monetary returns? We must avoid concepts that tacitly intermingle scientific and value questions, for such intermingling is "an affair of the devil." Of course we should discuss the logical coherence of value preferences and their possible interdependence. As social scientists, we might be able to convict policy opponents of inconsistency, or of risking unfavorable side effects. There is nothing unscientific or futile about intensive controversy over policy questions. What must be avoided is only the confounding of logical or empirical claims with value judgments, along with the justification of complex measures in terms of ambiguous standards of "productivity."[59]

Indeed, the critical examination of "average judgments" seemed to Weber a significant task of the social sciences: "Not that I underestimate [the importance of] value questions; on the contrary: . . . I cannot bear [to see] . . . the weightiest problems that can move a human heart . . . turned into technically economic questions of 'productivity.'" The Social Policy Association, Weber repeated, has always insisted upon the non-economic causes of human action, but it has ended by permitting the confusion of scientific with normative issues. Both science and practice would surely benefit from a reaffirmation of the relevant distinctions. "And if we have to recognize with a certain regret that among ourselves too, differences in value judgments have become greater than they used to be, then honesty demands that we openly acknowledge the fact. We do not know of any demonstrable ideals."[60] This was Weber's position as of 1909. It implied the possibility of scientific agreement among partisans of divergent value orientations, and it thus had little to do with the issues initially raised by Rickert.

The controversy over value judgments within the Social Policy Association reached a climax in 1914, when the association's executive committee held a closed meeting on the subject. To prepare for this meeting, Weber and others submitted memoranda that were printed in manuscript in 1913. A revised and slightly expanded version of Weber's memorandum was published in 1917. Objecting to "prophecy" in the classroom, Weber sought to dissuade his academic colleagues from preaching their value preferences from the lectern. Admitting that it might be difficult to keep one's scholarly work free of personal bias, he nevertheless insisted upon value neutrality as a *regulative ideal* of *Wissenschaft*. He particularly disliked the suggestion that, while the line between scholarship and value judgment is difficult to draw in practice, university teachers should avoid excessively "partisan" positions. The view that the classroom is no place for "passion" struck him as a "bureaucrat's opinion that every independent teacher would have to reject." The overt preaching of political creeds by such men as Heinrich von Treitschke seemed to him less dangerous to the students' autonomy than the covert suggestion of ideologies in nominally "dispassionate" ways. Along with specialized knowledge, he thought, the universities should practice the purely scholarly virtue of "intellectual rectitude." At the same time, far from wanting to turn all students into mere specialists, Weber wrote, he meant to leave them free to make their own ultimate "life decisions" without interference from their professors.[61]

Weber expressly challenged Schmoller's quest for a broad *consensus* on social policy objectives. As Weber reported, Schmoller used to insist that university lectures be exempted from public discussion. But Weber could accept this "privilege" only with respect to specialized analyses in the professor's field of competence. Surely the academic should not exploit his institutional authority to impose sociopolitical preferences upon a dependent audience. Would-be prophets should face the overt contest of views in the public arena.

Characteristically, Schmoller once proposed to exclude "Marxists" and "Manchesterites" from university chairs, while a jurist drew the line at "anarchists." But if political orientations *were* to be discussed at the universities, Weber argued, then all standpoints had to be represented. It was admittedly hard to imagine heterodox views being expressed in an academic system that still excluded criticism of the monarchy. Yet in principle, Weber wrote, an anarchist may be a good student of the law. "And if he is, then his . . . standpoint outside the conventions and presuppositions we take for granted . . . will enable him to discern problematic aspects in the foundations of the usual legal doctrines that elude all those for whom they are too self-evident. For the most radical doubt is the father of insight." Weber sharply repudiated the view that "the path to scientific 'objectivity' may be entered by weighing the divergent value positions and [reaching] a 'statesmanlike' compromise."[62]

Extending his argument against consensual commitments, Weber also opposed the notion that ethical or social norms may be deduced from the direction of historical development. He was thinking of German historical economists who took their "ethical" orientation to be consistent with the actual evolution of capitalism. In response, Weber granted that particular policies must be chosen in the light of changing circumstances, but he could not agree that policy objectives should be altered to accommodate historical trends.

> Human beings are sufficiently inclined . . . to adjust to . . . the promise of success, not only in the means by which they seek to realize their . . . ideals, but by abandoning these ideals themselves. . . . It is hard to see why . . . [academics] should feel the need to support [this inclination]. . . . [Politics may be] the art of the possible. But . . . the possible has often been attained only because people aimed beyond it. . . . It has not, after all, been the . . . ethic of "adjustment" . . . that has created the . . . positive . . . qualities of our culture.[63]

Here again, Weber was mainly concerned with the human and cultural threat of *conformism*.

The conceptual core of Weber's case for value neutrality, however, was the logical distinction between descriptive and prescriptive propositions, is and ought. He argued that the "formal" principles of Kant's practical philosophy did have substantive implications, but he did not believe that the guidance they provided was sufficiently specific in all situations. In the tradition of the German theory of *Bildung*, moreover, he thought it possible to imagine human values that transcended the framework of Kantian ethics. Above all, he believed that different individuals could be deeply committed to radically *divergent cultural values,* from the aesthetic to the erotic. Accordingly, value judgments could and should be intensely debated, preferably in the public forum, but they should not be confounded with empirical and causal questions. "The validity of a practical imperative as a norm and . . . the truth value of an empirical proposition lie on absolutely heterogeneous problem levels. . . . The empirical-psychological and historical investigation of a certain value standpoint . . . can never lead to anything other than its interpretive explanation." To understand the value judgments of others is of course crucial for fruitful debates about normative questions—and about the objectives of social policy. Still, Weber saw value orientations as individual choices, which is why he adopted John Stuart Mill's image of pluralism or "polytheism" in the moral realm. "The . . . unavoidable fruit from the tree of knowledge is none other than this: to . . . [see] the contradictions [among possible normative orientations], and thus to . . . recognize that every important action and . . . life as a whole, if it is consciously lived . . . [involves] ultimate decisions, through which the soul . . . chooses . . . its own fate."[64] The image of the "soul choosing its fate" through "ultimate decisions" served as an alternative to the vision of a consensually or historically grounded policy science.

Weber's evocation of John Stuart Mill's "polytheism" signals how closely his methodological position was linked to his liberal pluralism. Even more important *for us,* however, is his clear separation of cultural interests in the formulation of scientific questions from the rigorous objectivity of the inquiries that follow. The results of such inquiries must be *universally binding,* regardless of the cultural commitments of the investigator. In our own age, when the unchecked competition among cognitive interests threatens to engulf us in a bottomless relativism, Weber's call for objectivity offers a return to sanity.[65]

CHAPTER FOUR

The Protestant Ethic

Max Weber took Karl Marx very seriously, not only because he considered him the creator of an extremely fruitful ideal type, but also because he respected his practice as an economic and social historian. On the other hand, he flatly rejected the notion that all causal connections in history can ultimately be traced back to economic conditions, however defined, or that all historical processes are essentially unidirectional. At the 1910 meeting of the Social Policy Association, he stated his case against monocausal economism with characteristic directness.

> I . . . want to register a protest against . . . the proposition . . . that anything, be it technology or economics, is the . . . "ultimate" or "essential" cause of anything else. . . . The chain of causation . . . runs sometimes from technological to economic and political, sometimes from political to religious and then to economic matters, etc. At no point do we come to a resting place.

As a legitimate heir of the German historical school, Weber believed that the discipline of economics should deal not only with the economic "codetermination of all social phenomena," but also, conversely, with the "conditioning of economic processes and . . . systems" by noneconomic factors. He saw the historical "chain of causation" running in divergent and occasionally contrary directions.[1]

Among Weber's substantive works, none is further removed from the economism he opposed than his famous study *The Protestant Ethic and the*

Spirit of Capitalism, first published in 1904–1905. The study provoked critical reactions from several colleagues, to which Weber responded in what became an extended controversy. Weber's subsequent research program, moreover, was profoundly affected by what he learned about the contribution of ascetic Protestantism to the "spirit" of modern capitalism. He prolonged the approach of *The Protestant Ethic* into a vast investigation of the "economic ethics of the world religions," which became the core of a comparative universal history. In 1920, the first of three volumes of his *Collected Essays on the Sociology of Religion* contained a revised version of his *Protestant Ethic,* now heavily annotated to deal with the objections of his critics. Let us begin by studying this famous essay in its definitive version of 1920.[2]

THE DEFINITIVE TEXT

Weber began his *Protestant Ethic* by commenting upon comparative statistics on the occupation and education of the three main German confessional groups of his day. In his confessionally mixed home state of Baden, he observed, Protestants were substantially overrepresented, as compared to Catholics, in various entrepreneurial and technical positions, among skilled industrial workers, among secondary school pupils, and especially in the nonclassical, "modern" or "realistic" secondary streams. The confessional statistics on Baden also revealed that German Jews decisively outstripped German Protestants and Catholics in virtually every measure Weber considered. They were far better represented among secondary students—and in "realistic" secondary schools—than other Germans. Weber proposed to explain this phenomenon by noting that minorities, excluded from positions of political power, tend to channel their energies into business and related occupations (21–23).

Before attempting to account for the characteristics of Protestants that caught his attention, Weber repudiated the popular misconception that Protestants were more "worldly" than Catholics, and more receptive to Enlightenment optimism about human progress. He cited anecdotal evidence of deeply religious individuals who came from business families, especially in the seventeenth century, within the Calvinist diaspora of that time. In the light of these examples, he suggested an "affinity" between ascetic piety and active participation in economic life, or between the "spirit of work" and "progress" (24–30).

Pausing to reflect on methodological principles, he wrote of the historian's study of "individuals," complexes of interrelationships in historical reality that we isolate because of their cultural significance. The "spirit of capitalism" is such an "individual," not a member of a "class" of phenomena. We therefore cannot precisely define it at the outset of our investigation. All we can do is offer such illustrative examples as the maxims of Benjamin Franklin's early eighteenth-century texts: Time is money, and so is credit; money has a productive, fruitful character. The man who promptly repays his debts, who is honest, able and industrious—and who is seen to have these qualities—can have the use of others' money for extended periods of time. But he must not regard the capital he invests as his own; he must live frugally, while keeping scrupulous accounts of his transactions (30–32).

This "philosophy of avarice," for Weber, was not just advice on how to make money. What Franklin conveyed was an "ethically colored maxim" for the "conduct of life." What he urged, in fact, was the spirit of modern capitalism. Thus he explicitly prohibited the *enjoyment* of wealth. The goal he recommended transcended not just personal pleasure, but "individual happiness" in general; it was "irrational" in that sense. Citing his father's biblical injunction against idleness, Franklin clearly saw monetary success as a confirmation of proficiency in one's calling (33, 35). Here lay the origins of the often unreflected sense of *duty to one's profession* that sustains the culture of contemporary capitalism.

To be sure, as Weber explained, today's human beings are simply born into the "cosmos" of the capitalist order; it is the inescapable "housing" (*Gehäuse*) in which they must live. Capitalism now selects the entrepreneurs and workers it needs. But the concept of "selection" has obvious limits, for the orientations and ways of life that suit modern capitalism had to be created before they could be perpetuated by way of adaptation and selection. The "youth" of such "ideas" as those expressed by Franklin is "thornier" and more complex than Marxist theorists of the "superstructure" imagine (37–38). And in Franklin's Massachusetts, at any rate, the "spirit of capitalism" existed before capitalism itself. Today's entrepreneur may say that he works for his heirs, or he may enjoy the power and prestige that accompany wealth. But the reality is that he *needs* the restless chase that fills his life. Nowadays, those who cannot adapt to capitalism are doomed to fail; but that is because capitalism, now firmly established, no longer needs its former sources of occupational commitment (54–56).

Not that the acquisitive drive was unknown before the rise of modern capitalism. On the contrary, as Weber pointed out, outright covetousness was characteristic of the Chinese mandarin and the Roman aristocrat, not to mention the East Elbian landowner of Weber's own time. Lack of scruple in petty commerce has been prevalent precisely in economically backward countries. At all times, when chances of profit were provided by war, piracy, or state monopolies, they have been ruthlessly exploited. Thus a species of "adventure capitalism" has prevailed since ancient times. Indeed, it has proved compatible with "traditionalism," a major obstacle to modern entrepreneurial capitalism. Weber's example of traditionalism dealt with the attempt to raise the output of industrial workers by increasing their wages. In an early capitalist environment, workers might work, not to maximize their wages, but just long enough to support their accustomed way of life. But that outlook is a symptom of "traditionalism"; it reminds us that human beings do not "by nature" seek to increase their earnings indefinitely. For "nature" is on the side of custom and habit—and of pleasure as well (41–46). Before modern capitalism can succeed, workers as well as capitalists must believe that work is a *duty*. The question is how such a conviction could arise.

Weber's analysis of "traditionalism" was partly a response to Werner Sombart's 1902 *Modern Capitalism,* which contrasted an older economic system oriented to the "satisfaction of needs" with a newer "capitalist" economy of unlimited "acquisition." But from Weber's point of view, the needs to be satisfied could only be defined by tradition, while "acquisition" as a goal of economic behavior was certainly not unique to modern capitalism. The "spirit of capitalism" and capitalism itself, for Weber, stood in an "adequate," not a necessary, relationship to each other. One could reinforce the other, but the two could also appear separately. From early modern times to the nineteenth century, Weber argued, the real economic innovators were men from modest, middle-class backgrounds, the *parvenus* of Manchester and of Rhenish Westphalia, not the merchant patricians of Liverpool and Hamburg. Acquisition through trade was compatible with the traditional exploitation of political monopolies, and even the early "putting out" system could be pursued in a traditional manner, with conventionally set wages and profits, and a customary level of comfort for the capitalist involved. All this changed only when a newcomer moved from the city to the country, rigorously supervised his weavers, directly retailed his product, and strove for increased sales at lower prices. The man who did this was not an adventurer, but "sober and steady," wholly committed to his task, with strictly bourgeois principles (48–54). His attitude resembled Franklin's and would have been unthinkable among the traders of Renaissance Florence.

Weber accepted Sombart's characterization of the modern economy as a product of "economic rationality," if that is defined as the expansion of productivity by the "scientific" restructuring of production. Those imbued with the "spirit of capitalism" made it their goal to rationalize the provision of material goods. Their spirit was an element in the overall development of modern "rationalism." The only difficulty with this line of analysis was that the *schedule* of rationalization did not coincide in the various realms of human activity. The rationalization of private law, Weber wrote, was well advanced in Roman times, but delayed in England, the pioneer of economic rationalization. The secular rationalism of the Enlightenment was certainly not restricted to countries that were the most advanced economically. Thus "rationalism" encompasses a variety of conflicting elements. What requires explanation, however, is the notion of *duty to one's calling,* a notion that is "irrational" from the commonsense standpoint of "human nature" (60–62).

The idea of "the calling" Weber argued, originated in Luther's Bible translation. The German *Beruf* and the English "calling" came to signify a task ordered by God. There are no full equivalents of *Beruf* and of "calling" in the languages of predominantly Catholic countries. For Luther, the Christian's worldly occupation was at first a matter of indifference, since life itself was transitory. But over time and with the growing emphasis upon faith, the believer was asked to stay in his *Beruf,* and to accept the discipline it imposed. Ultimately, Luther became fearful of disorder, but the conservative element in Lutheranism was not transmitted to the other Protestant denominations, along with the vision of the calling as ordained by God. In any case, Luther for the first time extended the call for active asceticism beyond the monastic realm to every Christian. Not that he shared in the "spirit of capitalism"; his hostility to trading companies and usury signaled an economically regressive outlook. Nonetheless, Luther originated the idea of the *Beruf* as a religious duty, which thus became available for further interpretations, including substantially more strenuous ones (63–79).

Weber turned to Calvinism and to its offshoots, especially to the English Puritans, to find a radical commitment to work in this life. He cited the dramatic passage from Milton's *Paradise Lost* in which Adam and Eve, though expelled from Eden, enter a world that is theirs to transform. The vision of heroic labor *in this world*—and of self-discipline in its service—diverged sharply from Lutheran passivity and of course from Catholic doctrine. The question was how to explain this divergence. After all, the great religious reformers did not *intend* to awaken the spirit of capitalism; they were interested in the fate of human souls. But as happens so often in history, their ideas had unintended consequences. We cannot hope to show, Weber argued, that the "spirit of capitalism" could have arisen *only* from the Reformation, or that the capitalist system itself was a product of the religious upheaval, if only because capitalism existed before the Reformation began. We can only ask to what extent religious influences contributed to the spread of the capitalist spirit, and what aspects of modern culture were affected (79–83).

The historical "bearers" of ascetic Protestantism, according to Weber, were religious movements and sects that overlapped and interpenetrated each other in various ways. The most important among them was Calvinism as it developed over the course of the seventeenth century, and as it was articulated at the Synods of Dordrecht and of Westminster. "Pietism," inclusively defined, was an offshoot of Calvinism in England and especially in Holland; but a form of it also affected late seventeenth- and early eighteenth-century Lutheranism. It remained a movement of renewal *within* established religions rather than a distinctive denomination, and only the Moravians (*Herrnhuter*) under Count Zinzendorf took on some of the character of a separate sect. *Methodism* too was originally a reform direction within the Anglican Church of the eighteenth century; but it ultimately became a sect, especially as it extended into the United States. "Baptism," broadly speaking, grew out of the radical Anabaptist movements of the Reformation but absorbed elements of Calvinist doctrine during the seventeenth century. The term "Puritanism" initially referred to Dutch and English movements of ascetic revival; but again, tensions arose with the established churches. A series of separate denominations emerged, in which divergent emphases in church constitutional and doctrinal questions interacted and converged in a common commitment to an ethically rigorous "conduct of life." The English "Independents" were "Puritans," and so were the Baptists, including the Quakers and Mennonites. To understand all these forms of Protestant asceticism, Weber argued, one has to study their practices of pastoral care, as reflected in the compendia and reflections of active ministers. Even more important, for Weber, were the dogmatic foundations that gave rise to the *psychological impetus* behind the quest for a rigorous conduct of life (84–86).

In what might be called the ideal-typical application of Weber's method, he proceeded to construct an *ideal type* that encompassed a *logical* argument and a *psychological* process. He began with Calvin's doctrine of predestination, emphasizing its logical rigor. An all-powerful, transcendent God preordains the mass of mankind to damnation and an elect few to eternal salvation. Because the grace he confers upon the elect is gratuitous and irresistible, ordinary human beings cannot know whether they are damned or saved; nor can human institutions or individuals affect their fates. What is really a *double* predestination—to election or perdition—cannot be understood; the divine is *inscrutable* and *transcends* earthly concerns. The awful power of this distant

God has no purpose other than his glory. Indeed, as Weber moved on to the psychological implications of this "dark" doctrine, his language took on a chilling intensity: "In its . . . inhumanity, this teaching had to have one chief consequence for a generation that submitted to . . . [it]: a feeling of *unprecedented inner isolation of the individual*" (93). No one could help the Calvinist who confronted his unknown fate: no preacher, no sacrament, no church. There was no institutional transmission of grace, and even Christ died only for the elect. "[The] exclusion of the church's sacramental grace was absolutely decisive in the contrast with Catholicism. That great process in religious history, the *removal of magic from* (*Entzauberung*) the world, which began in ancient Jewish prophecy and, joined with Hellenic scientific thought, rejected all *magical* means in the quest for salvation . . . here reached its conclusion" (94–95). Rigorous Calvinism left the individual whom God had damned without recourse of a "magical-sacramental" kind (87–95).

This harsh doctrine of a remote God, Weber added, radically devalued the earthly realm of the "creaturely"—and thus engendered the Puritan distrust of everything sensual in religious and cultural life. At the same time, the "inner isolation" of the human being before God lay at the root of the "sober and pessimistically colored individualism" that can still be detected in the "national character" of people with a Puritan past. In English Puritanism, the dogma of gratuitous election enjoined exclusive trust in God, as against reliance upon human aid and friendship. The resulting mood, a kind of salvation panic, had extraordinary consequences. In John Bunyan's widely read *Pilgrim's Progress,* "Christian" stops his ears against the voices of his wife and children as he flees them in pursuit of eternal life. Paradoxically, the separation of the individual from his fellow humans, including the nearest and dearest among them, accounts for the Calvinists' superiority in social organization. Given the solitude, the loss of ordinary fellow feeling, and the gulf between God and his creatures, the Calvinist's action in this world could only be guided by the duty to increase God's glory through strenuous exertion in a vocation or in behalf of the "common good (95–97, 101)." In either case, the objective pursued took on an *impersonal* character.

The real question raised by the Calvinist doctrine, Weber insisted, was how its adherents could "bear it." The religious "virtuosi" might find personally satisfying solutions: Luther was able to experience a mystical union with God, while Calvin saw himself as God's instrument. But ordinary human beings faced greater difficulties. For Calvinists, the idea of the divine entering the soul was inconsistent with God's absolute transcendence. The exclusion of "magic" from the world of religion deprived most men of psychological relief, even by way of repentance. Puritan pastoral literature reflected the torments of the religious rank and file (105). Spiritual leaders could urge their charges to believe in their election as a matter of duty. More often, they counseled unremitting work in one's calling as a way to enhance the glory of God. The only hope of ordinary mortals lay in whatever *objective symptoms* they could detect that their efforts were truly "efficacious." In the emotional economy of Puritanism, the ability to perform laudable deeds from time to time was no sign of grace. Only continuous and methodical *self-control* could bear fruit in the *systematic* performance of good works. And that, according to Weber's ideal type, produced the "steel" saints of the heroic age of modern capitalism (111, 113).

In a pregnant aside, Weber reflected upon the history of Christian asceticism. In contrast to Oriental forms of the ascetic life, Western monasticism—and its antecedents in antiquity—took a distinctively *rational* direction. In a way that proved decisive for subsequent developments, the Christian monastic movement of the Middle Ages aimed at a systematically controlled *conduct of life,* one designed to *subdue nature* in man. Strenuous self-control was to free the monk from the dominance of irrational instincts. Through self-discipline, the exemplary Christian was to attain the capacity for conscious *volition,* for the rational planning of his actions, and the weighing of their *ethical consequences.* The suppression of instinctual affects and the strengthening of *constant* motives culminated in Puritanism—and still informs the *self-control* and *reserve* of the Anglo-American "gentleman." *Constant motives* can be sustained by conscious *practice,* and may thus produce what Weber called a "personality" (116–17).

The medieval monk's asceticism, of course, was meant to surpass the everyday ethic of the ordinary Christian. It was this circumstance that allowed the Catholic Church to draw upon a treasure of surplus holiness in the dispensation of *indulgences,* which became a principal target of Protestant contestation. The strict Calvinist doctrine of predestination in effect stopped the leakage of ascetic energy from the everyday realm to the monastic enclave, while adding an incentive for the asceticism of the ordinary individual in his need to discern *outward symptoms* of his salvation (118–21).

The norms for the Puritan's ascetic conduct of life, Weber observed, were taken from the Bible, and particularly from the Old Testament, which the Puritans read in the light of their Calvinist commitments. The ancient Judaic emphasis upon *the law* was thus revived in the Puritan's "Hebraicism," which contrasted sharply with Luther's emphasis upon the "freedom" of the Christian from the law. Without the aid of the church, of the sacraments, or of a personal mentor, the individual Puritan "felt his own pulse," keeping track of his capacity for methodically ethical conduct (123). The ordinary Lutheran lived in a less radically ascetic atmosphere, since he was less affected by the "dreadful teaching of Calvinism." Once again, Weber pointed to a divergence between Anglo-American and German national traits, which he traced to religious differences. To the extent that German Lutherans were less intent upon ascetic self-control, they also remained closer in their emotional lives to the "state of nature." They could thus seem more natural and even *gemütlich* than the Anglo-Americans, whose deportment reflected a certain "inner restraint" (127).

Some of the most vivid and telling passages in Weber's essay drew upon the writings of such Puritan spiritual counselors as Robert Barclay and Richard Baxter. One of the themes Weber found in the writings of these preachers was a suspicion of "mammon." What they really feared, however, was not the *acquisition* but the *enjoyment* of wealth. The ethical danger lay in the passive acceptance of acquired property, which led to leisure and sensual pleasure. Against this threat, Baxter and his colleagues preached uninterrupted work for the glory of God, which meant "the common good" or, quite explicitly, "the good of the many." The *acquisition* of wealth increased God's glory; it was only idleness and luxury, *resting* upon one's riches, that imperiled the soul. Against this danger—and against all sensual indulgence—the spiritual leaders of the Puritans and Pietists urged strenuous labor as a means of ascetic self-discipline. The suppression of the state of nature in man, which had been the aim of Western monasticism, was thus extended in principle to all of the faithful. Even the sexual drive was to be strictly confined to "sober" procreation, and work in one's calling became the favored ascetic technique (167–71).

Thomas Aquinas assigned the duty to labor to the whole human species; for the Puritans, however, every *individual,* including the man of wealth, was obliged to work. Luther enjoined the faithful to accept the occupation—and the estate—into which God had placed them; for Baxter, however, the division of labor was not only providential, but a positive good, in that it was *fruitful.* As Weber pointed out, Baxter thus anticipated the thought of Adam Smith; indeed, the emphasis upon the "good of the many" foreshadowed Jeremy Bentham's secular utilitarianism. Without a firm vocation, Baxter argued, man's life was confused and unstable; work had to be steady and orderly. The Puritan's calling was valued not only as a discipline, but also for its "profitableness." Offered a business opportunity by God, the believer was *obliged* to make good use of it, since he was God's steward. To earn a profit and to acquire riches in one's calling was praiseworthy, as long as it was the result of an active life in behalf of God's glory (171–77).

Just as the ascetic significance of the calling ethically justified the modern occupational specialist (*Fachmensch*), so the providential interpretation of opportunities for profit justified the modern businessman. The elegant indolence of the *seigneur* and the ostentation of the *parvenu* were equally hateful to the Protestant ascetic. By contrast, the fullest ethical approval surrounded the sober self-made man: "God blesseth his trade." Ascetic Protestantism in fact resurrected a version of the Old Testament tradition in which God rewards the just even in this life. In what commentators called "English Hebraism," the Judaic insistence upon legality found an echo (178). Yet Weber saw no relationship between this adaptation of ancient Judaism and the "pariah capitalism" of the Jewish Diaspora. For he associated medieval and early modern Jewish investment with speculative and political "adventure capitalism," rather than with the rational and entrepreneurial capitalism of the Protestant bourgeoisie. The rationalism of the ascetic entrepreneur required the systematic organization of productive work, and its spirit, like that of the Kantian ethic, was one of "loveless duty." The "total habitus" of the Puritan derived from his sense of being *chosen* by God; it expressed itself in the perfection of his conduct, and in the "hard" and correct character of the early capitalists (181–82). What the ascetic Protestant rejected, above all, was the naive enjoyment of life.

The Puritans were not hostile to all aspects of culture. They believed in empirical science, though not in scholastic reasoning; they approved the amateur study of nature as a leisure pursuit, and both seventeenth-century England and colonial New England were rich in university graduates. Yet "the saints" distrusted the sensual in art, along with the indiscipline of popular festivals. Shakespeare despised the Puritans, who disliked all theatrical display. Their hatred of finery and their insistence upon simplicity of dress foreshadowed the sober uniformity of modern apparel. For the Protestant believer, the possession of wealth entailed an obligation to God—or to the common good. The duty to increase and to account for the use of resources encouraged the distinction between domestic and business expenditures, while also ensuring parsimony in the satisfaction of personal needs. In sum, Protestant asceticism restrained consumption, while "unchaining the acquisitive drive," while the combination of unfettered acquisition with limited consumption aided *capital accumulation* (184–92).

Of course, riches were a temptation even for the "saints," as their pastors knew only too well. John Wesley wondered how genuine religiosity could be sustained, even while religion fostered industry and frugality, and therefore wealth, along with pride and worldliness: "Is there no way to prevent the continuous decline of pure religion? We must not prevent people from being hard working and thrifty. We must urge all Christians to gain and save as much as they can, but that means in effect to become rich." Wesley's anxious recommendation was that the faithful also "give all they can," so as to accumulate treasure in heaven (197).

Noting that Wesley wrote in the eighteenth century, Weber acknowledged that the economic consequences of ascetic Protestantism may have manifested themselves most markedly at a time when its religious roots were already being replaced by more routine forms of vocational virtue. Even so, the great seventeenth century left its utilitarian heirs a powerful legacy. The vocational ethos of the Protestant entrepreneurial bourgeoisie was reinforced by "a *pharisaically* good conscience" in the earning of money, as long as it remained within the bounds of legality. Protestant asceticism also provided conscientious and industrious workers who believed that their duty to labor was ordained by God. Finally, it contributed the "reassuring" conviction that the unequal distribution of the goods of this world was as holy and mysterious as double predestination itself. Begging was tolerated and even glorified during the Middle Ages, but from the Elizabethan poor laws forward, a new and "harder" view of mendicancy came to prevail, and poverty became a *moral failing* (198–99).

"The thought that modern work in a vocation has an ascetic character," Weber concluded, is not new. "That the limitation of occupational specialization, with the sacrifice of Faustian universal humanity that it entails, is a precondition of any worth-while work in the modern world . . . is what Goethe . . . too wished to teach us. . . . [It] meant a farewell to a time of full and beautiful humanity. . . . The Puritan *wanted* to be a vocational man; we *must* be vocational men." For when asceticism left the monastery and entered the world at large, it helped to create the "mighty cosmos of the modern economic order" along with its technical and mechanical underpinnings, which today determine the lifestyle of every individual and will continue to do so "until the last ton of fossil fuel has turned to ash" (202–3).

Baxter believed that care for the goods of this world should rest lightly on the shoulders of the saints. But *for us,* fate has turned this coat into a "steel housing." The outward goods of the world have acquired more power over humanity today than ever before, although "the spirit has escaped from this housing," so that the idea of vocation as a duty persists in our lives as "a specter of former religious beliefs." Where the commitment to a calling cannot be related to the highest cultural values, it will either be experienced as an economic necessity, or else the individual will not reflect upon it at all. Now that capitalism is firmly in the saddle, the "impersonality" and "senselessness" of work has lost its religious aura. In the most advanced country, the United States, the acquisitive drive tends to become a competitive sport.

> Nobody knows . . . whether, at the end of this enormous development, new prophets will arise, or there will be a revival of old ideas, *or*—if [neither occurs]—there will be mechanical ossification, veiled in a convulsive sort of self-importance. In that case . . . of the "last men" in this cultural development it may truly be said, "specialists without spirit, sensualists without heart: this nullity pretends to have reached a whole new level of humanity." (203–4)

With that dismissive gesture, Weber admitted, he had left the field of historical analysis and entered the realm of value judgments. As his readers, we should notice that his last sentence was written in the conditional mode. Like many of Weber's darkest pronouncements, it was a cautionary *provocation,* not a passive acceptance of cultural exhaustion.[3]

CONTROVERSIES: WEBER AND SOMBART

In a way, the controversy over Weber's *Protestant Ethic* began even before the essay was first published; for Weber extended a debate that had started among his scholarly predecessors. Well before 1905, German historians of theology had pointed to the Protestant vision of faithful work in one's station and to the Protestant contribution to German culture more generally. Under the influence of the "cultural conflict" (*Kulturkampf*) against political Catholicism, this Protestant perspective helped to provoke the public discussion of occupational statistics that Weber continued in his argument. In addition, Weber's friend Jellinek had launched the argument that the "rights of man" had originated, not in the Enlightenment or in the French Revolution, but in the religious distrust of secular authority that also fostered the demand for religious toleration. Jellinek pointed to the Puritan milieu of early modern Britain and of colonial New England. Weber acknowledged his obligation to prior scholarship, along with the influence of his friend Ernst Troeltsch, whose work on the social teachings of the Christian churches evolved concurrently with Weber's *Protestant Ethic* (18).[4]

Weber certainly aimed at value-free analysis; but he clearly preferred the ascetic rigor of the Puritans to the emotional and quietist religiosity of the Lutherans. He argued that Puritanism formed the "hard" entrepreneurial activists of early modern capitalism, whereas Lutheranism produced "patriarchal employers" and "faithful" officials and employees. He believed that religious traditions helped to shape national character traits, and he clearly admired the "reserve" of the Anglo-American "gentleman." A kind of Anglophilia probably heightened his distrust of German Lutheran *Gemütlichkeit* and of the Lutheran outlook he detected in the "habitus" of educated office holders in Imperial Germany. In a 1906 letter to Adolf Harnack, he admitted that he considered German Lutheranism "the horror of horrors": "That our nation never in *any* form went through the school of hard asceticism is . . . the source of everything I find hateful in it (and in myself)."[5] Thus Anglophilia and a distrust of Lutheranism were partly self-critical themes in Weber's works.

Upon its first publication in 1904–1905, Weber's *Protestant Ethic* attracted a good deal of attention. Along with favorable reactions, criticisms appeared as well. Some of his more radical critics overstated his claims, so as to make room for their objections. In 1913, Weber's respected senior colleague Lujo Brentano addressed the Bavarian Academy of Sciences on the origins of capitalism. In a sweeping evolutionary perspective, he touched upon the expansion of feudal holdings by military or other means, upon the accumulation of monetary fortunes by mercantile capitalists from the late Middle Ages on, and indeed upon every form of unlimited acquisition. From a distinguished Catholic family himself, Brentano argued that medieval Christian restraints upon usury—and upon acquisitive individualism more generally—had been gradually relaxed under the pressure of both pre-Christian and post-Christian secular attitudes. Against the background of this gradualist perspective, Brentano challenged particular aspects of Weber's essay, including his reading of Franklin, and his focus upon the rationalization of what Brentano considered an *irrational* way of life. Beyond that, he was troubled by the very idea that intense religious commitments could encourage acquisitive behavior, given the unanimous warnings of Christian theologians against the pursuit of wealth. In the face of Weber's attempt to link the traits of modern entrepreneurship to the rationalist "spirit" of the Puritan ethic, he suggested that Weber had defined the major terms of his arguments so that they really included each other. While this was a serious challenge, Brentano also reinforced the misleading impression created by his less expert critics that Weber had portrayed ascetic Protestantism as *the major cause* of modern capitalism.[6] Weber could only respond by restating his case (17–18n1, 33n2, 35n1, 41n, 42n1).

What really stands out in Weber's notes to the final version of the *Protestant Ethic,* however, is his running argument with Sombart. Indeed, the relationship between Weber and Sombart is almost a parable of German academic culture in Weber's lifetime. As a promising young academic, Sombart became a public spokesman for social reform. Impressed by Marx, he sympathized with Social Democratic revisionists and trade unionists. Yet despite Tönnies' urgings, he never joined the Social Democratic Party, and he refused to speak out in support of the Hamburg Dock Strike of 1897–1898. He considered the capitalist system a framework for further social progress. For a time, he nonetheless associated with such left-wing intellectuals as Heinrich Braun, editor of the *Archive for Social Legislation and Statistics* until its demise in 1903. He participated in the Society for Social Reform and wrote for the journal *Social Practice.* He saw himself as a major spokesman for the "young ones" (*die Jungen*) within the Social Policy Association, a group that included the brothers Max and Alfred Weber and Gerhart von Schulze-Gaevernitz, among others. This younger generation was impatient with the conservatism of the older generation around Gustav Schmoller. Perhaps some sort of bridge could have been built between the "young ones" and the reformist wing of the Social Democratic Party, as Tönnies certainly hoped; but that did not happen. Instead, Sombart was sharply attacked by conservative historians, and Weber failed in his attempt to obtain a position for him at the University of Freiburg. Sombart had to accept a less distinguished appointment at the University of Breslau and was not promoted to a full professorship until the First World War. Indeed, Sombart's alleged "demagogy" helped to provoke a serious political attack upon the "Socialists of the Lectern," and upon academic freedom more generally. Sombart could hardly fail to recognize that his academic career was in danger.[7]

From the 1890s to the early years of the new century, Weber and Sombart were political allies, and they shared certain methodological preferences as well. Jointly, they campaigned against the "ethical" approach to social policy questions, while Sombart briefly embraced the economic imperative of "productivity." Both scholars accepted industrialization; they called for progressive adjustments in German labor law, and in 1909 they jointly and strenuously urged the separation of scholarship from value judgment within the Social Policy Association. When Edgar Jaffe bought Heinrich Braun's journal and renamed it *Archive for Social Science and Social Policy* in 1904, Weber and Sombart became editors of the new review. Their programmatic introduction to the opening issue was jointly conceived, but written by Sombart. Yet the collaboration between the two sociologists did not last, because Sombart soon sharply diverged from Weber's intellectual path. In 1897, with the publication of his lectures on *Socialism and the Social Movement,* Sombart stood out as one of the most radical spokesmen of the "young ones" in social policy questions; to some, he looked like a socialist. In his two-volume *History of Modern Capitalism,* he still wrote as a critical champion of large-scale enterprise and capitalist productivity, but various countervailing themes had begun to make their appearance. In 1907, three years after beginning his collaboration with Weber and Jaffe in the *Archiv,* Sombart began to express his lack of interest in routine editorial labors. He also started to contribute to the literary journal the *Morning* as a disenchanted critic of modern rationalism, urbanization, and mass culture. A superficial lecture of 1910 on the tension between classical music and modernity drew a dismissive reaction from Weber. Sombart's *The Jews and Economic Life* (1911), which was written partly as a response to Weber's *Protestant Ethic,* exploited anti-Semitic stereotypes. During the First World War, Sombart produced one of the most flamboyant contributions to the German "cultural war" against the West, by contrasting English "traders" with German "heroes," and that was not the end of his trail.[8]

It is hard to escape the impression that Sombart lacked the moral strength and seriousness to develop and defend a coherent intellectual position. He could not endure the savage attacks upon him by a whole cluster of conservative historians. When he began to experience the personal costs of heterodoxy in his academic career, his course became erratic. He was unusually sensitive to the moods and slogans prevalent in his environment, and he excelled at embellishing upon the ideologically loaded antitheses that agitated the German academic world during these years: culture versus civilization, intuition versus calculation, and the idyllic rural past versus the "asphalt culture" of modernity. Characteristically, Sombart's virtuosity as a cultural critic led him into the rhetoric of anti-Semitism as well. Career anxieties probably aggravated his need to exchange the role of the controversial professor for that of the popular genius and man of the world. In 1907 and 1908, while writing for the *Morning,* Sombart repeatedly threatened to resign as editor of Jaffe's *Archiv.* Weber, who had steadily supported the young Sombart, managed to persuade him to continue his collaboration. But in July 1908, Weber's negative reaction to Sombart's new course became partly explicit. In a personal letter, Weber responded to Sombart's complaints about his academic reputation by trying to reassure him about his achievements. But he also asked him whether a full professorship really meant "everything" to him, and he urged him to shake off his *Weltschmerz.* Referring to a passage from a previous letter,

Weber wrote that he was not offended at Sombart's dismissal of editorial labor as "cobbler's work"; but he also registered substantial differences in their points of view.

> You want to write personal books. I am convinced that the distinctive personality . . . comes to expression invariably and *only* when it is *unintended,* when it retreats behind the book and its objectivity (*Sachlichkeit*), as all great masters have retreated behind their work. Where one *wants* to be "personal," one . . . almost always drifts into the path of the "typical." What you deliberately show the public as your Self has . . . thoroughly typical and few "personal" traits; precisely what is *significant* about the personal disappears, and everyone merely has the impression of having to do with one of the many representatives of the usual "aestheticism" and of the correspondingly *typical* "aristocratism."

For almost three years after sending this admonition, Weber did not write to Sombart at all, and then he conveyed a hurried apology for being unwell and too busy to comment upon Sombart's *Jews and Economic Life;* he merely registered unspecified objections, along with vague approval.[9] It seems safe to conclude that Weber saw Sombart's turn toward the rhetorical enhancement of the commonplace as a character flaw.

If Sombart ever engaged in serious scholarly work, it was in the two volumes of his *Modern Capitalism,* published in 1902. Among other things, Sombart here offered a detailed and extended account of early modern artisanal production, and of the economic life of the towns since the late Middle Ages. Like Marx, he saw modern capitalism emerging in a precapitalist environment, and he was concerned with the problem of primitive accumulation as well. His method was partly theoretical and partly historical, in the sense of the historically "individual." Like Weber, though less articulately, he believed in causal analysis, but not in timeless regularities. More important for the subsequent discussion, however, was his attempt to discern divergent economic "principles" or "motives," and thus to arrive at an overarching contrast between precapitalist economic systems designed to meet "needs" (*Bedarfsdeckung*) and early capitalist economies in pursuit of unlimited "acquisition" (*Erwerb*). This binary construct allowed Sombart to move easily from the "origins of capitalism" to the "genesis of the capitalist spirit," which, for Sombart, encompassed a "calculating" and "speculative" form of "rationalism" that partly expressed itself in double-entry bookkeeping. The practice of "money calculation" was thus linked to the awakening of the "acquisitive" drive. As Simmel had suggested earlier, economic rationalism affected forms of thought even beyond the economic realm itself, and thus helped to fuel the rise of modern science. Reducing Simmel's complex reflections to a simple formula, Sombart saw money advancing from a "means" to the "highest purpose" of human life.[10]

Against this background, Sombart introduced a set of loosely related and occasionally contradictory themes that were "typical" of his culture in the bad sense intended by Weber. While the natural economy of the precapitalist epoch was guided by human needs, he argued, the motives of early capitalism were impersonal: acquisition for its own sake—and such "abstractions" as profit and the accumulation of capital. Sombart doubted that "religious affiliation" played a role in the origins of capitalism. Yet, following Eberhard Gothein, he described the fact that "Protestantism, especially in its Calvinist and Quaker variants, substantially favored the development of capitalism" as "too well known to require further explanation." Elsewhere, he stressed the role of the "better shopkeepers" and "petty usurers," by way of underlining the *parvenu* traits of the early capitalists. Capitalism, he argued, "came from below, out of the depths of society." Since economic exploitation was presumably easiest to justify in relationships with foreign groups, *Sombart* called attention to the penetration of European peoples by "ethnically alien elements (the Jews)." He referred not only to the Jews' position as a disadvantaged minority, but also to their "racial characteristics."[11]

Some of these themes pointed the way to Sombart's evolution after 1902, which came to partial expression in his 1911 *The Jews and Economic Life.* Sombart himself characterized this tract as "personal," while still insisting that it was strictly scholarly. He acknowledged that he was influenced by Weber's interest in religious factors, and by Weber's account of "traditionalism." He saw a connection between the geographic distribution of the Jews and the stimulation of economic activity. Drawing uncritically upon reported hostile perceptions of Jews, he noted the "schematic similarity" of these judgments, suggesting that it testified to their *reliability.* Circumventing Weber's distinction between "adventure" and entrepreneurial capitalism, he characterized the early capitalist as a cross between an Arctic explorer and a "trader," who asks only "what things cost" and "yield." Offering a further alternative, he wrote that "Jews are money lenders; but capitalism grew out of money lending." As an "alien" minority, he claimed, the Jews developed a certain indifference to the state, so that "conflicts among nations" became a "major source for Jewish acquisition." The Jewish religion, according to Sombart, is a "mechanically artful" product of "rationalism" or "intellectualism," designed to "destroy everything natural in the world"; its morality is that of the "virtuous grocer." The social isolation of the Jews arose from their exclusiveness, their conviction that they were "superior to the common people in their environment." With that, Sombart moved on to posit a "distinctive Jewish character," which included the lack of an "intuitive" or "instinctual understanding" and of an "emotional relationship to the world." The Jews' thinking is "mechanical-rational," not "organic-creative"; they are "restless" but quick to adapt. "Capitalism, liberalism, Judaism are intimately related." While the racial theorists have so far failed to prove their case, Sombart concluded, he and others were convinced of the "anthropological distinctiveness" of the Jews and of "the significance of the 'race factor' in history." In a scathing reaction to Sombart's book, Brentano objected to his willful handling of the sources, his "sophistries," and his apparent contempt for the serious reader.[12] My own sense is that Sombart behaved just as Weber predicted. He displayed his "personal" virtuosity by rhetorically heightening "typical" themes already present in his environment, and he abandoned all scholarly standards.

Returning to Weber, we can now assess his formal response to Sombart, which was expressed mainly in a series of notes to the final version of the *Protestant Ethic,* and which were surprisingly mild. Both Sombart's 1911 essay on the Jews and his slightly later *The Bourgeois* struck Weber as flimsy; but while he joined Brentano's negative assessment in principle, he thought it too harsh (27n2, 56–57n). Instead of exposing Sombart's stereotypes, Weber focused upon threats to his own argument. Even those who disagreed with Sombart, he remarked, were obligated to him for raising questions about the "capitalist spirit" (42n2). He largely ignored Sombart's anti-Semitism, associating the "pariah" role of the Jews with that of marginalized groups more generally and with political and speculative "adventure capitalism" in particular (182n). What troubled him about Sombart's work—and about that of Brentano as well—was that it was based upon an overly general definition of "capitalism" and that it failed to distinguish various forms of "acquisition" from the *ethos* of modern entrepreneurial capitalism (48–49). He saw no similarity between the rules of prudence that guided the head of a Renaissance household and the maxims enjoined by Franklin (38–40n). He was not interested in Catholic anti-mammonism, its attenuation in practice, or its revival among the Puritans (165n3).

Weber traced Sombart's emphasis upon the rational character of capitalism to Simmel's *Philosophy of Money;* however, he also commented upon the fact that the rationalization of law, for example, followed a chronology quite different from that of economic rationalization (60–62). Against Sombart, who treated modern rationalism essentially as an *effect* of capitalist development, Weber insisted upon the rationalization of *conduct* as a contributing *cause* of that development (167n2). In response to Brentano, he explicitly conceded that it was possible to rationalize an *irrational* way of life (34n1). What he repeatedly underlined, against Brentano as well as against Sombart, was the decisive impact of the ascetic Protestant's need for symptoms of his salvation as a *psychological impetus* to self-control and achievement (86n1). What required explanation, after all, was not just "acquisition" and "calculation," but a religiously grounded *duty* to subdue the natural self through strenuous work in one's calling (190n1). Sombart may have been the first to identify the capitalist "spirit" as a subject of analysis, but he really had little to say about it. In a way, his theory of "acquisitiveness" merely enlarged upon the inherited assumption that the motives of "economic man" were given in "human nature"—and thus required no separate analysis.[13]

Unlike Sombart's speculations, the "Weber thesis" has left an enduring legacy. It has drawn a good many criticisms over the years, and I do not have the competence to evaluate them all. I agree that Weber in fact offered little *direct evidence* on the attitudes of early modern entrepreneurs; he saw their motives through the eyes of their spiritual advisers. I am unable to assess the claim that, following Jellinek, Weber overstated the role of the Protestant ascetics in the genesis of the "rights of man," just as I cannot comment on Brentano's claim that Weber misunderstood Franklin. But I am inclined to resist critics who stress the explicit conviction of Puritan divines that one cannot serve both God and mammon. For Weber convincingly argued that Calvinist theology could have *psychological* consequences that were certainly not contained in its doctrinal *logic*. The idea that Weber offered a kind of "spiritualist" *cause* of modern capitalism is certainly based upon a misunderstanding, not only because Weber meant to account primarily for a certain *occupational ethos*, but also because his multicausal model left plenty of room for the role of material factors. James Henretta has written a brief but complex account of economic life in colonial New England in which he stresses the tension between town and country. Yet Henretta believes that Weber rightly understood Franklin, and that the Weber thesis is applicable to at least some of the agents in the gradual emergence of capitalism in the northeastern United States.[14] To explain why the *Protestant Ethic* has long outlasted its critics *despite* its empirical flaws, I am inclined to point to its compelling "verisimilitude," its *adequacy at the level of meaning.*[15]

In late 1904, Max and Marianne Weber spent about four months in the United States. In connection with the Saint Louis World's Fair, the German-American philosopher and psychologist Hugo Münsterberg had helped to organize an international scholarly congress. A sizeable German delegation to that congress included Max Weber, Ernst Troeltsch, and Werner Sombart. Accompanied by Troeltsch and another colleague, the Webers sailed to New York in late August. From New York, they traveled north along the Hudson River, then to Niagara Falls and Chicago, south and west to Saint Louis and Oklahoma, and finally north again from New Orleans, by way of North Carolina and the major eastern cities, back to New York. In Marianne Weber's subsequent account of the trip, she quoted extensively, not only from her own letters home, but also from Max Weber's notes and reports, which are not yet separately published. Marianne expressed her delight at Max's full recovery from his nervous exhaustion, at his sound sleep and healthy appetite on shipboard and after, and at his lively interest in everything they saw in their travels.[16]

Weber's presentation in Saint Louis was on "The Relations of the Rural Community to other Branches of Social Science." If the intent was to have him comment upon "community" in Tönnies' sense, he quickly disabused his audience, proposing to talk about "rural society" instead. He then linked the agriculture of the wheat-producing states in America to "the absolute individualism of the farmers' economics" and "the quality of the farmer as a mere businessman." But that brought up the contrasting characteristics of agriculture on the European Continent. Given the scarcity of land and the role of tradition in its distribution, it used to be based upon a relationship between aristocratic landowners and peasants that was largely independent of the market. The rise of capitalism, however, led to a contest between an economy of sustenance for a large agrarian population and labor-saving agricultural production for the market.

Meantime, the *social* value of membership in the landowning elite drove rents to extraordinary levels. "Because ownership of land confers social position, the price of the large estates rises high above the value of their productivity. . . . And, in fact, rents are the economic basis of all aristocracies that need a gentlemanly, workless income for their existence." Under capitalist pressures, the agrarian elite loses ground *politically;* it can no longer "live for politics," and power passes into the hands of professional politicians and civil servants. "The importance of . . . state officials is and must be much greater in Europe than in the United States. The much more complicated social organization makes a host of specially trained officials . . . indispensable in Europe, which will exist in the United States only in a much smaller number even after the movement for civil service reform." Because of the cost of legal credentials, the German official must come from a wealthy family. Together with the officer corps, the civil service supports the monarchy, which "has a natural affinity with the holders of other social privileges." The Catholic and Lutheran churches, unlike Calvinism, further increase the influence of conservative and anti-capitalist attitudes.[17]

Before moving on to a fuller discussion of East Elbian agrarian conditions, Weber inserted a striking passage on the educated elite.

> In an old civilized country, the "aristocracy of education," the *Bildungsaristokratie* as it likes to be called . . . views more skeptically and criticizes more sharply the triumphant procession of capitalism than can be naturally and justly the case in . . . the United States. As soon as intellectual and esthetic education has become a profession, their representatives are bound by an inner affinity to all the carriers of ancient social culture.

They distrust gain—and the loss of cultural traditions, of "ethical and esthetic values." They do not believe that capitalism will guarantee either "personal liberty" or the "culture which they represent." "They want to be ruled only by persons whose social culture they consider equivalent to their own; therefore they prefer the domination of the economically independent aristocracy to the dominion of the professional politician." The result, in "civilized countries," Weber explained, is "serious" in several respects. "The representatives of the highest interests of culture . . . stand . . . opposed to the inevitable development of capitalism, and refuse to cooperate in the rearing of the structure of the future." Infelicities of translation aside, one cannot miss the extraordinary breadth of Weber's sketch. Starting with agrarian conditions narrowly defined, he offers his American audience a summary of German social, political, and cultural life. In the process, he highlights a topic that never lost its fascination for him. That topic, to be more fully discussed in a later chapter, is the relationship between advanced education, social status, bureaucracy, and political leadership.[18]

During his travels, Weber found it easy to interact with ordinary Americans from all sorts of backgrounds. He traded stories, asked good questions, and listened sympathetically. Not so Sombart, whose reactions were typically "mandarin." Shortly after debarking in New York, he sent greetings home from "this dreadful cultural hell," while also commenting upon the "*Götter-dämmerung* of culture," and the "chamber of horrors of capitalism." Ernst Troeltsch and Marianne also felt uneasy from time to time, but Max was fascinated. Marianne remarked upon his ability—and willingness—to identify with the new and unknown, and his aversion to uninformed criticism. "I am irritated at German travel companions," he wrote, "who groan about America after a day and a half in New York." Even the skyscrapers of Manhattan struck him as "beyond" beautiful and ugly, "symbols of what is happening here." Thus Weber took in a wide range of experiences about the United States, and reflected upon a great variety of topics, from race and bureaucracy to social stratification and American democracy. As for the scholarly yield of the trip, it was set down in two 1906 articles: "Churches and Sects," and "Churches and Sects in North America." These two pieces were later joined and expanded as "The Protestant Sects and the Spirit of Capitalism" for the first volume of his *Collected Essays on the Sociology of Religion,* published in 1920.[19]

Weber's 1920 article "The Protestant Sects" was divided into two parts. The second of these dealt with the origins of the Protestant sects in the seventeenth century, which he had already touched upon in his *Protestant Ethic.* The sectarian movement grew out of the idea of the "believers' church," the *voluntary* community of "the elect." In contrast to the *visible church,* the institutional vehicle of grace and of discipline for saints and sinners alike, the Protestant sectarians wanted to share communion only with true Christians. For some groups, the ceremony of adult baptism signified the believer's reception into the ranks of the reborn. The desire to separate the saved from the damned did not always lead to the formation of sects. In some denominations, the spiritually qualified formed conventicles of full members, who jointly administered the discipline of their weaker brothers. The institution of "the elders" in some of the sects reflected a similar sense of hierarchical differences of spiritual qualification. Since the sects meant to ensure the "purity" of the Lord's Supper by excluding the unjustified, those of their members who traveled or moved had to show letters of recommendation or "tickets" to gain access to communion at congregations away from home. Needless to say, the community of the elect could not accept the administration of the sacrament by an unworthy minister. Once grace was thought to be vested in the person of the minister, rather than the office of the priesthood, the lay members of the sect became the real guardians of sanctity within the community. Even apart from the Calvinist doctrine of predestination, the sects thus served as independent sources of Protestant asceticism, self-control, and moral rigor.[20]

Both the voluntary principle and the idea of the lay community's collective responsibility raised a number of constitutional problems. The sects could not allow secular authorities to override their authority in matters of faith and discipline. Moreover, the strict surveillance of conduct by a particular congregation could raise questions about less rigorous standards in other congregations, with serious implications for the mutuality of admission to communion. Religious communities in New England and elsewhere took on a local character; a certain exclusiveness toward outsiders was a possible result. The authority of ministers was generally weakened, as compared with that of the laity or of "the elders," and theological education itself lost in importance, as compared with demonstrated sanctity of life. In many sects, migrant or "circuit" preachers supported by voluntary contributions took the place of permanent and certified ministers. As in the early Christian church, the charisma of inspired spiritual leaders played an important role; indeed, it recaptured some of the ground that had been ceded to more institutional forms of religious authority. Within particular sects, believers felt an obligation to assist each other, especially in times of need. To some degree, therefore, the sects were able to guarantee both the rectitude and the economic viability of their members.[21]

Weber was primarily interested in the *practical consequences* of doctrinal and church constitutional positions. He noted that members of seventeenth-century sects, like other ascetic Protestants, found it easy to borrow money. Even non-Protestants were willing to give them credit, partly because they were known to be honest, and partly because their sects helped to insure them against economic failure. In Imperial Germany, Prussian officers and members of student fraternities were considered particularly worthy of credit, because codes of honor forced them to repay their debts. Members of the early Protestant sects enjoyed similar advantages, but for better reasons. The communities that certified their reliability also trained them in the middle-class virtues. They were imbued with a vocational ethos that dictated the *opposite* of an aristocratic life style. Sect members not only underwent an intensive moral scrutiny prior to their acceptance into the community; they also had to *prove themselves* permanently worthy in their personal and business conduct. And the qualities they had to demonstrate were those of the early capitalists. The Protestant sects enforced a discipline far more rigorous than that of the universal church. Indeed, they linked the social identity of the believer to his standing in his religious community. They thus created a situation in which the individual's interest in self-esteem and approval steered him toward the spirit of rational capitalism. Again, Weber insisted upon the psychological impulse provided by the quest for salvation—and for community approval. The medieval guilds also tried to control the economic behavior of their members;

but their aim was to *limit* the enterprises of fellow guildsmen, and thus to ensure the satisfaction of traditional needs, not to unchain the ascetic individualism of the early entrepreneurs.[22]

In the early portions of his essay on the Protestant sects, Weber focused upon the United States on the one hand and upon the eighteenth and nineteenth centuries on the other. With his trip to the United States in mind, he described an extended period of transition, in which secular clubs gradually took over the role played by the sects in American life until well into the nineteenth century. Given the strict separation between church and state in the United States, Weber wrote, no statistics were available on the religious affiliations of Americans. As of about 1880, nevertheless, only some 6 percent of the United States population was estimated to be "without a confession." Despite the fact that the state offered no advantages to members of established denominations, as it typically did in Europe, and although the cost of membership in American congregations was substantial, there were few overt nonbelievers in the United States. While the public authorities did not inquire into religious affiliations, ordinary Americans routinely asked new acquaintances what church they belonged to, or what service they attended away from home.[23]

In related anecdotes gathered during his travels, Weber told the story of an American patient who announced his membership in a nearby congregation to his doctor, in order to reassure him that his bill would be paid. A commercial traveler explained that he did not care what denominations his customers belonged to, but would not give credit to clients without religious affiliations. "Why pay me," he asked, "if [the client] doesn't believe in anything?" During an adult group baptism in North Carolina, Weber heard that one of the initiates was planning to open a bank in a neighboring town. To understand these incidents, according to Weber, one has to know that even in 1904, American sects accepted new members only after a thorough review of their conduct from childhood on. Did they drink or gamble; were they ever guilty of "disorderly conduct"—or late in repaying their debts? Anyone who had passed such an examination, who persisted in an orderly life under religious supervision, and who could expect emergency assistance from his community, was surely a good business risk. Unlike a church open to all, a sect could provide an economic and moral guarantee, because it elected its members, often by ballot, and because it watched over their subsequent conduct of life. Exclusion from a sect for ethical misconduct meant a reduction in "credit worthiness"—and a loss of social standing.[24]

Looking more closely at the American scene as of 1904, Weber noted the increasing importance of secular "orders" and clubs among the middle classes. These organizations also *elected* their members; they often provided health and burial insurance, and they sometimes extended emergency assistance as well. As in the case of the sects, the voluntary principle increased the ethical significance of club membership, which was often signaled by a badge in the buttonhole. Entry into a club could make a man "worthy of credit." True, the giants of American capitalism did not need such marks of respectability; they were "beyond good and evil." But the smaller entrepreneurs and prosperous tradesmen, the real bearers of the middle-class virtues, joined the clubs as they had joined the sects, especially in the northeastern states. In colonial New England, full membership in a religious community had been a de facto precondition of full citizenship. The Quakers had actually dominated Pennsylvania until the War of Independence. The sects had been powerful because they controlled access to Holy Communion. But the norms of conduct and the occupational ethos they fostered were ultimately perpetuated by an extensive network of secular orders and clubs.[25]

The thesis that the clubs continued the role of the sects was clearly an amendment of Weber's *Protestant Ethic.* It also provided a major theme of Weber's observations during his visit to the United States. Marianne's report on the American trip, with its direct quotations from Max, reflected his interest in both the sects and the clubs. At a Quaker meeting near Philadelphia, he was struck by the long periods of silence, and by the totally undecorated room. When someone was finally "moved" to speak, it was usually one of the "elders," who sat on a raised bench facing the rest of the congregation. Weber hoped to hear from an impressive white-haired woman, who was said to be a good speaker. "Unfortunately," he wrote, "the spirit instead moved the young librarian of Haverford College, a philologist who delivered a learned lecture on the various terms used to designate Christians in the New Testament." During an adult baptism in North Carolina, the preacher stood up to his hips in an ice-cold mountain stream, and eight people in formal dress completely submerged themselves in the water, with his assistance. The ceremony took place in October, but the Webers were told that baptisms occurred in winter as well, once the surface ice was broken. After the immersion, the initiates were congratulated, wrapped in blankets, and rushed away to their homes. Their faith was said to protect them against colds. At a regular service, the preacher, in ordinary dress, delivered a highly "practical" sermon with great passion, and those "awakened" went to kneel at the altar. Privately, the preacher acknowledged a decline in the frequency of revival meetings and of weekly "confessions" in the circle of one's neighbors. In the meantime, memberships in various "orders" and clubs steadily increased.[26]

Other scenes of American life also held Weber's attention. There was Chicago, the "unbelievable" city, with its contrasts between the weighty stone houses of the wealthy and the tenements of the working class, the incredible dirt of the unpaved streets in the center of the city, and the violet smog extending over the lake. Soft coal was the main fuel, and every major hotel had its steam elevator. Everywhere, the pace of work was intense. Along miles of ethnic shops and restaurants, workers traveled an hour to reach their work places in the filthy stockyards, the brutal assembly lines of the slaughterhouses and meat packing plants. The bankrupt trolley lines were in the hands of a receiver, who found it cheaper to reimburse some four hundred accident victims per day than to replace faulty equipment. A strike had just been defeated by Italian and African-American strikebreakers, and continuing violence led to deaths on both sides. In the mixture of nationalities, the Greeks shined the Yankees' boots, the Germans were their waiters, the Irish managed their politics, and the Italians did their earthwork. And in Chicago as in New York, a German and East European Jewish culture maintained its distinctive character; there was a Yiddish theater, and a privately funded institute offered educational, athletic, and cultural opportunities, especially for recent Jewish immigrants and for the young. "The absolute self-government of the children . . . is the most important means of Americanization. The rejection of authority by the young people . . . here bears its fruit."[27]

In sharp contrast with the landscape of Chicago, the American colleges were "oases," clusters of handsome buildings far from the urban centers, on carefully tended lawns and under old shade trees. For many Americans, the "magic memories of youth" were focused upon their college years. Along with all kinds of sports, the colleges offered "attractive forms of sociability, intellectual stimulation, enduring friendships, and especially a much more intensive habituation to work than that of our students." Many of the colleges, of course, were originally founded by religious sects. At Booker Washington's Tuskegee Institute, Weber found another remarkable cultural force. None of the students there were trained for purely intellectual work. The "conquest of the soil" was the ideal that inspired the enthusiasm of teachers and students alike. "Half, one-quarter, or one-hundredth Negroes," the graduates of Tuskegee were legally excluded from marriage and social intercourse with whites, restricted to their own waiting rooms, hotels, and parks, even when "no non-American could distinguish them from whites." Thus Tuskegee was an exceptional realm of social freedom, in "dreadful contrast with the half-apes one encounters in the plantations and huts of the cotton belt," but also with the "intellectual conditions of the whites in the South," who unanimously insisted that social ties across the racial barrier were impossible. "The only enthusiasm . . . in the South is to be found in that upper stratum of Negroes" represented at Tuskegee; the whites are reduced to "impotent rage against the Yankee."[28]

Visiting a frontier town in Oklahoma, Weber took lodging with a half-caste Indian. He was fascinated by the outwardly peaceful conquest of formerly Indian territory—and of the wilderness—by migrants from the north and east, who were "mostly poor devils and could actually become rich in a few years." Weber solicited a commentary on the despoliation of the Indians for the *Archiv* from his half-Indian acquaintance. The "boom" was "colossal," and land speculation rampant "in spite of laws." Open range and cotton fields in the prairies alternated with oil wells, wild rivers, and untamed land. "Nowhere else is there such a mixture of old Indian lore and modern capitalist culture."

> It is a fabulous hubbub here, and I can't help myself, I find a powerful magic in it, despite petroleum stench, smoke, spitting Yankees, and the dreadful noise of the many little trains. Nor can I deny that I find these fellows—generally—pleasant. Officials naturally received me in shirtsleeves, and we all stretched our legs on the window bench. The lawyers make a rather rakish impression—there is a fabulous informality, which nonetheless preserves mutual respect. . . . I haven't had so much fun since my [student days] as here with these naive and childlike fellows, who can nevertheless cope with any situation. . . . [Yet] it is wrong to believe that one can behave however one likes: Politeness lies in the tone (of what is said), and the humor is delightful. . . . Too bad: in a year this place will look like . . . any other town in America. With frantic haste, everything is ground up that might stand in the way of capitalist culture.[29]

At a minimum, Weber's reactions were more specific, livelier—and more ambivalent—than Sombart's account of the American *Götterdämmerung*.

In last-minute notes to the second, 1905 portion of his *Protestant Ethic,* Weber first broached the subject of American democracy.

> The traditional American aversion against performing personal services is probably linked to the . . . [Puritan emphasis upon] the "public" welfare or "the good of the many" as against the "personal" or "private" benefit of individuals, as well as to other weighty reasons that

follow from "democratic" sentiments. . . . [This is true also of] the relatively greater immunity of formerly Puritan peoples against Caesarism, and of the inwardly freer propensity to accept the standing of the great, on the one hand, and to reject any hysterical doting upon them, on the other.

Weber found a contrast here with "what we have experienced in Germany since 1878." He traced the Americans' "lack of respect" to the Puritan "hostility to authority," and its impact upon contemporary Anglo-American political culture. Along similar lines, he called attention to the Americans' middle-class glorification of business success as an *achievement*, and their reluctance to defer to (possibly inherited) *wealth* as such. The gradual "Europeanization" of the United States, Weber believed, would eventually reduce the differences between democratic America and post-"feudal" Europe, but that process was far from complete in 1904 (99n, 155n, 178n2).

Weber summarized his reflections on the United States in two dense pages of his 1906 essay "The Protestant Sects." Until very recently, he wrote, the "typical Yankee" was guided through life by a series of exclusive voluntary associations, from the Boys' Club in school and the Athletic Club, the Greek Letter Society or other student club at college, to the numerous honorary clubs of the business community—and of the plutocratic elite in the major cities.

> To gain admission to [these associations] . . . signified social advancement and . . . the sense of having "proved" oneself. A college student who did not gain entrance into a club . . . was usually a kind of pariah. In the past and into the present, these honorary associations were characteristic of the "specifically American *democracy*," which was "not a formless sand-heap of individuals, but a maze of strictly exclusive but voluntary associations."[30]

Until recently, Americans did not accord much recognition to "the prestige of high birth and of *inherited* wealth, of office and of certified education." Yet they were "far from accepting anyone at all as an equal." True, even a decade and a half ago, "an American farmer would not have led a guest past a laborer" without "introducing him and having him shake hands." In a "typical American club," members who played billiards together might be employer and employee in the "outside" world; within the club, however, "the equality of gentlemen" prevailed. Finally, there was little difference of dress or manner between the American trade unionist's wife and the middle-class lady with whom she had lunch. "But whoever . . . wanted to be fully accepted in this democracy not only had to submit to the conventions of middle-class society, . . . he also had to be able to demonstrate . . . that he had been voted into a . . . recognized sect, club, or association . . . and thus *proved* himself a gentleman."[31] Weber saw the fabric of American society much as Alexis de Tocqueville had seen it, but I have found no evidence that he learned from his illustrious predecessor.

When Weber asked young German-American businessmen ("with the best Hanseatic names") why they preferred the purely American to the German-American clubs, they said that their boss might play billiards with them in the German club as well, but he would think it nice of himself to do so. The entry into an American club, Weber added, was always an important moment in the separation from the German tradition. By the turn of the century, in any case, American society was undergoing a process of Europeanization. Weber detected the beginnings of "aristocratic" tendencies in the American clubs; he described them as vehicles of "status" *(ständisch)* developments that were an "antithesis to naked plutocracy."

> Even in America, mere "money" may buy power, but not social honor. Of course it is a means of getting power. It is the same with us and everywhere. But the indicated path with us has been: the purchase of an . . . entailed estate [and] letters of nobility, which then allow the grandchildren to be accepted into aristocratic "society." [In America] the *old* traditions respected the man who had acquired wealth *himself* more highly than the inheritor. And the path to social honor was: a distinguished fraternity in a distinguished college, formerly: in a distinguished sect . . . now mainly: a distinguished club. In addition now the kind of residence, dress, sport. Only recently: descent from the Pilgrim Fathers, from Pocahontas or other Indian ladies.

Weber may have been misinformed about the "other Indian ladies"; but he was not misguided in the parallels he drew. The reserve officer corps and the student fraternities were to Germany what the sects and clubs were to the United States. Of course the two forms of stratification were not simply identical. "The phenomenon is the same, but the *direction* and the material *consequence* differ in characteristic ways."[32]

Bismarck's Caesarism, the reserve officer corps and the student (fencing) fraternities: these, for Weber, were the characteristic institutions of the Imperial social system, in which "the great" were too much worshiped and status was transmitted by pseudo-aristocratic means. American democracy, a network of voluntary associations, provided the perfect contrast; for social honor was conferred by sects and clubs, which certified the *proven achievement* of their elected members. Weber did not pursue all the implications of the divergence between the two societies at this stage of his studies. The whole issue of social stratification, of status and social honor, and of the impact of advanced education upon the social hierarchy—these topics were to occupy him in several of his later works. Those works also expanded upon the *comparative* analysis that he had begun to practice in *The Protestant Ethic,* and that became the hallmark of his systematic sociology of religion.[33]

CHAPTER FIVE

Weber's Comparative Sociology of Religion

Soon after his last contribution to the debate over his *Protestant Ethic,* Weber began to plan a series of comparative studies in the sociology of religion, as well as a set of theoretical essays on the same subject. His work on this project was under way by 1913, and a study on Chinese religion appeared in the *Archiv* in 1915. During the First World War, Weber continued to write and revise these essays, while conceiving a multivolume series on *The Economic Ethics of the World Religions,* which was not fully published until after his death in 1920. We consider here the introduction and the section entitled "Intermediate Reflection" that Weber included in the opening volume of his huge project in comparative sociology and universal history, along with his studies on the religions of China and of India.[1]

FRAMING A COMPARATIVE WORLD HISTORY

Weber opened the introduction to his *Economic Ethics of the World Religions* with an explicit definition of the "world religions" as the five systems for the "regulation of life" that have attracted large followings, namely Confucianism, Hinduism, Buddhism, Christianity, and Islam. To these five, Weber added Judaism, partly because of its influence upon Christianity and Islam, and partly because of its possibly distinctive significance for the evolution of the modern Western economic ethic. Weber also emphasized that he was not interested in the theories included in theological compendia, but in the "practical incentives to action" that were formed in the psychological and pragmatic contexts of particular religions. Outwardly similar forms of economic organization have been compatible with divergent economic ethics, producing different historical consequences, and religious orientations in turn have influenced economic ethics only in conjunction with other social, economic, and political factors.[2]

While the influence of social groups has never been exclusive, Weber argued, it is possible to identify strata that have been the "bearers" of particular religions, either in their origins or in their subsequent histories. Thus Confucianism was originally linked to the status ethic of an office-holding literary elite; Hinduism was propagated by the classically learned Brahmin caste; Buddhism was perpetuated by mendicant monks that fled the world in strict contemplation; Islam was a knightly order of world-conquering warriors; post-exilic Judaism was the religion of a middle-class "pariah people," while Christianity began as a creed of wandering journeymen and thrived as an urban and "burgher" religion. Yet Weber cautioned against a dogmatic view of these connections: "It is in no way (my) thesis . . . that the distinctive character of a religion is merely a function of the social position of the stratum that seems its characteristic bearer . . . or a "reflection" of its material or ideal interests" (86–88). The reference to "ideal interests" is significant, for it acknowledges that social groups compete not only for economic and political advantages, but also about status issues and other forms of *symbolic power*. Much of what is characteristic of Weber's analytical practice grew out of his insistence upon an enlarged conception of social "interests."

Changes in the principal "bearers" of religions do have far-reaching consequences. Yet once a religion is formed, it can affect "quite heterogeneous strata." Weber's warning to that effect was directed not so much against "historical materialism" as against Friedrich Nietzsche's theory about the "resentment" of the disadvantaged. Weber believed that such resentment "often has absolutely nothing to do" with the religious "rationalizations of the conduct of life." Yet the valuation of suffering in religious ethics has undoubtedly undergone a historical transformation, which lends Nietzsche's theory a touch of legitimacy. In primitive religions, the sick or unhappy individual was considered possessed by a demon, or stricken by the anger of a god he had offended. That is how primitive religions met the massively "pharisaical" needs of human beings (88–90).

The paths toward the reversal of this viewpoint, toward the idealization of suffering, Weber observed, have been circuitous. A primary role was played by the experience that various forms of asceticism, from self-mortification to abstinence, awakened the charisma of the ecstatic, as well as other extraordinary states that were valued as holy. The development of "salvation" cults then paved the way for a whole new position on suffering. Among the magicians and spiritual advisers—and the gods in whose name they performed miracles, some extended their influence beyond local and ethnic boundaries to form religious "communities." Dynasties or organizations of miracle workers evolved, whose chiefs were held to be either incarnations or "prophets" of God. The new religious communities provided the setting for a revised response to suffering—and to "salvation" from it. The religious message and promise now turned to the masses in need of salvation. Under the pressure of this recurring spiritual "need," a religiosity developed that presupposed a "savior myth" and an at least relatively rational worldview, the most important element in which was suffering. For a politically threatened people like the Israelites, "messianic" promises were initially attached to saviors from political oppression. In the case of this people alone, the suffering of a whole political community, rather than that of individuals, became the object of religious yearning (90–93).

Hopes for salvation almost always gave rise to a theodicy—or religious rationalization—of suffering. Where religious development was shaped by "prophecy," Weber argued, "sin" primarily meant lack of faith in the prophet and became the chief cause of misfortune. And while the prophet himself was rarely a representative of the dispriveleged, it was the disadvantaged, rather than the fortunate and powerful, who usually *needed* a prophet. Prophetic savior religions therefore most often attracted followings among the disadvantaged. The growing urge to attribute "meaning" to the distribution of good fortune among human beings tended to rationalize religious ethics and to eliminate residual elements of magic. But the consequence was that theodicy ran into increasing difficulties. "Undeserved" individual suffering was all too frequent, and this by no means only in the light of a (Nietzschean) "slave morality." For even according to the standards of the dominant strata, it was all too often not the best, but the worst who had their way in the world (93–95).

The ineradicable need for a "theodicy" produced only three satisfactory answers to the question raised by the incongruity between fate and merit: the Indian *karma* doctrine, Zarathustran dualism, and the predestination decreed by an inscrutable God. In the *karma* doctrine, the pious acceptance of disadvantages in this life was rewarded in a future one. Zarathustran dualism pictured an eternal battle between the powers of light and of darkness, in which the ultimate triumph of light did not preclude prior episodes of darkness. And the predestination eternally decreed by the Puritan's transcendent and inscrutable God elicited the active response of ascetic Protestantism.

In any case, Weber argued, resentment *could* color the theodicy of suffering; but did not always or primarily do so. The distrust of wealth and power usually characteristic of salvation religions found its causes in the experience of prophets and saviors that the "satiated" strata generally felt little need for salvation. Elites with a firm grasp upon power and honor tend to create legends about their *essential* and usually hereditary qualities. Socially underprivileged strata, by contrast, derive their sense of dignity from a "mission" or "task" assigned them by God. The promises offered by religions, Weber argued, should not be conceived as primarily "otherworldly." With the partial exception of Christianity and of similar ascetic creeds, most religions initially promised such this-worldly blessings as health, long life, and wealth. Only the religious virtuosi aspired to nonworldly goods. But even they primarily sought an immediate *this-worldly habitus*. The Puritan certitude of salvation, the secure state of grace, the sense of having "proven" oneself, was the psychologically tangible good offered by this ascetic religiosity. The Buddhist monk's feeling of cosmic love and the various forms of mystic union or immersion in the great unity: all these states were undoubtedly pursued for the emotional sustenance they directly provided to the believer (95–99).

Such extraordinary religious states could be temporary, but they could also be sought as enduring states of "salvation." Of the two highest religious aims—"rebirth" and "salvation"—"rebirth" was an ancient magical good. The state of blessedness promised by a religion was bound to differ with the character of the stratum that was its principal bearer. Knightly warrior classes, peasants, tradesmen, and intellectuals each had their own predilections. The intellectuals were invariably—and the merchants and artisans potentially—bearers of a theoretically or practically oriented rationalism. While no one cares whether contemporary intellectuals want to enjoy "religious experiences" as part of their stylish interior furnishings, Weber grumbled, the characteristics of past intellectual strata were of great consequence for religion. Their principal achievement was the sublimation of the religious quest into the belief in "salvation." For "salvation" took on a specific significance only when it became the expression of a systematically rationalized view of the world. Therein lay the power of religious beliefs. "Material and ideal interests, not ideas, directly dominate the actions of human beings. But . . . "ideas" have often served as switches, setting the tracks along which the dynamics of interest moved the actions forward." Even while reemphasizing the importance of "ideal interests," Weber here vividly restated his triadic scheme of singular causal analysis, with interests moving the historical process along a given path and "ideas" intervening to alter the direction of development. After all, Weber commented, it was one's worldview that determined from what—and to what—one sought to be saved (100–1).

Religious views of the world were always activated by something that was felt to be specifically "meaningless" about the real world—and by the demand that the world order be a "meaningful cosmos." This insistence, the source of religious rationalization, was carried forward by the intellectual strata. But the modern theoretical and practical rationalization of the world and of the conduct of life had ironic consequences; for the further religion pursued this rationalization, the more it was forced into a position that was intellectually irrational, and this for several reasons. On the one hand, the equations of consistent rationalism did not balance. The several great types of rational life conduct were characterized by the irrational presuppositions they had incorporated into themselves as simply given. What these irrational presuppositions were, however, was determined largely by the social and psychological *interest situation* of the strata that were the bearers of the pertinent methodologies of life during the decisive era of their formation. The irrepressible need of the intellectuals for supramundane values, moreover, was increasingly forced to retreat into these irrational elements within the rationalized reality as the world came to seem more denuded of such values. The unity of the primitive world image, in which everything was concrete magic, thus tended to split into knowledge and rational domination of nature on the one hand and "mystical" experiences on the other. Irrational mystical insight remained the only otherworldly alternative to the godless mechanism of the real world (102–3).

This phenomenon appeared in one form or another wherever human beings rationalized their world as a cosmos governed by impersonal laws, particularly in religions shaped by intellectual elites committed to the cognitive penetration of the world and of its "meaning," as in the Asian and especially the Indian world religions. For all of these, contemplation and the access it offered to the blessed stillness of the all became the highest religious good. This had far-reaching consequences for the relationship of religion to life—and to the economy. These derived from the character of the mystical experiences and from the psychological states involved in their pursuit.

The development of religion took a wholly different direction, however, where the relevant strata played an active role in life, as in the case of warrior heroes, political officials, or economically acquisitive classes—or, finally, where the religion was dominated by an organized hierocracy. "Hierocracies," the governing hierarchies of churches, have always attempted to monopolize control over religious goods through the institutional dispensation of grace. Secular political officials have distrusted religious quests for salvation, along with priestly sources of institutional grace, as a potential threat to the state. For government bureaucracies, religious duties were civil obligations to be regulated, so that religion took on a ritualistic character when it was shaped by government administrations. Knightly warrior strata too pursued this-worldly interests and avoided all forms of "mysticism." Like heroes generally, they lacked the need and the capacity for the rational mastery of reality; their lives were in the hands of "fate." Peasants, bound in their whole existence to the elementary forces of nature, tended toward magic to coerce natural spirits or simply to purchase divine favor (104–5).

The economically active strata of artisans, merchants, and entrepreneurs were seemingly the most diverse social groups in their religious orientations. Nevertheless, affinities with certain types of religiosity are discernible precisely within these occupations. What they shared was *practical* rationalism in their conduct of life. Their whole existence was based upon the technically and economically calculated domination of nature and of other men. The inherited form of life could rigidify into traditionalism in their case as well. But there was always the *possibility* that their technical and economic rationality would engender ethically rational conduct of life as well (106–7).

Where prophecy provided a religious foundation for them, they could adhere to either of the types of prophetic religion: to "exemplary" prophecy, which *demonstrated* an apathetic-ecstatic path to salvation, or to "missionary" prophecy, which *announced* demands of an ethical and ascetic character in God's name. Ethical missionary prophecy that called for action in the world found a receptive audience among these groups, most particularly where "burgher" strata were well represented. Their preferred religious habitus was not the possession of God, or the pious contemplative state that ranked highest among intellectual elites, but *active asceticism* as it came to predominate again and again in the West over contemplative mysticism and apathetic ecstasy. The kind of missionary prophecy in which the pious felt like God's tools, not like vessels of the divine, had a profound affinity for the conception of God as a supramundane, personal, angry, forgiving, and loving creator God, in contrast to the impersonal God of exemplary prophecy, who is accessible only as the object of contemplation. An impersonal God dominated the Indian and Chinese religions; a personal God predominated in the Iranian and Near Eastern religions, and in the Western religiosity derived from them (107–8).

From a certain contemporary point of view, Weber conceded, one could take emotions to be primary and thoughts no more than their secondary elaborations—and "psychological" connections as thus causally more significant than their "rational" interpretations. But that would be going too far in the case at hand; for the development of either a supramundane or an immanent conception of God was determined by a whole series of factors, some of them purely historical, which in turn shaped experiences of salvation. Moreover, as Weber argued, the rational element in religion, its doctrine, has a dynamic of its own, and the techniques of salvation that follow from conceptions of God may have far-reaching consequences for the conduct of life. If the religious goods sought have been strongly influenced by worldly interests, the reverse has been true as well. The orientation of the conduct of life, wherever it was systematically rationalized, was determined by the ultimate values that guided this rationalization. Often if not invariably, Weber argued, these values have been religious ones (108–10).

Important for the mutual connections between "inner" and "outer" interests was the circumstance that the highest goods offered by a religion were not also the most universal. The crucial fact that confronts us in every history of religion, Weber reemphasized, is the *unequal* religious *qualification* of human beings. The most highly esteemed religious goods, the ecstatic and visionary capacities of magicians, ascetics, and mystics of all kinds, were not accessible to everyone; their possession was a "charisma" that could be awakened in some, but not in all. The consequence was the tendency of every intense religiosity to adopt an estate-like rank order of religious qualifications. The religiosity of virtuosi stood opposed to the religiosity of the "masses," meaning the religiously "unmusical," rather than the socially disadvantaged. But the religion of the virtuosi has invariably been challenged by the officials of a hierocratic church, who have tried to organize mass religion into a system of institutional grace. In line with the interests of its officials, the church must be "democratic" in its provision of access to religious goods, just as political bureaucracies must combat the aristocratic privileges of feudal estates. What concessions the virtuosi actually made to average religiosity became decisive for the impact of religion upon everyday life. The virtuosi had much less influence if they left the masses immersed in magic, as in almost all Oriental religions, than if they undertook an ethical rationalization of everyday life, no matter how much they were forced to modify their ideals in the process. Of course the character of the virtuosi's own religiosity too was important for the conduct of the "masses," and therefore also for the economic ethic of the religion involved (110–12).

More specifically, the relationship of virtuoso religion to the economy differed according to the religious goods sought by the virtuosi. Where these were contemplative or orgiastic-ecstatic in character, according to Weber, no bridge led from them to everyday action in the world. A deep chasm thus separated the conduct of "laymen" from that of the virtuosi in Oriental religions. The dominance of the virtuosi within the religious community then easily led to magical "anthropolatry": the virtuosi were worshipped as holy men; their magic was purchased by laymen as means toward worldly or religious salvation. The conduct of the laymen could nonetheless undergo a certain regulation in the process. For the virtuoso was the obvious spiritual guide. Yet he often influenced the religiously "unmusical" only in the ritual and conventional details of his own conduct. The "charisma" of the pure mystic certainly served only himself (112–13).

The situation was altogether different, Weber argued, where the religious virtuosi formed ascetic sects committed to the transformation of *life within the world* according to God's will. For this to happen, the highest religious good could not be contemplative in character; it could not consist in an orgiastic or apathetic-ecstatic mystical union with the divine; nor could it adhere to magical or sacramental *means* of grace, for all these devalued action in the world. Both the exclusion of magic from the world and the redirection of the path to salvation from contemplative *flight from the world* to the actively ascetic *transformation of the world* were fully realized only in the great church and sect formations of Western ascetic Protestantism (113–14).

According to Weber, certain purely historical traits of Western religiosity converged to bring about this outcome. Among these was the role of the social stratum that was responsible for its development. But its theoretical character was just as important: its supramundane God and the distinctiveness of its path to salvation, which originated in Israelite prophecy and in the doctrine of the Torah. Where the religious virtuoso felt placed into the world as God's "tool," cut off from all magical means of salvation, and commanded to "prove" himself before God through the ethical quality of his actions, there the "world" was devalued as a vessel of sin and yet affirmed as the scene of God-willed action. For this inner-worldly asceticism rejected the world in the sense that it despised worldly dignity, beauty, and power as rivals to God's empire. Yet it did not mean to flee from the world into contemplation, but ethically to rationalize the world according to God's command. It was thus really more urgently *committed to the world* than the naïve "world acceptance" of antiquity or of lay Catholicism. The grace and election of the Protestant ascetic proved itself precisely in the everyday world: not in the world as it was, but in the world of ethically rationalized action within one's calling. The sects of religious virtuosi in the West provided the ferment for the methodical rationalization of the conduct of life, including economic action. The Asian communities of contemplative, orgiastic, or apathetic-ecstatic virtuosi, by contrast, provided means of escape from the senselessness of this-worldly action (114–15).

Between these two extremes, Weber noted, there was room for a great variety of transitions and combinations. For religions, like human beings, are historical products; they need not be logically or psychologically consistent. The religions he was about to consider, Weber wrote, cannot be lined up in a chain of types or stages of development. Rather, they are highly complex historical individuals, and they jointly exhaust only a small fraction of the possible combinations among the relevant factors. What follows is not a systematic "typology" of religions, but neither is it a purely empirical project. Rather, the descriptions Weber now introduced were meant to be "typological" in that they highlighted what was significant about the historical religious ethics for the major economic orientations, while neglecting other aspects. They were not intended to provide a fully rounded portrait of the religions they took up. More specifically, Weber proposed to focus upon the traits of religions that affected economic ethics exclusively from the viewpoint of their relationship to economic rationalization. Indeed, Weber was explicitly interested in the type of economic rationalism that began to predominate in the West as part of the middle-class rationalization of life from the sixteenth and seventeenth centuries on (115–17).

Weber thought it necessary to remind his readers, finally, that "rationalism" can have different meanings. It can refer either to the *cognitive* rationalization of the world, the mastery of reality by means of increasingly precise abstractions, or to its *practical* rationalization in the sense of the methodical pursuit of practical aims by means of increasingly precise calculations of the adequate means. These two are different, Weber wrote, despite their ultimate unity. The rationalization of the *conduct of life*, too, can take divergent forms. Confucianism was so rationalistic in its lack of religious grounding that it stood at the limits of what could still be called a "religious" ethic; it was more baldly utilitarian than any other ethical system, except perhaps that of Jeremy Bentham. Yet it differed radically from Benthamism and from all Western types of practical rationalism, despite the presence of certain analogues. "Rational" in the sense of belief in a valid "canon" was the highest artistic ideal of the Renaissance, which was also rationalistic in its sense of rejecting tradition and in its faith in the power of natural reason. "Rational" in the wholly different sense of "goal-directed" was the method of apathetic asceticism, in Yoga, or in the late Buddhist prayer machines. "Rational" in the sense of distinguishing between the normatively "valid" and the empirically given were all kinds of *practical* ethics that systematically aimed at defined goals of salvation (117–18). These last-named processes of rationalization, Weber wrote, are of particular interest for us.[3]

RELIGION AND THE WORLD

Weber's "Intermediate Reflection" was written about 1915, and inserted between his analyses of the Chinese and Indian religions. It was subtitled "Theory of the Stages and Directions of the Religious Rejection of the World." In it, Weber proposed to describe the conflicts between divergent religious rejections of the world, as well as between them and other values, in an "ideal-typically" *heightened* way. He deliberately characterized competing normative "spheres" as *rationally coherent* to a degree they have rarely reached in reality, though they could and did attain it in historically significant instances. Ideal-typical construction made it possible to assess the distance of historical phenomena from the posited types, and it could offer something more as well. For the *rationality,* the logical or teleological *coherence,* of a position has always had a certain power over human beings. For Weber, in any case, the suitable construction of rational types—and the isolation of the most "coherent" forms of practical conduct to be derived from given presuppositions—could facilitate the description of an otherwise infinite variety. Finally, this kind of thought experiment in the sociology of religion could also contribute to a typology and sociology of rationalism itself.[4]

Weber here recalled the importance of the supramundane creator God for the actively ascetic pursuit of salvation. But he added that the supramundane God alone did not determine the direction of Western asceticism. After all, the Christian Trinity, along with the Christian saints, was actually more involved in the world than the Judaic God or the Islamic Allah; yet Judaism developed nothing that really resembled Western asceticism. Thus the conception of a supramundane God, despite its affinity with ascetic action, played its role only in conjunction with other circumstances, chief among them the kind of religious promise and the means of salvation that followed from it. In his "Introduction," Weber had already noted the antithesis between ascetic action as God's tool and contemplative mysticism as the passive possession of a religious good. This antithesis is most radical when, on the one side, *inner-worldly asceticism* seeks rationally to master the world, and when mysticism on its side draws the consequence of *contemplative flight from the world.* The tension becomes milder when ascetic action confines itself to overcoming sin within the believer, performing the undoubtedly God-willed, even to the point of avoiding action in an *ascetic flight from the world* that outwardly resembles contemplative flight; or when, on the other hand, the contemplative mystic does not draw the consequence of flight from the world but remains within the world, like the inner-worldly ascetic. The antithesis may in both cases fade to make room for any combination of the two methods of salvation. For the genuine mystic, the creature must be silent, so that God may speak. For the inner-worldly ascetic, the behavior of the mystic is slothful self-indulgence; for the mystic, the behavior of the inner-worldly ascetic leads to entanglement in the godless world (*Z*, 481–83).

Proposing to consider the tensions between religion and the world in greater detail, Weber recalled that both ascetic and mystic orientations had their origins in magical practices designed to awaken charisma. Even in its antecedents, asceticism thus revealed its dual tendency to reject the world, on the one hand, and to dominate it by means of magic, on the other. The magician was the precursor of the prophet. Both the prophet and the savior legitimated themselves through the possession of magical charisma; this was just a way of gaining recognition for their exemplary status or the content of their mission. The content of their prophecy was the rational systematization of conduct with the aim of salvation. The salvation religions offered their followers freedom from suffering; they sought to attain a permanent habitus of assured salvation, rather than the transitory states induced by orgies, ascetic practices, or contemplation. Where prophecy created religious communities, the regulation of conduct was first assigned to the prophet's or savior's charismatic disciples, and later generally to a priestly order.

Prophetic or savior religions usually lived in a state of tension with the world, and this tension grew more intense as the religions moved from ritualism to a sublimated religious disposition, and as the rationalization of worldly goods increased as well. For the rationalization and sublimation of men's relationships to the various spheres of religious and worldly values tended to become conscious in their own distinctiveness, and this led to conflicts among them that were unknown in the initially naïve posture toward the world (*Z*, 483–85).

Where prophecy created purely religious communities that broke the ties of kinship, according to Weber, it developed an ethic of *brotherliness*. At first, this ethic simply took over the norms of conduct current in the traditional communities of neighborhood, village, and occupation. These norms were based upon two axioms: the dualism of internal and external morality, and simple reciprocity within the group. The economic implications of these axioms were emergency aid for one's neighbor and interest-free loans within the community. In prophetic salvation religions, however, the more rationally and ethically sublimated the idea of salvation became, the more heightened became the commands derived from the neighborly ethic of reciprocity—outwardly to cosmic brotherly love, and inwardly to charity, love of one's fellow human beings, and finally of one's enemies. Psychologically, this augmentation was aided by the peculiar euphoria that accompanies all forms of sublimated religious ecstasy. The ethic of universal brotherliness broke through all social boundaries. The more consistently it was realized, however, the more sharply it clashed with the orders and values of the world (*Z,* 485–87).

According to Weber, this clash became most overt in the *economic* sphere. All primitive attempts to influence spirits and gods in the interest of individuals included wealth among their objectives. Salvation religions, however, increasingly came into conflict with the economy. Rational enterprise requires market competition, money prices, and calculation, and money is the most "impersonal" element in modern life. The more rational capitalism followed its immanent laws, therefore, the less it became accessible to a religious ethic of brotherliness. Formal and substantive rationality conflicted, so that salvation religions came to regard the *impersonal* and specifically *unbrotherly* economic powers with profound suspicion. The ethic of world-rejecting asceticism reacted most radically by forbidding monks as individuals to own possessions. This triggered the paradox of all rational asceticism, which rejects wealth only to end by creating it. Thus temples and monasteries everywhere became centers of rational enterprise. There were only two ways to escape from the tensions between brotherliness and the economy. One of these was the paradox of the Puritan vocational ethic, which simply abandoned the universalism of love. At bottom, this position abandoned the goal of salvation for all human beings in favor of the salvation of particular individuals. This unbrotherly standpoint was really no longer that of a salvation religion, whose only option was the heightening of brotherliness to the cosmic love of the mystic (*Z,* 487–90).

A similar tension was bound to exist between the brotherly ethic of the salvation religions and the *political* orders of the world. In the political as in the economic sphere, Weber noted, the tension increased as the political order itself became more rational. The apparatus of the bureaucratic state, Weber argued, performs its tasks "without regard for persons," without hate but also without love. The state has become more impersonal and thus further removed from substantive ethical concerns than the patriarchal orders of the past. Despite its attention to "social policy," the state's domestic administration is ultimately regulated by objective reasons of state. And that is even more clearly the case in foreign policy. The ultimate recourse to violence is essential to every political organization. The estrangement between ethics and the political sphere is especially deep because, unlike economics, politics may become a direct rival of religious ethics. Precisely in modern political communities, *war* may release a powerful pathos that religions can match only in heroic communities of brotherliness. War offers the combatant something uniquely meaningful: the dignity of a consecrated death. But the way in which death thus takes on a communal meaning diverges radically from the theodicy of death in a religion of brotherliness. For such a religion, the brotherliness of comrades at war must seem a mere reflection of the technically sophisticated brutality of battle, and the inner-worldly consecration of death in war a perverse idealization of murder (*Z*, 490–93).

Here again, according to Weber, one consistent reaction is Puritan vocational asceticism, which holds that the commands of an incomprehensible God must be enforced in the world by worldly means. The other is the mysticism of cosmic love and brotherliness, which proposes "not to resist evil" or to "turn the other cheek" in a way that entirely evades the pragmatic rationale of power. Any universal church will feel the right and obligation ruthlessly to oppose the religious misleading of souls under its care, and any religious aristocracy burdened with God's command to tame the world will produce the "religious warrior" along with the distinction between the "holy" or "just" war, which is really a religious war, and all other worldly, and therefore unjust, wars. The religious warrior will respond to the violation of God's will with a religious revolt, on the grounds that one must obey God more than men. But the opposite reaction was characteristic of the Lutheran church, which knew only passive resistance and preached obedience to worldly authorities even when they ordered a war. The involvement of religious organizations in worldly power relationships, the use of religion for the political domestication of the masses, and the need for the religious legitimation of existing regimes: all these shaped the relationships of religions to politics that history reveals. The most important such relationship, according to Weber, was the "organic" social ethic. It too was committed to "brotherliness," but not to the universal mysticism of love. Its point of departure was the inequality of religious qualifications, yet it could not accept the idea that salvation was accessible only to a few. It therefore devised a system of religious and occupational estates, in which every individual and group was assigned its own distinctive task (*Z*, 494–96).

Just as economically and politically rational actions follow their own immanent laws, so every other kind of rational action is tied to the conditions of the world that are its means or ends, and it therefore comes into conflict with the ethic of brotherliness. But it carries a profound conflict within itself as well, for there seems to be no way to decide whether the moral value of an action lies in its result or in some ethical quality of the action itself. The religious ethic will incline toward the latter alternative, but that condemns one's actions to irrationality in their effects. Indeed, the religious ethic of cosmic love may reject purposive rational action in all its forms. The organic social ethic is always eminently conservative and anti-revolutionary. Virtuous religiosity itself, by contrast, may lead to revolutionary consequences in two ways. One of these emerges from inner-worldly asceticism when it confronts the empirical world with a divine "natural law," whose realization becomes a religious duty, as in the Puritan revolutions. The alternative occurs where the mystic makes the psychologically possible move from possessing God to being possessed by Him. This is possible when eschatological hopes become acute enough to suggest the immediate onset of the era of cosmic brotherliness. The mystic then becomes a savior or a prophet. All chiliastic revolutions, including that of the Anabaptists, have been based upon such foundations (Z, 497–99).

If the religious ethic of brotherliness is in conflict with purposive rationality, Weber added, it takes a similar stance with respect to those worldly powers that are fundamentally nonrational or antirational in character. The most important of these are the aesthetic and the erotic spheres. Magical religiosity was intimately linked to the aesthetic sphere, which long made religion an inexhaustible source of artistic innovation on the one hand and of stylistic traditions on the other. For the religious ethic of brotherliness and for rigorous asceticism, however, art became suspect as a form of magic. The sublimation of religious ethics on the one hand, and the autonomous development of art on the other, tended to engender a mutual tension in any case. Salvation religions are concerned with the meaning, not the form, of objects and actions relevant to salvation. Art may remain allied with religion as long as the viewer naively focuses upon its contents rather than its forms. But the situation is altered by the emergence of intellectualism and the rationalization of life. Art comes to constitute itself ever more consciously as a system of autonomous values. It offers its own kind of inner-worldly salvation from everyday life, especially from the increasing pressure of theoretical and practical rationalism. The more art follows its own laws, however, the more likely it is to come into conflict with virtuoso religion (Z, 499–500, 502).

The tension between sexual love and the ethic of brotherliness similarly increases, according to Weber, with the sublimation of sexuality into "eroticism," a distinctive sphere that is separated both from the naturalism of the peasant and from the everyday realm. The separation from naturalism was linked to the rationalization and intellectualization of culture. As eroticism became something consciously cultivated, it seemed to open a path to the irrational essence of life as against the mechanisms of rationalization. The possibility of a tragic tension stemmed from issues of responsibility that in the West originated in Christianity. The positive valuation of erotic sensation developed in the context of feudal conceptions of honor, as the symbolism of vassaldom was transferred to erotically sublimated sexual relationships. The knightly courtship of the Christian Middle Ages was an erotic vassal's service directed exclusively at other men's wives; it involved theoretically chaste nights of love and a conventional code of duties. A further heightening of eroticism took place during the shift from the still masculine conventions of the Renaissance to the increasingly unmilitary intellectualism of salon culture. But the final elevation of the erotic sphere occurred when it clashed with the unavoidably ascetic character of modern occupational life. Under the influence of this tension, an extramarital sexual relationship could seem the only bond that still connected modern man to the natural sources of life. The valuation of this inner-worldly salvation from rationality confronted the radical rejection of eroticism by every ethic of salvation (*Z*, 502–6).

This confrontation grew most acute where the erotic relationship appeared to achieve the direct linking of souls, the highest goal of love. In radical opposition to rationalism, unlimited devotion lends a unique meaning to the value an individual has for only one other human being. That meaning lies in a bond that can become a merging with the other, an experience overwhelming enough to be interpreted in *sacramental* terms. Eroticism can function as a psychological substitute for certain forms of piety, especially for mystic union with the divine. But for a religious ethic of brotherliness, Weber wrote, the erotic relationship remains subtly allied to brutality, to the violation of the less brutal partner that feigns devotion while enjoying the self in the other. The euphoria of the happy lover, who wants to extend his happiness to the whole world, therefore easily encounters the cool mockery of a religiously grounded ethic of brotherliness, as in the early works of Tolstoy. Erotic ecstasy is also consonant with orgiastic religiosity; the recognition of marriage as a "sacrament" by the Catholic Church is a concession to this fact. With mysticism, as indicated, eroticism can fall into an unstable relationship of psychological substitution or fusion, which easily leads to a collapse into the orgiastic. Inner-worldly vocational asceticism can accept only rationally regulated marriage as divinely ordered for creatures hopelessly corrupted by "concupiscence." The Quaker ethic, as represented in William Penn's letters to his wife, succeeded in replacing the coarse Lutheran conception of marriage with a genuinely human interpretation of its inner religious value. Only the idea of mutual responsibility, a category heterogeneous to the erotic sphere, can sustain the sense that a supreme value lies in forbearing and being indebted to one another throughout the organic course of life, "until the pianissimo of old age" (Z, 506–11).

The greatest tension, to be sure, is that between religiosity and the realm of cognition. A union between the two may occur within a worldview, as in China. Mutual acknowledgement is possible in metaphysical speculation, even though it easily leads to skepticism. That, Weber argued, is why religiosity, especially ascetic Protestantism, considers empirical science more compatible with its interests than philosophy. Wherever reasoning has thoroughly removed magic from the world by transforming the cosmos into a causal mechanism, an inescapable conflict emerges with the postulate that the world must be ethically meaningful. With every advance of scientific rationalism, religion is pushed further out of the realm of the rational and thus at last becomes *the* purely irrational or antirational power. And precisely because of this apparently irreconcilable conflict, both prophetic and priestly religions again and again seek relationships with rational intellectualism; the more they become "doctrines," the more they need rational defenses. Because priesthoods are capable of preserving traditions, they undertook the schooling of the young, especially in writing and arithmetic. At the same time, the literary character of scriptural religion encouraged nonpriestly thought, which everywhere produced not only antipriestly mystics and sectarians, but also skeptics and philosophical opponents of religion. Every religion took a somewhat different stance toward intellectualism, but without ever avoiding the fundamental conflict that was grounded in the divergence of worldviews. There has been *no* functioning religion, Weber wrote, that has not been forced to demand the sacrifice of the intellect (Z, 512–14).

The "world " can come into conflict with various aspects of religion, but the aspect involved is always central to the quest for *salvation.* Indeed, that quest followed from the practical rationalization of life, or from the demand that the world process be *meaningful,* at least where it affects human affairs. This demand originated in the issue of unjust suffering but soon advanced toward an ever further devaluation of the world. For the more rational thought dealt with the problem of compensatory justice, the less an inner-worldly solution seemed possible, or an otherworldly one probable or meaningful. The fact of suffering itself, Weber observed, had to remain irrational, for it could be superseded only by the even more irrational problem of the origin of sin. A sinful world had to appear ethically even more imperfect than one condemned to suffering. That death and decay equally affected the best and the worst human beings devalued precisely the highest inner-worldly goods. As God and the world order were considered eternal, the highest values were idealized as "timeless," which reinforced the ethical rejection of the empirical world. For religion now faced considerations that were far graver than the imperfections of the world, since they concerned the highest "cultural goods." These depended upon intellectual or aesthetic *qualifications,* the cultivation of which required the unbrotherliness of social *inequality.* Barriers between levels of education and aesthetic culture are the most internalized and insurmountable of status differences. Precisely the highest goods the world can offer are thus weighed down with guilt, for the social order is everywhere maintained by force, with little regard for justice (*Z,* 515–17).

The objectified economic cosmos, the rational provision of material goods necessary for an inner-worldly culture, was rooted in lovelessness. Sublimated brutality, unbrotherly idiosyncrasy, and illusion inevitably accompanied sexual love. Rational cognition followed its own norms in constructing a cosmos that had nothing to do with the religious demand that the world must have a "meaning." Indeed, as Weber observed again, the cosmos of natural causality and the cosmos of ethical compensation stood in radical opposition to each other. And even though the science that created the natural cosmos seemed unable to account for its own ultimate presuppositions, it claimed, in the name of intellectual rectitude, to be the only possible way of thinking about the world. Like all cultural values, intellectualism created an unbrotherly aristocracy of cultural property that was independent of all ethical qualities. But this cultural possession, the highest value for inner-worldly man, was tainted not only by guilt, but also by ultimate meaninglessness (*Z,* 517–18).

The pointless character of the cultivated man's self-perfection followed for religious thought from the senselessness of death, precisely in the context of "culture." The peasant could die "sated with life," and so could the warrior. But not so the "cultivated" man, who strove for self-perfection by appropriating or creating "cultural goods"; for his perfectibility, like that of the cultural goods themselves, extended into the infinite. And the more these goods and the paths of self-enhancement multiplied, the smaller the portion became that the individual could encompass in the course of his life. "Culture," for the individual, did not consist of the *quantity* of cultural goods appropriated, but of a coherent *selection* among them. But there was no guarantee that this selection would reach a *meaningful* completion at the "accidental" time of the individual's death. Thus all "culture" became incongruent with the organic cycle of natural life and thus condemned to meaninglessness. Similarly, work on the objects of culture, the more it became a "vocation," turned into a senseless hastening in pursuit of mutually antagonistic goals (*Z*, 518–19).

As thought about the meaning of the world became more systematic, its outward organization more rationalized, and the experience of its irrational contents more sublimated, according to Weber, otherworldly religion grew ever more hostile. And it was not only the removal of magic from the world that led onto this path, but also the attempt at its ethical rationalization. Indeed, the intellectual search for mystic salvation itself succumbed to the reign of unbrotherliness. Since its charisma was not equally accessible to everyone, it necessarily created a religious aristocracy. Modern occupational life certainly leaves little room for the cultivation of cosmic brotherliness. The issue of theodicy, moreover, created tensions of its own. Of the three consistent kinds of theodicy named in Weber's "Introduction," Zarathustran *dualism* drew upon the magic antithesis between the "clean" and the "unclean," but the subsistence of the "unclean" implied an unacceptable limitation of God's power. The second coherent theodicy abandoned the vision of a benign God. The belief in *predestination* made God's decrees inscrutable, and accepted damnation for the greater part of humanity. But this un-brotherly consequence was endured only by the religious virtuosi of ascetic Protestantism. The third consistent theodicy combined the virtuosity of self-salvation with its universal accessibility, rejection of the world with an organic social ethic, and contemplation as the path to salvation with an inner-worldly ethic. But only the religion of the Indian intellectuals encompassed this outstanding form of theodicy (*Z*, 519–21).

Weber's "Intermediate Reflection" drew much of its force from his sense of an ineradicable conflict among ultimate values, which reflected his value pluralism. Beyond that, the essay was built around Tolstoy's ideal of indiscriminately universal love and "brotherliness," which evoked a powerful response from Weber. Part of that response grew out of the contrast between Tolstoy's religious ethic and the guilt associated with the unjust inequalities of the social order, with the objectified rationality of the acquisitive market economy, and even with culture, humanity's highest this-worldly good. Weber drew upon Simmel's sense of the increasing disproportion between the objectified world of cultural objects and the human capacity for "subjective culture." But Weber dramatically heightened that incongruity by locating it in the finite human lifespan. The darkest passages in Weber's "Intermediate Reflection" judged the empirical world, following Tolstoy, as not only "un-brotherly" and "loveless," but also devoid of "meaning." While he insisted that religion must ultimately ask for the "sacrifice of the intellect," Weber considered the demand that the world must be "meaningful" a postulate of religious thought. Some of us nowadays believe that our world is both finite and without "meaning," other than as a setting for various human projects. Indeed, we are no longer greatly shocked by these realities; but for Weber, there was an irreconcilable conflict between the competing "spheres" of life, and particularly between our scientific knowledge of the world as a "causal mechanism," and the religious postulate of "meaning." Weber made no effort to resolve that conflict; but he clearly experienced it as a tragic one.[5]

THE RELIGIONS OF CHINA AND OF INDIA

Weber devoted close to half of his extended essay entitled *Confucianism and Taoism* to a discussion of sociological foundations. He discussed the cities of China, which began as fortresses and princely residences, and were therefore soon inhabited by patrimonial officials. Along with their relationships to the agrarian countryside, the towns engaged in river trade exclusively with each other. Commercial contact with the West, when it came, was confined to a single port. Guilds arose to regulate the economic life of the towns, but they were dominated by the clans, and they encouraged economic "traditionalism," rather than capitalist enterprise. One of the main reasons was that the Chinese towns were not political communes; they knew no individual or property rights, no city "freedoms," and no municipal self-government. They were largely administered by a patrimonial bureaucracy that, in China as in Egypt, grew out of the early need for the central control of river water.[6]

Chinese religion consisted of ritual ancestor and spirit cults, and of a single impersonal divinity that was embodied, after the pacification of the realm, in the person of a theocratic emperor, the "son of heaven." The emperor's holy charisma had to "prove itself" in the welfare of his subjects. He did public penance when bad harvests or other natural disasters visited his realm, and he could be deposed if divine favor continued to elude him. He was expected to guarantee order and harmony within his domain. The centrality of his position in Chinese politics and religion helped to ensure the administrative control of the imperial bureaucracy. The Chinese officials were "literati," schooled in calligraphy and in Chinese classical literature. Beginning in the second century B.C., this "mandarin" elite gained control of access to public offices, which were increasingly allocated on the basis of educational qualifications—via a complex system of public examinations—rather than by birth or inherited rank. As provincial governors, the Chinese officials collected taxes that had been converted into monetary form; they kept much of what they collected, and they thus evolved a system of office benefices. This reinforced economic traditionalism, since any interference in the existing arrangements threatened the incomes of the officials (*K*, 166–79, 194–201, 207, 216–26).

The role of family clans in Chinese life was particularly dominant in the Chinese villages. Unlike the cities, which were dominated by the centralized bureaucracy, the villages enjoyed a degree of autonomy. While the cities were governed by mandarins, Weber wrote, the villages were "self-governing localities without mandarins." The village elder had significant powers, and the village temple was an important institution, even economically. Above all, the village was the location of every clan's ancestral land and thus of the ancestor cult as well. The clans took care of their members, insured and buried them, lent them money when necessary, and kept a degree of control even of those members who took up a trade or moved to a city. The petty artisanal production that arose, however, remained strictly traditional in orientation. A kind of patrimonial political capitalism prospered for a while, but the barriers between clans ultimately limited economic interactions. In any case, there was no privately owned manufacture, and no entrepreneurial capitalism. A further obstacle was the irrationality of patrimonial justice and the absence of formally rational and predictable law (*K*, 256–84, esp. 266).

The subjects tested in the Chinese examinations were the classical texts of the Confucian tradition, which originated in the works of Kung-tse (Confucius) in the fifth century B.C. Confucianism was not based upon a personal God, but upon the impersonal dualism of a heavenly *Shin* and an earthly *Kwei* principle, that extended into the life of every individual. The *purely* literary schooling of the Chinese mandarins profoundly affected their outlook—as well as Chinese thought more generally. It retarded progress in mathematics and logic. Orthodox Confucian philosophy knew no radical evil and no salvation. It was essentially a compendium of practical wisdom—and more a set of parables than a theological system or a coherent cosmology. Its aim was dignified acceptance of the world and graceful adjustment to it. There was no conception of natural law, of individual rights, or of personal "freedom." The formal development of law was undercut by the patrimonial tradition of substantive justice. Thus Confucian orthodoxy impeded the development of legal as well as of scientific rationalism. The dominant purpose of the Chinese "gentleman" was his own self-perfection, which also assured the propriety of his conduct in worldly affairs (*K*, 286–88, 292–94, 297–99, 310–13, 317–18, 339–46, 350–51, 355–57).

Not surprisingly, the Chinese mandarins despised the merely *wealthy*. The status ethic of the official elite, moreover, focused upon problems of *consumption*, rather than production. While the *possession* of wealth was perfectly acceptable, active involvement in its *acquisition* was ethically problematic. Confucius himself would reportedly have engaged in the pursuit of riches, if success had been certain. Since *risks* had to be taken, however, acquisitive activity was bound to disturb the balance of the soul. The position of the office beneficiary was thus idealized, according to Weber, because it alone permitted the self-perfection of the educated man. The Confucian gentleman, or "man of distinction," sought the universality offered by the classical literary curriculum, which is why Chinese patrimonial officials did without the specialized skills developed by their European counterparts. It was the principle of the Chinese mandarins that "the dignified man is not a tool" (*K*, 354–56).

Confucian orthodoxy was the doctrine of an educated and socially dominant elite of officials. But it was challenged by a more popular religious heterodoxy in the form of Taoism, founded by the anchorite Laotse, a contemporary of Confucius. Laotse's religious goal was ascetic flight from the world and, indeed, from the body. He drew upon ancient ascetic techniques designed to economize breath and to repress bodily functions, so as to attain a state of "emptiness," or apathetic ecstasy. This was a path to mystic union with the all-one. Laotse challenged Confucius' commitment to learning, along with his involvement in politics. Strictly apolitical, Laotse was interested only in extricating himself from the world. While he did not form a school or a doctrinal tradition, he served as the nominal father of a whole cluster of heterodox cults and practices that came to be known as Taoism. Most Taoists dismissed learning. Their anti-literary stance brought them a following among merchant groups, but they could hardly encourage economic rationality. Instead, Taoism sponsored the rationalization of such magic "sciences" as geomancy, which allowed the lucrative hawking of advice on auspicious building sites and the like. While turning the world into a "magic garden," the Taoists also fostered anchorite settlements of learners grouped around reincarnated spiritual guides. Orthodox Confucians accused them of founding unauthorized societies, begging to support them, worshipping holy men who promised eternal life, and—worst of all—separating themselves from their families and ancestor cults to live as monks. On the whole, the Confucian state religion was successful in controlling the Taoist heterodoxy, which remained a loose confederation of magicians and never became a religious community (*K*, 370–83, 387, 392–97, 402–7, 433–35, 448–49).

In the concluding section of his essay on Chinese religion, Weber contrasted Confucianism and Taoism with ascetic Protestantism. The Puritans had stripped magic from the world or banned it to the devil's realm, while systematically rationalizing God's relationship to the world, along with their own religious rejection and practical domination of it. In sharpest contrast, the Taoists' "magic garden" excluded economic and technological rationality, while Confucianism *accepted* the world in both theory and practice. Philosophic and literary education served it as a means of self-perfection; its aim was gentlemanly adjustment to the prevailing cosmic and social order. Orthodox Confucianism knew nothing of radical evil or of the yearning for salvation, and it despised ascetic flight from the world as sloth (*K*, 450–53).

A true prophecy, Weber argued, engenders the systematic assessment of conduct in terms of an inner ethical norm, which guides the individual's critical orientation toward the "world." Confucianism, by contrast, called for an adjustment to worldly realities. But a human being who is rationalized *only* in the light of the need for adjustment, Weber argued, is not a coherent unity; he is just a collection of useful qualities. Confucianism provided for the domestication of the masses and the dignified bearing of the gentleman. But the style of life it fostered could not generate the striving for inner unity that we associate with the concept of the "personality." Life remained a series of events, rather than a whole coherently oriented toward a transcendent end. Therein lay a sharp contrast between Confucianism and all Western religions, for no Christian ethic could as completely eliminate the tension between the world and man's ultimate destiny as the Confucian system of radical optimism about the world. Confucianism lacked any tension between nature and God, ethical obligation and human inadequacy, religious duty and sociopolitical reality. Thus the only power it could provide for the guidance of conduct was familial piety based upon the belief in ancestral spirits (*K*, 460–61).

A Confucian spiritual leader explicitly rejected the universal love of humanity, since it would be a threat to piety and justice: Only animals know neither father nor brothers. The primary duty of every Confucian was piety toward specific human beings, living or dead, who stood near him in the prevailing order. He knew no obligation to a supramundane God, and no commitment to a holy and objective task or idea. This *personal* obstacle to objectification also impeded economic rationalization, since it tended to bind the individual to "persons," rather than to objective enterprises.

The great achievement of the ethical religions, especially of the ethical and ascetic Protestant sects, was to *break through* clan ties, and to establish the predominance of the community of faith and *ethical* conduct over the community of *blood,* and to a great extent even over the family. In economic terms, this was to base *business confidence upon the ethical qualities* of individuals who had proven themselves in their *occupational* work.

For Weber, this was a decisive achievement (*K,* 462–63, esp. 463).

In a further contrast, Weber pointed to the Puritan's rejection of the world and of sinful human nature, which condemned the Confucian's ideal of self-perfection as the blasphemous deification of the creaturely, his enjoyment of wealth as the archetype of temptation, and his reliance upon his literary education as sinful pride. The ascetic Protestant could not earn his salvation, but he could hope that his permanent commitment to the doing of God's work would bring him the assurance of his election as God's instrument. The "doing the work of him who sent me while it is day" thus became a duty, and the works commanded were of a rationally ethical character, rather than a ritual one.

> The contrast to Confucianism is clear. Both ethics had their irrational roots: there (among the Confucians) in magic, here in the ultimately undiscoverable decisions of a supramundane God. But magic led to . . . the sanctity of tradition. The relationship to a supramundane God and to an . . . ethically irrational world, by contrast, led to . . . unceasing . . . work for the ethically rational mastery and domination of the existing world: for rational . . . "progress." . . . Confucianism demanded constantly alert self-control . . . to preserve the dignity of the . . . perfected man of the world; the Puritan ethic [did so to sustain] the unified orientation to the will of God.

Weber's portrait of Confucianism was colored by his passionate aversion to everything that smacked of conformity and "adjustment" (*Anpassung*) to the environment (*K,* 465–67, esp. 467).

The Puritan reconstructed his world in terms of objectively rational "enterprises" and "business" relationships, of rational law and rational contracts, whereas the Confucian remained attached to tradition, to local customs, and to the good will of individual officials. In China, worldly utilitarianism and the belief in the ethical value of wealth as a means of all-sided self-perfection, coupled with immense population density, led to high degrees of economic "calculation," and there were recurrent complaints of "materialism." Politically oriented capitalism prevailed, along with office usury, profits from wholesale trade, and even large workshops. But there were no *methodically* rational business conceptions, no bourgeois capitalism of a late medieval European type, not to mention the productive "enterprise" of modern scientific capitalism. Chinese wealth was derived from the exploitation of bureaucratic offices; there was no capital formation, no rational business organization, no adequate legal framework, no economic use of technical inventions, and no method of bookkeeping (*K,* 468–70). Weber's point was that economic activity and acquisitive behavior do not automatically or "naturally" lead to the rise of modern capitalism; they certainly did not do so in China.

For the Puritan, the acquisition of wealth was an unintended consequence, and an important symptom, of his virtue, but the consumption of wealth was sinful immersion in the creaturely world. Confucius, however, would not have objected to the acquisition of wealth, if its uncertainties did not threaten the balance of the soul. Work in a specialized occupation could not be reconciled with the dignity of the well-rounded gentleman, who was an end in himself rather than a "tool." This central principle of the Confucian ethic ruled out all forms of specialization and specialized training, especially in preparation for economic acquisition. The Confucian was a man of literary education, and more specifically a man of texts and of writing. Most Puritans, by contrast, though regular readers of the Bible, rejected philosophical and literary education as a waste of time and a danger to the soul. They distrusted Aristotelian and scholastic dialectics, preferring the empirical knowledge of nature, along with sober clarity of thought and specialized occupational skills as products of education (473–75).

"Confucian rationalism," Weber wrote, "meant rational adjustment to the world; Puritan rationalism, the rational *domination* of the world."

> Nothing was so thoroughly in conflict with the Confucian ideal of dignity as the thought of an "occupation." The "princely" man was an aesthetic value, and thus *not* the "instrument" of a God. But the genuine Christian, and above all the . . . ascetic desired to be nothing other than just that. For in that alone he sought his dignity. And because that is what he wanted, he was a useful instrument for the rational transformation and domination of the world.

Human outlooks of this kind, while partly shaped by economic and political conditions, Weber remarked, also had their own impact upon human affairs (*K*, 476, 478, esp. 476).

Turning to the historical context in *Hinduism and Buddhism,* Weber described India as a land of villages but also of towns and of trade. All forms of political capitalism and tax farming thrived there as well as in the West, and Indian city development paralleled medieval European patterns, at least for a time. The modern number system originated in India, along with significant work in the natural sciences, and lively debates took place among competing philosophical schools in a generally tolerant environment. Indian legal institutions could have favored early capitalism, much as they did in Europe. The achievements of Indian artisans were remarkable, as was the degree of occupational specialization. Yet modern capitalism did not emerge in India but was finally imported from the West. Weber's question was to what degree the religions of India contributed to this outcome. As of 1911, according to a British census, some 70 percent of Indians were Hindus, and about 21 percent were Muslims. The rest of the population was divided over several minority religions, among them the Buddhists at just over 3 percent. Weber's interest, of course, was in Hinduism and Buddhism.[7]

Hinduism, Weber explained, was an absolutely exclusive religion: the individual was simply born into one of the hierarchically ordered Hindu castes, from the highest-ranking Brahmins on down. Yet entire new peoples could be and were absorbed into the Hindu religion, which engaged in active propaganda and expansion through much of its history. In a typical case, the dominant strata of an animistic tribe or population began by imitating Hindu customs, while refusing to allow their daughters to marry into lower-ranking strata. They then either replaced their priests with Brahmins, usually not the best established among them, or their priests simply claimed to be Brahmins. Finally, there were cases in which so-called "guest peoples" practiced their trades in Hindu communities. If they were considered "unclean" and excluded from intermarriage and joint meals with Hindus, Weber called them "pariah peoples." Though "negatively privileged," they were integrated into the Hindu religion and caste system, and they often ended by requiring the ritual services of Brahmins. Indeed, along with rulers and nobles, whose positions were legitimated by such processes of integration, the Brahmins themselves were the chief beneficiaries of Hindu expansion (*H*, 56–57, 60–71).

The Hindu religion promised its followers several apparently irreconcilable future states: (1) rebirth to a further finite life on earth in a situation at least as favorable as the present one, or rebirth in a paradise, or as a God, again for a finite period, followed by rebirth on earth; (2) rebirth to eternal life in the presence of God, and thus immortality of the soul; or (3) cessation of individual existence through the submersion of the individual soul, either in the "all-one" or in an impersonal "nirvana." For the most distinguished Brahmin sect, the third of these alternatives was the most orthodox, while personal immortality (option 2) was "unclassical," if not actually non-Hindu. Yet even the most "classical" Hindu had the choice between (1) rebirth on earth and (3) cessation of individual existence. Moreover, the means of attaining these religious rewards varied; they could encompass ascetic contemplation, ritual practices, good works, and occupational virtue, or faith. Weber commented upon the extreme tolerance of divergent paths *within* Hinduism, which was clearly not strictly a religion in the Western sense. There were even religious associations open to all comers, and not exclusively determined by birth into a caste. But these movements, which included Buddhism, were considered heterodox by the Brahmins and other Hindu castes (*H,* 77–78).

The heterodoxy of the Buddhists and comparable groups lay in the fact that they freed the individual from his *ritual duties* to his caste, to which Hinduism was more deeply committed than to any element in its doctrine or teaching. Officially, Hinduism had a holy book, the *Veda;* but this was just a collection of more or less ancient songs and ritual formulas. It did not contain anything like a rational ethic, and it failed to mention either the migration of souls, or the *karma* doctrine of reward or retribution in a future life for the believer's actions in this one. Indeed, the *Veda* only belatedly and partly recognized the key institution of the *caste.* The role of the caste within the Hindu social system was dictated by its objective relationship to the highest-ranking caste of the Brahmins. A caste usually encompassed a limited range of occupations, and it thus defined a hereditary social rank, along with specific religious duties (*H,* 80, 82–83, 85–87, 89).

There was a period in Indian history when cities and urban guilds emerged much as they did in the West. But because these institutions rested upon the possibility of common meals and fraternal relationships among urban occupational groups, their further evolution was undercut by the caste system. Merely being seen by a man from a low caste while taking food or drink was ritually damaging to a Brahmin, and intermarriage among castes and subcastes was rare and problematic. Indian rulers and the Brahmins themselves were the chief beneficiaries of the developmental path that essentially replaced guilds and city communes with the ritual exclusivity of the castes. The rank of every caste and subcaste was defined by whether or not the member of a high caste—ultimately a Brahmin—would take food or drink from one of its members, whether the two castes could eat or smoke together, and whether or not the Brahmins would serve members of the lower-ranking caste in the performance of religious rituals (*H*, 92, 94–95, 97–99, 103).

The four main castes—or classes of castes—in the Indian social system were the Brahmins, the nobles or "knights," the "reborn" free men, and the servile castes. The Brahmins were expected to engage in the study of the *Veda*, in ascetic and ritual practices, and the acceptance of gifts or grants of land, never of salaries; the nobles performed military functions and exercised political power. Both the Brahmins and the nobles normally avoided agricultural work, along with the commercial and artisanal trades, which they left to the "free men" and to "pariah peoples," if not to other servile castes. There was a great demand for members of the highest castes in domestic service, since domestics had to be ritually qualified to interact with their employers, and especially to serve them drink. The education of a young Brahmin entailed the memorization of ritual formulas and *Veda* passages, which were orally transmitted by a senior Brahmin. The novice was also subjected to an ascetic regime. His schooling could be considered the awakening of charisma, but the hereditary character of caste membership ultimately overrode more personal views of his qualifications (*H*, 117–23).

In its impact upon the economy, Weber argued, the caste system did not actually forbid the bringing together of workers in a single factory; but it generally reinforced the characteristic traditionalism of the artisans. Where changes of occupation or technology could lead to ritual degradation, innovation of any kind was bound to be unlikely. Even under English rule, only about one-third of 1 percent of the population consisted of industrial workers. These workers were hard to recruit, and their traditional attitudes resembled those of early industrial laborers in Europe. Once they had earned enough to sustain themselves for a time, they retreated to their villages. The only advantage they provided to employers is that caste barriers prevented them from forming trade unions (*H*, 193–97).

The basic axioms common to all of Hinduism, according to Weber, were the transmigration of souls and the associated *karma* doctrine of retribution or reward in a future life for actions performed in this one. In conjunction, these two dogmas provided a social "theodicy," a theological rationalization and symbolic reinforcement of the prevailing social order. Similar theories have appeared in other cultures. But the rationalism of the Brahmins increased its force by emphasizing the *karma* principle that no good or bad action was ever "lost," and that it ultimately affected the place of the agent in the hierarchy of castes. Since it was hard to imagine the individual's ethical balance sheet altering his current life, retribution or reward in a future life was the obvious solution. Birth, in the Hindu social system, was never an accident. Birth in a low caste reflected moral failings in a former life. There was no changing one's social position during one's lifetime, for the caste system was sacrosanct and eternal. The only option, therefore, was the resigned acceptance of one's caste and the pious performance of one's social and ritual duties, with the hope of reward in a future life. Weber characterized the *karma* doctrine as the most rigorously consistent theodicy known to history. It was certainly more effective than the Lutheran injunction to stay in one's profession. Moreover, the lowest castes had most to gain from the pious acceptance of their disadvantages. They were therefore most committed to the caste system as a whole—and thus also to the strictest traditionalism in economic affairs (*H*, 202–8).

Weber warned against reducing the Hindu caste system to racial differences. There certainly were correspondences between caste and skin color: the highest castes were lighter-skinned than the lowest ones. This was partly a consequence of ethnic differences between ancient conquerors and conquered on the Indian subcontinent; but it also reflected the well-known tendency of socially dominant elites to resist the marriage of their daughters to the sons of lower-ranking social groups. Religiously and ritually reinforced by Hinduism, this tendency produced not only enduring ethnic differences, but relatively stable links between castes and ranges of occupations as well. Here again, Weber sought the relevant causes in the retardation of city and guild development, of burgher fraternization, and thus ultimately in the interests of the Indian rulers and Brahmins. The doctrines of Hinduism were not effects of economic conditions, he wrote, but products of the ethical rationalism of an intellectual elite (*H*, 208–9, 211, 213–14, 217–18).

The most threatening aspect of the Hindu world view, for Weber, was the fearful prospect of repeated rebirths or, more specifically, of recurrent deaths. The idea of a future life to compensate for the present one might be reassuring in itself. But what if one reflected upon the total sequence of repeated lives—and deaths? Again and again, the soul was immersed in the interests of a particular life, attached to concerns—and especially to loved ones—only to be torn away from them again, so as to be transported into another life, only to be wrenched away again. It was this senseless prospect that inspired all Hindu salvation religions, including Buddhism. Their quest was for salvation from the senseless "wheel" of recurrent deaths—and thus also of repeated rebirths, or of existence itself (*H*, 219–20).

Like the Confucian mandarins, the Brahmins were a highly educated and dignified literary elite, whose charisma rested upon *knowledge* of rituals and ceremonies laid down in a holy and esoteric literature. Both elites were proud of their learning; both were convinced that knowledge was the cardinal virtue and the source of all blessing, just as ignorance was the cardinal vice. For both elites, what followed was a form of "rationalism" that excluded orgiastic magic, along with all irrational means of salvation. But both elites paid a price for their posture. Particularly at the level of popular religiosity, the Confucian literati faced competition from the magic of Taoist heterodoxy. The Brahmins succeeded in preventing the rise of a hierarchy of priests without schooling in the *Veda*. But they could not stop the development of magic sects and cults, even within their own stratum, which threatened the unity and coherence of their dogma. Whereas the Chinese mandarins were an elite of officials serving a theocratic emperor, moreover, the Brahmins remained a strictly literary elite and lacked all influence in political affairs (*H*, 221, 225–27, 229–33).

The heterodox Indian salvation religions, including Buddhism, developed partly on the basis of Brahmin doctrines and partly in reaction against them. Though well protected against irrational magic, the Brahmins were less on their guard against asceticism and mysticism. The Brahmin novice underwent an ascetic discipline, and the aging Brahmin often retreated from the world as a wandering beggar. The ordinary conduct of the Brahmin too was characterized by ascetic restraint. The routine performance of ritual duties and pious works, however, sufficed only to improve one's chances of a favorable rebirth; it did not lead to "salvation." To be saved from the "wheel" of existence itself, the Brahmins therefore developed rational methods of asceticism and contemplative flight from the world. They pursued extraordinary states of blessed insight, of apathetic ecstasy, and of mystical union with the divine, which ultimately took on an impersonal character (*H*, 239–42, 245–47).

Hindu monasticism originated in voluntary communities formed by revered teachers and their pupils, along with lay sponsors and supporters. There were few formal regulations of monastic life, and even presence in a settlement could be temporary. The whole institution was founded upon the pious bond between a *guru*, a saintly teacher and spiritual leader, and his disciples and clients. The authority of the *guru* over his followers took precedence over the parental authority of the father. The monks were initially wandering beggars, typically Brahmins who chose to "live in the forest," away from worldly duties, so as to spend their old age in contemplation. The religious literature of classical Brahmin asceticism consisted of the products of such contemplation, chiefly interpretive commentaries upon the *Veda*. The "secret" teachings and speculations of Hindu religious literature were couched in a deliberately esoteric sacral language, the Sanskrit. In contrast to the holy writings of the Confucians, however, they were typically transmitted in spoken form. This led to the use of epigrammatic and repetitive formulas and refrains, which facilitated memorization and recitation. The emphasis upon rhetorical metaphors and spiritual meanings reduced the empirical content of Hindu thought. This retarded the development of the natural sciences in India, which also failed to benefit from the decisive Hellenic gift of mathematics (*H*, 251–53, 255–59, 262).

The ascetic practices of Hindu intellectuals, according to Weber, were based upon ancient magic techniques of restricted breathing and self-hypnosis. The inhibition of bodily functions was to serve the goal of contemplation. Yoga was one among a variety of methods used to regulate breathing in pursuit of apathetic ecstasy. Like Buddhism, it unfolded outside the orthodox Brahmin tradition, and its practitioners ultimately formed a caste of their own. The Brahmins themselves adopted techniques designed to "empty consciousness," but their objective was to make room for a mystic *knowledge* rather than an irrationally blissful *feeling* of the divine, although the divide between the two was fluid. In any case, Hindu salvation techniques were meant to offer an escape from everyday life and even from existence itself. The Brahmins' rejection of the world was more radical than that of the Chinese mystics, because the yearning for salvation from the senseless "wheel" of recurrent birth and death was thoroughly grounded in the dominant cosmology. The central question of Hindu philosophy, after all, was how the soul could extricate itself from the world of recurrence in which it was immersed. Outside Brahmin circles, Weber commented, the techniques of Yoga and its irrational aims were linked to belief in a "savior." Such a belief was hard to reconcile with the orthodox *karma* doctrine and the transmigration of souls. At a popular level, nevertheless, savior cults played an important if incongruous role among Indian religions (*H*, 262–70).

Focusing more specifically upon Buddhism, Weber briefly referred to Siddharta or Gautama, who became the Buddha, "the enlightened." Without offering a precise date, Weber associated his flight from the parental home into solitude with the era of Indian city development. In contrast to Confucianism, Buddhism was a strictly apolitical or antipolitical cult. Aided by Yoga techniques and propagated by wandering beggar monks, the cult of the Buddha accepted much of Hindu doctrine while carrying the Brahmins' contemplative retreat from the world to its logical extreme. Though committed to the most radical pursuit of salvation, Buddhism was not properly a salvation religion, because it knew no ethic, no divinity, and no eternal life. The salvation it sought was exclusively a product of the believer's own effort. And what it promised was escape not only from the senseless attachment to existence—and from the recurrence of death—but also from the individual soul. It called for detachment, not from worldly evil, but from the ephemeral beauty and passion of life, including the passion for ideas and the love of one's neighbor. What the Buddhist had to conquer was the "thirst" for life—for desire, action, power, and knowledge—that tied him to a persistent individual soul, and thus to a metaphysically senseless "wheel" of recurrent existence. To liberate himself, he had to overcome stupidity, the cardinal vice of the Buddhists. "Enlightenment," however, was a free gift of grace, a reward for contemplative immersion in the truth that banished illusion and stilled the yearning for life. Salvation could be attained *in this life,* along with a cosmic love of humanity that nevertheless remained detached, at least in theory (*H,* 326, 329–33, 337–40).

The highest stages of Buddhist salvation were open only to monks. But the Buddhist monasteries were not highly regulated, and their influence upon lay followers was not systematically planned. Buddhist communities were thus left with a lack of doctrinal coherence that led to heresies and sect formations. Buddhism was in no way linked to movements of social reform; it tacitly accepted the existing social order, rather than challenging it. The Buddha himself came from a patrician background. On the whole, therefore, Buddhism was a product of positively privileged strata. Nevertheless, it became one of the world's greatest missionary religions. This is hard to explain, unless one recognizes that the virtuosi of the Buddhist path were *psychologically* inclined, regardless of their doctrine, to proselytize in behalf of the euphoric stillness that was the aim of their quest (*H,* 356–58, 361–63, 365–66).

Toward the end of "Hinduism and Buddhism," Weber drew a series of conclusions about Asian salvation doctrines in general while treating the Indian religions as outstanding exemplars of Asian thought. Asian salvation doctrines, he argued, almost invariably held out one set of religious promises for those able to live exemplary lives and another for ordinary laymen. This was true partly because of the divide that separated the educated elites from the rest of the population, but it also reflected the related presupposition that salvation originated in *knowledge.* The knowledge involved, to be sure, was not about this world, about the laws of nature or of social life; rather, it was knowledge about the "meaning" of existence. Such knowledge was neither sought nor attained by Western science or scholarship; it did not convey means of rationally mastering the world and other men. Instead, it offered a "worldview," an essentially mystical knowledge attained by means of rigorous techniques of ascetic contemplation. It not only taught believers how to act; it also brought them the blissful possession of a state that was described as "emptiness" and detachment from the world. Asian intellectuals could never believe that actions in a finite life could be rewarded or punished for eternity. For them, the world was governed by the determinism of the *karma* doctrine. What they primarily sought was escape from the wheel of existence. But they had little to offer to the economically active groups within their populations. The Hindu caste system was the most consistent "organic" social theory ever devised, but it also perpetuated an extreme economic traditionalism. Beyond that, the esoteric doctrines of the Asian intellectuals channeled the less educated members of their societies toward the popular "savior" cults or into the world of the magicians (*H*, 528–33).

No path led from the Asian "garden of magic" to the rationalization of conduct. There was a contrast between the divine and the worldly. But in Asia, that contrast was never a confrontation between an ethical God and the power of "sin" that could be transcended through active engagement in the world. Instead, the opposition was between ecstatic passivity and a senseless reality, which could not be overcome through rational action. Whenever an intellectual stratum has sought to discern the "meaning" of the world, Weber wrote, it has been led into the realm of Indian mysticism. And wherever it has deliberately pursued the beauty and dignity of worldly perfection, it has been led to the Confucian ideal. Asian culture has been composed of these intersecting and complementary strivings. The active response to the "demands of the day" that characterizes the Western "personality" was as far removed from Asian conceptions as the rationalism that seeks to master the world by uncovering the impersonal laws that govern it. Since neither the mystic nor the aesthetic goals of Asian intellectuals spoke to the mass of their active fellow men, moreover, a gulf opened between the educated elites and the "masses." While the Asian intellectuals followed "exemplary" prophets and wise men, the uneducated were left without a "missionary prophecy." A unique constellation of historical circumstances led to the rise of such a prophecy in the Near East—and thus in the West (*H*, 534–36, 542–44). Without that constellation, the development of the West would have followed the Asian path.[8]

CHAPTER SIX

From History to Sociology

There was a shift in Max Weber's approach about 1909–1910, a change in his emphasis and in the breadth of his perspective, if not in his method. We have already considered his comparative study on the "economic ethics of the world religions," which became a kind of universal history. But even while pursuing that project during the last decade of his life, he also worked on a massive handbook on the interrelationships between the economy and other sectors of the social system, including law, politics, and social stratification. One way to describe his shift of emphasis is to say that he moved from history to sociology.

The year 1909 was marked by two outward occasions that signaled Weber's change of direction. In August of that year, he declined an invitation to join the Baden Academy of Sciences, expressing his dissatisfaction with the disciplinary emphasis within that organization. Apart from the natural sciences, he argued, the Academy really represented only philosophy, philology, and especially history. The systematic social sciences, by contrast were totally neglected, and this was unlikely to change, given the "stifling overemphasis upon the historical approach" [*Historismus*]. Throughout 1909, in fact, Weber worked to organize the German Society for Sociology. He tried to bring together a wide range of views on the study of society, including racist theories he personally rejected. A rigorous distinction between science and value judgment, he hoped, would permit scholars of radically divergent commitments to work together, as he explained in his report to the first annual conference of the society. Unfortunately, his efforts proved fruitless. Personal sensitivies and the vexed issue of value judgments led to the disruption of meetings, and Weber resigned from the society in 1912. Nevertheless, the whole episode reflected his determination to encourage systematic work in the social sciences.[1]

ECONOMY AND SOCIETY

In 1910, as Wolfgang Schluchter has demonstrated, Weber began to draft contributions to the handbook we have come to know as *Economy and Society*. One of his earliest contributions was an essay on the sociology of religion that reflected his concurrent project on the economic ethics of the world religions. After Weber's death in 1920, his wife Marianne and the Weber scholar Johannes Winckelmann published all the handbook manuscripts he had left behind as if they formed a single unit. They believed that Weber had always intended to offer a systematic conceptual exposition, followed by a collection of empirical examples. They applied this binary scheme to supplement the theoretical chapters Weber had written since the war (which they called part 1) with every older, presumably illustrative text they could find (as part 2), despite the repetitions and incongruities that resulted. They substituted the title *Economy and Society* for Weber's own *The Economy and the Social Orders and Powers*.[2] For us, the shorter title may serve, but we will focus upon the later part 1, and only occasionally draw upon congruent portions of the earlier part 2.

The new elements in Weber's later works were his frequent recourse to comparison and his predominant interest in persistent historical structures. Remember, however, that his model of singular causal analysis could be applied not only to such small-scale events as the Defenestration of Prague, but also to such large-scale structural conditions and developments as "feudalism" and the rise of modern capitalism. After all, there is no clear divide between microscopic and macroscopic events, conditions, and processes. No matter how broad the questions he addressed, therefore, Weber could remain a methodological individualist. At least in principle, his focus was upon the actions and beliefs of individuals, and this preference grew directly out of his commitment to the interpretive method. Single individuals and their actions are the atoms of sociology, he argued, precisely because they are the objects of interpretation. For other analytical purposes, human beings may be bundles of psychophysical processes, but as the performers of actions and holders of beliefs, they cannot be reduced below the level of the individual. "For the same reason, the individual is also . . . the upper limit [of analysis], and the sole bearer of meaningful behavior." Jurists might find it helpful to refer to states and other organizations *as if* they were individuals. For the interpretive sociologist, however, social entities and structures are strictly patterns of individual actions. An "action," to recall Weber's definition, is linked to a "subjective meaning"; a "social action" is "oriented in its progression to the behavior of others," and sociology as a discipline "seeks interpretively to understand social action and thereby causally to explain it in its progression and in its effects."[3]

In practice, Weber transcended the limits laid down in these initial stipulations, and he did so partly by aggregating the actions to be interpreted. "Understanding . . . signifies the interpretation of the meaning or complex of meanings (a) actually intended in a particular case, or (b) intended on the average and approximately, or (c) to be constructed . . . for the pure type (ideal type) of a frequent phenomenon. The concepts and 'laws' posited by pure economic theory, for example, are such ideal-typical constructions" (4). One of the functions of the ideal type, in other words, was hypothetically to characterize collective actions as more or less rational responses to given situations and thus causally to ascribe aspects of actual group behavior to the circumstances and orientations covered by the type. As we know, ideal-typical analysis could move through several stages, aiming at successively closer approximations to observed sequences of behavior.

Of further consequence was Weber's definition of "social action" in terms of the expectations of others. And from social actions Weber moved naturally and easily to "social relationships" and "social formations." A "social relationship," in Weber's definition, consists of "behaviors of several persons that are adjusted and oriented in their meanings to their mutual interdependence." Social relationships may be as open and transitory as an economic exchange, or they may be relatively closed and enduring "formations" *(Gebilde)*, as in the case of an artisanal guild or a political state. "The social relationship consists . . . exclusively of the chance that actions specifically oriented to each other in their meanings have taken place, even when [the relationships] are such . . . "social formations" as a "state." . . . [Thus] a "state" . . . ceases to exist sociologically as soon as the chance has faded that certain kinds of meaningfully oriented social actions will take place." The recourse to "chance" or probability is highly characteristic of Weber; his tactics of definition were designed to replace essentialist conceptions of social institutions and collectivities. His line of analysis allowed him to move from individual behaviors to complex social interactions and organizations. He could stipulate that a state exists or "has ceased to exist," and that was surely to make a statement about a structured collectivity (13).

One must also remember that Weber's theory of action extended well beyond the realm of deliberate and reflected agency. Like action generally, Weber held, social action may be "purposively rational"; "value-rational" (motivated by "conscious belief in the . . . value of a certain behavior . . . independently of its success"); "emotional"; or "traditional," sustained by accustomed usage. And of course he took real actions to be mixtures of these "pure" types. In any case, rational action itself, while methodologically significant as a point of departure, was never more than a limiting case in Weber's overall scheme. Indeed, he repeatedly called attention to actions performed in a less than fully conscious way. "In the vast majority of cases," he wrote, "action takes place in dull semi-consciousness or unconsciousness." Only occasionally do some individuals raise the meanings of their actions to full consciousness. It is therefore often the sociologists, rather than the agents they seek to understand, who conceptualize behaviors by classifying them in terms of "possibly intended meanings." As Weber knew perfectly well, finally, most human actions have consequences other than those anticipated by the agents involved, and this even if the actions are performed in a fully deliberate way (10 – 12).

In sum, Weber's account of human action provides for a wide spectrum of motives and behaviors. He never abandoned his commitment to the rational individual as the starting heuristic of the interpretive method. Yet his theory of action ultimately extended well beyond this foundation, to a complex model in which behaviors may be not only irrational or habitual, but also largely unconscious—and productive of outcomes that bear little relationship to the motives and beliefs of the agents involved. From 1910 on, Weber explicitly distinguished the work of the sociologist from that of the historian. He thought it possible to detect "regularities" in the realm of social action, cases in which similar "meanings" lead to similar "progressions" of behavior. Sociology, he argued, is concerned with such "types" of progressions, whereas history engages in the causal analysis of significant "singular relationships": "Sociology develops . . . typological concepts and seeks general rules about events. This in contrast to history, which pursues the causal analysis . . . of individual, culturally significant actions, structures and personalities. . . . [Sociology] forms its concepts and seeks its rules primarily with a view to whether it can thereby serve the causal attribution of . . . [singular] historical phenomena" (9). Sociology is here plainly described as a generalizing, regularity-seeking discipline, rather than a historical one; a clear line is drawn between the two approaches. On the other hand, sociology is assigned the task of facilitating the causal analysis of singular historical phenomena. The objects of historical understanding are still contemporary outcomes that strike the investigator as culturally significant. There is no suggestion that the historian's findings are interesting primarily as elements in the generalizations of the sociologist. Nor is sociology subordinated to history; the two disciplines are thoroughly interdefined. The difference between them is more a matter of emphasis than of principle, especially since Weber's account of causal analysis in history always encompassed typological tactics and the recourse to "nomological" knowledge.

Turning to the special domain of sociology in the opening chapter of *Economy and Society*, Weber considered the sources of observed *regularities* in both the inner meanings and the outward progressions of human actions. Such regularities could reflect the mere fact of unthinking repetition, or *usage (Brauch)*; or it could be imbedded in long-accustomed practice, or *custom (Sitte)*. Custom, in contrast to *convention* and *law*, Weber wrote, is not supported by external sanctions of any kind, though the transition from custom to convention and law may be gradual. A wholly different set of regularities of action, on the other hand, may occur if multiple agents pursue identical ends in a purposively rational *(zweckrational)* way. The actions of economic agents in a "free" market environment are obvious examples. The discipline of (neoclassical) economics emerged as the study of such behavior. But in other realms as well, unthinking immersion in inherited custom, like affective action, may be replaced by the deliberate adjustment to interest constellations. That is one form of the "rationalization" of action. "Value rationalization" *(Wertrationalisierung)* is another (15–16).

Actions, particularly social actions and social relationships, Weber continued, may be affected by the agents' belief in the existence of a legitimate *order (Ordnung)*; the "chance" of their being thus affected constitutes the *validity (Geltung)* of the order. The order encompasses identifiable norms or rules of conduct, and the agents believe that these maxims are binding. This will lead to regularities in the orientation of action even apart from custom and interest, and even though some individuals may circumvent the stipulated rules of conduct, rather than follow them. The legitimacy of an order may be subjectively guaranteed in a purely *affective* manner, through emotional devotion to it; or in a *value-rational (wertrational)* way, through belief in its validity as the expression of ultimate values; or *religiously*, through the belief that salvation depends upon it. Or it may be guaranteed by the expectation of certain external consequences. Thus a convention is externally guaranteed by the chance that deviation from it will meet with disapproval, while law is externally guaranteed by the chance of physical or psychological coercion by a staff of people assigned the task of such coercion (16–17, 19).

A social relationship, as Weber further stipulated, shall be termed *communal (Vergemeinschaftung)* where the orientation of social action rests upon the subjective (affective or traditional) feeling among the participants that they belong together. The relationship shall be termed *societal (Vergesellschaftung)* where the orientation rests upon a rationally motivated adjustment or conjunction of interests. It is typically based upon mutual consent; social action under such an agreement is oriented value-rationally, through the agent's sense of obligation, or means-ends rationally *(zweckrational)*, in the expectation that the other participants will conform as well. Weber here deliberately narrowed and specified Tönnies's contrasts in *Community and Society*. The purest types of societal relationships, he wrote, are market exchanges and organized interest groups, but also value-rational sects, for example. The family is the most obvious example of a communal relationship. The large majority of real social relationships are partly communal and partly societal in character (21–23).

Power (Macht), for Weber, is the chance of asserting one's own will even against the resistance of others within a social relationship, regardless of what it is based upon. *Domination (Herrschaft)* is the chance of obtaining obedience among certain persons for an order with a given content. An organization is a *ruling organization* in so far as its members are subject to domination by virtue of an established order. Such an organization is termed *political* if its existence and the validity of its order are continuously guaranteed within a certain territory by the application or threat of physical force by an administrative staff. A compulsory political organization is termed a *state (Staat)* if its administrative staff successfully maintains the monopoly of legitimate physical violence for the enforcement of its orders. A *hierocratic organization* guarantees its order by offering or denying religious benefits, rather than through the use of force. A *church* is a hierocratic organization that claims a monopoly of hierocratic coercion. In concluding the first chapter of *Economy and* Society in a section entitled "Basic Concepts," Weber explicitly rejected traditional attempts to define the state in terms of its purposes in favor of the focus upon "violence" as the "indispensable means" (28–30).

In the second chapter of *Economy and Society,* Weber dealt with *economic action (Wirtschaften),* which he defined as the peaceful exploitation of the power of disposition over resources in a purposively rational way. An *economic enterprise (Wirtschaftsbetrieb)* is a continuously acting economic organization. Weber emphasized the importance of having disposition over resources. He observed that in any type of economy, this power of disposition must be allocated to someone, though the principles of its distribution in a private economy will differ from those prevailing under socialism. Following the Austrian school of marginal utility economics, Weber defined *utilities (Nutzleistungen)* as *chances* of present or future use that become objects of *provision (Fürsorge)* for one or more economic agents. Such utilities may be objects or *goods,* or they may be human *services. Economic chances* are the chances offered an economic agent or enterprise by custom, by the constellation of interests, or by a conventionally or legally guaranteed order. The orientation of economic action is usually rational, but the influence of tradition may be significant even when economic action has been extensively rationalized. Typical measures of rational economic action are (1) the systematic allocation of utilities between present and future uses *(saving),* or (2) between several possible uses in the order of their urgency, according to the principle of marginal utility; (3) the systematic procurement (through production or transport) of utilities for which the means of procurement are at the disposition of the enterprise; (4) the systematic acquisition of the power to manage utilities, including through *exchange (Tausch).* Such exchange is an economic compromise between the partners to it, and it may be traditional or economically rational in orientation.[4]

Weber distinguished between two types of economically active organizations: a *wirtschaftender Verband,* which acts economically in pursuit of primarily non-economic objectives, and a *Wirtschaftsverband,* which acts primarily in pursuit of economic objectives. But even more important to him was the divide between such economically active organizations and organizations that either *regulate* the economic activity of their members *(wirschaftsregulierender Verbände)* or merely provide an *order* of formal norms and rules for the autonomous economic action of their members and guarantee the chances thus offered *(Ordnungsverbände).* As examples of such *regulative organization,* he cited medieval towns and village associations, guilds, trade unions, and cartels, but also modern states that seek to control economic activity in comparable ways. As a pure *Ordnungsverband,* he cited the modern "legal state" *(Rechtsstaat),* which takes a laissez-faire attitude toward the economic activity of households and enterprises, merely maintaining a legal framework for the settlement of disputes about contractual obligations.[5]

Analyzing *means of exchange,* Weber briefly dealt with exchanges in kind and with symbolic tokens and the grounds of their acceptance within certain regions and periods. But he moved on fairly quickly to various types of money, which can be issued, guaranteed (and manipulated) by dominant organizations of various kinds. The primary consequence of the use of money, Weber wrote, is *indirect exchange* as a means of meeting the needs of consumers, that is, the possibility of separating the goods desired from those offered in exchange, not only in place, in time, and in the persons involved, but also in the quantities desired and offered. Following Simmel, Weber stressed the immense expansion of exchange that resulted from this separation, along with the option of deferring obligations in the form of monetary debts. Moreover, money can be *stored,* either in specie or in claims to payment on demand. Economic chances are increasingly transformed into dispositions over money. A qualitative *individuation* and a corresponding expansion of consumption follow for the economically advantaged. There are other consequences of the use of money, but the most important among them is the possibility of *monetary calculation (Geldrechnung),* that is, of estimating the money value of all goods and services that may be exchanged. Indeed, the *market situation (Marktlage)* of an object of exchange is the chance of exchanging it for money as estimated by all participants in the competitive struggle for economic advantage.[6]

In a particularly interesting passage, Weber characterized the *formal rationality* of an economic action as the degree to which *calculation* is technically possible and actually applied in it. The *substantive rationality,* by contrast, is the degree to which the provisioning of human groups is shaped by *normative postulates.* Substantive rationality, Weber observed, judges economic action and its consequences in terms of "ethical, political, utilitarian, status, egalitarian," or other "demands" in a "substantively value-rational" way. The possible standards of such value-rationality are numerous. Money is technically the most perfect means of economic calculation, and thus the most formally rational means of orienting economic action. *Monetary calculation,* not the actual use of money, is what matters. Its consequences include the prior quantitative estimation of the chances of any projected economic action and the subsequent recalculation of its results in terms of *cost* and *yield,* along with the adjustment of consumption to the calculated data on the principle of marginal utility. Weber added that any economic unit engaged in the use and procurement of goods, whether through production or exchange, for consumption or further production, must have a *budget (Haushaltsplan).*[7]

Rounding out his roster of the basic concepts of economic action, Weber dealt with *acquisition (Erwerb),* by which he meant the making of economic gains. He defined *Erwerben,* or profit-making, as oriented to the chances of gaining additional powers of disposition over goods. Economic acquisition is peaceful and usually oriented to the exploitation of the market situation of goods. *Capital accounting (Kapitalrechnung),* a form of monetary calculation, is the assessment of the chances for profit-making ventures by means of a comparison between the money value of the total assets initially committed to a venture and those still at hand or newly acquired at its end.[8] Capital accounting as the basic form of economic calculation, Weber observed, arose only in the West.[9]

Having defined *domination* as the chance of obtaining obedience to specific orders among a given group of people, Weber added that in all but marginal cases of enslavement, obedience is at least partly voluntary. Routine compliance may be based upon custom and material interest. Yet domination is likely to prove unstable, unless it is believed to be *legitimate* in some valid sense. Weber distinguished three "pure types of legitimate domination" or "authority," depending upon whether their claims to legitimacy are primarily "rational" and "legal," "traditional," or "charismatic" in character. The scheme of three "pure" or "ideal" types, he hastened to add, cannot encompass the whole of historical reality.[10]

Deliberately beginning with the most modern form of authority, so as to prepare the way for comparisons and contrasts, Weber first fully characterized "legal domination with a bureaucratic administrative staff." Legal or "rational" authority rests upon the acceptance of several interconnected ideas, among them the belief that any set of laws (a) may be established by agreement or imposition, on purposively rational or value-rational grounds, (b) with a claim to obedience, at least among members of the relevant organization, and (c) that law is a complex of internally consistent abstract rules applied to particular cases in legal practice and binding upon the administration of the organization. It follows that the person in authority is also governed by an "impersonal order," and that the members of the organization (including the citizens of a state) merely obey "the law." Rational legal domination entails the rule-bound conduct of official business, within specified spheres of competence or jurisdiction, by an "administrative agency" *(Behörde)*. There is a hierarchy of offices: lower-ranking offices are under the supervision of higher ones, to which they have the right to appeal. The rule-bound conduct of office requires "specialized training" *(Fachschulung)*. Modern rational organizations of all kinds normally depend upon an administrative staff of trained officials. These officials are in principle "expropriated" from ownership of the means of production or administration. The "purest type" of rational legal domination, Weber wrote, employs a bureaucratic administrative staff. Only the head of the organization holds his position by virtue of appropriation, election, or succession. His subordinates are individual officials (not collegial bodies) recruited into a fixed hierarchy of offices on the basis of qualifications that may be ascertained by examinations and certified by diplomas. They are salaried and often pensioned, and they regard their work as a full-time career (*T*, 124–27).

Weber wrote with something like anxiety about the "fatefulness" of bureaucracy in modern life. Bureaucracy is inescapable, he argued, because it is the most efficient, the most calculable, and thus "formally the most rational" means of exercising authority. One may grumble about it, but there is no escaping it, no alternative to the specialized knowledge that sustains it. Historically, the development of bureaucratic administration was the breeding ground of the modern state. Modern technology and the modern economic system could not function without bureaucracy as the indispensable means of control. At bottom, bureaucracy means domination by means of knowledge, and that accounts for its specifically rational character. Though its technical mastery and its control of the relevant documents would suffice to ensure its predominance, it also deploys the concept of "official secrets" to ward off interference from "amateurs"—who may be its political superiors. The decisive question is always, who controls the bureaucratic apparatus? and the capitalist entrepreneur alone is "relatively" immune from bureaucratic domination within his domain. The outlook of the official is shaped by a sense of duty to the office; he acts in a spirit of "impersonality," without hatred and passion, but also without love and enthusiasm. In that sense too, his approach is "formal," though he may be tempted to imagine himself the beneficiary of his clients (*T*, 128–30).

The second type of legitimate domination or authority, according to Weber, rests upon belief in the sanctity of rules and powers that have "always existed." "Reverent loyalty," sustained in the simplest case by common upbringing, is directed toward a personal "lord"; the administrative staff consists of personal "servants," rather than officials; and the ruled are not "members" of the organization, but either "comrades" *(Genossen)* or "subjects" *(Untertanen)*. Obedience is due not to rules but to the person of the ruler, who either occupies his position by tradition or has been chosen for it by a traditional lord. His commands are obeyed either because they follow from tradition, whose transgression could endanger his position, or in virtue of his discretion within limits set by tradition. If the ruler's actions provoke resistance, it is directed against the person of the lord who has exceeded the bounds of tradition, not against tradition itself. Laws or rules cannot be newly created under traditional authority; they can only be "recognized" to have always existed by "wise insight" *(Weistum)*, and legal findings can be based only upon precedent (*T*, 130–31).

The most primitive types of traditional authority are "gerontocracy," the primacy of elders within loosely affiliated groups, and "patriarchalism," hereditary rule within familial or economic households. Both of these function without a staff. Under "patrimonialism," by contrast, the traditional lord rules with an administrative staff that is recruited either among kinsmen, clients, and holders of household offices ("ministeriales"), or among personal favorites, vassals, and free men who become patrimonial officials out of loyalty to the lord. As Weber points out, bureaucracy originated in patrimonial states, but the officials initially lacked fixed spheres of competence, a rational hierarchy of offices and of advancement, money salaries, and specialized training. Administrative tasks and powers were individually assigned by the lord, often as extensions of household offices. "Sultanism" was a variant of patrimonialism in which the discretionary power of the ruler reached a maximum (*T*, 131–33).

"Estate-type domination" *(ständische Herrschaft),* in Weber's scheme, is an interestingly limited form of patrimonial authority, in which the administrative staff appropriates certain ruling powers and economic chances. An association or an individual may appropriate such powers and chances, whether for life, on a hereditary basis, or as outright property. The lord's discretion in the selection of his administrative staff is accordingly limited. The holders of military powers and chiefs of feudal armies may equip themselves and possibly their followers as well. The appropriators may meet the costs of administration from their own resources, or the provision of the means of administration may become the object of an enterprise based upon fixed contributions from the lord, as in the mercenary armies of early modern Europe (*T*, 134). Patrimonial retainers may eat at the lord's table, or they may hold "benefices," drawing their support from the lord's magazines or treasury, from the use of "service land," or from appropriated rents, fees, or taxes, all in a pattern Weber termed "prebendalism" (*T*, 136–37). Under "feudalism," seigneurial powers are granted to qualified individuals as "fiefs," in exchange for military and administrative services, by way of *personal* contracts between the vassal and the lord that are oriented to conventional concepts of knightly status, honor, and mutual loyalty. Under "prebendalism," resources are committed to followers by way of rent-yielding *fiscal* contracts. Weber called attention to the precarious character of patrimonial power under "feudalism," "prebendalism," and "estate-type division of power," in which individuals or organizations of those holding appropriated seigneurial powers reach unstable compromises with their overlords in political and administrative matters (*T*, 148–51).

In its impact upon economic action, traditional authority usually strengthens traditional attitudes, especially under gerontocracy and patriarchalism, where in the absence of an administrative staff, legitimacy depends exclusively upon all-pervasive tradition. Beyond that, much depends upon the economic means by which patrimonial rule is sustained. Production by an extended household (*oikos*), exchanges in kind, and an emphasis upon consumption will tend to limit the use of money and thus reduce the calculability of economic enterprise. The monopolies of patrimonial rulers and of their partly independent retainers may irrationally restrain the development of the market and of capitalism. Patriarchal and patrimonial rulers may also be tempted to regulate economic action in the name of commitments to social welfare and other forms of substantive rationality, at the expense of the formal rationality of law. For all these reasons, patrimonial rule normally encourages political and adventure capitalism, rather than modern market capitalism and the rational organization of free labor (*T*, 137–39).

One of the most difficult passages in *Economy and Society* deals with "charismatic domination" or authority. Weber's analysis is complex enough to encourage simplifications and misunderstandings, so that a really close reading is called for. Inspired by Rudolf Sohm's historical account of ancient Christian concepts, Weber initially defined charisma as a "quality" of a personality that "is considered extraordinary" *(eine als ausseralltäglich geltende Qualität)*. This quality consists of supernatural or superhuman gifts, and its "God-sent" possessor is esteemed a "leader" (*T*, 124). Weber noted that the quality may originally have been "magically" grounded, and he offered a variety of examples, from prophets to heroic warlords, and from ancient shamans to the revolutionary "litterateur" Kurt Eisner, undone by his "success as a demagogue." In any case, the "validity" *(Geltung)* of charismatic authority depends upon the "recognition" *(Anerkennung)* of those subject to it. Such recognition is born of devotion to a revelation, hero worship, or trust in the leader; it is guaranteed by "proof" *(Bewährung)* that was originally a miracle. But if charisma is genuine, recognition is not considered the basis of the claim to legitimacy. Instead, those subject to charismatic authority are in duty bound to recognize and obey it. On the other hand, if the leader's charisma fails to prove itself, in that it does not ensure the subjects' well-being, then it is likely to fade (*T*, 140).

In some sense, all legitimacy rests upon the subjects' acceptance of it, but a leader's charisma, it seems to me, is more specifically an *attributed* quality, rather than one "objectively" lodged in his personality. The active role played by the subjects of charismatic domination is underlined by Weber's emphasis upon the "psychological" origins of their "personal devotion" to the leader in "enthusiasm or need and hope." If we consult a couple of pages from the earlier part 2 of *Economy and Society*, we find Weber writing about the "natural" leaders who emerge under conditions of desperate "psychological, physical, economic, ethical, religious [or] political need" *(Not)*. If a charismatic leader arises in such an "extraordinary situation," it seems to me, he must credibly define the relevant *need* and display the extraordinary gifts that will allow him to overcome it. If those to whom he feels sent do not recognize his mission, his claim to legitimacy "collapses," as Weber suggested, almost immediately. Thus it may be as important to understand the "extraordinary situation" to which the charismatic leader responds—and the psychology of those in need—as it is to comprehend the extraordinary qualities they recognize in him. Perhaps more than one candidate for charismatic leadership will come forward under conditions extraordinary enough to raise messianic hopes, though Weber does not say so. Still, the whole phenomenon of "charisma" may be best understood as a social interaction rather than a miracle.[11]

Those subject to charismatic authority, according to Weber, form an emotional "community" *(Gemeinde)*. The charismatic leader's staff is not made up of officials. It is not selected on the basis of specialized training, of status privilege, or of personal or household dependency. Instead, the staff is chosen for its own charismatic qualities. The prophet has his "disciples"; the warrior hero, his military guard; and the leader more generally, his trusted advisers. There are no designated spheres of competence, no hierarchy of offices, no salary, but also no benefices to be exploited. The leader designates or "calls" his closest followers, who live with him in a communism of love or comradeship, from means provided by voluntary benefactors. There are neither abstract legal rules nor precedents to be interpreted in rational or traditional legal practice, for the charismatic leader issues new substantive commandments from case to case, according to the proposition "It is written, but I say unto you." Obedience to his commandments is a duty. In its extraordinary character, charismatic authority stands in sharp contrast not only to rational legal, but also to traditional authority. Both are everyday forms of authority, whereas charismatic authority is extraordinary. Bureaucratic domination is specifically rational, in that it is bound to discursive rules that are subject to analysis, whereas charismatic authority is irrational in its freedom from rules. Traditional authority is tied to the precedents of the past, whereas charismatic authority overthrows the past and is in that sense specifically revolutionary (*T*, 141).

Pure charisma ignores economic considerations; it constitutes a calling in the emphatic sense of a mission. A charismatic warrior hero and his guard may seek "booty"; a plebiscitarian ruler or charismatic party leader needs material means of power and prestige. But all genuinely charismatic prophets and leaders repudiate the entanglement in the everyday world that inevitably accompanies the routine, traditional, or rational pursuit of economic gain. Members of mendicant orders refused to hold church offices, and most prophets were originally sustained by gifts from wealthy believers. Among the disciples of a modern aesthetic prophet like Stefan George (whom Weber disliked), economic independence may consist in living on income from property as a "rentier." In epochs bound to tradition, however, charisma is the most important revolutionary power. It differs from the equally revolutionary power of "reason," which either works from without, through changes in the conditions and problems of life, and thus indirectly in orientations toward them, or else through the "intellectualization" of the individual. Charisma, born of "need and enthusiasm," however, means a transformation *from within,* a change in the main direction of action and concern, a complete reorientation of attitudes to all aspects of life and to the world itself. In pre-rationalistic epochs, tradition and charisma between them divided up almost the whole range of orientations to action (*T,* 142).

To the extent that charismatic authority lies outside the everyday realm, Weber argued, it really exists in "ideal-typical purity" only *in statu nascendi;* it is inherently short-lived. If, nevertheless, it is to become an enduring social relationship, its character must change. The motives behind its transformation are the ideal or material interests of the followers in the continuation of the community, and the even stronger interests of the staff of immediate followers, disciples, or advisers, who want to perpetuate the existing social relationship in a way that will put their own positions on an enduring basis. These interests become particularly pressing at the death of the charismatic leader, given the unavoidable problem of succession. The way in which that problem is solved will decisively shape subsequent social relationships. As Weber specified possible solutions, he also observed that charismatic legitimacy was shifted in each case from the person of the leader to aspects of its transmission or "routinization" *(Veralltäglichung).* Thus if a charismatic successor is chosen because he has certain characteristics, then his legitimacy will be associated with the rules that are used to identify those characteristics. If there is recourse to an oracle, the drawing of lots, or other techniques designed to reveal the new leader, then his legitimacy will depend upon the correct application of these techniques. If a charismatic leader or the charismatic staff designate a successor who is then accepted by the community, such acceptance must not be misconstrued as a "vote," partly because a "false" designation is a wrong that calls for expiation. The symbolic means of designation, however, will come to be regarded as the source of the legitimacy that is conferred. A partial "traditionalization" and/or "legalization" of charismatic legitimacy will be the result. In two important approaches to the problem of succession, finally, charisma is held to be either a quality of the "blood" ("hereditary charisma") or a characteristic attached to an office ("charisma of office"). Hereditary charisma derives from law and tradition, and is not attached to the personality of the heir. The elevation of an aspirant to the priesthood or the ministry through the laying on of hands or other symbolic rituals is a good example of the "objectification" *(Versachlichung)* of charisma and of its investment in an office (*T*, 142–44).

Most of the disciples and immediate followers of the charismatic leader, too, must make a living out of their calling. The routinization of charisma therefore also leads to the appropriation of power and of economic chances by the followers, and to the regulation of their recruitment. Since genuine charismatic recruitment seeks charismatic qualities in persons, its routinization must set traditional or rational norms for the training and assessment of recruits. Charisma cannot be "taught" or "instilled"; it can only be "awakened" and "tested." All forms of ascetic preparation and all "novitiates" tend to regulate access to the administrative staff, since only the proven novice is allowed to exercise authority. Indeed, charismatic selection may easily give rise to traditional estate-type authority, particularly on the basis of "hereditary charisma." Weber defined a "clan state" *(Geschlechterstaat)* as one in which all governing powers, benefices, and economic chances are held on the principle of hereditary charisma. The creation and appropriation of ruling positions and economic chances for individual members of a charismatic staff may variously produce benefices, patrimonial or bureaucratic offices, or fiefs. The stream of originally charismatic authority is thus ultimately channeled into any of the several forms of traditional and rational authority. In the process of this channeling, however, charisma is invariably adjusted to everyday conditions, including the economic ones it originally ignored. The charismatic origins of the resulting forms of authority do leave a trace in the "status honor" *(ständische Ehre)* or prestige of those exercising various levels of authority (*T*, 144–46).

Toward the end of his extended discussion of legitimate domination, Weber repeated what he had written at the outset: that the three "pure types" of authority are rarely if ever to be found in reality. Virtually all ruling organizations are mixtures of the pure types. The basis of voluntary obedience, after all, is the belief in the legitimacy of the ruling powers, and this belief is never quite free of ambiguity. The belief in the legality of the ruler, for example, is likely to be at least partly grounded in habit and lived experience, which makes it partly traditional in character. Similarly, as we have seen, purely charismatic authority is inherently transitory; its routinization engenders partly traditional, and partly rational and legal forms of authority. All organized domination is further characterized by the development of the crucial relationship between the ruler and his administrative staff. Indeed, the social origins and especially the education of the administrative staff decisively affect the whole course of cultural development, because they jointly define the status order (*T*, 153–55).

Following upon his analysis of charismatic authority, finally, Weber wrote of the "anti-authoritarian reinterpretation" *(herrschaftsfremde Umdeutung)* of charisma. The label is odd, since it seems to break with Weber's whole conception of "authority" or legitimate domination as one capable of eliciting a degree of voluntary obedience. Yet Weber's meaning is clear enough. He recalls that a genuine charismatic community is in duty bound to recognize the authority of a proven charismatic leader, and he then suggests that this recognition may be "rationalized" and transformed into the vote of a democratic constituency. The "reinterpretation" lies in the fact that this vote now becomes the source of charismatic authority, rather than a consequence of its obligatory acceptance. A democratic electorate, in short, may appoint or dismiss its leader at will. One possible outcome is "plebiscitary" rule of the Napoleonic type; another is the rule of mass party leaders in modern democracies. Where the "voting principle" is extended to the administrative staff, as in the United States, the leader will be served by political clients and benefactors, rather than by a professional hierarchy of trained officials. As a "precision instrument," Weber comments, such a politically constituted staff, will rank well below a bureaucracy of appointed and salaried officials (*T*, 155–56).

"Plebiscitary democracy," in Weber's account, is the most important type of what he called "leadership democracy." The authority of the political chief, mass party leader, or demagogue is based upon the personal trust and devotion of his followers. Like other charismatic leaders, revolutionary dictators from antiquity to modern times have been indifferent to tradition and legality, but they have not escaped the routinization of their charisma. The impact of democratically transformed charisma upon the economy may be positive if it gives rise to rationality, to *formal* legality, and to an efficient bureaucracy; it will be negative if the plebiscitary leader pursues *substantively* rational objectives through inspired summary, or "khadi justice," or if he relies upon an elected staff of political patrons and clients. Plebiscitary leadership democracy, for Weber, is just the opposite of "leaderless democracy," and has to be understood in the broader context of Weber's politics, which we took up in an earlier chapter.[12] That leaves the contrast between an appointed bureaucracy as a "precision instrument" and an elected staff of clients and patrons. The "paradigm," of the latter, Weber wrote, is the United States: "Asked why they allowed themselves to be governed by corrupt party men, an Anglo-American worker answered . . . because 'in our big country,' millions could be stolen [without harm], and because . . . we can 'spit on' these 'professionals,' whereas trained officials of the German kind would 'spit on us'" (T, 158). In telling this memorable story, Weber meant to suggest that corruption is affordable only where resources are virtually unlimited. Yet he was also alert to the status issues at the heart of the American workers' objection to the rule of officials. It really echoed his ambivalence about bureaucracy, which will concern us again in a later chapter.

A section entitled "Collegiality and the Division of Powers" allowed Weber to consider the ways in which a form of domination can be traditionally or rationally limited or restrained. Thus patrimonial or feudal domination can be limited by means of estate-type privileges or divisions of power. Bureaucratic domination, particularly in its legal form, can be forced to adhere to fixed rules of administration by independent political bodies empowered to supervise it, to define its competences and procedures, and to control its budget (T, 158– 59). Any kind of domination can be prevented from taking on a "monocratic" or purely personal character by the introduction of various collegial bodies and procedures. Patrimonial rule can be softened and controlled in a particularly effective way by means of a "specified or constitutional division of powers," in which rationally subdivided "functions" of government are assigned to separate persons or bodies within a constitutional order. Such constitutional division of power, as Weber conceded, is an unstable arrangement. To determine the real structure of domination under it, one has to ask what would happen if a compromise necessary to its survival could not be reached in a crisis. Before the First World War, for example, an English monarch trying to govern without a budget would have risked his crown, but a Prussian monarch would have prevailed, and the dynastic powers would have emerged dominant in Germany (T, 165–66).

In the concluding pages of his chapter entitled "Types of Domination," Weber came back to the important role of political parties as voluntary associations that seek to attract more or less permanent followings on "charismatic," "traditional," or "purposively or value-rational" principles. Political parties may be organized to defend specific "world views," or "status and class interests," or they may (and increasingly do) seek electoral victories as means of access to the patronage of offices (as "patronage parties"). Like other political and voluntary associations, parties may try to limit the powers of their leaders or administrators by restricting them to the role of more or less temporary and more or less specifically instructed "servants" of their constituencies. If the administrators are actually elected at full membership meetings of the associations, as in certain American "townships" and small Swiss cantons, administration may take the form of "direct democracy." In other cases, the administration of associations or political parties may be in the hands of "notables" *(Honoratioren)*, who serve on a voluntary, part-time basis, and who usually hold full-time occupations, such as those of landowners or lawyers, that allow them to be "available" *(abkömmlich)* for such honorary part-time positions. Weber observed that both direct democracy and administration by notables may become technically inadequate for voluntary associations of very large memberships or where their tasks are complex enough to require specialized education. Their functions will then pass into the hands of political professionals. In any case, "representation" is typical of modern politics (*T,* 167–72). While delegates or representatives may be more or less strictly "bound" to the instructions of their constituencies, "free representation" is generally characteristic of modern parliamentary politics, which could not function without the active intervention of the political parties.[13]

THE SOCIOLOGY OF LAW

Weber's long chapter entitled "Sociology of Law" in the earlier part 2 of *Economy and Society* is difficult and complex, but it addresses issues that the reader cannot neglect. In particular, Weber analyzes the process of rationalization in the realm of law along with the impact of relatively autonomous legal developments upon the economy. He characterizes these developments as products of a triangular relationship between the legal professionals or "notables" *(Honoratioren)*, the dominant political powers, and the emerging entrepreneurial middle class.

The legal notables, in Weber's model, comprise legal scholars, various participants in the process of enunciating and applying law, and the practical advisers and "advocates" of the interested parties. Increased demands upon the expertise of these legal professionals originate in the needs of those involved in the expanding exchange economy. The consequent "rationalization" of the law, however, is only indirectly affected by socioeconomic factors. Its course is primarily shaped by such "intralegal" conditions as the characteristics of the legal professionals, especially their education. The development of a specialized legal curriculum, and therefore of legal thought, Weber argued, can take two almost diametrically opposed directions. Law can be taught either "empirically," as a craft, by the legal practitioners themselves, or *systematically*, in specialized schools of law, by means of rational or "scientific" analysis. A "rather pure type" of the first alternative was the guildlike training offered by the legal practitioners in England, who dealt in the commonsense "facts" of daily life and were moved in part by their interest in fees.[14]

The "purest type" of the second kind of legal schooling and thought, according to Weber, is modern, rational, university education in law. It holds a monopoly position where, as in Germany, only those are admitted to the practice of law who successfully pass through law faculties or schools. Additional years of apprenticeship do add some experience of legal practice. Nevertheless, university education in law is based upon abstract concepts or norms that are formed and delimited, at least in principle, by means of strictly logical interpretation and reasoning. The systematically rational character of such schooling may largely estrange legal thought from the everyday needs of interested clients, as well as from the descriptive terms of common sense. The Italian notaries of the early medieval cities formed an important stratum of legal professionals within the urban upper middle class *(popolo grasso)*, but under the influence of the early Italian universities, they perpetuated a modern form of Roman law. In medieval France and Germany, given a more rural and seigneurial environment, legal professionals held various appointments and offices but did not form a powerful guild or status group. Their thought was reflected in legal anthologies *(Rechtsbücher)* that were partly speculative and imaginary in character (*R*, 458–59, 461–62).

Weber repeatedly underlined the crucial distinction between *formal* and *substantive (materiale)* rationality in law, just as he did in the case of economic action. Theocratic regimes and patrimonial rulers have favored laws that followed from substantive norms of welfare or justice, and democratic forces have sometimes been ideologically committed to similar principles. Middle-class interests in Roman, late medieval, and modern times, however, have favored the formal rationalization of law, whether under the influence of religious forces or of patrimonial officials and administrators. What matters to middle-class interests is the predictability or calculability that follows from the systematic internal consistency of formally rationalized law, for it provides the optimal environment for peaceful economic competition and purposively rational action. Of course formal equality before the law may be accompanied by substantive inequalities of wealth and economic power. That is why patriarchal rulers have tended to identify with the substantive "welfare" of their subjects, and why democratic regimes from ancient Greece forward have had recourse to popular "khadi justice" in pursuit of substantively rational de-mands. They have understood that formal rationality in law has tended to confirm and stabilize the existing distribution of economic advantages (*R*, 468–70).

Against the background of these initial definitions and distinctions, Weber devoted the last three sections of his chapter on law to the emergence of the modern legal system. In addition to the Church and Canon Law, he argued, it was the patrimonial rulers and their officials who ultimately broke through the irrational forms of the old popular administration of justice. In England, the dominance of the royal power led to the establishment of a common law more unified than the heterogeneous feudal arrangements of the Continent. The Italian statutes of the Middle Ages also created an integral law of the land *(lex terrae)*. But in Central Europe, nothing similar was achieved until the rise of princely absolutism, and even the princes did not fully replace existing special laws until the emergence of the modern state. Their encroachment upon es-tablished legal traditions took one of two forms: In one, the rulers treated their dominions as (proprietary) acquired rights, portions of which they then passed down to various subordinates, as subjective rights or "privileges" that they agreed to respect. In the "estate type" legal system that was created in this way, law was both objectively and subjectively a sum of "privileges." Alterna-tively, the princes opted for the opposite approach, granting no privileges, but simply issuing orders to their subjects or procedural rules to their officials. The "patriarchal" law that arose in this manner was a mere extension of princely administration, within which there was no place for subjective rights. This "estate-type" alternative, Weber wrote, was fully realized only in the po-litical organization of medieval Europe (*R*, 482–83. 485).

As for the patriarchal form of patrimonial justice idealized in the "Solo-monic judgment," Weber continued, it was substantively rational in the light of ethical or welfare norms, rather than formally rational in the sense of logical coherence and predictability. In any case, patrimonial law was in fact usually a mixture of *ständisch* and patriarchal components, and of older folk traditions as well. Against this inherited pattern, the advance of formal rationality in modern European law originated partly in the needs of the patrimonial ad-ministration, especially where the suppression of estate-type law and privilege was concerned. Increased formal rationality, including formal equality before the law, enhanced the power of the princely rulers at the expense of the privi-leged. The situation was different, however, where the arbitrariness of patriar-chal domination itself was to be limited by fixed rules, especially by the guar-anteed "subjective rights" of subjects. Yet such guaranteed rights were sought by economic interest groups, whose support the princes needed to enhance their fiscal and political power. Bourgeois interests in particular had to insist upon clear and predictable laws that would ensure the legal security of contracts against irrational interference by patrimonial administrators and special "privileges" alike. An alliance between the princes and bourgeois interests therefore functioned among the foremost sponsors of legal rationalization. To be sure, as Weber acknowledged, fixed rights protected against patrimonial interference have not been characteristic objectives either of patrimonial bureaucracies or of the older forms of political capitalism, which relied upon princely monopolies. Moreover, systematic legal codifications have followed not only from the conjunction of patrimonial and bourgeois interests, but also in the aftermath of radical social or political innovations (*R,* 485–88).

In a curious reversal of historical development, according to Weber, Roman law directly affected Europe in late Roman times, before the beginning of the feudal and estate-type decentralization of power and the consequent particularization of the law. Nevertheless, Roman law remained a formative intellectual influence in Central Europe from the Middle Ages to modern times. It played this role by shaping the legal curriculum of European universities, and thus the thought of their graduates, the legal notables. Given the absence of established national legal traditions, educated legal professionals cultivated a purely abstract form of legal rationalism. Their "intellectual needs" demanded a "logically correct," internally consistent, and all-encompassing system of legal norms that was applicable in all conceivable circumstances. Their "logicalization" *(Logizierung)* of the law proceeded quite independently of the interest of legal clients. The entrepreneurial middle classes in particular had no use for the *substantive* contents of the Roman law; they preferred the practical terms of the commercial and municipal law that began to emerge in the Middle Ages. Nevertheless, they profited from the *formal rationality* of the Roman legal tradition, which affected Europe from Spain to Scotland and Russia, with the exception of England, northern France, and Scandinavia. It was only with the advent of "enlightened absolutism" in the eighteenth century that patriarchal princes and their officials sought to replace the Roman tradition with the substantive rationality of the bureaucratic welfare state. Weber wrote with bitter irony about the Prussian General Code (Allgemeines Landrecht) of the 1890s as a monument to the patriarchal welfare state, and about the "duties" urged upon Prussian subjects by naively self-righteous officials (*R,* 490–94).

The perfect example of a post-revolutionary codification, Napoleon's Civil Code and its imitations in western and southern Europe, for Weber, was the third great power in modern law, along with Anglo-Saxon law (the product of legal practice) and Roman law (the inspiration of legal education). In contrast to such patrimonial and patriarchal systematizations as the Prussian General Code, the Civil Code was free of nonlegal components and strictly avoided didactic moralizing. Many of its propositions had an epigrammatic and monumental character reminiscent of the Mosaic Tables, and some became as popular as ancient legal proverbs. The force of the Civil Code stemmed from its formal qualities, from the extraordinary lucidity and logical precision of its provisions—or from the feigning of these qualities. Its specific rationalism derived from the sovereign conviction that here, for the first time, law was created free of all historical "prejudices," consistent with Bentham's ideal, and indebted only to human reason and to the genius of the *grande nation*. Its epigrammatic and theatrical character echoed analogous formulations about the "rights of man and citizen" in the American and French Constitutions. Legal axioms were thus postulated, along with the demand that no legitimate legal system could henceforth contradict them (*R*, 496).

From a sociological point of view, as Weber pointed out, ideas about the "rightness" of the law are relevant only where legal practice is affected by the conviction that certain legal maxims are legitimate independently of the inherited distribution of power. This conviction has in fact played a practical role at the beginning of the modern era, in the revolutionary epoch, and in America right up to the present. Leaving aside the Stoic and Christian *lex naturae*, one can define modern "natural law" as the sum total of norms that are valid independently of positive law and superior to it, in that the legitimacy of positive law depends upon these norms. "Natural law" in this sense is the only possible source of legal legitimacy that remains, once religious revelation and the sanctity of tradition have lost their force. It has therefore served as the basis for revolutionary regimes. The German historical school of law has sought to defend the preeminence of "customary law," along with historicist and naturalist theories about the "spirit of the people" and the validity of "organically" evolved law. The natural law axioms of legal rationalism, however, stand in opposition to that kind of irrationalism. Their development in modern times was affected by the rationalist sects, by Renaissance ideals about the canons of "nature," and by the English conception of the citizen's "birthright." As for the transition to the idea of human rights as the rights of all human beings, it took place, with the help of Anabaptist influences, only during the Enlightenment of the seventeenth and eighteenth centuries. In their "formal" aspect, the maxims of natural law gave rise to "contract theory," which stipulates that all legitimate law rests in principle upon enactment by agreement. Chief among the individual freedoms accordingly guaranteed by natural law is the freedom of contract. In their substantive implications, the axioms of natural law are consistent with "nature" and "reason"; the insights of human reason are considered identical with the "nature of things," what ought to be, with what factually prevails (*R*, 497–99).

In recent times, according to Weber, interpretations of natural law have become increasingly "substantive" in emphasis. The need to adjust to the existing order, including the reality of inheritable property, produced formulations of a substantively utilitarian kind. Even more important was the theoretical linkage between property rights and the form of their acquisition. The decisive transition to substantive natural law stemmed from socialist theories about the exclusive legitimacy of acquisition through one's own labor. This substantive principle stands opposed to the formal freedom of contract, and indeed to all rights acquired by contract. There are obvious connections between the class situations of various social groups and their ideological positions on these matters. Thus the formal freedom of contract, along with all rights derived from it, serve the interests of the bourgeois participants in the exchange market. In the Russian Revolution of 1905 and its aftermath, the spokesmen for the landless peasants drew divergent conclusions from the axiom that the land belongs to those who work it, which also conflicted with the theories of the Russian Marxists. For the non-agricultural working class, the individual's natural right to the full product of his labor really made sense only in an artisanal economy; its only possible equivalent under developed market capitalism is the collective right of the working class to a "living wage," which recalls the "just price" of medieval ethics. But even in the Canonic literature, the "just price" evolved to mean the price that "naturally" emerged from unfettered competition rather than under the influence of monopolies and other forms of arbitrary interference in the market (*R*, 499–500).

Natural law dogmas, Weber concluded, have more or less considerably influenced both the creation of law and legal findings. Formally, they have increased the preference for logical abstraction and, more generally, the force of logic in legal thought. Their substantive impact has been more diverse, but always significant. Even the codifications of pre-revolutionary states and officials often traced the legitimacy of the law they created to natural law conceptions about its "reasonable" character. Under patriarchal rulers, as we know, the reasonable easily became the substantively useful or beneficial. By contrast, the codifications of the revolutionary period, which took place under the influence of the middle classes, emphasized and strengthened the natural law guarantees of individual rights in the face of the existing political powers.

The emergence of socialism increased the importance of natural law dogmas in the minds of the masses and more particularly in those of the intellectual stratum that provided their theories. But this ideological current did not directly affect legal practice. Indeed, in the realm of revolutionary law, natural law theory was undermined by the evolutionary dogma of Marxism, even while it lost ground to Comtean developmental schemes and "organic" historicism in scholarly circles. Quite apart from the tension between formal and substantive natural law, and from the evolutionary challenges to it, the progressive dissolution and relativization of all metalegal principles, along with the inroads of modern skeptical intellectualism, have now brought the axioms of natural law into deep discredit. The result has been the apparently irreversible advance of legal positivism(*R,* 501–2).

In the final section of his "Sociology of Law," Weber focused more broadly upon "the formal qualities of modern law." He reviewed the four main stages in the overall development of modern law, from the revelations of charismatic prophets and the empirical findings of legal practitioners extending established precedents to the imposition of law by secular or theocratic powers and, finally, to the elaboration and expert administration of the law by formally educated legal professionals. The later stages in this progression were accompanied by increases in the logical systematization of the law and in the technical rationality of its application. In historical reality, deviations from this overall scheme have been occasioned by differences in political power relationships, in the relative strengths of theocratic and secular forces, and in the character and schooling of the legal notables. Among the sources of modern legal developments that Weber considered distinctive of the West, he cited the impact of rational enterprise, whose representatives initially allied with patrimonial rulers, only to turn against them during the revolutionary period. Along with the reception of Roman law, modern Western legal education, and the concept of "natural law," Weber also underlined the peculiar antecedents of Western law in the folk justice and the particularized rights that were characteristic of feudal and estate-type patrimonialism. Even though these older forms of special law were eventually superseded by the fundamentally formal systematization of modern Western law, the thrust toward legal formalism has not been unambiguous. Thus a new kind of legal particularism has arisen in the field of commercial law; the participants in commerce and enterprise have come from a distinctive occupational group or class, and there have been recent attempts to bypass the formalities of legal practice in the interest of quicker and more immediately applicable procedures(*R,* 503–5).

In its increasing logical sublimation, modern legal thought has increasingly shifted attention from the formal properties of outward behaviors to the rational "interpretation" *(Sinndeutung)* of the meanings of both legal norms and legally relevant actions. Such interpretation is intended to take into account the "real will" of contending parties, and it thus intrudes an individualizing and substantive element into the formalism of the law. Indeed, like the systematization of religious ethics, legal interpretation seeks to construe the relationships between parties in terms of the "inner core" of their behavior, their attitude, or their good faith, for example. Commodity exchange requires a degree of trust in the reliability of business partners. With the growing importance of commodity exchange, therefore, courts have increasingly had to weigh substantive standards of "fair dealing" and good practice, which required them to rely upon evidence of average expectations in these matters. But all such involvement in the substantive norms and expectations of clients are inconsistent with the purely formal logic of the law. With the emergence of the modern class problem, moreover, the working class and its ideological spokesmen have raised new substantive demands, calling for a "social law" based upon principles of "justice" and "human dignity." Such demands pose a radical challenge to legal formalism. Like the welfare ideology of the monarchical bureaucracy, the new social demands of democracy are not grounded either in tradition or in the logic of the law. In legal terms, they are amorphous and indeed irrational; they express substantive ethical claims (*R,* 505–7).

Among the contemporary French and German legal practitioners of Weber's time, he observed problematic symptoms of disappointed status ideologies. Legal professionals disliked the subaltern role of automats, in which the circumstances of a case and the appropriate fees are inserted at the top, and the ruling and its reasons are spit out at the bottom. Reacting against the formalism of the law and the principle of its comprehensiveness, they emphasize the "creative" role of the judge, at least where the law falls short of addressing a particular case. They exaggerate the importance of the article in the Swiss Code that instructs the judge to proceed in doubtful cases according to the rule he himself would promulgate in a given situation. Despite its Kantian formulation, Weber argued, this article could legitimate plainly irrational judgments. Yet some opponents of legal formalism have gone so far as to claim that general legal propositions are secondary abstractions of concrete decisions, or that precedents rank above legal norms. In a contrary direction, Weber noted a yearning to transcend the merely "technical" application of positive law through new normative commitments variously derived from Catholic "natural law," from insight into the "essence" *(Wesen)* of the law, from neo-Kantian constructions of the "right law," or from the Comtean empirical establishment of average expectations among legal clients. French and German legal scholars and practitioners have been particularly threatened in their dignity by the systematizations of the Civil Code and the Prussian General Code; their reactions have thus been the products of specific intellectual interests. At a broader level, however, all these reactions against the logical systematization of the law are themselves the consequences of legal rationalization; for even when they are not rationalistic in character, they are forms of flight into the irrational, comparable to the contemporary irrationalization of religion, and thus effects of rationalization. Above all, they represent the attempts by legal practitioners to raise their own status dignity and influence, as in the frequent references to the "distinction" of the English judges, who are not tied to a rational form of law (R, 507–9).

Commenting upon this German image of English law, Weber pointed out that modern capitalism was as compatible with it as the rational law of the Continent. English legal practice is still an essentially "empirical art," and precedent continues to be centrally relevant. In the colonial countries, especially in the United States, legal findings in fact retain a charismatic quality; important decisions are considered the personal creations of named judges. The degree of legal rationality is accordingly low, and there is, properly speaking, no "science" of the law. English legal practice is not, like its Continental counterpart, the application of legal propositions derived from the inner logic of the law. These differences between English and Continental practices have had certain economic and social consequences; yet these have had no influence upon the overall structure of the economy. Nor has there been a discernible English tendency to move in the direction of Continental conditions to suit the capitalist economy. On the contrary, where English and Continental law have competed, as in Canada, the English pattern has prevailed (R, 509–11).

On the other hand, modern social development has provided motives for weakening the formal rationalism of the law, even beyond the political orientations and the status concerns of legal professionals that Weber mentioned. Thus the role of lay jurors has intruded an element of direct "khadi justice" into criminal procedures. Protests against this dimension of popular justice have come from two directions. Its interest-bound character clashes with the matter-of-fact habitus of the legal expert. Since jurors are usually chosen from the strata of notables who are able to make themselves "available" *(abkömmlich)* for jury duty, even when they come from the upper working class, they are subject to the working-class charge of "class justice," and the opposite objection is raised by the propertied classes against working-class juries. Interests other than those of "class," incidentally, can affect jurors. In Germany, where the honor of women is held in low esteem, for example, male jurors can rarely be moved to convict members of their own gender of rape. All these tensions in the realm of legal practice stem only partly and indirectly from technological and economic developments that favor intellectualism. Primarily, they are consequences of the ineradicable antithesis between formal and substantive principles in the law. Judges that originate in a bureaucracy and are dependent, moreover, upon the political authorities cannot expect to be equated with Swiss or English judges, not to mention American federal judges. Only genuine prophets have been consciously and objectively "creative" in their relationship to the law. But as Weber insisted, precisely the most "creative" among them have subjectively felt themselves to be mere mouthpieces for independently valid norms, and not at all their "creators." Weber ended with the expectation that progressive bureaucratization would eventually alter the position of the English judge as well, and with an emphatic warning against the replacement of legal concepts with supposedly "creative" sociological, economic, or ethical pronouncements. The whole antiformal movement, he argued, is a characteristic "backlash" against the role of the "specialized expert" *(das Fachmenschentum)* and against modern "rationalism," which in turn is the real cause of that backlash (*R*, 511–12). Thus Weber's sociology of law touched upon themes he was to pursue more persistently in his famous postwar addresses, "Science as a Vocation" and "Politics as a Vocation."[15]

CHAPTER SEVEN

The City, Capitalism, Socialism, and Bureaucracy

Among Weber's later writings, there is an extended essay entitled *The City (Die Stadt),* which assigns a remarkably distinctive role to the "Western City." In an introduction to the essay as a whole, Weber described some characteristic varieties of urban settlements. He noted that there have been "agrarian cities" as well as "consumer cities," whose inhabitants lived from civil service salaries and rents of various kinds. On the other hand, cities as economic units have usually been based upon commerce ("merchant cities") or upon artisanal and other forms of production ("producer cities"). Most real cities, of course, have been mixtures of these variants. They have served as market centers for a surrounding agricultural hinterland. Some municipalities have at least partly functioned as economic enterprises in their own right, or they have "regulated" the economic life within their boundaries. Most have been equipped with fortifications or attached to a fortress *(Festung, Burg)* of a feudal lord or prince. Politically, Weber's Western city was a "commune" *(Gemeinde)* characterized by fortifications of some kind; the presence of a local or regional market, which was sometimes linked to interregional trade routes as well; a municipal judicial court, along with laws at least partly the city's own; and at least partial autonomy, with some form of "burgher" participation in the selection of the municipal authorities. With temporary or rudimentary exceptions, according to Weber, merchant or producer cities with the political attributes of "communes" existed only in the West.[1]

Weber's account of the Western city provides a historical background for his bourgeois liberalism, for it shows the burgher of the medieval West challenging his traditional overlords, appealing to a kind of contract theory of political legitimacy, and insisting upon the burghers' active participation in the polity. Thematically, Weber's essay was based primarily upon a contrast between Asian and European conditions and secondarily upon a less radical distinction between the ancient *polis,* on the one hand, and the *communes* of medieval Europe on the other. Fortified settlements that were sites of markets and of mercantile and artisanal enterprise, he pointed out, existed all over the world, along with the important difference between exchangeable urban and encumbered rural land. Similarly, feudal estates could be found within European town walls, along with aristocratic landowners and the officials of local rulers. Indeed, the labor of slaves and serfs could be exploited in the market to yield substantial money rents for their owners and lords. In the process, however, the slaves and serfs gained the chance to "buy themselves free" by means of enterprise and money. The communes of the European Middle Ages, and especially the inland cities of northern Europe, consciously usurped or broke through the traditional rights of the lords, and that *revolutionary innovation* set them apart from all other cities. The axiom thus came to prevail that "city air brings freedom" *(Stadtluft macht frei),* for after a relatively short time in the urban environment, the lords lost their proprietary rights over their slaves or dependents (100 – 5, esp. 105).

The Western cities of antiquity and of the Middle Ages were further distinguished, according to Weber, by the fact that they were organized associations of "burghers" with special administrative organs and subject to laws of their own. This character of the European "polis" or "commune" as a distinctive estate was not to be found in a more than incipient form in legal systems other than the Mediterranean and northern European ones. Above all, the fully developed city of the ancient and medieval West was constituted or interpreted as a *fraternal* association, which therefore usually had an appropriate religious symbol, the burghers' own god or saint (107–8).

From the beginning, Weber added, the populations of urban centers suffered from poor sanitary conditions and continually had to be replenished by further waves of new immigrants from the countryside. Among the consequences were significant status differences between newcomers and established groups. But even where political equality and the free election of city officials initially prevailed, as in the northern European cities, there gradually emerged a stratum of notables and patrician families who monopolized town offices because their economic security allowed them to devote themselves to politics. In other Western cities, especially in the south, status distances separated ordinary burghers from aristocrats with urban residences. On the other hand, the commonalities among city dwellers, including their participation in economic enterprise, tended to reduce the social differences between them, particularly in the eyes of the agrarian nobility. A leveling of distinctions among social groups within the urban population thus coexisted with a trend toward internal status differentiation, and it was the latter that usually prevailed in the long run (101, 105–7).

Considering the causes of the difference between Western and Asian cities, Weber pointed to cultural patterns he had investigated most thoroughly in his comparative studies of the Chinese and Indian religions. Thus magical restrictions and clan or caste barriers not only reduced the chances of economic cooperation, but also prevented shared meals among urban coreligionists, along with political fraternization. In the ancient *polis* of the Hellenic tradition, by contrast, a real or imagined act of "housing together" included a cultic meal among city founders that survived as a symbol of fraternity among urban clans and military associations. Thus the Western city of antiquity already had some of the features of a "commune" *(Gemeinde)*, and that term was even more fully applicable to the newly founded cities of medieval Europe, where the newcomer swore an oath *as an individual* to enter the burgher association (109–12, 117–18).

Only the Jews suffered the disprivileged role assigned to "guest people" in Asia. The rulers of cities might seek to recruit them as sources of wealth, but the ritual barriers to commensality—and the absence of the Jews from the Lord's Supper, the sacrament of Communion—prevented the development of fraternal relations between Jews and non-Jews. For the medieval city too was a religious cult community. The city church, the city saint, the common Lord's Supper, and the official celebration of the Christian holy days—all these were regular features of the medieval city. But Christianity had deprived the *clan* of all religious significance. The Christian community was essentially a religious association of individual believers, not a ritual association of clans. The Jews, however, remained outside the community of burghers from the beginning (118–19).

Yet while the medieval city needed the bond of the religious cult, it was nevertheless a secular foundation, like the city of Western antiquity. Together with the purely secular town council, the lay elders of the parishes and sometimes the merchant guilds represented the burghers in formal legal actions.

Full membership in the church community was the prerequisite of burgher status. "The Western City, especially the medieval city . . . was not only the economic site of commerce and production, politically . . . a fortress and possibly a military garrison, administratively a judicial district, and beyond that a sworn communal *fraternization*. . . . It was a sworn 'commune' and counted as a '*corporation*' in the legal sense" (119, and esp. 121). These are the central theses that Weber developed in his chapter on the Western city.

At their beginnings, the burgher organizations of the Western cities were treated as sources of tax revenue for their rulers. It was the local prince who was initially granted privileges by his overlord that indirectly benefited the burgher, while providing the prince or bishop with a reliable income from taxes upon urban enterprise. The judicial court of the city was the ruler's court; the city councilors and other functionaries served the ruler. But all that gradually changed. Increasingly, the city became an autonomous association, while its officials became city functionaries. At a time when their economic interests encouraged organized association, the burghers were *not* divided by magical or religious barriers or submerged in the rational administration of a larger political unit. The emergence of the autonomous city association headed by its own mayor or "burgher master" differed in essential respects from the development of cities in Asia and even in European antiquity (121–24).

In some medieval cities, the corporations of burghers were "legitimately" constituted through privileges granted by their overlords. In many other cities, however, what actually happened was a "revolutionary usurpation." According to Weber, one can distinguish *spontaneous* from *derived* formations of medieval city associations. In *spontaneous* cases, there was a revolutionary act of political association or fraternization *(conjuratio)* among burghers, *despite* and *against* the "legitimate" powers, or a whole series of such acts. *Derived* burgher associations arose through grants of autonomy given by city founders and their successors, most often to new settlers and their heirs. As a rule, spontaneous and derived processes took place in combination, but the imperial edicts directed against city autonomy explicitly prohibited not this or that isolated legal innovation, but the *conjurations* as such (124–26).

The real home of the *conjurations* was Italy. Despite the ambiguity of the sources, one can there most easily discern the sociological meaning of the city association. Its general precondition was the partly feudal and partly prebendal appropriation of power characteristic of the medieval West, in which a great variety of claims to authority stood side by side, *overlapping* or *conflicting* with each other. The complex feudal hierarchy that made up a loose network of power in medieval Europe offered room for the emergence of the Western city. The aim of the oath of fraternization was not only to allow the urban landowners to combine for mutual protection, the peaceful settlement of disputes, and the securing of legal practices consistent with the interests of the city inhabitants, but also to *monopolize the economic opportunities* offered by the city; for only members of the sworn association were allowed to participate in the commerce of the city. Additional objectives of the burgher associations were to substitute fixed sums for the lord's arbitrary taxation, as well as military organization to ensure the outward extension of the commune's political and economic power (127–29).

Thus everywhere toward the end of the eleventh century, "consuls" were annually elected by the burgher estate as a whole or by a body of notables. The consuls were salaried and had the right to collect fees. Completing the revolutionary usurpation, they seized the judicial authority and the supreme military command, and they ultimately managed all of the city's affairs. They were strictly supervised by councils of notables that were dominated by the wealthiest families. Status differences were initially maintained, but the animus against feudal relationships soon came to the fore. The consuls were forbidden to become vassals of a lord, and one of the first privileges bought or wrested from the emperor was the dismantling of feudal fortresses within the city. The legal achievements of the cities included prohibitions against calling burghers before courts outside the city and the establishment of an urban code of rational law (129–32).

In discussing the confraternities of northern Europe, especially those of Germany, Weber pointed out that the cities did not originate in the guilds, which were not the only city associations in any case. The guilds coexisted, rather, with religious associations on the one hand and with mercantile or craft associations on the other. The movement of religious unification and the creation of "confraternities" continued throughout the Middle Ages, along with the formation of occupational associations, and these processes interacted in a variety of ways. Some occupational associations pursued sociable or religious interests, or sought religious recognition. Thus the various associations were effective primarily by facilitating the coming together of the burghers in pursuit of common interests (136–39).

Once successive usurpations had succeeded in a few large cities, feudal overlords hastened to "compete" by offering chartered rights to their burghers voluntarily, without waiting for their formal association. As a result, the successes of the usurpations tended to become universal. The revolutionary achievements extended to burghers at the founding or privileging of cities everywhere primarily included the constitution of the cities as "communes" headed by their own administrative organs. In Germany, these were the "councils," and the burghers demanded autonomy in their selection. In some south German cities, the town magistrate *(Schultheiss)*, who depended upon the lord, remained the administrative head of the city, and the burghers could escape his control only by buying the office. Almost everywhere in southern Germany, on the other hand, the "burgher master," usually a representative of the burgher association, ultimately gained preeminence over the *Schultheiss* (139–42).

Asking once more why the city emerged in the Mediterranean basin and in northern Europe, rather than in Asia, Weber again argued that the fraternal associations could not be formed in China and India because magical and clan barriers stood in the way. In addition, the need to regulate rivers and access to water gave rise to royal bureaucracies in Asia, which also enabled kings to form and supply large armies as bases of centralized military might. In such an environment, political burgher communes could not become independent of the royal power. In the West, according to Weber, military units in principle equipped themselves, whether they were levies of farmers, knightly armies, or burgher militias. The ultimate consequence was the development of estate-type division of power on the one hand and of autonomous burgher communes on the other (143–45).

In two long concluding sections of *The City*, Weber dealt with "patrician," or aristocratic, cities; with "plebeian cities," or city "democracies"; and with city "tyrants" that were usually supported by democratic populations. But I will confine myself to sketching a few major themes that run through these sections of Weber's work. He pointed out, for example, that in Italy, the landowners and notables who participated in municipal governments often came to dominate them. Leadership naturally fell to men who had the wealth to arm themselves. The cities thus became a status association of notable "families," who during the period of "patrician domination" *(Geschlechterherrschaft)* cultivated a knightly style of life (146–48). In northern Europe, too, the rise of the patriciate was based upon economic and status differences that already existed at the time of the burgher associations (170–71).

The patrician cities of European antiquity contrasted with those of the Middle Ages; the names of their subdivisions did not signal economic differences, but were military or religious in character (188). Moreover, ancient and medieval cities emerged in different circumstances. The medieval communes arose within patrimonial realms, in opposition to feudal and patrimonial rulers; the cities of antiquity arose on the sea coast and confronted peasant and barbarian peoples. The ancient cities originated in monarchies; the medieval communes, in conflicts with feudal or episcopal city lords. The typical city patrician, however, was not an economic entrepreneur, whether in antiquity or in the Middle Ages. He lived primarily on income from rents, and he was sometimes secondarily an entrepreneur (195). The characteristics of urban patriciates were predominantly "status" characteristics, and they included descent from old aristocratic or office-holding families (198).

The destruction of patrician rule, according to Weber, took similar forms in ancient and medieval Europe, especially in Italy. After an interlude of rule by a *podesta*, the Italian city saw the rise of the *popolo*, which was made up primarily of entrepreneurs and artisans, much like the German guilds. In the battle against the patrician families, the entrepreneurs initially took the lead; they encouraged and financed the sworn confraternities, while the artisan guilds supplied the numbers. Yet the Italian *popolo* took on a political character as well. Within the urban communes, it had its own financial and military organization. It became a true "state within the state," the first deliberately *revolutionary* and *nonlegitimate* political association. In medieval Florence the patrician families joined with the *popolo grasso*, the propertied or university-educated burgher strata, which were grouped in the "upper guilds" *(arti maggiori)* of lawyers and notaries, bankers, cloth merchants, doctors, and apothecaries, usually joined by the urban nobility. For a time, all city officials had to be selected from these upper guilds, but then through additional insurrections, the "lower guilds"*(arti minori)* of the *popolo minuto,* the lesser tradesmen, acquired a significant share of power, and they were briefly joined by the artisans after the *Ciompi* revolt of the fourteenth century (199–200, 204–5).

In their politics, the Italian cities of the Middle Ages moved through a kind of cycle. After beginning as elements in a patrimonial and feudal structure, they passed through a phase of revolutionary independence, of autonomous government by notables and then by guilds, to rule by the *signoria,* and finally to reintegration into a relatively rational patrimonial system. This cycle, and especially the *signoria,* had no full equivalent elsewhere in the West. The cyclical development as a whole, however, was universal in one respect: The cities of the Carolingian period were scarcely more than administrative districts, and they eventually approached that condition again under the modern patrimonial state (233). During the interval between these two phases, however, they were everywhere to some degree "communes," with autonomous political rights and autonomous economic policies. The evolution in antiquity was quite similar, and yet neither modern capitalism nor the modern state originated in the ancient cities. But the development of the medieval communes, while not an indispensable antecedent, was certainly a decisive factor in the emergence of modern capitalism and of the modern state (288–89).

Altogether, Weber's extended essay on the city is rich enough to call for additional comment. To begin with, there is the paradox of political "illegitimacy." In the conceptual introduction to the chapter entitled "Types of Domination," Weber argued that all obedience is at least partly voluntary, and that domination is virtually impossible without the belief that it is "legitimate" in some "valid" sense of that term. Weber then defined the three "pure" types of "legitimate domination" or "authority" as "rational-legal," "traditional," or "charismatic" in character. But there really was very little room for "illegitimate" domination in that scheme. One is reminded of what Weber termed the "anti-authoritarian reinterpretation" of charismatic authority.[2] Certainly, Weber *could* have treated the medieval communes as early forms of rational-legal domination, perhaps by emphasizing the quasi-contractual character of the freedoms granted to the burgher associations by local rulers or feudal lords. The legal autonomy of the medieval cities might also have been interpreted as a symptom of the burghers' enduring interest in legal codification and in the "formal rationality" of codified patrimonial law. Asking myself why Weber did not approach his topic in this way, I can only imagine that he wanted to give the greatest possible emphasis to the *radical* nature of the *break* with the medieval form of *traditional* domination—and to the burgher as a revolutionary citizen.

The European Middle Ages certainly emerge from Weber's essay on the Western city as a critical phase in the history of modern Europe and of modern Western civilization more generally. The mixed system of patrimonialism, feudalism, and prebendalism that prevailed in medieval Europe represented an extreme degree of political decentralization, an extraordinary structure of dispersed and countervailing power. Like a porous fabric, it provided the framework for the rise of the "illegitimate" burgher associations, guilds, and communes. As Weber pointed out in his *Protestant Ethic,* moreover, medieval monasticism first set the conditions for the emergence of the modern "personality." The monk's ascetic and regulated regime of labor and piety provided an early opportunity for the systematic rationalization of conduct. In acquiring the ability to control his inner life, the monk learned to predict and thus rationally to plan his own actions. He became capable of conscious *volition,* of acting upon principle and in the light of the probable consequences. In a way, this made him the first modern man.[3] Taken together, in any case, the burgher communes and the monasteries made the European Middle Ages a crucial phase in the rise of Western rationalism. One has to imagine a medieval "passage" or "moment," one of those critical junctures at which the intervention of new *causal factors* brings about a culturally significant change in the direction of historical development. Weber himself explicitly considered the emergence of the medieval communes a decisive factor in the emergence of modern capitalism and of the modern state.

Finally, Weber's study of the Western city was a celebration of the European "burgher" in all of his variety. It must have pleased Weber to recall the antecedents of the burgher as a revolutionary in both the economic and the political realms. As an economic man, the medieval burgher was a merchant, an artisan, or a small producer, at once a member of a mercantile or craft guild and an early entrepreneur. As a political man, he gained his legal autonomy in a memorable conflict with his patrimonial and feudal lords. Above all, he was a revolutionary *citizen*. Unlike his weaker Asian equivalent, he learned to cooperate and to associate in pursuit of common interests. In his cultural life and sociability, he was a member of a range of "guilds" in the more inclusive sense of that term. And it was the Christian religion, his sharing in the Lord's Supper, that enabled him to break through barriers of clan and caste in fraternal association. It is worth noting here that the German word *Bürger* (burgher) has no full equivalent in other languages. Certainly the French or English term *bourgeois* rarely occurs in Weber's works. In translating or summarizing his texts, one has to look to the context to determine whether he is writing about the "burgher estate" *(Bürgertum)* as an *economic class,* or entrepreneurial elite; as a *status group* of the highly educated *(Bildungsbürgertum);* as a group of *political citizens;* or as the bearers of distinctive cultural, moral, or religious traditions and forms of life. Weber himself, one must remember, thought of himself as a class-conscious and sometimes embattled *Bürger,* and that too was reflected in *The City.*[4]

CAPITALISM, SOCIALISM, AND BUREAUCRACY

In his "Economy and Law (The Sociology of Law)," Weber introduced the important distinction between "formal" and "substantive" rationality. *Formal* rationality as an internal characteristic of legal systems was a type of logical consistency. Weber argued that formal legal rationality satisfied the interest of the middle class, and especially of its entrepreneurial elements, in predictability and *calculability* in the legal environment of economic enterprise. In general, the European economic middle classes therefore generally supported the codification of law by patrimonial princes. Yet theocratic regimes and certain kinds of patrimonial rulers also showed a certain preference for *substantive* legal rationality, or for laws that pursued *substantive norms of welfare and justice*. According to Weber, this led to a tension between formal and substantive rationality in the law. Part of the problem was that formal equality before the law was perfectly compatible with substantive inequalities of wealth and power. Indeed, it tended to confirm and stabilize the existing distribution of economic advantages and disadvantages.

Elsewhere in *Economy and Society*, Weber devoted a whole series of passages to an analogous distinction between "formal" and "substantive" rationality in the economic realm. In the process, he developed complex critiques of both capitalism and socialism that cannot be adequately understood apart from that distinction. Thus he initially defined formal rationality in economic action as the degree to which calculation is technically possible and actually applied in it. He further specified that *money calculation* is the indispensable means of maximizing the formal rationality of an enterprise. Substantive rationality, by contrast, is the degree to which the provisioning of human groups through economic action is guided by "normative postulates." Here is the key passage from "Categories of Economic Action."

> The concept of substantive rationality is thoroughly ambiguous. It stipulates only . . . that the consideration [of economic action] does *not* limit itself to the purely formal . . . fact that there is purposively rational *calculation* with technically . . . adequate means, but puts forward *demands* of an ethical, political, utilitarian, hedonistic, status [*ständisch*], egalitarian, or any other kind, in terms of which the results of economic action are assessed in a *value-rational* . . . way. The possible standards of value are in principle infinite in number, and the . . . ethical and egalitarian standards of socialism and communism are . . . [just] one subgroup within this multiplicity.

Weber's listing of possible measures of the substantive rationality in economic action was deliberately comprehensive; even political or military considerations, he claimed, could figure among the "demands" put forward to assess economic outcomes. Nevertheless, he explicitly focused upon the "provisioning of human groups" as subject to judgments of substantive rationality.[5]

Money calculation, according to Weber, is the "technically" most perfect and thus "formally most rational" means of orienting economic action. It is used (1) to estimate the present and future market value of all means of producing utilities; (2) numerically to state the advantages of economic actions, whether intended or actually performed; (3) periodically to compare the goods and opportunities available to an economic unit with those available to it at an earlier time; (4) to estimate and subsequently to verify the gains and losses an economic unit can make available for use during a given period, while preserving its resources; and (5) to orient the actual use of utilities to these data, in accordance with the principle of marginal utility. To supplement this account of money calculation, Weber further considered the economic "making of profit" by an "enterprise," and offered relevant definitions of "capital," and "capital calculation," of "profit" and "loss," of "risk" and "profitability." While "households" as economic units act on the principle of marginal utility, he pointed out, "market enterprises" plan their actions by estimating the chances of their "profitability" and assess their results by means of *capital accounting*, which is a more elaborate form of money calculation. Capital accounting as the basis of economic calculation—and the budgetary separation of household and enterprise, which it presupposes, as Weber pointed out, has arisen only in the West. In its "*formally* most rational form," he added, it further assumes competition as a peaceful form of "conflict of man with man" (*G*, 45, 48–49).

A fascinating and crucial portion of Weber's "Sociological Categories of Economic Action" is devoted to *calculation in kind*. Where money calculation is *not* used, calculation in kind does have its uses, particularly when one wants to specify goods needed to satisfy the economic needs of a certain group of consumers. Households certainly make use of calculations in kind. But only differences of amount between qualitatively similar goods can be reliably assessed by means of calculations in kind. Problems arise as soon as one confronts economic goods of *divergent* kinds or uses, whether they are to be consumed directly or in further production. "The comparison of different processes of production with divergent means of acquisition and a plurality of uses is easily accomplished by today's enterprises in terms of money costs, whereas calculation in kind here encounters difficult and 'objectively' insoluble problems." Weber considered this the fundamental difficulty confronting "full socialization." One cannot talk of a rationally "planned economy," he wrote, as long as there is no rational means of establishing a relevant "plan" (*G*, 53–56, esp. 55).

Above all, calculation in kind cannot compare the *desire* or *demand (Begehrtheit)* for different *kinds* of economic goods whose production or acquisition is equally feasible under prevailing conditions. This is a problem that ultimately affects every single calculation of every economic unit, one that in the context of money calculation determines the profitability and thus the direction of production of every enterprise. But this crucial problem can *in principle* be resolved in the context of calculation in kind in only two ways. There must be recourse either to tradition or to an arbitrary dictatorial power that regulates the pattern of consumption—and finds obedience to its decrees. Even in that case, however, calculation in kind cannot rationally attribute the total output of an enterprise to the different "factors" and decisions involved in the process of production, a problem that is currently resolved through money calculations of profitability. In short, calculation in kind runs into insoluble technical difficulties and ends by having to resort to irrational tradition or arbitrary imposition (*G*, 56).

It was in connection with his comments on calculation in kind that Weber challenged the philosopher Otto Neurath, who advocated "*full* socialization" and a "planned economy." Neurath proposed to assess the economic needs of a population *in kind,* and to develop a plan to satisfy them without recourse to money prices, and thus also to money calculation and to market exchange. Weber claimed that there was no *rational* way to carry out Neurath's project. He conceded that his economic critique of that project could not undermine its "justification," since it was based upon "ethical and absolute postulates" that could not be "refuted" in scientific or scholarly terms. At the same time, Weber observed that the difference between Neurath and himself coincided with the divide between "full socialization" and the kind of social reform long advocated by the Socialists of the Lectern. We know that Weber found Gustav Schmoller's brand of "social policy" unsatisfactory, both in its conceptual foundations and in its paternalistic tendencies. But he consistently identified himself with the overall objectives of reformist "social policy," which he here described as the major alternative to full socialization. Finally and almost paradoxically, Weber also repeated a warning he had already issued in another context. "Mere" money calculation cannot tell us to what extent a given population is provided with the goods it needs. Money estimates of "national income" in particular are useful only for purposes of taxation. They tell us nothing about the distribution of family incomes within a given social group or geographical region. The obvious example is that of an agricultural area in which a few immensely wealthy landowners confront a large population of impoverished peasants (*G*, 56–57).

Weber further pointed out that the formal rationality of money calculation depends upon several substantive (not substantively rational) preconditions. Thus it requires market competition among independent economic units, in which money prices function both as means of competition and as expressions of the compromises actually reached. The highest degree of rationality in money calculation, Weber specified, is reached in capital accounting, which in turn depends upon the *substantive* precondition of maximal freedom of the market; there must be no monopolies, whether officially imposed and economically irrational, or voluntary and economically rational. The competition to sell goods under such conditions will generate costs of marketing and advertising that would be unnecessary in a planned economy or under complete monopoly conditions. Strict capital accounting also requires supervised discipline within economic enterprises, along with private appropriation of the means of production; in short, it presupposes a form of *domination*. As Weber further pointed out, it is not "demand" as such, but the *effective* demand for utilities that regulates the production of goods by means of capital accounting. The direction of production is thus determined by the marginal utility situation confronted by the income group that is typically able and willing to purchase a certain good at a given *distribution of income*. Joined—in a completely free market—to the absolute indifference of the formally most rational capital accounting to all substantive value postulates, these circumstances reveal the limitations of capital accounting. It is, after all, purely formal in character; but formal and substantive rationality always diverge in principle (*G*, 58–59).

In a "market economy," as Weber defined it, economic needs are satisfied by means of action oriented to advantages in exchanges between agents who interact for that purpose, and who are motivated by self-interest. In a planned economy, by contrast, needs are met through economic action that is systematically oriented to an established substantive order that is valid (and enforced) within a political organization, whether imposed or agreed upon. A rational market economy normally presupposes money calculation and, where capital accounting is used, the budgetary separation of the household from the enterprise. A planned economy normally depends upon calculation in kind as the ultimate basis for its substantive orientation; but it depends formally upon the directives of an administrative staff. Thus economic action in a planned economy is constrained by promulgated budgets, rules, special incentives, and sanctions. In a market economy, formally voluntary action may be analogously constrained where differences in the distribution of wealth, especially of capital goods, force those without property to submit to the authority of others in order to be compensated at all for the utilities they are able to offer. In a purely capitalist exchange economy, Weber wrote, submission to the owners of capital goods—or to their deputies—is the fate of the entire working class. A planned economy, he added, must tolerate the reduction in formal rationality that inevitably follows from the absence of money calculation and of capital accounting. Substantive and formal rationality, he insisted again, inevitably diverge. This fundamental and inescapable "irrationality" of the economy, he wrote, is one of the sources of the "social problem," and above all of socialism (*G,* 59–60).

Weber expanded upon this topic a little later in his chapter entitled "Categories of Economic Action." In a kind of dialogue with socialist theoreticians, he described the expropriation of the individual worker from the means of production as "*technically* conditioned." Among the examples he provided, the shared use of machines or sources of power by a plurality of workers in modern factory production most clearly demonstrates his point. Of course such expropriation of individual workers, as Weber pointed out, is perfectly compatible with the appropriation of the means of production by an *association* of workers, a producers' cooperative of the kind recommended by Ferdinand Tönnies. But Weber promptly turned to the expropriation of *all* the workers from the means of production. He described it as "economically conditioned," and he offered a wealth of examples to demonstrate its necessity in the light of the need for profitability in competitive enterprise. Among the economic considerations he cited, the applicability of capital accounting was probably the most important (*G,* 77–78).

At this point in his argument, Weber came back once more to the issue of formal and substantive rationality in the following formulation: "A further specific *substantive* irrationality of the economic order lies in the fact that the highest level of *formal* rationality through *capital accounting* requires the subjection of the workers to the domination of the entrepreneurs." Weber then offered examples of the *collective* expropriation of the workers from the means of production. It may involve the direction of the enterprise by an administrative staff, and that even, or indeed especially, in a fully socialized or planned economy; or it may involve the direction of the enterprise by its owners or their deputies. The direction of enterprises by deputies of the owners is formally rational, since it permits the selection of highly qualified executives. But it may also allow control over executive positions to pass into the hands of financiers, whose proprietary interests are "foreign" to those of the enterprise itself. Bankers and investors may be less interested in making enterprises more productive than in earning stable rent incomes from the shares they own. That could lead to a victory of rent over profit. In any case, the intrusion of interests "foreign" to enterprises into the disposition over executive positions, according to Weber, may maximize formal rationality in the selection of executives, but it is a "further specific *substantive* irrationality of the modern economic order (*G*, 78-79).

Notice that Weber described both the collective expropriation of the workers from the means of production and the advent of finance capital as correlates of formal rationality in economic action on the one hand, and as "further substantive irrationalities" of the modern economic order on the other. The use of the word *further* in this connection can only be interpreted as extending the earlier identification of the unequal distribution of economic goods as an outstanding substantive irrationality of market capitalism. Weber clearly recognized that data on per capita "national income" did not suffice to demonstrate that the economic needs of a population were adequately satisfied, and that serious economic inequality led to the incomplete provisioning of the poor, even while compelling the workers to sell their labor at minimal rates and to submit to the domination of the capitalists and their deputies. In most of his analytical passages, Weber wrote as an objective sociologist of economic action and a dispassionate observer of the great variety of norms used to assess the "substantive rationality" of economic outcomes. When he enumerated the "substantive irrationalities" of the market economy, however, he wrote as a serious critic of capitalism in his own name. The question is, how are we to reconcile his critique of the economic order of his time with his enthusiasm for the merchants, artisans, and small producers of the medieval commune, not to mention the heroes of inner-worldly asceticism among the Puritan entrepreneurs?

The answer is to be found in those dark passages in which Weber contrasted the world of the Puritans with that of his own time. "The Puritan *wanted* to be a vocational man," he wrote, "[but] we *must* be vocational men"; for we are inescapably confronted by the "mighty cosmos of the modern economic order," which will endure "until the last ton of fossil fuel has turned to ash." The Puritan pastor Richard Baxter believed that care for the goods of this world should rest lightly on the shoulders of the saints. But for us, fate has turned this world into a "steel housing." The outward goods of the world have acquired unprecedented power over humanity, even though "the spirit has escaped from this housing." With capitalism firmly in the saddle, the "impersonality" and "senselessness" of work have caused it to lose its "religious aura," and "nobody knows whether at the end of this enormous development, new prophets will arise," or whether "there will be a mechanical ossification, veiled in a convulsive sort of self-importance."[6]

As if to emphasize the theme of self-importance, Weber added that the Puritans had left their heirs a powerful legacy. The vocational ethos of the Protestant entrepreneurial bourgeoisie, he observed, was reinforced by a "pharisaically good conscience," and by the "reassuring" conviction that the unequal distribution of the goods of this world was as divinely ordained as double predestination itself. It followed, moreover, that the poor really "deserve" their disadvantages. Thus the difference between the rich and the poor can become a *moral* failing, at least in the eyes of the rich.[7] But if we find the ideology of triumphant capitalism hard to bear, should we respond by attending to the other striking example of "substantive irrationality" Weber offered? Should we try to reverse the collective separation of the workers from the means of production by turning to socialism?

Weber's answer was emphatically *no;* for he was much more radically critical of "planned economies" than he was of "market economies." His objections to "full socialization" were explicitly *technical* in character. He was as free of the urge to lament the "materialism" of the masses as he was of the disdain for "self-interest" in economic action—or for the "interest politics" of political parties and leaders. But the technical impossibility of arriving at a rational plan by compounding the economic "needs" of a population, for Weber, had truly ominous practical consequences. In the absence of a reasoned plan, the actual scheduling of consumption could only be *arbitrarily imposed* by the dominant political power. The administrative staff of a political organization or state had to regulate the economy by at least partly irrational means. They could not draw upon the wealth of information provided by the interacting equilibria of the market economy, and so their ultimate recourse could only be to force, if not also to corruption. Above all, the "planned economy" did not end the collective "separation of the workers from the means of production"; it merely replaced their subjection to the owners of capital and their deputies with the unrestrained rule of a public bureaucracy. "Full socialization" as a project was based upon value imperatives, but any attempt to convert it into practice was likely to lead to force and tyranny.

As we know, Weber also had an opportunity to address the issue of socialism in the rhetoric of a bourgeois politician. In the summer of 1918, he delivered a lecture before Viennese army officers that was meant to help them confront and refute the arguments of revolutionary workers or soldiers. He did this by challenging the central predictions contained in the *Communist Manifesto* along lines reminiscent of Eduard Bernstein's "revisionism." In sum, the capitalist class has not shrunk, and economic crises have not deepened. Instead, finance and monopoly capitalism have evolved new forms of organization; small producers have survived, especially in agriculture; joint stock companies have created a rent-earning stratum; and the members of a rapidly expanding white-collar hierarchy have refused to identify with the working class. A system of collaboration between private enterprise and public authority, far from controlling big industry, has increased the political power of capital, even while the advance of bureaucratization has transformed the landscape of early entrepreneurial capitalism. Weber explicitly sympathized with the effort of labor unions to improve the workers' lot in a capitalist framework, along with the revisionist direction within the Social Democratic Party. His sharpest polemics were directed against the threat of revolutionary syndicalism and of the general strike as a weapon of disgruntled soldiers returning from the front.

At the same time, Weber used the opportunity presented by this political lecture of 1918 to point out again that socialism in almost any of its possible forms would in no way improve the actual situation of the workers themselves; it would certainly not end the "expropriation of the workers from the means of production." If the private ownership of capital goods were replaced by an economic system that dispensed with the role of the owner and entrepreneur, he asked, *who* exactly would take over the control of that system? If the "anarchy of production" embodied in the market competition among entrepreneurs were superseded by some kind of "communal economy," the direction of the economy would simply be transferred into the hands of government officials. In publicly owned enterprises too, it would be the officials, and not the workers, who would rule. "What is hidden behind the most frequently cited socialist slogan—the slogan about the 'separation of the worker from the means of production'—is . . . inescapable universal bureaucratization." Weber cited the advance of bureaucratic organization within the political parties, the separation of university scholars and scientists from the means of research, the apparently irreversible separation of the soldier from the means of warfare, and even the separation of the official from the means of administration. He argued that these trends could be traced to the complexity of modern technology and to the increasing need for *discipline* in modern organizations. "It is a serious error to regard this separation of the worker from the means of the enterprise as characteristic only of the economy, and particularly of the *private* economy. Nothing fundamental changes, after all . . . if a president or minister of a state . . . [is put in charge]." Weber concluded his lecture by observing that no rule of the proletariat, from the Paris Commune to the Bolshevik revolution, had been able to survive without recourse to the immediate force of executions.[8] But his central theme remained the threat of universal bureaucratization.[9]

Max Weber can be interpreted as a champion of bureaucracy. Some of what he wrote comes close to an idealization of bureaucratic administration. In other portions of his work, however, Weber also drew an extraordinarily negative portrait of bureaucracy as a stifling force in modern life. It was as if he had two different perceptions of the bureaucratic phenomenon, or if that phenomenon had two different faces. One cannot help asking whether these two faces of bureaucracy were ever fully reconciled in Weber's thought, and how one is to account for the divergence between them. I want to address these questions in the remainder of this chapter, and I need to begin by reviewing some of Weber's most important passages on bureaucracy and its implications.

At the very beginning of his chapter on the three "pure types" of domination and legitimacy, Weber deliberately focused upon the most modern form of authority, which he defined as "legal domination with a bureaucratic administrative staff." Among the characteristics of rational or legal authority, he emphasized the conception of law as a system of internally consistent, abstract rules, an "impersonal order" that is binding upon the head as well as the members of a political organization or state. The "purest type" of rational legal domination relies upon a "bureaucratic" administrative staff, in which there are specified spheres of competence or jurisdiction, along with a strict hierarchy of offices. The decisions of lower-ranking officials may be appealed to their supervisors higher up. The rule-bound conduct of official business requires specialized schooling. The educational qualifications of officials are ascertained by examinations and certified by diplomas. The officials are salaried and pensioned. Their offices are not exploitable benefices; the officials are "separated" from the means of administration. Finally, they typically regard their work as a lifetime career.[10]

Weber wrote with extraordinary intensity about the fatefulness of bureaucracy in modern life. He saw bureaucratic organization advancing in the state, in the church and the army, in mass political parties, business enterprises, interest groups, and other associations of all kinds. Bureaucracy is inescapable, he argued, because it is the most efficient, the most calculable, and thus "formally" the most *rational* means of exercising authority in every form of organization. There is no escape from it; for modern technology and modern enterprise would be impossible without bureaucracy as the indispensable means of control. If socialism were to replace capitalism, the dependence upon bureaucracy would not decrease, but actually *increase*. If a group of individuals wanted to challenge a bureaucracy, they could do so only by creating a counter-organization, which would be bureaucratic in character. At bottom, bureaucracy means domination by means of specialized knowledge, and that accounts for its rational character. In addition to the officials' technical mastery and their control of the relevant documents, bureaucracies may deploy the concept of "official secrets" to ward off interference from "amateurs." Even a ruler or political leader may find himself at the mercy of his expert officials. Only the capitalist entrepreneur is *relatively* free of bureaucratic domination within his own domain. The outlook of the official is shaped by a sense of duty to the office; he acts in a spirit of "impersonality," without hatred or passion, but also without love or enthusiasm. In that sense too, his approach is "formal," though he may imagine himself the beneficiary of his clients.[11]

In other contexts as well, Weber stressed the steady advance of bureaucracy. Just as modern economic organization is equivalent to progress toward entrepreneurial capitalism, so the modernization of the state entails the growth of bureaucracy. The parallel development of capitalism and of bureaucracy is no accident; for modern Western capitalism rests upon rational *calculation*. It therefore urgently needs a system of public administration and of justice whose workings are predictable, like the workings of a machine. As modern mass political parties have escaped from the traditional control of notables, they have increasingly come under the control of salaried officials. Of course the parties must still compete for voter support, but ordinary voters and party members have played a shrinking role in determining party programs. Notables have continued to be important as patrons or figureheads; but their former influence has passed to party secretaries, publicists, and other professionals. In what were clearly foundational passages, Weber thus characterized bureaucracy as a crucial element in the rationalization of modern political and economic institutions: technically efficient, sustained by specialized knowledge, and indispensable as an organizational device in every realm of modern life. The face of bureaucracy Weber described in these passages was the face of *rationality*, whose advance is not only inevitable, but ultimately desirable as well.

Yet there are many paragraphs, especially in his political commentaries, in which Weber portrayed bureaucracy in a much more negative light. The face of bureaucracy he examined and displayed in these portions of his work exposed it as a threat to individual freedom, equality, and cultural vitality. Toward the end of his commentary on the Russian revolution of 1905, for example, he observed that current developments were pointing away from democracy and individualism. "Everywhere," he wrote, "the steel housing for the new bondage stands ready." He cited what seemed to him a slowing down of technical and economic progress, the victory of rent over profit, and the exhaustion of the remaining free soil and free markets, even in America. He certainly distrusted the human and social consequences of contemporary capitalism. He thought it "ridiculous to ascribe to high capitalism" an elective affinity with "democracy" or "freedom," when all signs pointed in the opposite direction.[12]

In a somewhat later passage, Weber called up a dark vision of the ancient Egyptian bureaucracy, and anxiously wondered whether something like it might be reincarnated in his own world. Honorable and able individuals might have a chance to make their way in the hierarchy of officialdom, he noted; but that brought up the "dreadful" thought that the world might some day be inhabited only "by those little cogwheels," those human beings "glued to a little post and striving for a little better one." Yet he detected symptoms of that disheartening pattern, not only in the German civil service of his day, but also "among its heirs, *our students.*"

> [It is as if we were] human beings who need "order" and nothing but order, who become nervous and cowardly when that order is weakened for a moment. . . . That the world should know nothing but such men of order—that is the development in which we are involved . . . and the central question is not how we are to reinforce . . . it, but what we have to *set against* [it] . . . to preserve a remainder of humanity . . . from this total domination of bureaucratic ideals.[13]

This was both a frightening portrait of bureaucracy and a passionate plea to resist it.

More than other people, Weber argued elsewhere, the Germans have displayed a talent for rational administration in every field. They have *applauded* bureaucratization as a "form of life." That is what the German "literati" really meant when they celebrated the "ideas of 1914" and the "communal economy" during the First World War. They apparently believed that private capitalism should be domesticated through state control, and they thus helped to pave the way for universal bureaucratization. But future human beings will be forced to enter "the housing for the new bondage"—if "rational bureaucratic administration" is their "ultimate value." One can only "smile at the fear of our literati," Weber wrote, that we might have too much individualism or too much democracy. Given the advance of universal bureaucratization, the burning political question was how one might nevertheless "salvage" some individual freedom of movement, or how the "growing stratum" of "state officialdom" could be kept under effective control. That is why he reminded his readers that modern

Europeans would find it hard to live without the "rights of man." That, too, is what moved him to look to English political models and to advocate parliamentary commissions of inquiry that could override the bureaucratic concept of "official secrets," force officials to testify before them under oath, and thus gain some measure of control over the bureaucratic apparatus.

No careful reader of Weber, I would argue, could see him *only* as a champion of bureaucratic administration. The presence of two competing perceptions—or faces—of bureaucracy in Weber's texts is just too hard to miss. The only open question is how he managed simultaneously to hold two such divergent views of bureaucracy, and the answer has a great deal to do with his context. When Weber wrote as a champion of bureaucracy, he wrote as a progressive historian, one who perceived the use of salaried officials by patrimonial rulers as decidedly superior to the alienation of public offices as exploitable benefices that helped to destroy the monarchy in France. The modern state and modern rational legal authority, Weber believed, grew out of the creation of a patrimonial civil service that was recruited *on merit principles,* and at least partly from the burgher stratum, whose members were interested in the *predictability* of public administration, both as potential entrepreneurs and as private citizens. The power of bureaucracy, for Weber, was based upon the authority of specialized knowledge.

When Weber wrote as a critic of bureaucracy, by contrast, when he warned his readers against the human threat of universal bureaucratization as a "steel housing," he was primarily moved by his liberal individualism—and by his revulsion against aspects of the German sociopolitical order in general and of German academic culture in particular. He came close to idealizing British parliamentary government, which managed not only to train and test genuine political leaders, but also to keep its public servants firmly under control. The pseudo-constitutional regime of Wilhelmian Germany, by contrast, enhanced and glorified the authority of a paternalistic bureaucracy. It was surely his own immediate environment that Weber had in mind when he wrote of those holders of "little posts" who yearned for slightly bigger ones. Above all, it was the German educated burgher stratum, the *Bildungsbürgertum* and its spokesmen among his orthodox colleagues, that Weber meant to challenge when he wrote of the German "literati," their disdain for capitalist "profit" and for "partisan" politics, their love of order, and their reactionary illusions about the "ideas of 1914," about a distinctively German political system, about a "communal economy," and the like.

Weber never explicitly argued that divergent forms of the bureaucratic phenomenon might in fact be possible in different sociocultural settings. But he repeatedly told a story that strongly suggests such a possibility. In his Vienna lecture on socialism, he came back again to an incident that occurred during his American tour, and that had to do with the overt corruption that prevailed during contests among political "patronage" parties in the United States. When Weber asked an American worker why he and his colleagues allowed themselves to be governed by corrupt politicians, the American worker explained that "in our country," millions are available to be stolen without it doing much harm. Besides, the worker added, "we can spit" on our corrupt party professionals; but if we had trained and honest officials of the German kind, "they would spit on us." Weber was clearly impressed by the American worker's attitude, which he reported along with other examples of American informality and egalitarianism.[14]

What I take away from Weber's "spitting story" is the suggestion that there are at least two different versions of the bureaucratic phenomenon. The hierarchic combination of highly specialized skills and functions may occur in an environment that does not otherwise dramatize the social distances between participants in the enterprise. I am thinking of the launching of a missile by a NASA team. But I can also imagine situations in which "bureaucracy" is either *designed* to emphasize the social distances between members of an organization or social group, or actually *produced* by such distances. Thus members of a trade union might want to specify and delimit not only their obligations to their employers, but also the channels of communication between the "bosses," the "supervisors," and the rank and file. Where sociopolitical regimes make an attempt at centralized economic planning without recourse to market mechanisms, of course, differences of political influence are likely to determine the distribution of social advantages and disadvantages. In less exceptional settings, the dramatization of social distances in our ordinary experience of the bureaucratic phenomenon is exemplified by the attitude of American customs officials toward would-be immigrants or by that of Parisian municipal police officials toward foreigners forced to seek their permission to stay in Paris for extended periods.

Uppermost in Weber's mind, however, was the blatantly paternalistic relationship of the German bureaucracy to its "clients." In his angriest moods, Weber inveighed against the dominance and condescension of German government officials—and of its heirs, *"our students."* Weber understood, in short, that the outlook of German officials of his time was intimately related to certain status differences based on advanced education, and thus also to the place of education—and of the educated elites—in German society. These are issues we need to consider more fully in the next chapter.[15]

Education, Knowledge, and Vocation

Some of Weber's most compelling texts deal with distinctive conceptions of education and of knowledge, and with the impact of education upon the status order. Short but weighty passages in *Economy and Society* are devoted to these subjects, as are portions of his comments upon "value freedom" in the historical and social sciences. His extended study "Confucianism and Taoism," as we will see, is relevant as well. My aim in this chapter is to assemble and analyze Weber's views on education and on social status, and thus also to prepare the way for close readings of the two famous addresses he delivered to student audiences, toward the end of his life: "Science as a Vocation" and "Politics as a Vocation."

CULTIVATION AND SPECIALIZATION, CLASS AND STATUS

Almost alone among German academics of his time, Weber believed that the German universities of the early twentieth century had to abandon the traditional ideal of personal *Bildung* and confine themselves to conveying specialized knowledge to future professionals and officials. While his colleagues agonized about the need to preserve or to recover the old link between *Wissenschaft, Bildung, and Weltanschauung,* to derive morally and socially profitable insights from learning by means of "synthesis" or the "viewing" of "essential" meanings, Weber opted for a deliberately modest view of *Wissenschaft.* He repudiated the neo-humanist ideal of "cultivation" as self-perfection and focused exclusively upon the transmission of expert knowledge and the exercise in logical analysis. Indeed, he took a position quite similar to that of his French colleague Emile Durkheim, who scoffed at the yen to turn the isolated individual into a self-sufficient work of art by means of "general culture" *(culture generale).* [1] In Weber's methodological writings, as we know, he pursued ethically neutral forms of causal analysis and rational interpretation. His lecture "Science as a Vocation," to which we will turn in a moment, stressed the limitations of science as a human enterprise. He apparently believed that although the ideal of *Bildung* had once played an important role in German academic ideology, its time was now definitely past. Unfortunately, he never wrote a detailed critique of the concept of *Bildung* as an element in the German scholarly tradition.

On the other hand, Weber commented upon the classical literary education of the Confucian "mandarin" in his essay on Chinese religion, and it is hard to miss the references to German *Bildung* in his account of Confucian literary education.

> For twelve centuries, social rank in China has been determined far less by property than by the qualification for office established by *Bildung,* and specifically by examinations. China has made literary education the exclusive measure of social esteem; it has done so far more exclusively than Renaissance humanism and, most recently, Germany has done. [The Chinese examinations] ascertained the possession of a thorough literary cultivation, and of what followed from it: *the style of thought* appropriate for the dignified man. . . . As far as one can judge from the questions put to pupils in the examinations, these . . . resembled the themes of essays assigned in the highest grade of a German *Gymnasium* or, perhaps more accurately, of a German girls' secondary school. [2]

Obviously, Weber considered Chinese literary education an extreme instance of a pattern that was present in Germany as well. In one of his political essays, as we know, he actually characterized the attitude of German civil servants toward their "subjects" as one of "mandarin haughtiness." [3]

Indeed, Weber explicitly located Chinese literary education in a systematic typology of educational aims. The two extremes in this field, he argued, were the awakening of heroic or magic charisma and the transmission of specialized knowledge. The first of these corresponded to charismatic domination and the second to modern bureaucratic rule. Among the intermediates on the scale between the two extremes, Weber included all those types of education that mean to cultivate the pupil to a specific conduct of life. The charismatic training of magicians or of warrior heroes helped aspirants to attain a personal "rebirth"; specialized schooling turned pupils into useful members of public and private administrative organizations of all kinds. Finally, the "pedagogy of cultivation," according to Weber formed a "man of culture," in line with prevailing ideals, to a certain inner and outer conduct of life. The Chinese literary curriculum offered the kind of "general education" that in Germany until recently had opened the way to the highest offices, while also classifying its beneficiaries as members of a distinctive stratum of the highly educated. But whereas German education had taken on an increasingly specialized character in recent times, China remained totally committed to its classical literary sources.[4]

The spirit of the Chinese examinations reflected the fundamental assumptions of orthodox Confucianism.

> The dualism of Shen and Kwei . . . of the heavenly Yang and the earthly Yin substances . . . was bound to make it seem the sole object of education to unfold the Yang substance within the human soul. . . . The . . . "princely man" . . . has attained self-perfection; he is a "work of art" in the sense of the classical . . . canon of inner beauty planted by the inherited literary classics in the soul of its pupils.

Again I am struck by the parallels between the German model of *Bildung* and Weber's account of Chinese "self-perfection" by means of immersion in an inherited canon of classical literary sources.[5]

Weber's own position on the tension between *Bildung* and specialized knowledge is most clearly expressed in his commentary upon "value freedom" in the social sciences. Whether or not one chooses to make value judgments in one's teaching, he wrote, really depends upon one's normative vision of the university. There were academics who still claimed, both for the universities and for themselves, the right to "form human beings" (in the traditional sense of *Bildung*). But there were others, including himself, who felt compelled to face the fact that academic lectures nowadays essentially transmitted specialized knowledge *(Fachwissen)*. The former, he argued might consider it appropriate to "propagate political, ethical, artistic, cultural or other normative viewpoints." But the latter knew that they could exercise a salutary influence only by inculcating the specifically cognitive virtue of "intellectual rectitude" *(intellektuelle Rechtschaffenheit)*. Weber explained that one could take this position, as he clearly did, even on the basis of a decidedly "modest" estimate of specialized knowledge: *not* because one wanted all human beings to become mere "specialists" *(Fachmenschen)*, but precisely because one did not want the individual's "ultimate personal life decisions" taken out of his own hands by means of suggestions from the lectern. It seems to me useful to recall this passage in one of Weber's methodological essays, because it displays his view of scientific knowledge as a deliberate and explicit challenge to the traditional ideal of *Bildung*.

The implications of advanced education for the social order are most fully discussed in a fragment Weber added to the later part 2 of *Economy and Society* entitled "Status and Class." Applying his usual tactics of definition, he there characterized an individual's "class position" as his "typical chance" of deriving advantages from his disposition over goods and services. He further distinguished between "property classes" and "income classes." "Privileged *property* classes," he stipulated, enjoy monopolistic market advantages as buyers and sellers, in the accumulation of capital, in the owners' or shareholders' control over enterprises, and in access to expensive advanced education. "Negatively privileged property classes," by contrast, are typically impoverished debtors, serfs, or proletarian workers. Situated between the positively and the negatively privileged property classes, the "middle strata" *(Mittelstandsklassen)* derive revenues from various combinations of property ownership and educational qualifications. "Positively privileged *income* classes" monopolize the management of economic enterprises. They are typically entrepreneurs, merchants, bankers, agricultural managers, members of the "liberal professions," or highly skilled workers. "Negatively privileged income classes" are workers of various sorts. Between the positively and the negatively privileged income classes, the "middle classes" *(Mittelklassen)* are independent farmers or specialized workers.[6]

A "social class," in Weber's definition, is a set of "class positions" that are *similar,* in the sense that individual or inter-generational mobility among them is possible and actually takes place. Movement from one social class to another, on the other hand, is relatively rare. Weber distinguished four "social classes," namely, (1) the working class; (2) the lower middle class (*Kleinbürgertum);* (3) unpropertied but highly educated intellectuals, technical specialists, white-collar employees, and civil servants, all of them differentiated by levels of qualification; and (4) the class of those privileged by property ownership or high levels of education. Weber specified, as usual, that the transitions between social classes were gradual. Quite independently of individual experiences, nevertheless, "social classes" are relatively enduring features of social systems, and they are primarily economic in origin.

While making this point, Weber cautioned his readers against overly simple theories of revolution. Similar class positions, he pointed out, *may but need not* generate concerted social action. The differences between property classes are not "dynamic"; they do not necessarily lead to class conflicts and revolutions. The specific and overt tensions between creditors and debtors, landowners and the dispossessed, to be sure, may sharpen into revolutionary clashes; but these need not transform the prevailing economic order. More generally, class-based social action is easiest to organize (1) against such immediately visible opponents as managing entrepreneurs, not against company owners and shareholders (the real recipients of unearned income), and not by peasants against landowners; (2) in the presence of massively similar class positions; (3) where class action is easiest to organize, as in a common workplace; and (4) where convincing goals of action are proposed by an intellectual leadership that regularly comes from outside the relevant class.

[handwritten margin note: Economic tension do not necessarily lead to revolution of economic order]

Returning to his tactics of classification, Weber then defined "status position" as a typically effective claim to "social esteem" that is based upon an appropriate "style of life," upon an education that forms that style, or upon prestige of birth or occupation. In practice, similarity of "status position" expresses itself in "connubium" and "commensality," in the monopolization of privileged income sources or the rejection of certain kinds of economic acquisition, as well as in other status conventions or "traditions." Status position, Weber pointed out, can be based upon class position, but not exclusively so. Thus wealth and entrepreneurship are not status qualifications in themselves, although they may lead to status advantages, and the reverse is true of poverty. Conversely, status position can affect class position, without being identical with it. Thus the class position or wealth of an officer, civil servant, or student can vary widely, without altering his status position, since the conduct of life, instilled by his education, is identical in the relevant respects. A "status group" *(Stand),* Weber continued, holds specific status advantages within a given social system, which may be grounded in a variety of historical antecedents. Whereas income classes develop in the context of market-oriented economic systems, status groups originate and persist primarily in feudal or "estate-type patrimonial" societies. Indeed, a society may be termed a "status" or "estate society," or a "class society," depending upon which kind of social differentiation predominates within it. A status or estate society is conventionally ordered by rules of conduct that are economically *irrational.*[7]

The relationship between class position and status position *within* a given society is the subject of a fascinating paragraph in the older part 2 of *Economy and Society.* Weber there argues that the "status order" normally predominates during periods of economic stability, whereas technological or economic change tends to threaten it and to bring the "class" system into the foreground. Periods in which "naked class positions" reach maximal significance are usually ages of technological and economic transformation, whereas the slowing down of economic change encourages the reemergence of the "status" hierarchy and reaffirms the importance of social "honor." In other words, class and status hierarchies change at different *rates*. Economic development can bring about rapid redistributions of class advantages and disadvantages, but the status order cannot be quickly transformed. It evolves only slowly, with a kind of inertia or cultural lag, and this can lead to more or less temporary *incongruities* between the hierarchies of economic class and of sociocultural status. High-status styles of life—and of education—are typically those of formerly dominant elites. The status order can both reinforce and modify or complicate the hierarchy of class.[8] In the Germany of Weber's own time, in fact, accelerated economic growth threatened the status position of the formerly dominant educated elite, which brought on painful experiences of social incongruity and cultural unease, as the high industrial class society threatened inherited status rankings.

In any case, Weber considered status differences—and their roots in educational differences—particularly significant in Germany. "Differences of education are one of the strongest barriers in society, *especially in Germany*, where privileged positions within and outside the civil service are tied not only to specialized knowledge, but also to 'general *Bildung*.' . . . All our examination diplomas also and primarily certify this important *status* quality."[9] With that, we are back at the significance of *Bildung* in the German tradition, with its emphasis upon the sources of classical antiquity, especially Greece, and with the attendant vision of cultivation as self-perfection through the interpretive interaction with these sources. That interaction could be conceived simply as an absorbing of values from what Georg Simmel termed the realm of "objective culture," or it could be imagined in a more complex image as a *selective* interaction. Weber really followed Simmel in picturing the "knowledge of cultivation" as the awakening of charisma or the fulfillment of a potential already present in the personality of the learner. On the other hand, as we also know, he believed the German "doctoral factories" of his day could no longer claim to confer *Bildung* and were well advised to concentrate on the specific virtue of "intellectual rectitude."[10]

SCIENCE AS A VOCATION

The major themes in Max Weber's work came together for one last time in his two famous addresses, "Science as a Vocation" and "Politics as a Vocation."

The two lectures were famous even in their own time as deliberate challenges to the methodological and political irrationalism in the German academic community of that time. Both were invited lectures sponsored by a liberal student organization. The first was initially delivered from handwritten notes in November 1917; the second was given over a year later, and both were revised for publication in mid-1919. In the first of the two titles, the word *Wissenschaft* could have been translated as "Scholarship" or "Learning," but I prefer "Science," a term Weber explicitly reserved for systematic knowledge based upon *causal analysis*, including the analysis of human actions. "Vocation" *(Beruf)*, used in both titles, evokes the sense of a "calling," or a commitment to a an objective task or "cause" *(Sache)*, as Weber first described it in his *Protestant Ethic*. For a principled individualist, one has to realize, a "vocation" is also a *social identity*, in that it projects a set of purely personal commitments into the dimensions of a social role or function. When Weber talked about "science" and "politics" as "vocations," in other words, he meant to relate his identity as an individual to the social world in which he lived.

Weber opened "Science as a Vocation" with a comparison between the German and the American university systems, focusing upon how they affected young people contemplating academic careers. In America, he reported, beginning academics are given modest salaries as "assistants," much like assistants at large German research institutes in the natural sciences. Once salaried, young American faculty are asked to teach the large introductory courses and expected to attract big audiences. Their positions are not automatically renewed; they are judged in part on their teaching performance, and they are not left with much time for their own research. In Germany, a young academic must earn the right to teach *(venia legendi)* in a specified subject as an instructor *(Privatdozent);* the "need" for additional faculty is sometimes considered in the appointment of *Privatdozenten,* and influential senior professors may favor their own students in awarding these positions. Even scientific research assistants have to work toward the *venia legendi.* Once awarded the right to teach, German instructors are expected to teach only small courses in their own specialties, so as not to compete with their senior colleagues for the obligatory fees paid by students in the large lecture courses that prepare for the main qualifying examinations. As a result, German *Privatdozenten* have time for their own research but virtually no earnings from their teaching. They almost have to be independently wealthy, which accounts for a "plutocratic" element in the recruitment of German university faculty.[11]

On the other hand, the German universities are gradually being "Americanized": German senior faculty, especially full professors *(Ordinarien),* are becoming directors of huge, state-supported research organizations, even while the large majority of junior faculty are being forced into the dependent position of salaried employees. Occasioned by the rapidly increasing complexity and cost of research technology, this trend is part of the all-pervasive advance of bureaucracy and of state capitalism. In Germany as in America, it separates the large majority of researchers from the means of research, and it makes the position of the junior faculty a vaguely proletarian one. The transformation in progress has altered the spirit of the German university, turning its inherited constitution into a fiction. Certainly the chiefs of the gigantic new research institutes have nothing left in common with the German *Ordinarius* of former times (74–75).

One thing, however, has remained unchanged, or has actually worsened, Weber insisted, and that is the situation of young people proposing to enter the academic profession. Whether a research assistant or *Privatdozent* will ever attain the rank of full professor, not to mention the directorship of an institute, is more a matter of chance than of individual ability. The fact that so many mediocrities play prominent roles at the universities cannot justly be blamed upon the personal deficiencies of individual faculty members or ministerial officials. The fault lies, rather, in the laws of human collaboration among a plurality of corporate organizations—in this case the faculties that recommend candidates and the ministries that make the final selections. The real surprise is that, despite everything, a substantial number of good appointments are actually made, except where parliaments or monarchs have interfered in the process, or present-day revolutionary powers meddle for political reasons, thus making room for conformist mediocrities (75–77).

The accidental element in the fate of the young German academic is due also to the fact that he must be an able teacher *and* a good scholar, even though the skills required for the two tasks rarely coincide in the same person. Weber distrusted large student audiences as symptoms of good teaching. Of course the laying out of scientific issues in a way that allows unschooled but receptive minds to understand them—and to think independently about them—is a great gift. Yet one may be good at that even without attracting high enrollments. Democracy is fine where it belongs, Weber said, but scientific training in the tradition of the German universities is an intellectually aristocratic task, and that should not be overlooked. In sum, success in an academic career is an accident for a variety of reasons; one hardly dares to encourage young people to enter the profession. If they are Jews, of course, one must tell them, in Dante's language, to "leave all hope behind." But all of them must ask themselves whether they will be able to see mediocrities outstrip them again and again without bitterness or emotional damage (78–80).

Weber then turned to what he called the "inner vocation" for *Wissenschaft*, which he associated with the passionate desire to make an original and permanent contribution to human knowledge. To satisfy this passion under present conditions, he argued, is possible only by means of strict scientific specialization. To cross the boundaries between different research fields, as sociologists do, is to run the risk of discovering no more than new lines of inquiry for others to pursue. On the other hand, the passion for discovery alone does not guarantee the scientist what he really needs: a fruitful idea or "intuition" *(Eingebung)*. Young people nowadays imagine that *Wissenschaft* is like a mathematical calculation, a factory product of "cool reason," rather than of the "whole soul." But that view is false. For nothing is ever achieved in science— or in other fields—without an "intuition" or new idea. Fruitful hunches usually present themselves only after much work has been done. Yet in science as in other fields, dilettantes sometimes have productive intuitions, although they lack the training to confirm them (80–83).

Whether or not fruitful ideas come to us is partly a question of fate beyond our ken, but it also depends upon the individual's "gifts." That fact in turn helps to account for the popularity among young people of a cult that is widely celebrated today. The idols of that cult, Weber said, are the idols of "personality" and of "vital experience" *(Erleben)*. The impression prevails that the two are interdependent, since the having of "experiences" is held to be a defining characteristic of the "personality." But an old and adequate German term for this "experiencing" is "sensation"; for to legitimate yourself by means of "vital experience," and self-consciously to reach for radically new insights is just to make a spectacle of yourself. The only way to become a personality in science, in art, and in all other fields, he insisted, is to commit yourself to a task or problem *(Sache)*, and to meet the demands it makes upon you (84–85).

But there is a crucial difference between the work of the artist and that of the scientist. A work of art can reach perfection within the technical and stylistic frameworks of its time, but that is not true of scientific work, which is subject to the laws of "progress." Our scientific findings, Weber told his audience, will be outdated in ten, twenty, or fifty years; this is their fate, and indeed their "sense." Every "fulfillment" in our research raises new questions and *wants to be* superseded. And this progress extends into the infinite, which surely raises a problem of meaning. Why should we engage in a project that is inherently endless? Part of the answer may be practical or technical: We are helped to attain our immediate ends. But what if we seek scientific knowledge "for its own sake," without regard for commercial or technical benefits? What meaningful end do we pursue when we enter into the infinite sequence of "progress"? Weber characterized the advance of science as the central element in the process of "intellectualization" that has been under way for thousands of years. Before asking what it means for our lives, he points out that the modern individual understands less about the workings of a streetcar—and of the science and technology that surround him—than the "savage" knew about his tools. What modern man gains from the ongoing process of intellectualization and rationalization, therefore, is just the conviction that he *could* understand the conditions of his life if he *wanted* to, or that no mysterious forces are at work around him. In principle, therefore, he could calculate, predict, and thus dominate his environment. That is "the removal of magic from the world." But again, what "sense" does it make beyond the realm of practical applications? (85–87).

It was Leo Tolstoy, Weber reported, who posed this question while pondering the significance of death for the modern individual. Abraham, or a farmer of ancient times, died "old and sated with life." But the man immersed in modern culture, in the unending growth of knowledge, can become "tired of life," never "sated," for he cannot appropriate more than a tiny fraction of what has been made available to him in modern civilization. In the face of this infinite wealth, the death of the individual has become an abrupt and pointless interruption of his potential development. "Progress" has made death a contradiction, and thus the boundless increase of knowledge itself has lost its meaning. With that, Weber said, we have moved beyond the problem of the individual's vocation for *Wissenschaft.* Now we are questioning the meaning of scientific inquiry itself: What, ultimately, is the meaning of *Wissenschaft* for the life of humanity? (87–88).

There were times in the past when this question seemed to have a satisfying answer, and Weber vividly recalled them. There was Plato's wonderful image of prisoners chained in a cave who can see only shadows against the wall they face. But then one of them frees himself, sees the sun, and takes on the philosopher's task of leading his companions upward to the light of scientific truth and to the knowledge of "true being." Weber traced the enthusiasm of Plato's vision to Socrates' discovery of *concepts,* the basic tools of systematic inquiry. If one discovered the concept of the beautiful, or of the good, or of the soul, Plato believed, then one could reach the essential truths they encompass. It also seemed to follow that one could learn how to act, as a citizen for instance, and that was decisive. Today's youth, Weber observed, hold views diametrically opposed to those of Plato. They regard scientific concepts as bloodless abstractions that never succeed in capturing the reality of life (88–90).

To the discovery of the concept in the Hellenic era, Weber continued, the European Renaissance added the rational experiment, the second great element in the scientific method. Such artistic innovators as Leonardo da Vinci, along with the musical practitioners of the sixteenth century, saw the experiment as a path to "true art" and thus also to "true nature." The rational experiment was absorbed into the emerging natural sciences by Galileo in practice, and by Roger Bacon in theory. And again Weber contrasted the optimism of the early experimenters with the attitudes prevalent among the young people of his time. The idea of "science as a path to nature" strikes them as blasphemy, since they seek relief from the intellectualism of the sciences, so as to return to their own true nature—and to nature itself (90–91).

In the seventeenth century, finally, the advance of the empirical sciences raised even greater expectations. Weber cited the naturalist Swammerdam, who found "proof of God's providence in the anatomy of a louse." Indirectly influenced by Puritan and Pietist religious beliefs, the scientists of those times distrusted philosophical deduction but thought it possible to detect God's purposes in physical nature. How vast a gulf separated that age from our own! With few exceptions, Weber said, no one nowadays believes that the sciences can teach us anything about the meaning of the world. If anything, they tend to eradicate the belief that there is such a meaning. Far from pointing the way to God, modern science has become the chief *enemy* of religion. Contemporary youth yearns to escape from scientific rationalism, whether in religious experience or in the realm of the irrational. As for the naive hope that science and technology can transform our lives and bring us happiness, it is surely subject to Nietzsche's devastating critique of "the last human beings who have invented happiness" (91–92).

Summarizing this part of his argument, Weber arrived at the issues that really concerned him:

> What is . . . the meaning of science as a vocation now that all these earlier illusions—"the way to true being," "the way to true art," "the way to true nature," "the way to the true God," "the way to true happiness"— have faded. The simplest answer was given by Tolstoy . . . "It is meaningless, since it does not answer the only question that is important for us: "What shall we do? How shall we live?" The fact that it does not

provide an answer is plainly incontestable. The only question is in what sense it provides "no" answer, and whether it does not, after all, offer something to those who ask the question properly.

Commenting upon the idea of a science free of presuppositions, Weber argued that all scientific work presupposes valid rules of logic and of method, the foundations of our orientation in the world. "But there is the further presupposition that the results of scientific work are *important* in the sense of 'worth knowing.' And that obviously raises all sorts of problems. For this presupposition itself cannot be scientifically demonstrated. It can only be *interpreted* in its ultimate meaning." One can only accept or reject this presupposition, depending upon one's own orientation to life (93).

Indeed, different kinds of scientific work also differ in their relationships to their presuppositions. Thus the natural sciences presuppose that the laws of events in the cosmos are worth knowing, quite apart from their practical applications, and this presupposition is not scientifically demonstrable. And of course there is no way of proving that the world described by science is worthy of existence, not to mention whether one can meaningfully exist within it. The technical sciences may allow us to dominate the world, but they cannot prove that we should do so. In medicine, one assumes that life should be preserved and suffering ameliorated, but the medical sciences do not tell us whether life is worth living, and analogous problems confront us in jurisprudence. The historical sciences of culture seek to understand political, artistic, literary, and social phenomena in the context of their origins; but they cannot decide whether these phenomena are either valuable in themselves, or worth the effort to understand them. They presuppose that it is of interest to participate in the community of cultures, but they do not scientifically defend that position (94–95).

As he turned more specifically to his own fields of specialization, Weber also shifted focus to the issue of politics in the classroom. He reacted negatively to reports of noisy student demonstrations at the lectures of pacifist professors, although he did not share their pacifist views. But he mainly repeated his earlier arguments against the expression or tacit suggestion of political preferences by professors in the classroom.

What one can demand from [university teachers] is the intellectual rectitude to recognize that it is one thing to ascertain facts, mathematical or logical relationships, or [the] inner structure of cultural goods, and quite another to ask questions about the *value* of culture and of its several contents, or how one should *act* within cultural communities and political organizations. If [the colleague] then asks why he should not address both in the lecture hall, one must answer: because the prophet and the demagogue do not belong there. . . . "Go out into the streets and speak in public." Speak, that is, where criticism is possible.

The individual academic may not fully succeed in bracketing his subjective sympathy, but that "proves nothing, since other, purely factual errors are possible as well, and yet prove nothing against the duty to seek the truth." For good measure, Weber offered to show in the work of historians that "wherever the man of science intrudes his own value judgment, there the full understanding of the facts comes to an end." If both a believer and a nonbeliever are to profit from a course on the history of religion, he added, then the teacher must be able to focus upon what can be known apart from all faith (95–98, esp. 97–98).

Scientifically grounded value preferences were impossible, for Weber, because the various possible value orientations confronted each other in an irreconcilable conflict. This was a major thesis of his "Intermediate Reflection," and he reintroduced it here. He approvingly cited John Stuart Mill's claim that experience suggests polytheism, or a plurality of ultimate values. From Nietzsche and from Baudelaire, Weber said, we have relearned that "something may be holy" precisely to the extent that "it is not beautiful . . . and beautiful . . . in that it is not good. And of course the true need be neither holy, nor beautiful, nor good. Reading Weber today, we may be struck by the echo of Kant in this foursome, but Weber saw it as part of a more extended diversity of mutually contradictory "gods" or normative orders. The battle among these gods, he argued, was governed by "fate." In any case, he did not see how a classroom teacher could "disprove" the Sermon on the Mount or the injunction to "turn the other cheek." He clearly preferred the "manful dignity" of "resisting evil," lest one share responsibility for its persistence. Yet he was deeply aware of the diversity of possible ethical orientations in the post-Christian era, and his rhetoric primarily dramatized the difficulty of choosing among contending "gods" (99–101).

Directly addressing his young listeners, Weber urged them not to expect their professors to be "leaders" as well. In a deliberate exaggeration, he described the attitude of the American student, who learns little, takes many tests, but still resists the German student's obsession with official examinations, largely because bureaucratization has not yet fully conquered the American continent. The young American respects nothing but personal achievement; that is his version of "democracy." He expects his teachers to "sell" him their knowledge and method, in exchange for his father's money, but it would not occur to him to seek rules of conduct or a *Weltanschauung* from them, although he might regard his coach as a personal leader. But in America as in Germany, Weber insisted, an excellent scholar and teacher may not have the qualities of a leader, whether in matters of practical orientation or in politics. It is therefore problematic to attribute such qualities to him—or to have him presume to play the role of a leader. The professor who feels qualified to advise the young may want to interact with them on a personal level. But if he wants to take a position in the battle of worldviews and party opinions, he should do so in the public marketplace, where his listeners will not be forced to remain silent (101–3).

Having thus stated his case for an irreducible conflict of values—and against politics in the classroom—Weber turned at last to the positive services that *Wissenschaft* could provide. The teacher who made his students face facts that were inconvenient in the light of their preferences, he thought, could be credited with an intellectual achievement and an ethical one as well. Beyond that, he named four ways in which systematic inquiry can guide the individual in his practical and personal life: It can offer technical advice on how to calculate, to predict, and thus to act upon both physical objects and human beings. It can supply methods of analysis and tools of thought. It can help the individual to understand the consequences of his own projects, especially the relationships between means and ends. With respect to social questions, for example, if you take a certain position and wish to achieve certain outcomes, controlled experience can inform you that you must choose specific means to achieve your objectives, and that you will obtain a particular set of side effects as well. You may find either the means or the side effects morally problematic, but that judgment lies beyond the bounds of science. Still, there is one last service that systematic knowledge can offer you: It can help you to reach "clarity" about the internal consistence of your commitments, it can tell you what positions can be logically derived from any given ultimate worldview or evaluative axiom. "For you will necessarily come to these or those ultimate meaningful consequences if you remain true to yourself. . . . We can oblige or help the individual to *account to himself about the ultimate meaning of his own actions.* . . . Of the teacher who achieves this, I am again tempted to say he serves ethical powers: the duty to foster clarity and a sense of responsibility." Of course, as Weber insisted, all this still assumes the eternal and irreconcilable conflict between the ultimate value orientations, and thus also the necessity of deciding among them (103–5).

Weber asked his audience to reflect whether, under the circumstances, *Wissenschaft* made sense as a vocation or, indeed, whether it had a vocation itself. Science could not answer these questions either, although Weber announced his own choice in favor of the search for truth. Today's science, he said served reflection and the detection of factual relationships; it would *not* offer revelation, the gift of prophecy, or the speculations of wise men about the meaning of the world.

> And if Tolstoy again rises within you and asks, Who . . . will answer the question, "What shall we do?" . . . or "Which one of the competing gods shall we serve?" . . . then the answer must be, "Only a prophet or a savior." And if he does not exist, or his gospel is no longer believed, then you will certainly not bring him back to earth by having thousands of professors . . . try to take over his role in their lecture halls. . . . The prophet after whom so many in our youngest generation yearn is just *not* there. . . . The innermost interest of a religiously "musical" human being can in no way be served, if the fundamental fact that he is fated to live in an age without God and without . . . prophets is hidden from him . . . by surrogate prophecies from the lectern.

Honest religious sentiment itself, Weber said, would have to rebel against false prophecy (105–6).

But what of theology and of its claim to the status of a *Wissenschaft*? To the presuppositions of all other disciplines, Weber argued, the theologians add the assumption that the world has a meaning, which leaves them with the Kantian question of how this is possible. In addition, theology usually assumes a specific "revelation," which invests life with meaning, but which lies beyond the bounds of *Wissenschaft*. All positive theology must eventually demand the Augustinian "belief in the absurd," the "sacrifice of the intellect," which accounts for the unbridgeable chasm between religion and science. That sacrifice is brought by the disciple to the prophet, or by the believer to his church. "But a new prophecy has never arisen from the fact . . . that some modern intellectuals feel the need to furnish their souls with genuine antiques . . . and playfully decorate their domestic chapel . . . with little icons from all parts of the world, or create a surrogate through all kinds of vital experience." Unlike religious youth communities, which Weber took more seriously, he regarded the surrogate religions of the intellectuals as "fraud and self-deception" (106–9).

It was characteristic of the "fate of our age," given rationalization and the removal of magic from the world, Weber thought, that its highest values had retreated from public life into the mystic realm or the brotherliness of intimate personal relationships. It is no accident, he said, that our attempts at monumental art are miserable failures, and the same will be true of attempts to invent a new religion in the absence of genuine prophecy. "And prophecy from the lectern will create only fanatical sects, but never a genuine religious community. Those who cannot manfully bear this fate of our time must be told: It would be better if you returned quietly . . . into the wide and charitably open arms of the church." For that is more honest than intellectual evasion, and certainly than false academic prophecy. The only virtue that belongs in the lecture hall is "simple intellectual rectitude."

> For all those who today wait for saviors and prophets, the situation is as . . . [described in] the Edomitic watchman's song, . . . "There comes a call from Seir in Edom: Watchman, how long yet the night? The watchman answers: The morning is coming, but still it is night. If you want to ask, come again another time."

The people who were told that, Weber commented, asked and waited for more than two millennia, and we know their fate. Let us conclude that it is not enough to yearn and to wait. Let us go to work and do justice to the "demands of the day," both humanly and in our professions. "But that is simple and easy if everyone finds and obeys the demon who holds the threads of his life" (110–11).

Weber's "Science as a Vocation" was intensely vivid. But it also raised a number of difficult questions that must be considered. And to begin with, Weber's talk of "fate" and of "demons" suggests what might be called a *post-religious* position. While he absolutely rejected the "sacrifice of the intellect," he was clearly not at ease in an age without God and without genuine prophecy. The Edomitic watchman knew not only that it was night, but also that day was coming. In "Science as a Vocation," as in the "Intermediate Reflection," Tolstoy and the salvation religion of "cosmic love" powerfully exemplified the Christian challenge to a purely scientific view of the world. To be sure, Weber did not need the Sermon on the Mount to make the judgment that free market capitalism is "substantively irrational." Nor did he invoke "fate" when he warned young scholars of the "accidents" they would encounter in their careers. Yet what he meant by "fate" at the end of his lecture cannot simply be rendered as "the accidental." For the "demons" who hold the "threads" of our lives have something in common with God's inexorable Providence. Today, some of us are fully convinced that there is no God—and no nonhuman "meaning" in the awesome history of the universe. But that is certainly not what Weber felt. He knew that he lived in a godless age, but God and "meaning" still lived in some part of his memory, as the painful echo of a loss.

The question that follows is how much Weber owed to Nietzsche, and it is not easy to answer. In the letters Weber wrote from 1906 to 1912 (those that have so far been published), there is only one reference to Nietzsche.[12] Almost certainly following Simmel, Weber approvingly mentions Nietzsche's "ethic of human dignity" (*Vornehmheit*), while dismissing his "biological" speculations. In his sociology of religion, as we know, Weber largely rejected Nietzsche's "slave revolt in morals," although he partly accepted the role of "resentment" in post-exilic Judaism. Beyond that, Weber twice explicitly followed Nietzsche in his contempt for "the last human beings, who have invented happiness," and there is something strenuous in that gesture. It is one thing for Weber to announce that he is less interested in the "comfort" of future generations than in the fostering of "human greatness." But the slap at "happiness" still seems excessive. It reminds me of the striking passage in *The Red and the Black*, in which Stendhal steps out of his narrator's role, so as gently to remind his exalted young hero that there is nothing wrong with a little happiness. One wants to say that to Max Weber as well. On the other hand, in Weber's remarks about the relationship between infinite "progress" and the "life of humanity," he was probably following Simmel, rather than Nietzsche; for his emphasis was upon the *disproportion* between the endless growth of knowledge and the brevity of the individual life, which Simmel had described as an incongruity between "objective" and "subjective culture."

One might ask, moreover, whether anything in Weber's writings resembles Carl Schmitt's "decisionism," even outside the realm of political commitments, or whether he was a liberal "pluralist," as I have suggested. The force of the question stems from Weber's own persistent emphasis upon the conflict among rival "gods" or norms. Again and again, he suggested that the individual must choose or "decide" among competing value axioms, and one can easily get the impression that the choice to be made is largely gratuitous. Yet that impression cannot be accurate, since Weber offers a substantial framework of scientific consideration that the individual should take into account before entering upon a course of action: He must reach "clarity" about *all* the consequences of the steps he contemplates; that is a requirement of "intellectual rectitude." In addition, he must be logically consistent; his ultimate principles must be reflected and consistent with each other. Finally, as Weber explained in a letter to Ferdinand Tönnies, he believed in Kant's categorical imperative, though he considered its purely "formal" character insufficient as a basis for a fully substantive ethic. How much room would be left, after all that, for the play of gratuitous "decisions"?[13]

The historical approach to the thought of the past is fruitful only to the extent that the traditions and the immediate context in which it originated can help us to understand its meaning. But Weber stood in the tradition of Wilhelm von Humboldt and of John Stuart Mill, both of whom celebrated the benefits of individual and cultural diversity. But if *they* were liberal pluralists, then why not Max Weber?—In his immediate intellectual environment, moreover, Weber was primarily concerned with the crucial distinction between *Wissenschaft* and value judgment, and with false "prophecy" in the classroom and elsewhere, because they were irrational currents in the "cultural crisis" of his age. Indeed, that brings us back again to the conflict between *Bildung* and intellectual specialization, and to the traditional link between *Wissenschaft* and *Weltanschauung,* for the large majority of his colleagues really *wanted* to offer their students more than information and method, and to convey something like wisdom and evaluative insight.

In any case, the reactions of Weber's colleagues to "Science as a Vocation" were almost uniformly negative. Thus Ernst Troeltsch countered with Ernst Husserl's phenomenology as a new form of philosophy that permitted the "viewing" *(erschauen)* of experiences and ideas in their "essence." Arthur Salz and Eduard Spranger, who stood closer to the orthodox center of the academic spectrum, expressed their regret at the excessive modesty of Weber's position, and sought to extend the scope of *Wissenschaft* by means of "synthesis," and "vital experience" *(erleben).* What followed during the 1920s was an intense search for morally profitable insights, especially in humanistic scholarship, that ultimately converted the "cultural crisis" into a "crisis of *Wissenschaft*" as well.

Eduard Spranger was a prominent professor of philosophy, psychology, and pedagogy. In a 1921 lecture entitled "The Present State of the *Geisteswissenschaften* and the School," he totally transformed Weber's message to Germany's young people. "Today more than ever before, the young adult . . . lives through the fullness of his intellectual faculties. . . . [There is] a drive toward wholeness . . . [and] a religious yearning: a groping back from the artificial and mechanical circumstances to the eternal spring of the metaphysical." Spranger believed that some of the new methods in the humanistic disciplines would allow scholars to arrive at new ethical perspectives.

> [We can] establish total ethical norms for given cultural situations on the basis of our empathetic understanding.

> Every teacher of the humanistic disciplines ought to realize that his
> task entails not only the presentation of his own . . . value judgments,
> but the penetration of the possible fundamental standpoints as such.
> . . . The only question is whether this is the last word.[14]

Of course it wasn't; for Spranger was one of those prophetic opponents of the
Weimar Republic who helped to bring it down.[15]

POLITICS AS A VOCATION

The opening third of Weber's lecture entitled "Politics as a Vocation" was devoted to the familiar concepts of his political sociology, including his theories
of legitimacy and of bureaucracy, his history of the Western city, and his sociology of law. It took him a long time to turn to the actual occupations available
to members of his audience with an interest in politics, and the first profession
he considered in any detail was that of journalism. For Weber, the journalist
was the modern "demagogue," who used the written word, rather than the
Periclean oration. The journalist suffered from a lack of social esteem, but he
was at least equal to the academic intellectually and in his sense of responsibility, as was evident during the World War. On the other hand, journalism
was of limited promise as a path to political leadership. Even among the Social
Democrats, political editors had trouble asserting themselves, and their
chances were apparently declining in the middle-class parties as well. Journalists did not have the free time to engage in part-time political activity, and their
influence was being outstripped by that of the great press magnates to boot. In
Germany, at any rate, journalism was no longer—or not yet—a good stepping
stone to political leadership. The career of the young journalist was even more
subject to "pure accident" than that of the young academic. The surprise, under the circumstances, was that so many serious and talented individuals were
nevertheless attracted to journalism as a vocation.[16]

Before turning to the professional politician and the party official, Weber
reviewed the role of the traditional "notables" *(Honoratioren)* and parliamentary deputies, particularly in Germany. The arrival of the middle classes in European politics, he argued, led to the formation of political clubs and parties
dominated by an educated and propertied elite of clergymen, teachers, professors, lawyers, doctors, well-to-do landowners, and manufacturers. In England, all those considered "gentlemen" were included in this group. Most of
these notables were part-time politicians, and their influence was primarily local. National political parties had not yet been formed, so that policy decisions

were made by the leaders of political clubs and parliamentary delegations. Even when the desire for nationwide platforms and increased impact led to the emergence of disciplined political parties, the party apparatus long remained in the hands of the notables. While programs were increasingly defined by a national party press, and while membership contributions helped to strengthen central party offices, the party activists were rarely full-time professional politicians (*P*, 201–2).

There is the sharpest possible contrast, Weber continued, between the "idyllic" rule of the notables and parliamentarians, and the most modern forms of party organization. These forms are the products of mass democracy and of the need for mass organization, for centralized leadership, and for strict party discipline. Full-time politicians *outside* the parliaments now take charge, either as political entrepreneurs, like the American "boss" and the English "election agent," or as salaried party officials. There is a degree of formal democratization, in that open party meetings elect delegates to higher-level party conferences. Nevertheless, the real power lies in the hands of those who occupy permanent positions within the organization or who are large financial contributors. On the other hand, the party absolutely depends upon effective popular leaders, whom the "machine" will follow even over the heads of the parliamentary delegation. The development of mass parties thus also means the emergence of *plebiscitary democracy*. The party's rank and file naturally expect to benefit from the leader's success at the polls, both "materially," from political appointments and other benefits, and "ideally," in commitment to a personal leader, rather than to abstract programs and political mediocrities. There have been Social Democrats who feared the "bureaucratization" of their party by its officials. But Weber argued that "the material and ideal interests" of party functionaries would normally move them to follow an outstanding leader. Thus the rise of popular leaders was most difficult in the middle-class parties under the control of part-time political notables. Fresh from his own defeat at the hands of Democratic Party notables in his home state of Baden, Weber expressed his contempt for men who derived their importance from their "little posts" and who of course resented the demagogue as an upstart (*P*, 202–5).

Reflecting upon the environment in which mass parties, party professionals and political entrepreneurs emerged, Weber once again recalled the story of the American worker who would rather "spit on" corrupt politicians than have honest officials "spit on him." That, Weber said, was American "democracy," though the Civil Service Reform was bringing educated officials to the fore in the United States as well. German political conditions, meantime, have been characterized by powerless parliaments unable to attract political talents, by the immense importance of trained officials, who took over the ministerial positions as well; and by two political parties, the Social Democrats and the Catholic Center, that sought to represent *Weltanschauungen,* deliberately played minority roles, and rejected parliamentary compromise (217–20). As a result, no responsible political leaders could rise to power, and both the middle-class parties and the parliament itself became petty "guilds." The postwar revolution might bring changes, but Weber noted that the old party organizations were continuing their work as usual. Nevertheless, the alternatives remained what they had always been. "The only choice is leadership democracy with a "machine" or leaderless democracy, that is, the rule of professional politicians without the inner charismatic qualities that make a leader." The plebiscitary president of the Reich offered a possible escape from the passivity of the inherited "guild system." For students forced to earn their living from politics, in any case, the careers of the journalist and of the party official were still the major options (*P,* 222–26, esp. 224).

With almost three-quarters of his lecture behind him, Weber finally turned to the personal "vocation" for politics and the "inner joys" it could offer. Above all, he asked what "qualities" his listeners needed to "do justice" to the "responsibility" that comes with power. He raised the "ethical question" about "what sort of human being one must be to put one's hand on the wheel of history." And he named the three principal qualities of "passion, the feeling of responsibility, and judgment." The passion he had in mind was "passionate commitment to a cause" *(Sache),* rather than the "sterile excitement" that Weber's "late friend Georg Simmel" used to dismiss . . . or the aimless "romanticism" of some contemporary intellectuals: "a 'romanticism of the intellectually interesting,' without any . . . feeling of responsibility. For mere . . . passion will not do . . . if it does not . . . make *responsibility* toward a cause its guide to action. And that requires . . . *judgment,* the ability to confront the realities with inner concentration." Vanity, Weber observed, is a common trait, and among academics it is "a kind of occupational disease"; fortunately, however, it does no harm to the advance of science. But the situation is different for the politician, who uses "the striving for power as an indispensable means."

> The sin against the holy ghost of his profession begins where this striving for power becomes subjective *(unsachlich)* and an object of purely personal self-intoxication, . . . For there are only two deadly sins in the field of politics: subjectivity *(Unsachlichkeit)* and . . . lack of responsibility.

The *unsachlich* politician, Weber said, takes the brilliant appearance of power for power itself, and the irresponsible politician enjoys power for its own sake, without regard for any substantive purpose. The mere "power politician" may *seem* strong; but the recent collapse of his type has taught us how much inner weakness is hidden behind his empty gestures (*P*, 226–29).

To what cause a politician commits himself is up to his own convictions. He may choose to serve purposes that are national or human, social, ethical or cultural, this-worldly or other-worldly; he may accept or reject the belief in progress, or stand for an idea; but he must have some kind of faith or purpose. And that brought Weber back to the conflict of ultimate worldviews and to the need to choose among them. But he paused at this point to reject what he considered a false application of ethics to politics. He found it hard to tolerate the talk, among both the winners and the losers of the war, about the "guilt" of having caused it. He preferred an emphatically masculine rhetoric of "dignity" and "chivalry," in which both victors and vanquished simply accepted the military outcome, and resolutely turned their attention to the *consequences*, which, incidentally, were mainly the victors' responsibility (*P*, 231–32).

Weber also insisted that the revolutionary Councils' use of power backed by force was no more ethical than its use by the dictatorial masters of the old regime. The revolutionaries might emphasize the moral excellence of their ends, but their opponents were likely to lay claim to noble intentions with equal subjective honesty. It was the use of power as a means that was at issue: "He who lives by the sword will die by the sword, and conflict remains conflict. And so: the ethic of the *Sermon on the Mount*?" The choice of that ethic, Weber argued, is a more serious matter than some of its current advocates seem to realize. A saint may "turn the other cheek"; the "ethic of cosmic love" may forbid resistance to evil. But the opposite holds for the politician; he must resist evil—or be responsible for its ascendancy. The Christian pacifist may lay down his arms, as some Germans lately did, so as to put an end to war. But the politician will recognize that only a peace on the basis of the status quo would have discredited war, since nations would have questioned its purpose. That is not possible now that the victors—or some of them—have profited from the war. And that is partly the responsibility of those who made it impossible for Germany to resist. Now "the *peace will be discredited, not the war*" (*P*, 233–36).

The absolute ethic does not "*ask* about consequences." But all ethically oriented action can be guided by two radically divergent maxims: by an "ethic of ultimate ends" *(Gesinnungsethik)*, or by an "ethic of responsibility" *(Verantwortungsethik)*. Of course the ethic of ultimate ends is not identical with irresponsibility, just as the ethic of responsibility does not mean lack of conviction. But there is a vast difference between acting in the name of ultimate values, like the Christian who "does the good and leaves the result to God," and acting in the light of one's "responsibility for the foreseeable *consequences* of one's actions." If you convince a "syndicalist," for example, that his behavior will increase the chances of sociopolitical reaction and retard the advance of his class, you will make no impression upon him, for he will attribute what evil comes of the actions that flow from his ethic to the imperfections of the world and the "stupidity of humanity." The responsible agent, by contrast, will count upon "the average defects of human beings," and not feel entitled to ascribe the consequences of his actions to the failings of others. The only responsibility consistent with the ethic of ultimate ends is "the duty to keep alive the flame of protest" against the injustice of the social order. The actions it calls for may be irrational, as long as they have *"exemplary* value" (*P,* 237–38).

Yet the problem extends even further. For "good" ends may be reached by problematic or dangerous means, and no ethic in the world can specify when and to what extent valid ends will justify the acceptance of defective means or of imperfect side effects. Weber used the revolutionary socialists of the "Zimmerwald faction" as a relevant example: Confronted by the choice between a few more years of war followed by a revolution, and an immediate peace without a revolution, they opted for "a few more years of war." And at least according to Weber, they knew perfectly well that the revolution would not bring about true socialism, but merely another version of the "bourgeois economy, with a few feudal elements and dynastic remnants stripped off." Indeed, this problem of the ends justifying the means seems to signal the defeat of the ethic of ultimate ends. In the real world, if not in logic, of course, that ethic may suddenly turn into "chiliastic prophecy," so that the injunction of "love against violence" becomes a call for "violence to end all violence." The pacifist F. W. Förster, an upright man with faulty views, believes that "only good can come of the good, and bad out of the bad." But the whole history of the world demonstrates the opposite, and all religions have had to deal with the problem of "theodicy," the question of how a perfect God could create so imperfect a world (*P,* 238–41).

Indeed, religion has dealt in various ways with the diversity of ethical commitments and qualifications in the world. The vision of an organically differentiated order of paths to salvation, Weber observed, was less consistently carried out in Christianity than in Hinduism. The Christian church permitted the recourse to violence as "a means of discipline against sin." Yet the "ethic of cosmic love" embodied in the Sermon on the Mount, together with the Christian doctrine of natural law, retained their revolutionary force, "reasserting themselves during periods of social upheaval" and creating such pacifist sects as the Quakers. Ordinary Protestantism, by contrast, "legitimated the state" and thus also the means of violence as "divine institutions," especially for the "legitimate authoritarian state." Calvinism, finally, sanctioned force in defense of the faith, and thus also the holy war, which was a vital element in Islam from the beginning. Thus it was not modern unbelief that first raised the problem of political ethics: "All religions have wrestled with it" (*P*, 242–45).

If you want to achieve "absolute justice in the world by means of force," Weber told his audience, you will need an "apparatus" of followers, and you will have to offer your revolutionary followers both "inner" and "outer" rewards. The inner reward will consist of the satisfaction of their class "hatred," their "resentment," and their self-righteous need to "slander their opponents." The outer rewards will be "adventure, victory, booty, power, and prebends." What you accomplish under these circumstances will not depend upon your own motives but upon those of your followers. Even their belief in you as a leader may be a rationalization of their desire for revenge, power, and spoils. "For the materialistic interpretation" of events applies to its believers as well. He who wants to engage in "politics as a vocation" must be "aware of these paradoxes" and of his "responsibility for what he himself can become under their pressure." The "great virtuosi of cosmic love" could ignore political means, since their empire was "not of this world." But all political action that "works with violent means" in accordance with the "ethic of responsibility endangers the salvation of the soul" (*P*, 245–48).

One cannot tell anyone whether and when to follow "the ethic of ultimate ends" or the "ethic of responsibility." But confronted with a sudden increase in politicians who hold others responsible for the consequences of their actions, one may question their seriousness. "In nine of ten cases," Weber said, they seem to me "windbags."

> [They] intoxicate themselves with romantic sensations. I do not find that very interesting. . . . Whereas it is deeply moving when a *mature* human being . . . who really and fully feels this responsibility for the consequences, and who acts from the ethic of responsibility says at some point, "Here I stand; I cannot do otherwise." . . . For this situation should *be able* to arise . . . for anyone who is not dead in spirit. To that extent, the ethic of ultimate ends and the ethic of responsibility are not absolute opposites . . . but jointly characterize the human being who *can* have the "vocation for politics."

"We will speak to each other again in *ten* years," Weber told the young people in his audience. By that time, he rightly predicted, "the age of reaction will long have closed in upon us" (*P*, 249–50).

What lies before us, Weber concluded, is a polar night of icy darkness and severity. And what will become of each of you? Will you succumb to bitterness or to philistinism, a dull acceptance of the world—or flight from the world?

> In each of these cases I will conclude: They did *not* measure up to their own actions, and *not* to the world as it really is. . . . They did not have the vocation for politics. . . . They would have done better simply to cultivate brotherly relationships between human beings.
>
> Politics is a slow drilling of hard boards with both passion and measure. It is quite right, after all, and all of historical experience confirms it, that one would not achieve the possible, if people had not reached again and again for the impossible. But he who can do that must be a leader (and) . . . a hero. And those too who are neither of these must arm themselves with that stoutness of heart that measures up to the disappointment of all hopes, . . . or they will never achieve what is possible today. (*P*, 250–51)

Only he who will not falter if the world seems too stupid and mean for what he wants to offer—"only he has the 'vocation' for politics."[17]

A Man for Our Time

I have been reading Max Weber—and writing about his multidimensional view of the social order as a historically changing mixture of "class position" and "status position," and about the function of advanced education as a source of "social honor." Nothing is intellectually more liberating, surely, than Weber's comprehensive approach to the individual's social identity in terms of "ideal" as well as "material" interests, or than his vision of conflict between competing social roles and self-definitions. I am glad to acknowledge what I have learned from Pierre Bourdieu about the threefold hierarchy of "economic," "social," and "cultural capital," and about "symbolic power" more generally. As the reader knows, I have also drawn upon Bourdieu's concept of the "intellectual field" in the organization of this book. An intellectual field, for Bourdieu, is a network of intellectual positions that have *relational* properties, in that they are defined by their relationships to each other and their place in the overall field. There are differences of symbolic power or authority within an intellectual field, in which dominant orthodoxies confront more heterodox positions. The intellectual field as a whole, finally, is rooted in a "cultural preconscious" that is tacitly perpetuated by inherited institutions, practices, and social relations. I briefly restate all this because I have read Weber's texts in the light of their partly deliberate relationship to the ideology of his orthodox "mandarin" colleagues. With Bourdieu's help, in other words, I have attempted a Weberian reading of Weber. I have tried to understand Weber *in his own time*.

Yet from the beginning, I have also been fascinated by the substance of Weber's arguments. I have read him for his relevance to the concerns of our own time, as someone whose texts are worth reading today, as pungent comments upon our own social and cultural world. Far from having surpassed his thought, we still have much to learn, for example, from his views on politics and economics. Thus many of us have struggled with the problems of capitalism and of socialism. Some of us have been attached to a vision of the individual as a rationally innovative entrepreneur; some have dreamt of a socialist society; while others have rejected socialism as incompatible with human freedom. But what happens when we begin to read Weber?

Calmly but convincingly, Weber tells us that a centrally planned economy is a technical impossibility. Without building up an ideological defense of capitalism, he draws upon his distinction between *formal* and *substantive* rationality, which he originally developed in his sociology of law. To work at all, capitalism depends upon the information and the calculated adjustments that only the market can provide. Given even a modest shift in the felt "needs" of consumers, the most powerful mind in the world could not predict all of the resulting adjustments in the equilibrium relationships that jointly make up the market system. Yet the capitalist absolutely needs a degree of predictability to invest in the factors of production and—at least normally—to profit from providing goods and services at prevailing market prices. The question is not what the entrepreneur "deserves" or what he "owes" to the community. What matters is just the "fact" that he cannot and will not perform unless he can rationally predict the consequences of his economic actions with a reasonable degree of accuracy. What prevents him from acting in his own interests is neither anti-capitalist sentiment nor "government interference" as such, but an excess of unpredictability. The paradox of the market is precisely this: that the individual economic agent must be able to predict the results of his actions within his own sector of the economy with reasonable accuracy; yet no one can predict what "needs" the economy as a whole will have to meet and how.

Having thus insisted upon the need for *formal rationality* in market enterprise, Weber proceeded to characterize functioning capitalism as *substantively irrational*. What he meant is that capitalism falls short of meeting a variety of human normative standards. Not only does it separate the worker from the means of production and force the vast majority of the working population into an incurably marginal bargaining position in their relationship with their employers, but it also creates unbearable differences of wealth and economic power, both among nations and within them. That it does this is simply incontestable, and we can see the disastrous human consequences around us every day. Must we learn to be insensitive to the coexistence of mass starvation, human degradation, and the obtrusive display of senseless luxury? Weber does not choose to preach a secular sermon about these matters; he merely tells us that capitalism is "substantively irrational," and we can only begin to reflect upon ways in which these irrationalities could be reduced. He leaves it to us to decide what measures a liberal polity might legislate to compensate for these humanly unacceptable consequences of capitalism.

Weber was a habitual champion of heterodoxy, a radical individualist, and a liberal pluralist. But he was emphatically *not* an *economic* individualist. True to the German tradition of "social policy" in this respect, he had no sympathy with laissez-faire economic liberalism, not to mention the scientistic economism of some of his pro-entrepreneurial colleagues. The only question he asked himself is what *goals* social policy ought to set for itself, other than a vague mixture of historicist and "ethical" ones. His answer, as we know, was the cause of "the nation," along with the "qualities that make for human greatness," rather than for the "comfort" of future generations. Since the age of liberal nationalism is now behind us, and since Weber himself envisaged a diversity of national cultures, we cannot today make much of his German nationalism. So we are left with his ultimate commitment to a principled cultural individualism and to human greatness, both conceived explicitly as alternatives to the purely economic individualism that seems to have become our surrogate for all human values. Beyond that, I have tried to show that Weber was a liberal pluralist in the tradition of Wilhelm von Humboldt and John Stuart Mill, both of whom were interested in human and cultural diversity, rather than in the inalienable rights of the acquisitive individual.

As a political theorist, Weber believed in democracy, in liberalism, and in fundamental human rights. He also envisaged a competition among "plebiscitary" leaders, who solicit votes in behalf of measures selected to bring about specific outcomes with a high degree of probability. This was Weber's *consequentialism*, the liberal "ethic of responsibility" he recommended to future politicians. It had nothing left in common with the traditional vision of German academics as direct advisers to public officials and to ministries staffed by their former students. It was emphatically democratic in its acknowledgement of mass party organization; it was pluralist in its emphasis upon conflict in the public arena; and it was liberal in its commitment to responsible parliamentary government as a training ground for future leaders. It has troubled some readers because it emphasizes the creative role of charismatic leaders in the courting of a typically passive electorate. But I believe Weber's view was realistic with respect to contemporary democracies, and I cannot see this exceptional academic champion of the Weimar Republic as its gravedigger, unwitting or otherwise.

There are not many serious Marxists left among us, and yet we seem to live in a world in which only the economy matters. Thus when we read Weber, we rediscover the historical and causal significance of *culture,* and indeed of *religion.* In his *Protestant Ethic,* Weber not only explained why the Puritans had to dominate the sinful world in God's honor, but also why modern vocational man strives to succeed—without suspecting the source of his drive. Weber thus also accounted for what he called the "pharisaical good conscience" of those who succeed in the contemporary economic world. Explicitly or not, they believe that their wealth is a reflection of their moral excellence and that the less fortunate *deserve* their failure.

At a deeper level, Weber allows us to understand what it meant for our lives that the Western religious ascetic, starting with the medieval monk, learned to *observe and to control* his inner life—and thus acquired the all-important ability to *predict* and to *plan* a course of action. Weber further offers a convincing portrait of the medieval commune as a revolutionary stage in the rise of the modern "burgher" stratum—and of the role of Christian participation in the Lord's Supper in the emerging "confraternities." And of course Weber teaches us to appreciate the constitutive role of the Protestant sects in American associational life.

It is not easy to assess the adequacy of Weber's contrast between the rise of capitalism and rationalism in the West, and the obstacles to comparable developments in China and India. But he does convince us that deep-seated cultural, familial, and religious differences crucially affected this divergence. Above all, I am enthralled and converted by Weber's comprehensive history of human *reason* in the evolution of human culture. The gradual "removal of magic from the world," which began in religious thought, came to assert itself over all kinds of obstacles, until it encompassed the systematic rationalization of *life conduct* as well as of thought. Weber experienced the ultimate outcome of that process as a tragedy, because he was not as "unmusical" with respect to religion as he believed. And he allows us to be moved by the sharpening conflict between science and religion that was the trauma of his time. He deeply felt the tension between the unconditional imperative of Tolstoy's "cosmic love," even while remaining committed to science—and to the view of religion as the "sacrifice of the intellect." But what I mainly want to highlight here is his profound awareness of the *cultural* foundations of modern life, which we are increasingly predisposed to overlook.

Weber's probabilistic account of singular causal analysis continues to command our respect and allegiance even today, as does his grounding of interpretive understanding in the heuristic attribution of rationality. His grand defense of objectivity and of "intellectual rectitude" against the historical relativism, the methodological irrationalism, and the false prophecies of his time is still very much needed. For we are beset by a new brand of militant relativism that replaces the commitment to truth and to rational debate with a self-destructive "cultural war" among conflicting ideological perspectives, which are selected and proclaimed without recourse to either evidence or logic. Weber may help us to stand firm against this tide.

As I have tried to show, Weber held a deliberately modest view of science, arguing that it required an independently grounded presupposition about what was worth knowing. Indeed, Weber's science could give no definitive answer to questions about "how we should live." And yet Weber's science could reveal connections between actions and their consequences, and expose logical inconsistencies in an agent's principles and value commitments. That left room for a liberal value pluralism and for an ethic of responsibility in politics. But I have found nothing in Weber that would resemble anything like nihilism or gratuitous "decisionism."

The other great benefit one can derive from reading Weber is a fuller awareness of the complexity, not only of social relationships in general, but of the elusive role of advanced education and of intellectual specialization in modern social systems. We seem unable to avoid the advance of intellectual specialization and of bureaucracy in modern life. I do not see Weber as a man in flight from the "steel housing" of modern occupational life. He certainly warned his contemporaries against unthinking submission to the anxious struggle for advancement from the "little post" one has to the slightly better post one hopes to reach. He warned, above all, against all forms of human "dependency," and he clearly dreamt of individuals who were moved by conscious principle and by commitment to a "cause," rather than by the all-too-human tendency to "adjust."

Finally, I have tried to describe Weber's attitude to modern bureaucracy, which was as ambivalent as the phenomenon is ambiguous—and inescapable. Our only hope is that *equality* may lighten its burden, as Weber suggests in his recurrent evocation of the American worker who preferred corrupt politicians he could "spit on" to officials who would "spit on him." But what shall we do to preserve and enhance the American style of equality that caught Weber's attention almost a century ago? As a minimum, it seems to me, we must strive to recover a greater *equality of opportunity,* whether in access to education, to occupational status, or to wealth. It is our only chance to recapture the informal egalitarianism that so impressed Weber when he visited the United States a century ago.

NOTES

INTRODUCTION

1. Abbreviated forms of citation are used throughout for titles more fully spelled out in the bibliography (see the headnote to the bibliography). In addition to Marianne Weber, *Max Weber*, see Bendix, *Max Weber*, 1–6.

2. Mitzman, in *Iron Cage*, portrays Helene Weber as a victim. But my own reading of Marianne Weber's biography of her husband—and the daunting moral presence of Helene Weber in that biography—have made me wonder whether Mitzman rightly interpreted the incident in which Weber broke with his father. My hunch is that Helene was an expert manipulator of her family. I ask myself how it came about that her husband was explicitly excluded from her visits to her son, and how Marianne Weber was convinced, against her own best interests, to play the role of Helene's dutiful daughter. See also Krüger's sensitive study, *Max und Marianne Weber*.

CHAPTER ONE

1. Bourdieu is cited in Ringer, *Fields of Knowledge*, 4–12.

2. Humboldt, "Über die . . . Organisation."

3. See Bruford, *German Tradition;* and Ringer, Review of Buford, *Central European History,* 11 (1978): 107–13.

4. Ringer, *German Mandarins*, 109, 287–88.

5. Weber, *Protestantische Ethik,* in *GAR* 1: 14.

6. See Ringer, *Fields of Knowledge,* 95–96.

7. Ranke, *Die grossen Mächte,* 22, 60.

8. Ranke, *Das politische Gespräch,* 19, 22, 25.

9. Droysen, *Grundriss der Historik,* 422–24, 435, 441–44, 461–68.

10. Knies, *Politische Oekonomie,* 1–35, 321–55, esp. 19, 343, 354.

11. Ibid., 111–16, 334–47, 352.

12. Menger, *Untersuchungen,* 3–59, esp. 10.

13. Ibid., 3, 6–7, 17, 25–26, 34–42.

14. Lamprecht, *Moderne Geschichtswissenschaft,* 1–2, 15–16, 18, 44–45, 49, 52, 62, 65.

15. See Chickering, *Lamprecht.*

16. Meyer, *Zur Theorie und Methodik,* 3–11, 13–28.

17. Dilthey, *Einleitung in die Geisteswissenschaften,* bk. 1, 5–6, 9–17, 26–38, 64–68, 90–92, 116; Dilthey, "Ideen," 139–240. Dilthey traced the word *Geisteswissenschaften* to John Stuart Mill; Weber noted its use in German by Hermann von Helmholtz in "Roscher und Knies," 44.

18. Dilthey, *Aufbau der geschichtlichen Welt,* chaps. 2–3, 84–88, 130–62, 197, 205–20; Ermarth, *Dilthey.*

19. Simmel, *Probleme der Geschichtsphilosophie,* 1, 4–6, 14–17, 20–21.

20. Ibid., 34–44, 54–56, 60, 64–65.

21. Ibid., 71–72, 81–84, 92.

22. Windelband, "Geschichte und Naturwissenschaft," 357, 361–64

23. Rickert, *Grenzen der naturwissenschaftlichen Begriffsbildung,* 33–146, 228–48. Hereafter cited by page numbers in parentheses in the text.

24. Tönnies, *Gemeinschaft und Gesellschaft.* The subtitle, from the second edition on, was *Grundbegriffe der reinen Soziologie.* See also Bickel, *Ferdinand Tönnies;* Heberle, "Sociological System"; and König, "Begriffe Gemeinschaft und Gesellschaft."

25. Tönnies, *Gemeinschaft und Gesellschaft,* 208–9.

26. Ibid., 214. See also Tönnies, "Ferdinand Tönnies," in Schmidt, ed., *Philosophie der Gegenwart,* vol. 3, 1–36; Tönnies and Paulsen, *Briefwechsel.*

27. Simmel, "Über soziale Differenzierung," 169–75.

28. Simmel, *Soziologie,* 3–17; Tenbruck, "Formal Sociology."

29. Simmel, *Soziologie,* 32–100; "Über soziale Differenzierung," 239.

30. Simmel, *Soziologie,* 186–255, 305–44,

31. Simmel, *Philosophie des Geldes,* v—viii, 4–61, 86–126, 456–79.

32. Ibid., 127–28, 160–89, 311–15, 371–82.

33. Ibid., 220–25.

34. Ibid., 480–551.

35. Simmel, "Das Individuum und die Freiheit"; *Schopenhauer und Nietzsche,* 41–56, 262–335.

36. Simmel, "Vom Wesen der Kultur," and "Begriff und Tragödie der Kultur," esp. 197.

CHAPTER TWO

1. I draw, where possible, upon the editors' introductions to the volumes of the *Max Weber Gesamtausgabe* (henceforth *MWG*).

2. Weber, *MWG* I: 3, 61–81, 886–929; "Erhebung des Vereins" and "Ländliche Arbeitsverfassung" in *MWG* I: 4.

3. Weber, *MWG* I: 3, 916.

4. Ibid., 917; "Ländliche Arbeitsverfassung," in *MWG* I: 4, 173–91.

5. Weber, *MWG* I: 3, 920.

6. Weber, "Ländliche Arbeitsverfassung," in *MWG* I: 4, 176, 183.

7. Weber, "Die deutschen Landarbeiter," in *MWG* I: 4, 319, 325–27, 333, 335.

8. Ibid., 339–40.

9. Weber, "Entwickelungstendenzen," in *MWG* I: 4, 425–43, 448.

10. Ibid., 459–62.

11. Weber, "Fideikommisfrage," in *MWG* I: 8, 92–156, 173–75. The draft law was shelved in 1911 but briefly revived in 1917, whereupon Weber protested the "ennobling of war profits"; see Weber, "Deutschlands Nobilitierung," in *MWG* I: 15.

12. Weber, "Deutschlands Nobilitierung," 170, 173–74, 183–85, 187.

13. Weber, "Antrittsrede," in *MWG* I: 4, 547, 552–53.

14. Ibid., 548, 551, 553–55.

15. Ibid., 558–59, 561, 564.

16. Ibid., 570, 573.

17. Weber, "Diskussionsrede . . . Ploetz," 458, and "Diskussionsrede . . . Barth," in *GASS,* 458, 484.

18. Weber, "Ethnische Gemeinschaften," in *MWG* I: 22, bk. 1, 168–82, esp. 168.

19. Ibid., 184–85, 187.

20. Weber, "Machtprestige und Nationalgefühl," in *MWG* I: 22, bk. 1, 228–40.

21. Ibid., 240–46.

22. Weber, "Zwischen zwei Gesetzen," in *MWG* I: 15, 96.

23. Ringer, *Decline of the German Mandarins,* 189–99.

24. Weber, "Bismarcks Aussenpolitik," in *MWG* I: 15, 77–79, 83–91; see also "Deutschlands . . . : I. Polenpolitik," in *MWG* I: 15.

25. Weber, "Der verschärfte U-Boot Krieg," in *MWG* I: 15, 115–16, 118–19, 122–24.

26. Weber, "Deutschland unter den europäischen Weltmächten," in *MWG* I: 15, 169–70, 182–83, 185–89.

27. Ibid., 192–93, 162–65, 168.

28. There are three sections in each chapter. The note at the end of each section in chapters 2–8 lists relevant English translations. In addition, a note at the end of each of these chapters identifies original Weber texts that might usefully be translated. Of the original Weber texts discussed in this section, the following are available in translation: "The Nation State and Economic Policy" ["Antrittsrede"] and "Between Two Laws" ["Zwischen zwei Gesetzen"], both in *Political Writings;* and "Ethnic Groups" ["Ethnische Gemeinschaften"] and the passages from "Power Prestige" to "The Nation" ["Machtprestige und Nationalgefühl"], both in *Economy and Society.*

29. See Weber, *MWG* II: 5, 6, and 7 for Michels and others.

30. Weber, "Sogenannte 'Lehrfreiheit'"; "Lehrfreiheit der Universitäten," 89–91.

31. Weber, *MWG* II: 5, 467–73, 482–83, 492–96.

32. Weber, *MWG* II: 5, 568–71, 585–86, 644; *MWG* II: 5, 542, 625; see Mommsen

and Schwentker, *Weber und seine Zeitgenossen*, 196–215, 285–95, 419–33, 506–23, 682–702.

33. Jellinek, *Menschen- und Bürgerrechte*.

34. Weber, "Russland," in *MWG* I: 10, 164–267, esp. 164.

35. Ibid., 269–70.

36. Ibid., 268–69, 272–73.

37. Weber, "Arbeitsverhältnisse," in *MWG* I: 8, 251, 254–57, 259.

38. Weber, "Verhältnis der Kartelle," in *MWG* I: 8, 267–69, 277.

39. Weber, "Verfassung der Städte," in *MWG* I: 8, 304–14, esp. 310; see also *MWG* II: 5, 407, 423.

40. Weber, "Unternehmungen der Gemeinden," in *MWG* I: 8, 360–66.

41. Ibid., 362–63.

42. Weber, "Fall Bernhard"; *MWG* II: 5, 594–95; *MWG* II: 7, 575–77, 580–84, 587–88, 591–93, 605, 608, 621, 646, 649, 709, 712, 726, 733, 755, 773, 807–10.

43. Of the original Weber texts discussed in this section, the following is available in English translation: "On the Situation of Constitutional Democracy in Russia" ["Russland"], in *Political Writings*.

44. Weber, "Preussische Wahlrecht," "Wahlrecht und Demokratie," and "Parlament und Regierung," in *MWG* I: 15, esp. 432–36 (hereafter cited parenthetically by page number in the text).

45. Weber, "Wahlrecht und Demokratie," in *MWG* I: 15, 347–48.

46. Mommsen, *Age of Bureaucracy*, 72–94, esp. 87, 89; see also Giddens, *Politics and Sociology*, 7–27; Turner, *Cambridge Companion*, 131–48.

47. Weber, "Typen der Herrschaft," in *Wirtschaft und Gesellschaft*, 158, 165, 169–73.

48. Weber, "Wahlrecht und Demokratie," in *MWG* I: 15, 349–50.

49. Weber, "Das preussische Wahlrecht," 229–31, and esp. "Wahlrecht und Demokratie," 350–51, both in *MWG* I: 15.

50. Weber, "Sozialismus," in *MWG* I: 15, 607–25.

51. Ibid., 626–30.

52. Again I am relying on Mommsen's introduction to *MWG* I: 16.

53. Weber, "Deutschlands künftige Staatsform," 110–12, 116–22, 125–30, 138–40; and "Reichspräsident," both in *MWG* I: 16. Weber's remark that the right to property might have to be modified was presumably tactical.

54. Weber, "Deutschlands künftige Staatsform," in *MWG* I: 16, 99–109, 112–16, 145–46, esp. 103, 105–9, 116.

55. Of the original Weber texts discussed in this section, the following are available in English translations: "Suffrage and Democracy in Germany" ["Wahlrecht und Demokratie"], "Parliament and Government in Germany under a New Political Order" ["Parlament und Regierung"], "Socialism" ["Sozialismus"], and "The President of the Reich" ["Der Reichspräsident"], all in *Political Writings;* "The Types of Legitimate Domination" ["Typen der Herrschaft"], in *Economy and Society*. In general, the English translations on Weber's politics are fairly complete.

1. This chapter is based upon my *Max Weber's Methodology*. Unless otherwise noted, all of the essay titles cited appear in Weber's *GAW*, except for his review article of Adolf Weber's work.

2. Weber, "Roscher und Knies," 4–5; "Objektivität," 146, 170–71, "Kritische Studien," 233.

3. Weber, "Objektivität," 176–178; "Kritische Studien," 237–43.

4. Weber, "Objektivität," 180, 184.

5. Ibid., 183–84; "Kritische Studien," 261.

6. Von Kries, "Ueber den Begriff," 180–201.

7. Ibid., 198, 201–3.

8. Ibid., 203–5, 212–13, 218–20.

9. Weber, "Objektivität," 179; "Kritische Studien," 266–68, 273–74.

10. "Kritische Studien," 271, 277, 282–85.

11. Weber, "Roscher und Knies," 65–70; "Kritische Studien," 284–85, both in *GAW*.

12. "Kritische Studien," 266, 274–75.

13. Ibid., 268, 273.

14. Ibid., 275–77.

15. Weber, "Objektivität," 170–71.

16. Weber, "Kritische Studien," 277–79.

17. Weber, "Objektivität," 178–80.

18. Weber, "Kritische Studien," 228–30, 267.

19. Weber, "Roscher und Knies," 65–66, 115; "Stammlers 'Überwindung,'" 322.

20. Weber, "Kritische Studien," 282–83; Weber, "Roscher und Knies," 134–36.

21. Weber, "Roscher und Knies," 68–70, 134.

22. Of the original Weber texts discussed in this section, the following are available in adequate English translations: "'Objectivity' in Social Science and Social Policy" ["Objektivität"], "Critical Studies in the Logic of the Cultural Sciences," and "Objective Possibility and Adequate Causation" ["Kritische Studien"], all in *Methodology of the Social Sciences*.

23. Weber, "Roscher und Knies," 9–24, 142–44.

24. Weber, "Objektivität," 172–74, 186–88; "Energetische Kulturtheorien"; *MWG* II: 5, 25; "Roscher und Knies," 7–8, 23–24, 56, 63.

25. Weber, "Objektivität," 188–189; "Roscher und Knies," 84.

26. Weber, "Grenznutzlehre," 384–97; *MWG* II: 5, 578–79, "Grundbegriffe," in *Wirtschaft und Gesellschaft*, 9; *MWG* II: 6, 108.

27. Weber, "Objektivität," 173, 183.

28. Weber, "Roscher und Knies," 34–37, 44–46, 137; "Kritische Studien," 218–19; "Nachtrag zu dem Aufsatz über R. Stammlers 'Überwindung,'" 364; hereafter cited as "Nachtrag."

29. Weber, "Roscher und Knies," 63–65, 136–37; "Nachtrag," 366–68.

30. Weber, "Kritische Studien," 221–22; "Nachtrag," 364–67.

31. Weber, "Roscher und Knies," 67, 132–33; "Kritische Studien," 226–27.

32. Weber, "Roscher und Knies," 92–95, 114–15, 134; "Kritische Studien," 282; "Wertfreiheit," 532.

33. Weber, "Roscher und Knies," 126–30.

34. Ibid., 83, 100, 111–13, 116–22.

35. Weber, "Dortselbst, Diskussionsrede zu dem Vortrag von H. Kantorowicz," in *GASS*, 482–83.

36. Weber, "Wertfreiheit," 532–33.

37. Weber,"Stammlers 'Überwindung,'" 322–33, 336–37, 342–43, 356–57; "Dortselbst, Diskussionsrede zu dem Vortrag von H. Kantorowicz," in *GASS*, 478.

38. Weber, "Grundbegriffe," in *Wirtschaft und Gesellschaft*, 1.

39. Ibid., 1–4.

40. Ibid., 2.

41. Ibid., 12–13.

42. Weber, "Kategorien," 428, 434, 437–38.

43. Weber, "Grundbegriffe," in *Wirtschaft und Gesellschaft*, 2; "Kategorien," 432.

44. "Kategorien," 435, 438.

45. Weber, "Grundbegriffe," in *Wirtschaft und Gesellschaft*, 4–5.

46. Weber, "Objektivität," 190–93.

47. Ibid., 195–200.

48. Weber, "Wertfreiheit," 534–36.

49. Weber, "Kategorien," 436.

50. Of the original Weber texts discussed in this section, the following are available in English translations: "Basic Sociological Terms" ["Grundbegriffe"], in *Economy and Society;* "'Objectivity' in Social Science and Social Policy" ["Objektivität"], "Critical Studies in the Logic of the Cultural Sciences," "Objective Possibility and Adequate Causation" ["Kritische Studien"], and "The Meaning of 'Ethical Neutrality' in Sociology and Economics" ["Wertfreiheit"], all in *Methodology of the Social Sciences.*

51. Weber, "Objektivität," 170–71.

52. Ibid., 214.

53. Weber, "Roscher und Knies," 122–25; see also "Kritische Studien," 246.

54. "Kritische Studien," 251.

55. Weber, "Objektivität," 183–84, 155.

56. Weber, "Debattenreden . . . in Wien 1909 . . . über die Produktivität der Volkswirtschaft," and "Dortselbst, Diskussionsrede zu dem Vortrag von H. Kantorowicz," in *GASS*, 420, and esp. 482.

57. Weber, "Objektivität," 149–55, 157–59.

58. Weber, [Review of] "Weber, Adolf, 'Die Aufgaben,'" 618.

59. Weber, "Debattenreden . . . in Wien 1909 . . . über die Produktivität der Volkswirtschaft," 416–20.

60. Ibid., 419–20.

61. Weber, "Wertfreiheit," 489–91.

62. Ibid., 496, 499.

63. Ibid., 513–14.

64. Ibid., 501, 503, 507–8.

65. Of the original Weber texts discussed in this section, the following are available in English translations: "'Objectivity' in Social Science and Social Policy" ["Objektivität"], "Critical Studies in the Logic of the Cultural Sciences" ["Kritische Studien"], and "The Meaning of 'Ethical Neutrality' in Sociology and Economics" ["Wertfreiheit"], all in *Methodology of the Social Sciences.*

CHAPTER FOUR

1. Weber, "Dortselbst, Diskussionsrede zu dem Vortrag von H. Kantorowicz," in *GASS,* 456; "Wertfreiheit," in *GAW,* 538.

2. Weber, *Protestantische Ethik,* in *GAR* 1. This work is hereafter cited parenthetically by page number in the text.

3. Of the original Weber texts discussed in this section, the following are available in English translation: "The Meaning of 'Ethical Neutrality' in Sociology and Economics" ["Wertfreiheit"], in *Methodology of the Social Sciences; The Protestant Ethic and the Spirit of Capitalism* [*Die protestantische Ethik und der Geist des Kapitalismus*], trans. Stephen Kalberg.

4. Jellinek, *Menschen- und Bürgerrechte;* Lehmann and Roth, *Protestant Ethic,* 27–49.

5. Lehmann and Roth, *Protestant Ethic,* 83–121; Weber, *MWG* II: 5, 33.

6. Brentano, *Anfänge,* 7–49, 117–99.

7. See Lenger's basic work, *Sombart.*

8. Ibid., 123–98.

9. Weber, *MWG* II: 5, 605; *MWG* II: 7, 154.

10. Sombart, *Der moderne Kapitalismus,* 1: esp. 369–97.

11. Ibid., esp. 380–81, 383, 389–91, 397.

12. Brentano, *Anfänge,* 159–60; Sombart, *Juden,* ix—xi, 137, 189–90, 212, 222, 227, 242, 282, 298, 316, 323, 329, 346, 353, 384.

13. See Lehmann and Roth, *Protestant Ethic,* 195–208.

14. Fischoff, "Protestantische Ethik"; Marshall, *Spirit of Capitalism;* see also Lehmann and Roth, *Protestant Ethic,* 83–121, 211–243, 245–72, 305–25, 327–46, and 347–65; and Turner, *Cambridge Companion,* 151–71.

15. Of the original Weber texts discussed in this section, the following is available in English translation: *The Protestant Ethic and the Spirit of Capitalism* [*Protestantische Ethik*], trans. Stephen Kalberg.

16. Marianne Weber, *Lebensbild,* 297–317; Lehmann and Roth, *Protestant Ethic,* 357–83.

17. Weber, "Relations of the Rural Community," in *MWG* I: 8, 213, 220–21.

18. Ibid., 224.

19. Lenger, *Sombart,* 148–49; Weber, *Lebensbild,* 294–95. Max Weber's "Kirchen und Sekten" and "Kirchen und Sekten in Nordamerica" were combined and expanded in "Die protestantischen Sekten," published in *GAR* 1.

20. Weber, "Protestantischen Sekten," *GAR* 1, 220–25.

21. Ibid., 226–32.

22. Ibid., 233–36.

23. Ibid., 207–9.

24. Ibid., 209–11.

25. Ibid., 212–14, 217–19.

26. Weber, *Lebensbild,* 301, 306, 311–12.

27. Ibid., 298–300, 315–17.

28. Ibid., 300–301, 307–9.

29. Ibid., 304–6.

30. Weber, "Protestantischen Sekten," in *GAR* 1, 215.

31. Ibid., 215–16

32. Ibid., 216.

33. Of the original Weber texts discussed in this section, the following is available in English translation: "The Protestant Sects and the Spirit of Capitalism" ["Die protestantischen Sekten"], in *From Max Weber.*

CHAPTER FIVE

1. Editorial introductions to relevant volumes of the *MWG* reflect the scholarship of Wolfgang Schluchter.

2. Weber, "Einleitung," in *MWG* I: 19, 83–86. This work is hereafter cited parenthetically by page number in the text.

3. Of the original Weber texts discussed in this section, the following is available in English translation: "The Social Psychology of the World Religions" ["Einleitung"], in *From Max Weber.*

4. Weber, "Zwischenbetrachtung," in *MWG* I: 19, 479–81. This work is hereafter cited parenthetically by the initial *Z* and page number in the text (e.g., *Z, 481–83*).

5. Of the original Weber texts discussed in this section, the following is available in English translation: "Religious Rejections of the World and Their Directions" ["Zwischenbetrachtung"], in *From Max Weber.*

6. Weber, *Konfuzianismus und Taoismus,* 128–30, 144–54, 158–59. This work is hereafter cited parenthetically by the initial *K* and page number in the text (e.g. *K, 166–79*).

7. Weber, *Hinduismus und Buddhismus,* 49–51, 53–55. This work is hereafter cited parenthetically by the initial *H* and page number in the text.

8. Of the original Weber texts discussed in this section, the following are *partly* available in English translations: "India: The Brahman and the Castes" [*Hinduismus und Buddhismus*] and "The Chinese Literati" [*Konfuzianismus und Taoismus*], in *From Max Weber*. In general, Weber's analytical and historical works on the world religions are fairly accessible in English.

CHAPTER SIX

1. Weber, *MWG* II: 6, 214–15, 220; "Rede auf dem ersten Deutschen Soziologentage."

2. Weiss, *Max Weber heute,* 55–89. Winckelmann even added a section entitled "The Modern Rational State," which he compiled from excerpts from other texts of Weber's.

3. Weber, "Grundbegriffe," in *Wirtschaft und Gesellschaft,* 1, 6–7. This work is hereafter cited parenthetically by page number in the text.

4. Weber, "Grundkategorien des Wirtschaftens," in *Wirtschaft und Gesellschaft,* 31–36.

5. Ibid., 37–38.

6. Ibid., 38–39, 41–43.

7. Ibid., 44–46.

8. Ibid., 48–49.

9. Of the original Weber texts discussed in this section, the following are available in English translation: "Basic Sociological Terms" ["Grundbegriffe"], and "Sociological Categories of Economic Action" ["Grundkategorien des Wirtschaftens"], both in *Economy and Society.*

10. Weber, "Typen der Herrschaft," in *Wirtschaft und Gesellschaft,* 122–24. This work is hereafter cited parenthetically by the initial *T* and page number in the text.

11. Weber, "Charismatische Herrschaft," in *Wirtschaft und Gesellschaft,* 654–55.

12. See Weber, "Parlament und Regierung," in *MWG* I: 15, 473, 488–91, 535–37, 539–40; and Mommsen, *Age of Bureaucracy,* 72–94, esp. 87, 89; see also Giddens, *Politics and Sociology,* 7–27; and Turner, *Cambridge Companion,* 131–48.

13. Of the original Weber texts discussed in this section, the following are available in English translations: "The Types of Legitimate Domination" ["Typen der Herrschaft"], and "Charisma and Its Transformation" ["Charismatische Herrschaft"], both in *Economy and Society.*

14. Weber, "Rechtssoziologie," in *Wirtschaft und Gesellschaft,* 455–58. This work is hereafter cited parenthetically by the initial *R* and page number in the text.

15. Of the original Weber texts discussed in this section, the following is available in English translation: "Economy and Law (The Sociology of Law)" ["Rechtssoziologie"], in *Economy and Society.* The subjects of this chapter are accessible in English translations, but we could use a briefer (one-volume) translation of central essays from *Economy and Society.*

1. Weber, *Die Stadt,* in *MWG* I: 22, bk. 5, 59–100, esp. 84. This work is hereafter cited parenthetically by page number in the text.

2. See Weber, "Typen der Herrschaft," in *Wirtschaft und Gesellschaft,* 153–55.

3 .See Weber, *Protestantische Ethik,* in *GAR* 1, 116–17.

4. Of the original Weber texts discussed in this section, the following is available in English translation: *The City (Non-Legitimate Domination)* [*Die Stadt*], in *Economy and Society.*

5. Weber, "Grundkategorien des Wirtschaftens," in *Wirtschaft und Gesellschaft,* 44–45. This work is hereafter cited parenthetically by the initial *G* and page number in the text.

6. Weber, *Protestantische Ethik,* in *GAR* 1: 202–4.

7. Ibid., 198–99.

8. Weber, "Der Sozialismus," in *MWG* I: 15, esp. 607, 609.

9. Of the original Weber texts discussed in this section, the following are available in English translations: "Sociological Categories of Economic Action" ["Grundkategorien des Wirtschaftens"], in *Economy and Society; The Protestant Ethic and the Spirit of Capitalism* [*Protestantische Ethik*], trans. Kalberg.

10. Weber, "Typen der Herrschaft," in *Wirtschaft und Gesellschaft,* 124–27.

11. Ibid., 128–29.

12. Weber, "Russland," in *MWG* I: 10, 269–71.

13. Weber, "Unternehmungen der Gemeinden," in *MWG* I: 8, 362–63.

14. Weber, "Der Sozialismus," in *MWG* I: 15, 604.

15. Of the original Weber texts discussed in this section, the following are available in English translations: "The Types of Legitimate Domination" ["Typen der Herrschaft"], in *Economy and Society;* "On the Situation of Constitutional Democracy in Russia" ["Russland"], and "Socialism" ["Der Sozialismus"], both in *Political Writings.* In general, the topics of this chapter are accessible in English, although the analysis draws interactively upon a variety of sources.

CHAPTER EIGHT

1. Ringer, *Fields of Knowledge,* 304–5.

2. Weber, "Konfuzianismus und Taoismus," in *MWG* I: 19, 28, 304–5.

3. See Weber, "Deutschlands Nobilitierung," in *MWG* I: 15, 170, 173–74, 183–85, 187.

4. Weber, "Konfuzianismus und Taoismus," in *MWG* I: 19, 302–4.

5. Ibid., 317–18.

6. Weber, "Stände und Klassen," in *Wirtschaft und Gesellschaft,* 177–79.

7. Ibid., 179–80.

8. Weber, "'Klassen,' 'Stände,' und 'Parteien,'" in *MWG* I: 22, bk. 1, 269.

9. Weber, "Wahlrecht und Demokratie," in *MWG* I: 15, 350–51.

10. Of the original Weber texts discussed in this section, the following are available in English translations: "The Chinese Literati" ["Konfuzianismus und Taoismus"], in *From Max Weber;* "Status Groups and Classes" ["Stände und Klassen"], in *Economy and Society;* "Suffrage and Democracy in Germany" ["Wahlrecht und Demokratie"], in *Political Writings.*

11. Weber, "Wissenschaft als Beruf," in *MWG* I: 17, 71–73. This work is hereafter cited parenthetically by page number in the text.

12. Weber, *MWG* II: 5, 402–3.

13. Weber, *MWG* II: 6, 63–64.

14. Ringer, *Decline of the German Mandarins,* 357–66, esp. 365.

15. Of the original Weber texts discussed in this section, the following is available in English translation: "Science as a Vocation" ["Wissenschaft als Beruf"], in *From Max Weber.*

16. Weber, "Politik als Beruf," in *MWG* I: 17, 191–96. This work is hereafter cited parenthetically by the initial *P* and page number in the text.

17. Of the original Weber texts discussed in this section, the following is available in English translation: "Politics as a Vocation" ["Politik als Beruf"], in *From Max Weber.* In general, the subjects discussed in this chapter are accessible in English, although the last section of the chapter draws interactively upon brief excerpts from a variety of sources.

BIBLIOGRAPHY

The first two subsections of primary sources list works by Max Weber. Primary sources by other authors are entered in the third section. The final section includes secondary sources that I read with particular interest, without necessarily sharing their perspectives. The best currently available editions of Weber's primary texts are listed, beginning with the most recent and authoritative, the *Max Weber Gesamtausgabe* (henceforth *MWG*), with its superb introductions and discussions of the textual sources. The volumes in Section I (*MWG* I) contain writings and speeches; Section II (*MWG* II) contains letters; and Section III includes lectures. In the following section of German texts, all currently available volumes are listed; those not cited in my text are preceded by an asterisk. In citations of *MWG* volumes, the roman section number is followed by a colon and the volume number in that section. Citations in the endnotes use the following abbreviations in addition to *MWG* I and *MWG* II:

- *GAR* 1: *Gesammelte Aufsätze zur Religionssoziologie,* vol. 1
- *GAR* 3: *Gesammelte Aufsätze zur Religionssoziologie,* vol. 3
- *GASS: Gesammelte Aufsätze zur Soziologie und Sozialpolitik*
- *GAW: Gesammelte Aufsätze zur Wissenschaftslehre*

English translations of Weber's works appear in the second section of primary sources. The separate titles of essays contained in anthologies listed in that section are alphabetized under the main entry for the anthology and include only those that are translations of German texts actually considered in this book.

Weber's German Texts

*MWG I: 2. *Die römische Agrargeschichte in ihrer Bedeutung für das Staats- und Privatrecht.* 1891. Reprint, ed. Juergen Deininger. Tübingen: J. C. B. Mohr, 1986.

MWG I: 3. *Die Lage der Landarbeiter im ostelbischen Deutschland.* 1892. Reprint, ed. Martin Riesebrodt. Tübingen: J. C. B. Mohr, 1984, 61–81, 886–929.

MWG I: 4. *Landarbeiterfrage, Nationalstaat und Volkswirtschaftspolitik. Schriften und Reden, 1892–1899.* Ed. Wolfgang J. Mommsen. Tübingen: J. C. B. Mohr, 1993. Contains the following:

"Die deutschen Landarbeiter: Korreferat und Diskussionsbeitrag auf dem fünften Evangelisch-sozialen Kongress am 16. Mai 1894," 313–41.

"Entwickelungstendenzen in der Lage der ostelbischen Landarbeiter." 1894, 425–62.

"Die Erhebung des Vereins für Sozialpolitik über die Lage der Landarbeiter." 1893, 123–53.

"Die ländliche Arbeitsverfassung: Referat und Diskussionsbeiträge auf der Generalversammlung des Vereins für Socialpolitik am 20. und 21. März 1893," 165–98.

"Der Nationalstaat und die Volkswirtschaftspolitik: Akademische Antrittsrede." 1895, 543–74.

*MWG I: 5. *Börsenwesen. Schriften und Reden, 1893–1898.* Ed. Knut Borchardt. Tübingen: J. C. B. Mohr, 1999.

MWG I: 8. *Wirtschaft, Staat und Sozialpolitik. Schriften und Reden, 1900–1912.* Ed. Wolfgang Schluchter. Tübingen: J. C. B. Mohr, 1998. Contains the following:

"Agrarstatistische und sozialpolitische Betrachtungen zur Fideikomissfrage in Preussen." 1904, 92–188.

"Das Arbeitsverhältnis in den privaten Riesenbetrieben: Diskussionsbeitrag auf der Generalversammlung des Vereins für Sozialpolitik am 26. September 1905," 249–59.

"The Relations of the Rural Community to Other Branches of Social Science." 1904, 212–43.

"Verfassung und Verwaltungsorganisation der Städte: Diskussionsbeitrag auf der Generalversammlung des Vereins für Sozialpolitik am 2. Oktober 1907," 304–15.

"Das Verhältnis der Kartelle zum Staate: Diskussionsbeitrag auf der Generalversammlung des Vereins für Sozialpolitik am 28. September 1905," 266–79.

"Die wirtschaftlichen Unternehmungen der Gemeinden: Diskussionsbeitrag auf der Generalversammlung des Vereins für Sozialpolitik am 28. September 1909," 360–66.

MWG I: 10. *Zur Russischen Revolution von 1905. Schriften und Reden, 1905-1912.* Ed. Wolfgang J. Mommsen. Tübingen: J. C. B. Mohr, 1989. Contains the following:

"Zur Lage der bürgerlichen Demokratie in Russland." 1906, 86-279.

*MWG I: 11. *Zur Psychophysik der industriellen Arbeit. Schriften und Reden, 1908-1912.* Ed. Wolfgang Schluchter. Tübingen: J. C. B. Mohr, 1995.

MWG I: 15. *Zur Politik im Weltkrieg. Schriften und Reden, 1914-1918.* Ed. Wolfgang J. Mommsen. Tübingen: J. C. B. Mohr, 1984. Contains the following:

"Bismarcks Aussenpolitik und die Gegenwart." 1915, 71-92.

"Deutschlands äussere und Preussens innere Politik: I. Die Polenpolitik." 1917, 197-203.

"Deutschlands äussere und Preussens innere Politik: II. Die Nobilitierung der Kriegsgewinne." 1917, 206-214.

"Deutschland unter den europäischen Weltmächten." 1916, 157-94.

"Parlament und Regierung im neugeordneten Deutschland." 1918, 432-596.

"Das preussische Wahlrecht." 1917, 224-35.

"Der Sozialismus." 1918, 599-633.

"Der verschärfte U-Boot-Krieg." 1916, 115-25.

"Wahlrecht und Demokratie in Deutschland." 1917, 347-96.

"Zwischen zwei Gesetzen." 1916, 95-98.

MWG I: 16. *Zur Neuordnung Deutschlands. Schriften und Reden, 1918-1920.* Ed. Wolfgang J. Mommsen. Tübingen: J. C. B. Mohr, 1988. Contains the following:

"Deutschlands künftige Staatsform." 1919, 98-146.

"Der Reichspräsident." 1919, 220-24.

MWG I: 17. *Wissenschaft als Beruf, 1917/19. Politik als Beruf, 1919.* Ed. Wolfgang J. Mommsen and Wolfgang Schluchter. Tübingen: J. C. B. Mohr, 1992. Contains the following:

"Politik als Beruf," 157-252.

"Wissenschaft als Beruf," 71-111.

MWG I: 19. *Die Wirtschaftsethik der Weltreligionen. Konfuzianismus und Taoismus: Schriften, 1915-1920.* Ed. Helwig Schmidt-Glintzer. Tübingen: J. C. B. Mohr, 1989. Contains the following:

Konfuzianismus und Taoismus. 1915, 128-478.

"Die Wirtschaftsethik der Weltreligionen. Vergleichende religionssoziologische Versuche. Einleitung." 1915, 83-127.

"Zwischenbetrachtung. Theorie der Stufen und Richtungen religiöser Weltablehnung." 1915, 479-522.

MWG I: 20. *Die Wirtschaftsethik der Weltreligionen. Hinduismus und Buddhisnus, 1916-1920.* Ed. Helwig Schmidt-Glintzer. Tübingen: J. C. B. Mohr, 1996. Contains the following:

Hinduismus und Buddhismus. 1916, 49-544.

MWG I: 22, bk. 1. *Wirtschaft und Gesellschaft: Die Wirtschaft und die*

gesellschaftlichen Ordnungen und Mächte. Nachlass. 1921. Bk. 1. Gemeinschaften.
Ed. Wolfgang J. Mommsen with Michael Meyer. Tübingen: J. C. B. Mohr, 2001.
Contains the following:
"Ethnische Gemeinschaften," 168–90.
"'Klassen,' 'Stände' und 'Parteien,'" 252–72.
"Machtprestige und Nationalgefühl," 222–47.
*MWG I: 22, bk. 2. Wirtschaft und Gesellschaft. Die Wirtschaft und die
gesellschaftlichen Ordnungen und Mächte. Nachlass. 1921. Bk. 2. Religiöse
Gemeinschaften.* Ed. Wolfgang J. Mommsen with Michael Meyer. Tübingen:
J. C. B. Mohr, 2001.
*MWG I: 22, Bk. 5. Wirtschaft und Gesellschaft. Die Wirtschaft und die
gesellschaftlichen Ordnungen und Mächte. Nachlass. 1921. Bk. 5. Die Stadt.* Ed.
Wilfried Nippel. Tübingen: J. C. B. Mohr, 1999.
MWG II: 5. Briefe, 1906–1908. Ed. M. Rainer Lepsius and Wolfgang J. Mommsen.
Tübingen: J. C. B. Mohr, 1990.
MWG II: 6. Briefe, 1909–1910. Ed. M. Rainer Lepsius and Wolfgang J. Mommsen.
Tübingen: J. C. B. Mohr, 1994.
MWG II: 7. Briefe, 1911–1912. Ed. M. Rainer Lepsius and Wolfgang J. Mommsen.
Tübingen: J. C. B. Mohr, 1998.
"Geleitwort." *Archiv für Sozialwissenschaft und Sozialpolitik* 1 (1904): i–vii.
"Der Fall Bernhard." *Frankfurter Zeitung* 52, no. 168 (June 1908): 1.
Gesammelte Aufsätze zur Religionssoziologie. Vol. 1. 7th ed. Tübingen: J. C. B. Mohr,
1978. Contains the following:
"Die protestantischen Sekten und der Geist des Kapitalismus." 1906, 207–36.
Die protestantische Ethik und der Geist des Kapitalismus. 1920, 17–206.
"Vorbemerkung." 1920, 1–16.
Gesammelte Aufsätze zur Religionssoziologie. Vol. 3. *Das antike Judentum.* 7th ed.
Tübingen: J. C. B. Mohr, 1983.
Gesammelte Aufsätze zur Soziologie und Sozialpolitik. Tübingen: J. C. B. Mohr, 1988.
Contains the following:
"Debattenreden auf der Tagung des Vereins für Sozialpolitik in Wien 1909 zu
den Verhandlungen über die Produktivität der Volkswirtschaft," 416–23.
"Diskussionsrede [auf der ersten Soziologentagung in Frankfurt 1910] zu dem
Vortrag von A. Ploetz über 'Die Begriffe Rasse und Gesellschaft,'" 456–62.
"Diskussionsrede auf dem zweiten deutschen Soziologentag zu Berlin zum
Vortrag von P. Barth über 'Die Nationalität in ihrer soziologischen Bedeu-
tung,'"and "Zum Vortrag von F. Schmid über 'Das Recht der National-
itäten,'" 484–88.
"Dortselbst, Diskussionsrede zu dem Vortrag von H. Kantorowicz,
'Rechtswissenschaft und Soziologie,'" 476–83.
"Rede auf dem ersten Deutschen Soziologentage in Frankfurt, 1910," 431–49.

Gesammelte Aufsätze zur Wissenschaftslehre. 4th ed. Tübingen: J. C. B. Mohr, 1973.
  Contains the following:
  "'Energetische' Kulturtheorien." 1909, 400–26.
  "Die Grenznutzlehre und das 'psychophysische Grundgesetz.'" 1908, 384–
  99.
  "Kritische Studien auf dem Gebiet der kuturwissenschaftlichen Logik." 1906,
  215–90.
  "Nachtrag zu dem Aufsatz über R. Stammlers 'Überwindung' der materialis-
  tischen Geschichtsauffassung." Nachlass. 1921, 360–83.
  "Die 'Objektivität' sozialwissenschaftlicher und sozialpolitischer Erkennis."
  1904, 146–214.
  "Roscher und Knies und die logischen Probleme der historischen National-
  ökonomie." 1903–1906, 1–145.
  "Der Sinn der 'Wertfreiheit' der soziologischen und ökonomischen Wis-
  senschaften." 1918, 489–540.
  "R. Stammlers 'Überwindung' der materialistischen Geschichtsauffassung."
  1907, 291–359.
  "Über einige Kategorien der verstehenden Soziologie." 1913, 427–74.
"Die Lehrfreiheit der Universitäten." *Hochschul-Nachrichten* 19, no. 4 (January
  1909): 89–91.
"Die sogenannte 'Lehrfreiheit' an den deutschen Universitäten." *Frankfurter
  Zeitung* 53, no. 262 (September 1908): 1.
[Review of] "Weber, Adolf, 'Die Aufgaben der Volkswirtschaftslehre als Wissen-
  schaft' (Tübingen, 1909)." *Archiv für Sozialwissenschaft und Sozialpolitik* 29
  (1909): 615–620.
Wirtschaft und Gesellschaft: Grundriss der verstehenden Soziologie. 1921. 5th ed.
  Tübingen: J. C. B. Mohr, 1976. Contains the following:
  "Die charismatische Herrschaft und ihre Umbildung," 654–87.
  "Rechtssoziologie," 387–513.
  "Soziologische Grundbegriffe," 1–30.
  "Soziologische Grundkategorien des Wirtschaftens," 31–121.
  "Stände und Klassen," 177–80.
  "Typen der Herrschaft," 122–76.

English Translations of Weber's Works

Political Writings. Ed. Peter Lassman and Ronald Speirs. Cambridge: Cambridge
  University Press, 1994. Contains the following:
  "Between Two Laws."
  "The Nation State and Economic Policy."
  "On the Situation of Constitutional Democracy in Russia."

"Parliament and Government in Germany under a New Political Order."
"The President of the Reich."
"Socialism."
"Suffrage and Democracy in Germany."
The Methodology of the Social Sciences. Trans. and ed. Edward A. Shils and Henry
    A. Finch. New York: Free Press, 1949. Contains the following:
    "The Meaning of 'Ethical Neutrality' in Sociology and Economics."
    "'Objectivity' in Social Science and Social Policy."
    "Critical Studies in the Logic of the Cultural Sciences."
    "Objective Possibility and Adequate Causation in Historical Explanation."
The Protestant Ethic and the Spirit of Capitalism. Trans. Stephen Kalberg. Los
    Angeles: Roxbury, 2002. Contains the following:
    The Protestant Ethic and the Spirit of Capitalism.
    "The Protestant Sects and the Spirit of Capitalism."
From Max Weber: Essays in Sociology. Trans. and ed. H. H. Gerth and C. Wright
    Mills. New York: Oxford University Press, 1946. Contains the following:
    "Bureaucracy."
    "The Chinese Literati."
    "Class, Status, Party."
    "India: The Brahman and the Castes."
    "Politics as a Vocation."
    "The Protestant Sects and the Spirit of Capitalism."
    "Religious Rejections of the World and Their Directions."
    "Science as a Vocation."
    "The Social Psychology of the World Religions."
    "The Sociology of Charismatic Authority."
    "Structures of Power."
Economy and Society. Ed. Guenther Roth and Claus Wittich. 2 vols. Berkeley and
    Los Angeles: University of California Press, 1978. Contains the following:
    "Basic Sociological Terms."
    "Bureaucracy."
    "Charisma and Its Transformation."
    The City (Non-Legitimate Domination).
    "Economy and Law (The Sociology of Law)."
    "Ethnic Groups."
    "Feudalism, Ständestaat and Patrimonialism."
    "Household, Neighborhood, and Kin Group."
    "Patriarchalism and Patrimonialism."
    "Political Communities."
    "Sociological Categories of Economic Action."
    "Status Groups and Classes."
    "The Types of Legitimate Domination."

Brentano, Lujo. *Die Anfänge des modernen Kapitalismus: Festrede gehalten in der . . . Akademie der Wissenschaften, . . . 1913.* München: Verlag der K. B. Akademie der Wissenschaften, 1916.

Dilthey, Wilhelm. *Der Aufbau der geschichtlichen Welt in den Geisteswissenschaften.* In *Gesammelte Schriften,* 7: 79–220. Stuttgart: Teubner, 1958.

———. *Einleitung in die Geisteswissenschaften.* In *Gesammelte Schriften,* 1: 3–120. Stuttgart: Teubner, 1959.

———. "Ideen zu einer vergleichenden und zergliedernden Psychologie." In *Gesammelte Schriften,* 5: 139–240. Stuttgart: Teubner, 1957.

Droysen, Johann Gustav. "Grundriss der Historik." 3rd ed. 1882. In *Historik,* by J. G. Droysen, ed. Peter Leyh, 415–88. Stuttgart: Frommann-Holzboog, 1977.

Humboldt, Wilhelm von. *Über die Grenzen der Wirksamkeit des Staates.* Nürnberg: Verlag Hans Carl, 1954.

———. "Über die innere und äussere Organisation der höheren Wissenschaftlichen Anstalten in Berlin." In *Die Idee der deutschen Universität.* Darmstadt: Hermann Gentner Verlag, 1956, 377–86.

Jellinek, Georg. *Die Erklärung der Menschen- und Bürgerrechte: Ein Beitrag zur modernen Verfassungsgeschichte.* 2nd ed. Leipzig, 1904, 1–64.

———. *Das Recht des modernen Staates.* Vol. 1. *Allgemeine Staatslehre.* Berlin, 1900, 3–39.

Knies, Karl. *Die politische Oekonomie vom Standpunkte der geschichtlichen Methode.* Braunschweig, 1853, 1–35, 70–123, 321–55.

Kries, J[ohannes] v[on]. "Ueber den Begriff der objektiven Möglichkeit." *Vierteljahrsschrift für wissenschaftliche Philosophie* 12 (1888): 180–222.

Lamprecht, Karl. *Moderne Geschichtswissenschaft: Fünf Vorträge.* Freiburg im Breisgau, 1905.

Lange, Friedrich Albert. *Geschichte des Materialismus und Kritik seiner Bedeutung in der Gegenwart.* Iserlohn, 1866, iii—xiv, 233–557.

Menger, Carl. *Untersuchungen über die Methode der Socialwissenschaften und der Politischen Oekonomie insbesondere.* Leipzig, 1883, 3–59.

Meyer, Eduard. *Zur Theorie und Methodik der Geschichte.* Halle, 1902.

Radbruch, Gustav. *Die Lehre von der adäquaten Verursachung.* Berlin, 1902.

Ranke, Leopold von. *Die grossen Mächte.* Ed. Friedrich Meinecke. Leipzig: Insel-Verlag, 1916, 13–61.

———. *Das politische Gespräch und andere Schriften zur Wissenschaftslehre.* Halle, Saale: Niemeyer, 1925, 10–36.

Rickert, Heinrich. *Die Grenzen der naturwissenschaftlichen Begriffsbildung.* Tübingen, 1902.

Simmel, Georg. "Der Begriff und die Tragödie der Kultur." In *Philosophische Kultur,* 195–219.

———. "Die Grosstädte und das Geistesleben." In *Das Individuum,*192–204.

———. *Das Individuum und die Freiheit: Essays.* Berlin: Verlag Klaus Wagenbach, 1984.

———. "Das Individuum und die Freiheit." In *Das Individuum,* 212–19.

———. *Philosophie des Geldes.* 1900. 7th ed. Berlin: Duncker and Humblot, 1977.

———. *Philosophische Kultur.* Berlin: Verlag Klaus Wagenbach, 1983.

———. *Probleme der Geschichtsphilosophie: Eine erkenntnistheoretische Studie.* 1892. 2nd ed. Leipzig, 1905.

———. *Schopenhauer und Nietzsche.* Leipzig, 1907.

———. *Soziologie: Untersuchungen über die Formen der Vergesellschaftung.* 1908. 5th ed. Berlin: Duncker and Humblot, 1968.

———. Über soziale Differenzierung: Soziologische und psychologische Untersuchungen [1892]. Vol. 2 of *Georg Simmel Gesamtausgabe,* ed. Otto Rammstedt. Frankfurt: Suhrkamp, 1989.

———. "Vom Wesen der Kultur." In *Das Individuum,* 84–91.

Sombart, Werner. *Die Juden und das Wirtschaftsleben.* Leipzig: Duncker and Humblot, 1911.

———. *Der moderne Kapitalismus.* Vol. 1. *Die Genesis des Kapitalismus.* Leipzig: Duncker and Humblot, 1902.

Tönnies, Ferdinand. "Ferdinand Tönnies." In *Philosophie der Gegenwart in Selbstdarstellungen,* ed. Raymund Schmidt, 3: 1–36. Leipzig: Meiner, 1922.

———. *Gemeinschaft und Gesellschaft: Grundbegriffe der reinen Soziologie.* 1887. Darmstadt: Wissenschaftliche Buchgesellschaft, 1979.

———, and Friedrich Paulsen. *Briefwechsel, 1876–1908.* Ed. O. Klose, E. G. Jacoby, and I. Fischer. Kiel: F. Hirt, 1961.

Windelband, Wilhelm. "Geschichte und Naturwissenschaft." 1894. In *Präludien,* 355–79. 3rd ed. Tübingen, 1907.

SELECTED SECONDARY SOURCES

Albrow, Martin. *Max Weber's Construction of Social Theory.* New York: St. Martin's Press, 1990.

Aron Raymond. *La Sociologie allemande contemporaine.* Paris: F. Alcan, 1935, 97–154.

Bendix, Reinhard. *Max Weber: An Intellectual Portrait.* Garden City, NY: Doubleday Anchor, 1962.

Bickel, Cornelius. *Ferdinand Tönnies: Soziologie als skeptische Aufklärung zwischen Historismus und Rationalismus.* Opladen: Westdeutscher Verlag, 1991.

Breuer, Stefan. *Bürokratie und Charisma: Zur politischen Soziologie Max Webers.* Darmstadt: Wissenschaftliche Buchgesellschaft, 1994.

Bruford, W. H. *The German Tradition of Self-Cultivation: "Bildung from Humboldt to Thomas Mann.* New York and London: Cambridge University Press, 1975.

Bruun, H. H. *Science, Values and Politics in Max Weber's Methodology.* Copenhagen: Munksgaard, 1972.

Chickering, Roger. *Karl Lamprecht: A Germanic Academic Life (1859–1915).* Atlantic Highlands, NJ: Humanities Press, 1993.

Collins, Randall. *Weberian Sociological Theory.* Cambridge: Cambridge University Press, 1986.

Ermarth, Michael. *Wilhelm Dilthey: The Critique of Historical Reason.* Chicago: University of Chicago Press, 1975, 3–178.

Fischoff, Ephraim. "Die protestantische Ethik und der Geist des Kapitalismus: Die Geschichte einer Kontroverse." In *Die protestantische Ethik,* by Max Weber, vol.2, *Kritiken und Antikritiken,* ed. J. Winckelmann, 346–79. Gütersloh: Mohn, 1978.

Germer, Andrea. *Wissenschaft und Leben: Max Webers Antwort auf eine Frage Friedrich Nietzsches.* Göttingen: Vandenhoeck and Ruprecht, 1994.

Giddens, Anthony. *Politics and Sociology in the Thought of Max Weber.* London: Macmillan, 1972.

Goldman, Harvey. *Max Weber and Thomas Mann: Calling and the Shaping of the Self.* Berkeley and Los Angeles: University of California Press, 1988.

Heberle, Rudolf. "The Sociological System of Ferdinand Tönnies: 'Community' and 'Society.'" In *An Introduction to the History of Sociology,* ed. Harry Elmer Barnes, 227–48. Chicago: University of Chicago Press, 1948.

Hennis, Wilhelm. *Max Webers Fragestellung: Studien zur Biographie des Werks.* Tübingen: J. C. B. Mohr, 1987.

Henrich, Dieter. *Die Einheit der Wissenschaftslehre Max Webers.* Tübingen: J. C. B. Mohr, 1952.

Honigsheim, Paul. "Max Weber in Heidelberg." In *Max Weber zum Gedächtnis: Materialien und Dokumente,* ed. Rene König and J. Winckelmann. Köln: Westdeutscher Verlag, 1963.

Jansen, Christian. *Professoren und Politik: Politisches Denken und Handeln der Heidelberger Hochschullehrer, 1914–1935.* Göttingen: Vandenhoeck and Ruprecht, 1992.

Kalberg, Stephen. *Max Weber's Comparative Historical Sociology.* Chicago: University of Chicago Press, 1994.

Käsler, Dirk. *Einführung in das Studium Max Webers.* München: C. H. Beck, 1979.

Kocka, Jürgen. "Otto Hintze, Max Weber und das Problem der Bürokratie." *Historische Zeitschrift* 233 (1981): 65–105.

———, ed. *Max Weber, der Historiker.* Göttingen: Vandenhoeck and Ruprecht, 1986, 13–27, 28–50, 119–50, 158–72, 173–92, 193–203.

Köhnke, Klaus Christian. *Entstehung und Aufstieg des Neukantianismus: Die deutsche Universitätsphilosophie zwischen Idealismus und Positivism.* Frankfurt: Suhrkamp, 1986, esp. 233–432.

König, Rene. "Die Begriffe Gemeinschaft und Gesellschaft." *Kölner Zeitschrift für Soziologie* 7 (1955): 248–420.

Krüger, Christa. *Max und Marianne Weber: Tag- und Nachtansichten einer Ehe.* Zürich: Pendo, 2001.

Lehmann, Hartmut, and Guenther Roth, eds. *Weber's Protestant Ethic: Origins, Evidence, Contexts.* Cambridge: Cambridge University Press, 1987.

Lenger, Friedrich. *Werner Sombart, 1863–1914: Eine Biographie.* München: Beck, 1994.

Lindenlaub, Dieter. *Richtungskämpfe im Verein für Sozialpolitik.* Wiesbaden: Frank Steiner, 1967.

Löwith, Karl. *Max Weber and Karl Marx.* Ed. T. Bottomore and W. Outhwaite. London: George Allen & Unwin, 1982.

Marshall, Gordon. *In Search of the Spirit of Capitalism.* New York: Columbia University Press, 1982.

Mitzman, Arthur. *The Iron Cage: An Historical Interpretation of Max Weber.* New York: Alfred A. Knopf, 1970.

Mommsen, Wolfgang J. *The Age of Bureaucracy: Perspectives on the Political Sociology of Max Weber.* Oxford: Blackwell, 1974.

———. *Max Weber and German Politics 1890-1920.* Trans. M. S. Steinberg. Chicago: University of Chicago Press, 1984.

———. *Max Weber: Gesellschaft, Politik und Geschichte.* Frankfurt: Suhrkamp, 1982.

———. *The Political and Social Theory of Max Weber: Collected Essays.* Chicago: University of Chicago Press, 1989.

———, and Wolfgang Schwentker, eds. *Max Weber und seine Zeitgenossen.* Göttingen: Vandenhoeck and Ruprecht, 1988, 84–97, 98–118, 119–36, 337–79.

Oakes, Guy. *Weber and Rickert: Concept Formation in the Cultural Sciences.* Cambridge, MA: MIT Press, 1988.

Ringer, Fritz. *The Decline of the German Mandarins.* Cambridge, MA: Harvard University Press, 1969.

———. *Fields of Knowledge: French Academic Culture in Comparative Perspective, 1890–1920.* Cambridge: Cambridge University Press, 1992.

———. *Max Weber's Methodology.* Cambridge, MA: Harvard University Press, 1997.

———. Review of Bruford [see entry for Bruford above]. *Central European History* 11 (1978): 107–13.

Roth, Guenther, and Wolfgang Schluchter. *Max Weber's Vision of History.* Berkeley and Los Angeles: University of California Press, 1979, esp. 119–27, 172–80.

Runciman, W. G. *A Critique of Max Weber's Philosophy of Social Science.* Cambridge: Cambridge University Press, 1972.

Scaff, Lawrence A. *Fleeing the Iron Cage: Culture, Politics, and Modernity in the Thought of Max Weber.* Berkeley and Los Angeles: University of California Press, 1989.

Schelting, Alexander von. *Max Webers Wissenschaftslehre.* Tübingen: J. C. B. Mohr (Paul Siebeck), 1934.

Schluchter, Wolfgang. *Die Entwicklung des okzidentalen Rationalismus. Eine Analyse von Max Webers Gesellschaftsgeschichte.* Tübingen: J. C. B. Mohr, 1979.
———. *Rationalismus der Weltbeherrschung: Studien zu Max Weber.* Frankfurt: Suhrkamp, 1980.
———. *Religion und Lebensführung.* Vol. 1. *Studien zu Max Webers Kultur- und Werttheorie.* Vol. 2. *Studien zu Max Webers Religions- und Herrschaftssoziologie.* Frankfurt: Suhrkamp, 1988.
Tenbruck, F. H. "Formal Sociology" In *Georg Simmel, 1858–1918: A Collection of Essays,* ed. Kurt Wolff. Columbus: Ohio State University Press, 1959, 61–99.
———. "Die Genesis der Methodologie Max Webers." *Kölner Zeitschrift für Soziologie und Sozialpsychologie* 2 (1959): 573–630.
———. "Das Werk Max Webers." *Kölner Zeitschrift für Soziologie* 27 (1995): 663–702.
Turner, Brian S. *For Weber: Essays on the Sociology of Fate.* Boston: Routledge, 1981.
Turner, Stephen P., ed. *The Cambridge Companion to Weber.* Cambridge: Cambridge University Press, 2000, 21–41.
Turner, Stephen P., and Regis A. Factor. "Decisionism and Politics: Weber as Constitutional Theorist." In *Max Weber, Rationality and Modernity,* ed. Scott Lash and Sam Whimster, 334–53. London: George Allen & Unwin, 1987.
———. "Objective Possibility and Adequate Causation in Weber's Methodological Writings." *Sociological Review* 29 (1981): 5–28.
Wagner, Gerhard, and Heinz Zipprian. "Methodologie und Ontologie: Zum Problem kausaler Erklärung bei Max Weber." *Zeitschrift für Soziologie* 14 (1985): 115–30.
Weber, Marianne. *Max Weber: Ein Lebensbild.* Heidelberg: L. Schneider, 1950.
Weiss, Johannes. "Kausale Durchsichtigkeit." In *Max Webers Wissenschaftslehre: Interpretation und Kritik,* ed. Gerhard Wagner and Heinz Zipprian. Frankfurt: Suhrkamp, 507–26.
———. *Max Weber heute: Erträge und Probleme der Forschung.* Frankfurt: Suhrkamp, 1989.

America (*continued*)

eral judges, 201; legal findings retain a charismatic quality, 200; middle-class glorification of business success, 140; secular clubs, 136–37; social honor conferred by sects and clubs, 141–42; town meetings, 69; townships, 192; university system, 138, 231–33; Weber's reflections on, 140–41

American presidency, as example of plebiscitarian democracy, 68

American university professors, 231

Anabaptists, 118, 156, 196

anarchist, 111

anarcho-syndicalists, 58

ancestor cult, 162

anchorite settlements, 163

Anglo-American, national traits, 121

Anglo-American "gentleman," 120, 125

Anglophilia, 125

Anglo-Saxon law, 196

animist beliefs, 100

annexationist hysteria, 3, 15

Anschütz, Gerhard, 55

anthropolatry, 150

anti-Semitism, 15, 127, 129, 130

antisocialist laws, 41, 64

apathetic asceticism, 151

apathetic ecstasy, 148, 151, 163, 171

Aquinas, Thomas, 121

Archiv für soziale Gesetzgebung und Statistik (*Archive for Social Legislation and Statistics*), 108, 126

Archiv für Sozialwissenschaft und Sozialpolitik (*Archive for Social Science and Social Policy*), 2, 126, 139, 143

arms manufacturers, 51

art: monumental, 240; as a system of autonomous values, 156

art historians, 96

artisan guilds, 209

asceticism: ability to observe and control inner life, 254; and active participation in economic life, 114, 144; Christian, history of, 117, 120; dual tendency to reject work and to dominate it by means of magic, 153; inner-worldly, 150; of medieval monk, 120; path to salvation as transformation of the world, 150; suspicion of art as a form of magic, 156; world-rejecting, 153, 154. *See also* Protestant asceticism

Asia: disprivileged role of Jews in, 205; need to regulate rivers and access to water, 208; salvation doctrines, 173

Austria-Hungary, 53

Bacon, Roger, 235

Baden, 114

Baden Academy of Sciences, 175

baptism, 118

Baptists, 118

Barclay, Robert, 121

Battle of Marathon, 82, 88

Baudelaire, Charles, 237

Bavaria, 74

Bavarian Academy of Sciences, 125

Baxter, Richard, 121–22, 123, 217

beggar monks, 172

begging, 123

Belgium, 53

Below, Georg von, 40

benefices, 60, 162, 185, 189

Bentham, Jeremy, 121, 151, 196

Bernhard, case of 1908, 63

Bernstein, Eduard, 73, 218

Bethmann Hollweg, 53

Bildung, 39, 111; change in meaning of between 1800 and 1900, 11; cultivation as self-perfection, 230; development of an incomparable individual, 18; differences in as societal barrier, 70–71; education in the sense of self-cultivation, 8, 38; educative effects similar to interpretation, 104; as effect of involvement in research, 9; emergence of as a new concept by around 1800, 10–11; as a higher form of selfishness by 1900–1920, 12; and intellectual specialization, 71, 242; linked to a universal vision of human salvation in 1800, 12; as a source of self-esteem and social honor, 9; used to challenge the notion that school and university places should be distributed on the basis of academic aptitude, 13; use of in defense of the status quo, 13

Bildungsbürgertum, 8, 211, 223

Bismarck, Otto Von, 41, 82; Caesarism, 48, 141; demagogic tactics, 1, 64; foreign policy, 53; heritage, 64; Reinsurance treaty with Russia, 53; universal suffrage, 70

"Bismarck legend," 64

Bloch, Ernst, 57

Bolshevik Revolution, 73, 219

Bourdieu, Pierre, 7, 251

bourgeois principles, 116

Brahmins, 144, 167; asceticism, 171–72; benefit from ritual exclusivity of the castes, 168–69; charisma based upon knowledge of rituals and ceremonies, 171; education of, 169; threat to unity and coherence of dogma by magic sects, 171

Braun, Heinrich, 126

Brentano, Lujo, 55, 60, 62, 63, 125, 130, 131

brotherliness, ethic of, 153–54, 247–48; conflict with purposive rationality, 156; and intellectuality (*Geistigkeit*), 159; lack of in empirical world, 160–61; mysticism of, 155; suspicion of art as a form of magic, 156; tension with aesthetic and erotic spheres, 156–

58; tension with economic and political spheres, 154–55; and Tolstoy, 160

Buckle, H. T., *History of Civilization in England,* 20

Buddha, "the enlightened," 172

Buddhism, 143, 172–75; apoliticality, 172; and Brahmin doctrines, 171; call for detachment, 173; as great missionary religion, 173; heterodoxy, 168; highest stages of salvation open only to monks, 173; monasteries, 173; not properly a salvation religion, 172–73; perpetuated by monks, 144; prayer machines, 151

budget (*Hauschaltsplan*), 182

Bunyan, John, *Pilgrim's Progress,* 119

bureaucratic administrative staff, 183, 185, 190, 215, 220

bureaucratic domination, 255; as crucial element in rationalization of modern political and economic institutions, 221; domination by means of specialized knowledge, 184, 221, 223, 226; as inescapable, 220–21; limitations on by political bodies, 191; "official secrets," 221, 223; origination in patrimonial states, 185; rationality, 187; "steel housing" of, 217, 221, 223, 255; two faces of, 220–24

bureaucratic offices, 189

bureaucratic state, impersonal, 154–55

bureaucratic welfare state, 195

burgher associations: oath, 205; quasi-contractual character of freedoms granted to, 210; sociological meaning of, 206; as sources of tax revenue for their rulers, 206; spontaneous vs. derived formations of, 206

burgher estate (*Bürgertum*), 211

burgher master, 206, 208

bürghers (burghers), 204, 210, 211, 254

business associations, 32

Caesarism, 48, 68, 141
calculation, in rational enterprise, 154, 221
calculation in kind, 213–14
calling (*Beruf*): ascetic significance of, 122; defined, 231; origination in Luther's Bible translation, 117; to subdue the natural self through strenuous work, 131
Calvin, John, 119
Calvinism, 117; doctrine of predestination, 118, 120; harsh doctrine of a remote God, 119; sanctioning of force in defense of the faith, 248; superiority in social organization, 119; unprecedented inner isolation of the individual, 119
Calvinist diaspora, 114
Canada, 200
Canon law, 194
capital accounting (*Kapitalrechnung*), 182, 213, 215, 216
capital accumulation, 122
capital and labor, antagonism between, 109
capitalism: adventure, 116, 122, 129, 186; agrarian, 43, 46, 47; and bureaucracy, 64, 65; and contest between sustenance economy for agrarian population and labor-saving agricultural production for the market, 132; and destruction of community, 33; and duty to one's profession, 115, 116; exchange economy, 215–16; impersonality and senselessness of work under, 217; inaccessible to a religious ethic of brotherliness, 154; mandarin view of, 14; medieval communes and emergence of, 211; "pariah capitalism," 122; political, 166, 167; among Protestant sects, 135; relation to "spirit of capitalism," 116; religious influences on, 118; rise of modern,

176; as substantively irrational, 217, 252–53; traditionalism as obstacle to, 116; Weber's analysis of, 3, 211–24
Carolingian period, 209
caste barriers, 205
Catania, 61
Catholic Center, 65, 245
Catholic Church: indulgences, 120; natural law, 199; political, 124; recognition of marriage as a sacrament, 157
Catholics, occupational representation in Baden, 114
causal analysis: abstract character of, 84; inherently nomological, 20; object of, 88
causal determination, 92
causal regression, 85
causation: adequate, 81–85, 86; two components of, 87
cause and effect, diagram of, 88
Central Europe, Roman law, 195
centralized economic planning, 224
cereal production, 42
change: alternate paths of, 85; dissensus as a source, 35; unfolding of preexistent potentialities, 19
charisma: anti-authoritarian reinterpretation (*herrschaftsfremde Umdeutung*), 190, 210; defined by Weber, 186; magical practices designed to awaken, 153; the most important revolutionary power, 188; of office, 189; of the pure mystic, 150; as religious qualification, 149; routinization of, 189, 190
charismatic domination: anti-authoritarian reinterpretation of, 190, 210; "ideal-typical purity," 188; inherently transitory, 190; training for in China, 68, 226–27; Weber's analysis of, 186–89
charismatic successor, 188–89
charity, 154

Chicago, 138
chiliastic prophecy, 247
chiliastic revolutions, 156
China: charismatic domination, 68,
    226–27; commercial contact with the
    West, 161; economic traditionalism
    encouraged by guilds, 161; examina-
    tions, 162; patrimonial bureaucracy,
    161; patrimonial tradition of substan-
    tive justice, 162; politically oriented
    capitalism, 166; public offices allo-
    cated on the basis of educational
    qualifications, 161–62; role of family
    clans in villages, 162; wealth derived
    from exploitation of bureaucratic
    offices, 166
Chinese emperor, and welfare of sub-
    jects, 161
Chinese "gentleman," self-perfection,
    162–63
Chinese mandarins: and access to pub-
    lic office, 161; acquisitive drive, 115;
    despised the merely wealthy, 163;
    purely literary schooling, 162
Chinese officials, office benefices, 162
Chinese religion: impersonal divinity
    embodied in theocratic emperor, 161;
    ritual ancestor and spirit cults, 161
choice, 93
Christianity: as an urban and "burgher"
    religion, 144; history of asceticism,
    117, 120; holy days, 205; influence of
    Judaism on, 143; saints, 152; Trinity,
    152
Christian Middle Ages, 157
church, as hierocratic organization, 149,
    180
church law, 194
Ciompi revolt, 209
"circuit" preachers, 135
cities: agrarian, 203; of antiquity and of
    Middle Ages, 204, 208–9; consumer,
    203; democracies, 208; Italian, 209–

10; medieval, 210; merchant, 203; pa-
    trician, 208; plebeian, 208; producer,
    203; tyrants, 208. *See also* Western
    city
Civil Code, 195–96, 200
civil law cases, 80
civil service, 62, 65, 66, 222
Civil Service Reform, 244
clan relationships, 32
clan state (*Geschlechterstaat*), 189
class antagonism, 45
classical Greece, 8
classical secondary schools, 12
cognitive rationalization, 151
collegial bodies, 191
Colmar museum, 51
commensality, 229
commercialism, opposed to German
    culture, 14
commercial law, 195, 198
commodity exchange, 199
common law, 194
communal law, 32
communal relationships: common ex-
    pectations and obligations, 32;
    defined, 50–51
communes (*Gemeinde*). *See* medieval
    communes (*Gemeinde*)
Communion, 205
Communist Manifesto of 1848, 73, 218
community, destruction of, 33
comparative sociology of religion, We-
    ber on, 143–74; Asian salvation doc-
    trines, 173; aversion to conformity
    and "adjustment," 165; "bearers" of
    particular religions, 144; conflict be-
    tween the competing spheres of life,
    161; contrast of Confucianism and
    Taoism with ascetic Protestantism,
    164–67; different meanings of ratio-
    nalization, 151–52; enlarged concep-
    tion of social "interests," 144; interest
    in economic rationalization in West

comparative sociology of religion (*continued*)

in sixteenth and seventeenth centuries, 151; relation of religions to politics, 155–56; religions of China and of India, 161–74; religions of the world, 152–60; sense of ineradicable conflict among ultimate values, 160; tension between brotherly ethic and aesthetic and erotic spheres, 156–58; tension between brotherly ethic and economic and political spheres, 154–55; tension between religion and intellectualism, 158–59; theodicy of suffering, 144–46; triadic scheme of singular causal analysis, 146

comparative world history, framing of, 143–52

compensatory justice, 158

competition, 35

compulsory political organization (state *[Staat]*), 180

Comte, Auguste, 17, 90

concept, discovery of, 234–35

conditions, comparative analyses of changing, 22

conduct of life: psychological impetus behind the quest for, 118; Puritan, 120–21; rationalization of, 151; rational systematization of with the aim of salvation, 153; systematically controlled, 120

conflict, limits and norms of, 35

conformism, 111

conformity to observable "rules," 87

confraternities, 207, 209, 254

Confucian gentleman, 166

Confucianism, 143; and acquisition of wealth, 163, 166; adjustment to worldly realities, 164; Chinese examinations, 227; and consumption of wealth, 163; doctrine of an educated and socially dominant elite of officials,

144, 163; ideal of self-perfection, 165; impediment to development of legal and scientific rationalism, 162; impersonal dualism, 162; mandarins, 171; no radical evil and no salvation, 162; radical optimism, 164; rationalism, 151, 166; rejection of universal love of humanity, 164; success in controlling the Taoist heterodoxy, 163; vs. Western religions, 164

conjurations, 206

connubium, 229

consequentialism, 253

conservatives: enlightened, 15–16; retarding of commercial and industrial development, 41; Romantic, 31

constant motives, 120

constitutional division of power, 96, 191

consuls, 207

consumer cities, 203

consumers' cooperatives, 33

consumption: arbitrarily imposed by the dominant political power, 218; Confucian, 163; emphasis upon, 186; Protestant limitation of, 122

contemplation, 147, 160

content, of social forms, 35

Continental Congress, 57

Continental law, 200

contract theory, 196–97

corporate boards, state representatives on, 60, 62

cosmic love. *See* brotherliness, ethic of

counterfactual reasoning: in causal analysis, 83–84, 85, 89, 101; Kries and, 81; and nomological knowledge, 88

courses of events, 87

covetousness, 115

cultivation (*Kultiviertheit*): defined by Simmel, 38–39; learning as, 39; pedagogy of, 227; as self-perfection, 159, 225, 230

cultural conflict (*Kulturkampf*), 124
cultural epochs, 22
cultural goods, ultimate meaninglessness, 159–60
cultural ideas, 108
cultural individualism, 11, 18, 57, 253
cultural nationalism, 44–45
cultural norms, validity of, 30
cultural pluralism, 5, 55, 105, 112
cultural sciences (*Kulturwissenschaften*), 78
cultural state (*Kulturstaat*), mandarin doctrine of, 10
cultural values, 29, 112
cultural war, German, 127
customary law, 196
customs, 32, 179

da Vinci, Leonardo, 235
decisionism, 241, 255
Defenestration of Prague, 176
demand (*Begehrtheit*), for different kinds of economic goods, 213
democracy: American, 139–40, 244; direct, 69, 192; leaderless, 190; plebiscitary leadership, 5, 190–91, 244
desiring self, distance from desired object, 36
determinism, 17, 29, 83, 92
deviation, 81, 83, 87, 88, 102
dignity (*Vornehmheit*), 32, 38
Dilthey, Wilhelm, 19; *Construction of the Historical World in the Humanistic Disciplines* (*Geisteswissenschaften*), 24; empathy as an element in interpretation, 25; explication of interpretation of intellectual structures, 24–25; on humanistic studies, 25; *Introduction to the Humanistic Disciplines* [*Geisteswissenschaften*], 23–24
direct democracy, 69, 192
disciplinary specialization. *See* specialized knowledge (*Fachwissen*)

dissensus, as a source of social change and vitality, 35
district administrators (*Landräte*), 67
divergences between alternate paths and outcomes, 87, 102
diversity, toleration of, 56
division of labor, 39, 40
division of power, constitutional, 69, 191
doctrine, 149, 158
domestic service, 37
domination (*Herrschaft*): characterized by the development of the crucial relationship between ruler and administrative staff, 190; defined, 183; estate-type (*ständische Herrschaf*), 185; legal, 183–84, 210; limited or restrained, 191; pure types of, 183–92, 210; Weber's definition of, 180
double-entry bookkeeping, 128
double predestination, 118, 123, 218
doxa, 7
dress, simplicity of, 122
Droysen, Johann Gustav, 19–20
duma, 58
Durkheim, Emile, 35, 40, 226

East Elbian provinces: agrarian conditions, 133; agriculture based upon the labor-intensive exploitation of land, 46; landowners, 41, 115; relationships between agricultural employers and workers, 43
economic action (*Wirtschaften*): defined by Weber, 180; formal rationality, 182; substantive rationality, 182
economic chances, 181
economic enterprise (*Wirtschaftbetrieb*), 180, 181
economic individualism, 253
economic modernization, equivalent with progress toward capitalism, 64
economic order, substantive irrationality, 216–17

German academic community
(*continued*)
commitment to bureaucratic monarchy, 11–12; commitment to concept of *Bildung,* 9; crisis of culture, 17; enthusiasm for First World War, 14, 52; natural spokesmen of the mandarin elite, 9; and "partisan" positions, 110; requirement of being able teachers and good scholars, 232; servility, 33; tradition, 8; two major groups, 15, 52–53

German-Americans, 141

German Austria, 74

German classical sociology, 30–40, 31

German Constitution of 1871, 66

German Democratic Party, 73

German Empire, 1; annexations in northern France, 54; bourgeoisie commitment to preservation of the status quo, 47; bureaucratic domination and condescension, 224; civil service, 62, 222; classical secondary schooling, 9; community, 33; confessional groups, 114; cultural war against the West, 127; eastern policy, 54; economics, 14; educational revolution, 8; education as primary concern of the new intellectual stratum, 11; historical economists, 111; historical school of law, 196; interpretive individualism, 31; legal philosophy, 80; legal practitioners, 199–200; municipal government, 61; national traits, 121; November Revolution, 73, 74; political conditions, 244–45; politics, 70; program of naval construction, 53; rational administration, 71–72, 222; research universities, 10; suzerainty in Belgium, 54; wartime values, 52

German Historical School of Economics, 20, 42

German historical tradition, 18–30, 89, 90, 92

German History (Lamprecht), 22

German Idealism, 8, 9, 12, 16, 17, 39, 90

German Jews, 114

German literati, 66, 67

German Lutheran *Gemütlichkeit,* 125

German Society for Sociology, 34, 175

German universities: academic system, 231–33; "doctoral factories," 230; funded by the territorial states, 10; ideal of personal *Bildung,* 225; researchers separated from the means of research, 232; research universities, 10; university teachers' day (*Hochschullehrertag*), 55

German workers: factory rules, 60; out-migration, 43

gerontocracy, 184, 185

God: conceptions of, 149; of Judaism, 152; personal, 148; remote, 119, 148; supramundane creator, 150, 152; wealth as increasing glory of, 121

Goethe, Johann Wolfgang von, 123

good works, systematic performance of, 120

Gothein, Eberhard, 129

grace: institutional dispensation of, 148, 149; means of, 150

grain tariffs, 47

great men, 92

Gresham's law, 77

group actions, 100–101

guilds, 32, 33, 135–36, 161, 207, 209, 210

guilt, associated with the unjust inequalities of the social order, 160

guru, 171

Gutsherr (lord), 43

Gymnasium, 12

Hamburg Dock Strike of 1897–1898, 126

Hannibal, 82

harmony of views (*Eintracht*), 32

Harnack, Adolf, 125
"Hebraicism," 120
Hegelian terminology, 24
Hellenic scientific thought, 119
Helmholtz, Hermann von, 258n17
Henretta, James, 131
hereditary charisma, 189
hermeneutic method, 16
hermeneutic studies, as primary source of *Bildung*, 9
"heroes," narratives organized around, 22
heterodoxies, 7
hierocracies, 147–48, 149, 180
Hindu caste system, 167, 168, 170, 174, 205
Hinduism, 143, 167–72; as an absolutely exclusive religion, 167; asceticism, 172; basic axioms, 169; extreme tolerance of divergent paths within, 168; guest peoples, 167; monasticism, 171–72; propagated by Brahmin caste, 144; question of how the soul could extricate itself from the world of recurrence, 172; rebirths, 170; salvation techniques, 172; several future states, 167–68; social theodicy, 169
historical change, alternate paths of, 85
historical individuals, defined in the light of their cultural significance, 28
historical study of culture (*historische Kulturwissenschaft*), 28
historiography, insistence on imitating the natural sciences, 23
history: adequate causal connections expressed in rules, 86; as applied psychology, 22–23, 90; centrality of the individual and the concrete, 20; debate about free will and determinism, 93; equation with applied psychology, 23; objectivity, 30; presuppositions, 236; relatively historical concepts, 28; as a science of reality

(*Wirklichkeitswissenschaft*), 26, 28, 78; study of "individuals," 114–15
Hitler, Adolph, 5
holism, 89–90
Holy Communion, sects controlled access to in America, 137
holy war, 248
Honigsheim, Paul, 56
honor, 54, 157
household, budgetary separation from the enterprise, 213, 215
human beings, unequal religious qualification of, 149
humanistic disciplines (*Geisteswissenschaften*), 17–18, 24, 28, 77, 258n17
humanities and social sciences, sense of crisis, 12
human mind (*Geist*), 24, 39–40
human rights, historical origins of the idea of, 57
Humboldt, Wilhelm von, 10–11, 13, 18–19, 57, 242, 253
Hume, David, 26, 81
Husserl, Ernst, 242

ideal gas law, 77
ideal type, 40, 101–4, 177
"ideas of 1914," 52, 71, 222, 223
idiographic knowledge, 27, 84
image of result, as cause of the action, 94
immediate experience (*Erlebnis*), 24
imperialism, theory of, 51
impersonal God, characteristic of Indian and Chinese religions, 148
import duties, 41
income classes, 228
Independent Commission for a German Peace, 52
India: caste system, 168, 169; modern number system, 167; occupational specialization, 167; political capitalism and tax farming, 167; retarded development of natural sciences and

comes, 46; economic position undermined by shifts in psychology of
their employees, 44; survey of, 42
jurors, 200–201
jury duty, 200

Kant, Immanuel, 33, 93, 241–42
Kantian ethics, 111, 122
Das Kapital, 106
Karlsruhe, 56
karma doctrine, 145, 168, 169–70, 172,
174
khadi justice, 190, 194, 200
Knies, Karl, 20–21, 23, 87, 89, 92
knightly courtship, and eroticism, 157
Kries, Johannes von, 80–81
Kulturstaat, 11–12
Kung-tse (Confucius), 162
Kürwille (arbitrary will), 31, 32
Kwei, 162, 227

laboratory science, 10
labor theory of value, 36
labor unions, 13, 33, 73, 126, 219, 224
laissez-faire economics, 14, 64, 253
Lamprecht, Karl, 22–23, 90
landowning elite, social value of membership in, 132
Laotse, ascetic flight from the world,
163
law: antithesis between formal and substantive principles in, 201; codification of, 211; defined by Simmel, 26;
development of modern, 198–201;
"essence" (*Wesen*) of, 199; formally
rationalized, 192, 193–94, 195, 196;
functioning as cause, 96; logical systematization of, 198–99; substantive
(*materiale*) rationality, 193, 212; substantive norms of welfare and justice,
212; university education in, 193;
weakening of formal rationalism, 200
law of differentiation, 26

law of the land (*lex terrae*), 194
lay community, collective responsibility,
134–35
lay jurors, 200–201
leaderless democracy, 190
leadership democracy, 190
League of Nations, 75
learning, as "cultivation," 39
learning and teaching, freedom of, 55–
56
Lederer, Emil, 56
legal anthologies (*Rechtsbücher*), 193
legal codifications, 195
legal curriculum, 192–93, 195
legal domination, 183–84, 210, 220
legal formalism, 198
legal norms, rational interpretation
(*Sinndeutung*), 199
legal professionals: education of, 195,
198; increased demands upon in
exchange economy, 192; reaction
against the formalism of the law,
199–200
legal state (*Rechtsstaat*), 181
legal system, emergence of, 194
Leipzig Circle, 90
Leninists, 58
lex naturae, 196
liberalism: Semstwo, 58, 59; Weber's, 5,
55–63, 112; widespread attacks on in
1920s, 34
liberal pluralism, 5, 55, 112
literati, 66, 67, 71, 72
logicalization (*Logizierung*), 195
Lord's Supper, 205, 211, 254
love: goal of direct linking of souls, 157;
of one's enemies, 154
lower guilds (*arti minori*), 209
lower middle class (*Kleinbürgertum*),
228
Lukacs, Georg, 57
Luther, Martin, 117, 119, 120, 121
Lutheranism, 118, 121, 155

magic: based on animist beliefs, 100; designed to awaken charisma, 153; removal from (*Entzauberung*) the world, 119, 234, 254; and Taoism, 163

magical religiosity, linked to the aesthetic sphere, 156

magical restrictions, 205

"magic garden," 163, 174

magicians, 145, 227

magic sects, threat to Brahmins, 171

mammon, suspicion of, 121

Manchester, 116

Manchesterite dogma, 109

mandarins: Chinese, 115, 161, 162, 163; Confucian, 171; deeply threatened by changes, 13; doctrine of cultural state (*Kulturstaat*), 10; German, owed social standing to educational qualifications, 8–9; role of cultural leadership during World War I, 14–15; university professors as spokespersons for, 9; view of capitalism, 14; Weber's dissent from views of, 30–31

Marathon, Battle of, 82, 88

marginal cost, 36

marginal utility theory, 21, 36, 91, 95, 180, 181, 213, 215

market capitalism, unequal distribution of economic goods as a substantive irrationality of, 217

market competition, 154

market economy: adjustments in equilibrium relationships, 252; formal rationality, 252; motivated by self-interest, 215; substantive irrationalities, 217

market exchanges, 180

market situation (*Marktlage*), 182

marriage, Lutheran conception of, 158

Marx, Karl, 31, 73, 113

Marxism, 17, 51, 59, 198

mass religion, 149

materialism, 17

maxim, 96

Max Weber Gesamtausgabe, 4

meaningless phenomena, 98

meaning relation, 104

means-ends relations, 32, 38

means of exchange, 181

medical sciences, 236

medieval communes (*Gemeinde*), 203, 204, 205, 208, 209, 210, 211, 254

mendicant orders, 144, 188

Menger, Carl: conception of theoretical economics, 21; critique of German historical economics, 23; distinction between abstract-but-exact and empirical-but-inexact regularities, 26; understanding of marginal utility theory, 95

Mennonites, 118

merchant cities, 203

metaphysical speculation, 158

Methodism, 118

methodological individualism, 91

methodology of the social sciences, Weber's, 77–112; attack upon "psychologism," 91; cautious about reliability of interpretation, 100–101; concept of "ideal type," 101–4; concern with description of singular objects, 85; conjectural ranking of possible causes, 84; critique of Eduard Meyer, 85, 106; critique of Stammler, 86, 96; definition of the "world religions," 143; distinction between adequacy of an interpretation of a singular causal claim, 104; distinction between descriptive and prescriptive propositions, 111; distinction between nomological sciences and sciences of reality, 78, 104; distinction between primary and secondary historical facts, 78; distinction between social science and value judgment, 9, 108, 109–10; distinction between subjectively motivated problem definitions and objective research results, 106–7; distinction between value analysis and historical interpretation, 106; on divergence between ideal type of right rationality and empirically observed beliefs and behavioral progressions, 100; economic theory as a hypothetical construct, 91; ethically neutral forms of causal analysis and rational interpretation, 226; four types of action, 98–99; interpretation as a form of causal analysis, 103; and liberal pluralism, 112; limits of interpretive understanding, 98; maxim that interpreters must begin by supposing that the actions and beliefs they seek to understand are "rational," 95; methodological individualism, 91; "motivational understanding" of actions, 94; objectivity of research results in the cultural and social sciences, 79, 105–7; opposition to naturalistic fallacies, 90–91; partial adaptation of Rickert's philosophy, 104; on political orientations in university classrooms, 110–11; problem of irrationality, 92–94; rationality model of interpretation, 78, 92, 94, 99; redefining the aim of an action as its cause, 92; repudiation of "holism," 89; review of Adolf Weber book, 109; "right rationality" (*Richtigkeitsrationalität*), 96; role of counterfactual reasoning in causal analysis, 83–84; role of description in the formulation of singular causal claims, 84; role of deviations from purposive and/or right rationality, 99–100; role of ideal type in model of singular causal analysis, 101–2; role of interpretation in the cultural and social sciences, 91–92; rules of experience, 84–85; several senses of the word "rule," 96;

singular causal analysis, 77–78, 80, 82–89, 254; systematic approach to the varieties of understanding, 98; triadic scheme of causal relationships, 87–89, 102; two components of causation, 87; "value analysis" (*Wertanalyse*), 105–6; value neutrality, 110–12

"methods controversy," 21

Meyer, Eduard: belief that laws are replaced in history by "analogies" that may be altered by human agency, 23; and "freedom" of actions, 93; on historical significance of Battle of Marathon, 82; view that causality implies lawfulness and determinism, 92; Weber's critique of, 81

Michels, Robert, 55

Middle Ages: cities of, 204, 208–9, 210; patrimonialism, 210; prebendalism, 210. *See also* medieval communes (*Gemeinde*)

middle classes (*Mittelklassen*), 228

middle strata (*Mittelstandsklassen*), 228

migrant laborers, 43–44, 46, 47

migration, of former peasants, 41

Mill, John Stuart: appeal of cultural individualism to, 11, 18, 242, 253; Geisteswissenschaften, 258n17; ideal of an open intellectual community, 57; polytheism, 112, 237

Milton, John, *Paradise Lost,* 117

minorities, channeling of energies into business and related occupations, 114

miracle, 186

miracle workers, 145

missionary prophecy, 148

Mitzman, Arthur, psychobiography of Weber, 2

modernists, 52, 55; call for reexamination of German intellectual tradition, 16; critical distance from mandarin orthodoxy, 16 modern societies, composed of many loosely integrated "social circles," 35–36

Mommsen, Wolfgang, 56, 68

monasteries, as centers of rational enterprise, 154

monasticism, 120; Hindu, 171–72; medieval, 120, 210; Western, 120, 121

monetary calculation (*Geldrechnung*), 182

monetary debts, 182

money: consequences of use of, 181–82; impact upon the modern "style of life," 37; in modern social systems, 36–37; purely symbolic role, 36–37; stored, 182

money calculation, 212–15

money prices, 154

monopoly conditions, 215

monumental art, 240

Moravians (*Herrnhuter*), 118

Morning, 127

Mosaic Tables, 196

motive: as the image of a desired outcome that is taken to be the cause for an action, 100; for Weber, 94

municipal government, 64

municipal law, 195

Münsterberg, Hugo, 132

mystic, as savior or prophet, 156

mysticism, 147, 148, 152

Nacherleben, 24

Napoleonic Civil Code, 195–96

national idealism, 10

national identity, based on the subjective belief in nationhood, 51

National Liberal Party, 1, 33

National Socialism, 5

naturalism, 89, 90–91

natural law, 32, 156, 248; and contract theory, 196–97; defined, 196; and emergence of socialism, 198; influence on creation of law and legal findings, 197; vs. religiously motivated restriction of state power, 57; substantive interpretations, 197

natural sciences: dramatic success of, 90; vs. historical disciplines, 28; laws of, 86; limitation, 27; presuppositions, 236; natural will, 32

Naumann, Friedrich, 45, 55

necessity, 20, 92, 93

needs, meeting of (*Bedarfsdeckung*), 128

negative politics, 67

neo-classical economics, 36, 91, 102, 179

neo-humanism, 8, 11, 12, 16

neo-mercantilist policies, 61

Neurath, Otto, 214

New England, full membership in a religious community a de facto precondition of full citizenship, 137

Nietzsche, Friedrich, 38, 144, 235, 237, 241

nirvana, 168

nomological (*naturgesetzlich*), 20

nomological (*naturwissenschaftlich*) laws, 25

nomological knowledge, 27, 80, 85–86, 87, 88

nomological sciences (*Gesetzeswissenschaften*), 78

normative postulates, 182

norms: of conflict, 35; inner ethical, 164; rules as, 96

notables (*Honoratioren*): administration by, 192; legal, 192, 195, 198; rule of, 243–44; status association of in Western city, 208

objectification (*Versachlichung*) or charisma, 24, 189

objective mind (*Geist*), 24, 39–40

objective probability, 82, 83, 85

objectivity, of social sciences, 17, 105

occupational associations, 207

occupational specialist (*Fachmensch*), 35, 122

Oklahoma, 139

Old Testament, 120, 122

order (*Ordnung*), 179

Ordinarien, 231, 232

organic historicism, 198

organic social ethic, 155, 156, 160

organized experience (*Erfahrung*), 24

organized interest groups, 180

Oriental religions, chasm between laymen and virtuosi, 150

Ornungsverband, 181

orthodoxies: perpetuated by inherited practices, 7; perpetuated the ideology of *Bildung*, 16; repudiation of modernity in all its aspects, 15

Ostwald, Wilhelm, 90

Pan-Slavism, 53, 54

"pariah peoples," 167, 169

Paris Commune, 219

parliament, right of inquiry (*Enqueterecht*), 67

parliamentary deputies, 243

parliamentary reform, 3

party politics, voluntary character of, 69

parvenu, 116, 122, 129

patriarchalism, 184, 185, 194

patriarchal welfare state, 195

patrician cities, 208

patrimonialism, 191; and bureaucratic domination, 185; in China, 161, 162; encourages political and adventure capitalism, 186; estate-type, 198, 229; in European Middle Ages, 210; law, 194

patronage parties, 65, 191

Paulsen, Friedrich, 33

pedagogy of cultivation, 227

Penn, William, 158

perfection, obstacles to, 39

personal culture, 39

personal dependence, 37–38

personal God, characteristic Near Eastern religions, 148

personality, 36, 164, 233

pharisaical good conscience, 254

phenomenological methods, 18

philosophy of avarice, 115

philosophy of life (*Lebensphilosophie*), 24

pietism, 118, 121

planned economy, 213, 214, 215, 216, 218, 252

Plato, 234

plebeian cities, 208

plebiscitary leadership democracy, 5, 68, 190–91, 244

pluralism, liberal, 5, 55, 105, 112

podesta, 209

polis, 204, 205

Polish agricultural immigrants, 43, 44, 46

Polish-German federation, 53

political education, 49

political leaders, lack of responsible, 65

political organizations, 155, 180

political parties: formation of, 243; increasingly bureaucratic in structure, 65; narrow interests of, 14; organization, 244; as voluntary associations, 191–92

political professionals, 192

political reforms, resistance of university professors, 15

politics, Weber on, 41–75; the agrarian question and Weber's nationalism, 42–55; animus against Polish immigrants, 46; articles from *Frankfurter Zeitung* outlining postwar political views, 74–75; assessment of the prospects for liberalism in Russia, 57–59; call for a plebiscitary presidency, 75; as a "class-conscious bourgeois," 45; commitment to con-

politics (*continued*)
stitutional democracy, 68; commitment to "human rights" (*Menschenrechte*), 57–59; contrast of parliamentary system of England with "negative politics" of Germany, 66–67; critique of existing German political system, 65–68; critique of the Wilhelmian sociopolitical system, 64; critique of ultra-annexationist program, 54; cultural individualism, 57; toward a democratic coalition, 63–75; distinction between living from and living for politics, 67–68; on draft law to establish entailed estates, 47; emphasis on technical training of the official, 72; enthusiasm for First World War, 52; on freedom of the autonomous personality, 60; inclusive nationalism, 49, 52; introduction of racial qualities into discussion of agrarian question, 48, 49; later rejection of reality of "racial qualities," 50–51; liberalism, 55–63; 1917 political essays, 70; opposition to outright territorial acquisitions, 53; opposition to unrestricted submarine workfare, 53–54; overview of the East Elbian situation, 46; political education lecture to Austro-Hungarian army officers, 73; on political maturity, 48–49; position on war aims, 53; and Protestant Social Congress survey of agrarian conditions, 45–46; recommendations of smallholdings in the eastern provinces, 44; on role of value judgments in social policy, 48; on social pretensions of the highly educated, 71; on steady advance of bureaucracy, 64; theory of imperialism, 51; two components of causation, 87; on ultimate cause of the war, 54
polytheism, 112, 237

poor laws, 123
popolo grasso, 209
popolo minuto, 209
popular leaders, rise of, 244
popular sovereignty, natural law conception of, 74
populist romanticism, 59
positivism, 17, 22, 90
post-religious position, 240
poverty, as a moral failing, 123
power (*Macht*), 180
practical rationalism, 148, 151
prebendalism, 185, 210
predestination, 118–19, 120, 134, 145, 160; double, 123, 218
presuppositions, and scientific work, 236
Preuss, Hugo, 75
prices, as intersubjective effects of exchange relationships, 36
primary historical facts, 78
primary historical individuals, 29
primitive religions, 144
princely absolutism, 194
Privatdozenten, 231
private law, rationalization of, 117
probabilistic reasoning, 80, 83
problem of *Historismus,* 18
"problem" of rationality, 92–94
producer cities, 203
producers' cooperatives, 13, 33, 216
progression of action, 97, 99, 100
property classes, 228, 229
property rights, 197
prophecy, 145, 188
prophet, magical charisma, 153
prophetic religions: conflict with the economy, 154; followers among disadvantaged, 145; neighborly ethic of reciprocity, 154; relationships with rational intellectualism, 158; tension with the world, 153; types of, 148
Protestant asceticism, 2, 57, 145; broke

through clan ties to establish community of faith, 165; combination of unfettered acquisition with limited consumption, 122; contrast to Confucianism, 165–67; empirical science more compatible with its interests than philosophy, 158; ethically rationalized action within one's calling, 150; need for symptoms of salvation as a psychological impetus to self-control and achievement, 131; provided conscientious and industrious workers, 123; role in genesis of the "rights of man," 131; and sober self-made man, 122

Protestant ethic, Weber and, 113–42; analysis of "traditionalism," 116; Anglophilia and distrust of Lutheranism, 125; argument with and response to Sombart, 124–42; case against monocausal economism, 113; construction of ideal type encompassing a logical argument and a psychological process, 118–20; distinction between "adventure" and entrepreneurial capitalism, 129; on economic consequences of Ascetic Protestantism, 123; on increasing importance of secular "orders" and clubs among American middle classes, 136–37; and Marx, 113; notion of duty to one's calling, 117–18; rationalization of conduct as a contribution to development of capitalism, 131; "spirit of capitalism" and capitalism in an adequate not a necessary relationship to each other, 116; "Weber thesis," 131

Protestant sects: accepted new members only after review of their conduct, 136; interest in practical consequences, 135; interest in self-esteem and approval steered members toward rational capitalism, 135; overrepresented in Baden, 114; in the United States, 136–39; vocational ethos, 135; Weber on, 134–37

Protestant Social Congress, survey of agrarian working conditions, 45

provision (*Fürsorge*), 181

Prussia: General Code (Allgemeines Landrecht), 195, 196, 200; military system, 43; Ministry of Culture, 63; three-class suffrage, 70; voting classes, 70

psychic differentiation, theory of, 22

psychologism, 89, 90–92

psychology, rules of commonsense, 103

psychophysical tradition, 91

Puritanism: acquisition of wealth as unintended consequence of virtue, 166; ascetic conduct of life, 120–21; belief in empirical science, 122; distrust of everything sensual in religious and cultural life, 119; English, 117, 119; paradox of vocational ethic, 154; poor blamed for their disadvantages, 218; powerful legacy, 217–18; psychologically tangible good offered by, 146; rationalism, 166; rationalization of God's relationship to the world, 164; rejection of philosophical and literary education, 166; rejection of the world and sinful human nature, 165; sense of being chosen by God, 122; strenuous labor as a means of ascetic self-discipline, 121; tension with established churches, 118; unremitting work in one's calling, 120; vocational asceticism, 155

Puritan Levelers, 57

Puritan revolutions, 156

purpose of life, 38

purposive rationality (*Zweckrationalität*), 98, 99, 100, 102

"putting out" system, 116

among historical individuals, 29; *Limits of Scientific Conceptualization*, 27; philosophy, 105; "philosophy of value" (*Wertphilosophie*), 79; and problem of interpretation, 30; and problem of values, 29; tendency to confound values that are with values that ought to be, 29–30; view that judgments of value relevance guide historians in the choice of objects of study, 79

"right law," 199

right rationality, ideal type of (*Richtigkeitstypus*), 96, 99, 100, 102, 103, 104

rights of man, 57, 124, 223

Roman aristocrat, 115

Roman law, 193, 195, 196, 198

Romantic conservatives, 31

Romanticism, 16, 38

Roscher, Wilhelm, 20, 89–90, 92

rules of experience (*Erfahrungsregeln*), 84, 88

ruling organization, 180

rural society, 132

Russia: fight for individual freedom in, 58; problem of land redistribution, 58

Russian Marxists, 197

Russian migrant workers, 43

Russian Revolution of 1905, 57, 197

Saint Louis World's Fair, 132

salon culture, 157

salvation: ascetic pursuit of, 152; concerned with meaning, 156; contemplation as the path to, 160; cults, 144; experiences of, 149; freedom from suffering, 153; organically differentiated order of paths, 247; originated in knowledge in Asian salvation doctrines, 173–74; quest for, 158; sublimation of the religious quest

into the belief in, 146; and suffering, 145

salvation religions, 146, 171

Salz, Arthur, 242

Sanskrit, 172

saving, 181

savior, magical charisma, 153

savior myth, 145

Schäfer, Dietrich, 56

Schluchter, Wolfgang, 176

Schmitt, Carl, 241

Schmoller, Gustav: and bureaucratic paternalism, 108; chair of Social Policy Association, 42; historical school of economics, 21; proposal to exclude Marxists and Manchesterites from university chairs, 111; quest for a broad consensus on social policy objectives, 110; seventieth birthday, 63; social policy, 214; view of state positions on corporate boards, 60; view that causality implies lawfulness and determinism, 92

Schnitger, Marianne. *See* Weber, Marianne

scholarly synthesis, call for, 17

scholarship, value judgments in, 21, 79, 104–11, 126, 227

Schopenhauer, Arthur, 38

Schulze-Gaevernitz, Gerhart von, 126

Schwentker, Wolfgang, 56

science (*Naturwissenschaft*), 86

sciences of reality (*Wirklichkeitswissenschaften*), 78

scientific rationalism, and religion as antirational power, 158

seasonal labor, demand for, 43–44

secondary historical facts, 78

secondary historical individuals, 29

secondary teachers, formal examination and credentials for, 8

Second Punic War, 81

self-control, 120

self-development, through textual interpretation, 106
self-discipline, in service of labor, 117
self-hypnosis, 172
self-salvation, 160
Semstwo liberalism, 58, 59
"sense" (*Sinn*), 95
serfs, 204
Sermon on the Mount, 106, 247
service land, 185
servile castes, 169
Seven Years' War, 81
sexuality, sublimation into eroticism, 156–57
Shakespeare, William, despised by Puritans, 122
Shin, 162, 227
Siddharta (Gautama), 172
signoria, 209
Silesia, 43
Simmel, Georg, 16, 31, 34–40, 78, 245; analyst of German academic culture, 40; disproportion between cultural objects and subjective culture, 160; economic rationalism helped to fuel the rise of modern science, 129; on the impact of money on social relationships, 44; influenced by Marx, 40; on interpretation, 30; on "laws in history," 26; objective culture, 230; observation that human behaviors are difficult to predict, 94; occasional essays, 38; "On Social Differentiation," 34; *Philosophy of Money,* 34, 36–38, 130; positive view of conflict and competition, 35; *Problems in the Philosophy of History,* 25–26; rejected by Heidelberg because of being Jewish, 56; rejected the notion of understanding as a kind of telepathic reproduction, 26; second founder of sociology in Germany, 34; *Sociology,* 34–36; subjective and objective

mind, 39–40; theory of action, 37–38; vision of formal sociology, 35
sin, 159
singular causal analysis, 77–78, 80, 82–89, 101–2, 104, 146, 254
skepticism, 158
slaves, 204
Smith, Adam, 121
social action: class-based, 229; defined by Weber, 97, 177, 178
social circles, 35–36
social class, defined by Weber, 228
social contract, 32
Social Darwinism, 90
Social Democratic Party, 5, 64, 245; bureaucratization, 61, 244; collaboratism in "negative politics," 67; exceptional legislation against, 41; expansion, 13; fixed substantive ends, 65; members barred from university positions in Prussia, 55; revisionists, 73, 126, 219
social inequality, 159
social interactions, "forms" and "contents" of, 34–35
socialism, 198, 216, 219, 224
"Socialists of the Lectern," 63, 109, 126, 214
social policy: German tradition of, 253; nationalism as the ultimate norm of, 49; paternalist, 14; reformist, 214; role of value judgments in, 48
Social Policy Association (Verein für Sozialpolitik), 60; confusion of scientific with normative issues, 110; controversy over value judgments within, 104, 107, 110, 126; discussion of public enterprises of municipalities, 61; founded to study and recommend reforms within a capitalist framework, 108; increasing tensions within, 62; Schmoller and, 21, 42; Weber's case against monocausal

economism, 113; Weber's report on agrarian conditions, 42; "young ones" (*die Jungen*), 126

Social Practice, 126

social psychology, 22–23

social relationships: categorical analysis of, 40; communal (*Vergemeinschaftung*), 179–80; Weber's definition of, 177

social sciences: guided by the values of the investigators, 105; interpretation and explanation of actions and beliefs of social agents, 96–97; more successful in their retrospective explanations than in their predictions, 86; value freedom in, 227. *See also* methodology of the social sciences, Weber's

"sociation" (*Vergesellschaftung*), 34

societal entities, 32

Society for Social Reform, 126

sociology, 177; defined by Weber, 97, 178; German classical, 30–40; and history, 178–79; of law, 192–201; linked to economics, 95; not inherently "rationalistic," 99

Socrates, 234

Sohm, Rudolf, 186

"Solomonic judgment," 194

Sombart, Werner, 132; anti-Semitism, 129, 130; appointment at the University of Breslau, 126; attacks upon by conservative historians, 127; *The Bourgeois,* 130; call for distinction between social sciences and value judgments, 109; doubt that "religious affiliation" played a role in origins of capitalism, 129; editor of *Archive for Social Science and Social Policy,* 2, 107–8, 126; *History of Modern Capitalism,* 116, 127, 128–29; *The Jews and Economic Life,* 127, 129–30; public spokesman for social reform,

126; saw money advancing from a "means" to the "highest purpose" of human life, 129; *Socialism and the Social Movement,* 127; travels in America, 133–34

soul, immortality of, 168

specialized knowledge (*Fachwissen*), 255; association with "positivism," 17; and *Bildung,* 71, 227–28, 242; and disjunction between subjective and objective mind, 39; threat to unity of knowledge, 16, 17

specialized research, widespread dissatisfaction with, 16–17

specialized training (*Fachschulung*), 72, 183

spiritual advisers, 145

spiritual leaders, charisma of, 135

Spranger, Eduard: "The Present State of the *Geisteswissenschaften* and the School," 242; on testing of academic aptitude, 13

Stammler, Rudolf: and "freedom" of actions, 93; "rule-governed" (*geregelt*), 96; view that causality implies lawfulness and determinism, 92

state creditors, 51

"state of nature," 121

status group (*Stand*), 229

status honor (*ständische Ehre*), 189

status position: defined by Weber, 229; slowly evolving, 230

status society, 229

"steel housing," 217, 221, 223, 255

"steel" saints, 120

Stendhal, *The Red and the Black,* 241

stupidity, cardinal vice of Buddhism, 173

subjective mind (soul), 39–40

subjective rights, 57, 194–95

subjectivist fallacy, 95

subjectivity, 105, 106–7

submarine warfare, 53, 70

subordination, 35, 37–38

universal validity, 29, 30
University of Berlin, 1
University of Freiburg, 1
University of Heidelberg, 1
University of Munich, 2
University of Turin, 55
university professors, American, 231
university students, American, 238
unjust suffering, irrationality, 158–59
unpropertied intellectuals, 228
upper guilds (*arti maggiori*), 209
upper middle class, 14
usage (*Brauch*), 179
usury, 37, 117, 125
utilitarian individualism, 14
utilitarianism, 121
utilities (*Nutzleistungen*), defined by
    Weber, 180–81

validity (*Geltung*), 179
value analysis, 105–6
value considerations, 79, 100
value judgments vs. judgments of value
    relatedness, 29
value neutrality, as a regulative ideal of
    Wissenschaft, 110
value rationalization (*Wertrational-
    isierung*), 179
value-rational sects, 180
value-rational (*wertrational*) action, 98,
    99
Veda, 168, 169, 171
venia legendi, 231
Versailles, 74
Verstehen, 24, 25, 92
villages, 32
Virginia, 57
virtuoso religion, relationship to the
    economy, 149–50
visible church, 134
vital experience (*Erleben*), 18, 233
vocation. *See* calling (*Beruf*)

voluntary associations, 35
voluntary obedience, 189, 190
voluntary political parties, 69
voluntary principle, 137

wage contract, 33
wage labor, 43, 46
Wagner, Adolf, 61
war, and dignity of a consecrated death,
    155
War of 1866, 82
warrior heroes, 227
wealth: acquisition of as increasing
    God's glory, 121; acquisition of in
    Confucianism, 163, 166; fear of enjoy-
    ment of, 121; as unintended conse-
    quence of virtue for Puritans, 166
Weber, Adolf, 108–9
Weber, Alfred, 2, 126
Weber, Helene Fallenstein, 1, 2
Weber, Marianne, 2, 132, 134, 137, 176
Weber, Max
    friends and colleagues: attempt to
        bring Georg Simmel to Heidel-
        berg, 56; close relationship with
        many junior faculty and students,
        55; influenced by aspects of Rick-
        ert's work, 30; influence of Sim-
        mel on, 25; negative reaction to
        Sombart's new course, 127–28;
        and Nietzsche, 241; reactions to
        "Science as a Vocation," 242–43;
        recommendation of Eulenburg
        for an associate professorship, 56;
        and Robert Michels, 55; running
        argument with Sombard, 126
    personal education, career, and gen-
        eral beliefs: academic career, 1;
        administration of military hospi-
        tal in Heidelberg, 3; champion
        of German industrialization, 2;
        change in direction of thought

Weber, Max (*continued*)

    after 1902, 2; critique of the German historical tradition, 18, 30; dissent from orthodox mandarin views, 30–31; distinctive intellectual personality, 55; doctoral dissertation on the history of medieval trading companies, 1; editor of *Archive for Social Science and Social Policy,* 108, 126; intellectual field, 8–18; interest in religion, 1; legal studies, 1; liberal pluralism, 5, 105, 112; resignation from teaching duties a the University of Heidelberg, 2; survey of agrarian working conditions, 1; survey of the psychophysical conditions of productivity among factory workers, 3; thesis on Roman agrarian history, 1; traditionally humanistic secondary schooling, 1; travels in America, 133–34

    personal life: birth, 1; bursts of manic energy, 2; conflict with his father in 1897, 2; death from pneumonia in 1920, 2; education, 1; extramarital affair, 2; marriage, 2; military service, 1; nationalism, 10; predisposition to manic-depressive illness, 2; as private scholar, 2; profound depression, 2; sleeplessness and nervous exhaustion, 2

    shift from history to sociology, 175–201; basic concepts of economic action, 180–82; commitment to the interpretive method, 176–77; definition of "social action" in terms of the expectations of others, 177; early skepticism of German sociology, 40; formal qualities of modern law, 198–201; founding of German Society for Sociology, 3, 34, 40, 175–76; frequent recourse to comparison and predominant interest in persistent historical structures, 176; and Social Policy Association, 61–63; sociology of law, 192–201; theory of action, 177–79; two types of economically active organizations, 181; types of legitimate domination (authority), 183–92

    works: "Basic Concepts of Sociology," 97–101, 180; "Categories of Economic Action," 212; "Churches and Sects," 134; "Churches and Sects in North America," 134; *The City (Die Stadt)*, 203–11; *Collected Essays on the Sociology of Religion,* 114, 134; "Collegiality and the Division of Powers," 191; *Confucianism and Taoism,* 161–74; *The Economic Ethics of the World Religions,* 143–52; "Economy and Law (The Sociology of Law)," 211; *Economy and Society,* 3, 40, 50–51, 68–70, 176–82; *The Economy and the Social Orders and Powers,* 176; Freiburg Inaugural Address of 1895, 47–49, 62; "Germany among the European World Powers," 54; *Hinduism and Buddhism,* 167–72; "Intermediate Reflection," 152–60; "Objective Probability and Adequate Causation in Historical Analysis," 81–85; "'Objectivity' in Social Science and Social Policy," 2, 81, 85–87, 92, 101–4, 108; "On the Situation of Constitutional Democracy in Russia," 2–3; "Parliament and Government in Germany under a New Political Order," 63–70, 71; "Politics as a Vocation," 74, 230–31, 243–49;

The Protestant Ethic and the Spirit of Capitalism, 2, 113–42, 210, 231, 254; "The Protestant Sects and the Spirit of Capitalism," 134–39, 140; "The Relations of the Rural Community to other Branches of Social Science," 132; "Science as a Vocation," 230–43; *Situation of the Agricultural Workers in East Elbian Germany,* 42–45; "Sociological Categories of Economic Action," 213; "Status and Class," 228–30

Weber, Max, Sr., 1, 2

Weimar Republic, 3, 5, 13, 15

Weltanschauung, 90, 225, 245

Wesenwille ("essential" or "natural will"), 31

Wesley, John, 122–23

Western asceticism, supramundane creator God, 150, 152

Western city: of antiquity and of the Middle Ages, 204; as an autonomous association, 206; as a commune, 203; difference from Asian cities, 205, 206; establishment of an urban code of rational law, 207; as a fraternal association, 204; leveling of distinctions among social groups with a trend toward internal status differentiation, 205; oath of fraternization, 207; as a religious cult community, 205; secular foundation, 205; status association of notable "families," 208

Western civilization, 14

Western legal education, 198

Western monasticism, 120, 121

Western rationalism, rise of, 210–11

West Prussia, outmigration of German laborers and increase in Polish immigrants, 47

Wilhelmian Germany, 223

William II, 41, 45, 65, 74

Williams, Roger, 57

Winckelmann, Johannes, 176

Windelband, Wilhelm: antithesis between "nomothetic" and "idiographic" knowledge, 27, 28; "History and the Natural Sciences," 27; principle of individuality, 27; and Simmel's rejection by Heidelberg, 56

Wirtschaftsverband, 180, 181

Wissenschaft: crisis of, 17; inner vocation for, 233; linked to objective of *Bildung,* 9; positive services of, 234, 238–40; among the products of the "rational will," 33; prohibition of openly "partisan" social and political views, 10; pure, as impractical, 10; systematic knowledge based upon causal analysis, 225–26, 231; and value neutrality, 110; and *Weltanschauung,* 225, 242

work, impersonality and senselessness of under capitalism, 217

workers: agricultural, 44, 46, 47; German, 43, 60; as product of Protestant asceticism, 123; separation from the means of production, 216, 217, 218, 219, 252

workers' organizations, police and judicial harassment of, 41

working class, 228; collective right of to a "living wage," 197; idealism, 64; new substantive demands, calling for a "social law," 199

worldview (*Weltanschauung*), 9

World War I, German enthusiasm for, 14, 52

Wundt, Wilhelm, 22–23, 90

Yoga, 151, 172

Zarathustran dualism, 145, 160

"Zimmerwald faction," 247

Zinzendort, Count, 118